Responsible Inve

This textbook provides the first holistic resource on Environmental, Social, and Governance (ESG) investing for undergraduate and graduate programs. It provides a thorough background and history of ESG investing, as well as cutting-edge industry developments, in a way that introduces the reader to the rapidly developing field of responsible investing.

Beginning with a comprehensive background of ESG investing and the development of models measuring risk and return, the book then discusses the development of ESG risks, and provides an overview of ESG rating systems. The textbook also outlines the current position of ESG investing in portfolio management through granular analysis, provides insight into common investor concerns about ESG investments, discloses qualitative theories relevant to ESG investing, and reviews literature attempting to model ESG investment performance. Finally, the authors provide readers with a foundation on the development of financial models measuring risk and return, which will be useful for measuring the performance of ESG investments. With case studies from contributors around the world, this textbook is the first of its kind to truly provide a compelling blend of quantitative and qualitative analysis supporting the incorporation of ESG investment strategies into investment portfolios.

Offering an excellent overview of the growing trends in ESG investing, as well as a close analysis of ESG theories and their practical application both today and in the future, this book will be a great resource for both undergraduates and graduate students.

Matthew W. Sherwood, Ph.D. is Director of Public Markets Investments at MMBB Financial Services. He is also an appointed Fellow in Business and Finance and an adjunct faculty member at The King's College, and a guest lecturer at Columbia University, where he lectures on ESG Investing and Derivatives. Sherwood is also an Investment Committee Member and Head of the ESG/SRI Working Group for the Plan Sponsor Council of America (PSCA).

Julia Pollard is Financial Associate with Bernstein Private Wealth Management, a division of AllianceBernstein (AB). Pollard recently published "Establishing ESG as Risk Premia," which was published in 2018 in the *Journal of Investment Management* and "The Risk Adjusted Return Potential of Integrating ESG Strategies into Emerging Market Equities," which was published in 2017 in the *Journal of Sustainable Finance and Investments*.

Responsible Investing

An Introduction to Environmental, Social, and Governance Investments

Matthew W. Sherwood, Ph.D.
and Julia Pollard

Routledge
Taylor & Francis Group

LONDON AND NEW YORK

First published 2019
by Routledge
2 Park Square, Milton Park, Abingdon, Oxon OX14 4RN

and by Routledge
711 Third Avenue, New York, NY 10017

Routledge is an imprint of the Taylor & Francis Group, an informa business

British Library Cataloguing-in-Publication Data
A catalogue record for this book is available from the British Library

Library of Congress Cataloging-in-Publication Data
Names: Sherwood, Matthew W., 1983– author. | Pollard, Julia, 1995– author.
Title: Responsible investing : an introduction to environmental, social, and
     governance investments / Matthew W. Sherwood and Julia Pollard.
Description: 1 Edition. | New York : Routledge, 2019. | Includes bibliographical
     references and index.
Identifiers: LCCN 2018025635 (print) | LCCN 2018028479 (ebook) | ISBN
     9780203712078 (Ebook) | ISBN 9781138560062 (hardback : alk. paper) |
     ISBN 9781138560079 (pbk. : alk. paper)
Subjects: LCSH: Investments—Social aspects. | Portfolio management.
Classification: LCC HG4515.13 (ebook) | LCC HG4515.13 .S34 2019 (print) |
     DDC 332.6—dc23
LC record available at https://lccn.loc.gov/2018025635

ISBN: 978-1-138-56006-2 (hbk)
ISBN: 978-1-138-56007-9 (pbk)
ISBN: 978-0-203-71207-8 (ebk)

Typeset in Joanna MT
by Apex CoVantage, LLC

Printed and bound in Great Britain by
TJ International Ltd, Padstow, Cornwall

Contents

Figures

Tables

About the authors

Co-authors Dr. Matthew W. Sherwood and Julia Pollard are recognized subject matter experts in the field. The authors have collaborated on empirical research in the ESG investing landscape and continue to conduct scholarly studies on the implementation and performance of ESG factors and the broader ESG research universe. Recent publications include "Establishing ESG as Risk Premia," which was published in 2018 in the *Journal of Investment Management* and "The Risk Adjusted Return Potential of Integrating ESG Strategies into Emerging Market Equities," which was published in 2017 in the *Journal of Sustainable Finance and Investments*.

Matthew W. Sherwood, Ph.D.

Dr. Matthew W. Sherwood is an accomplished investment professional with a strong track record of success. Dr. Sherwood began his asset management career at Morgan Stanley. Dr. Sherwood left Morgan Stanley for a full discretion Portfolio Manager position at Access Global Partners, where he was responsible for managing capital across all asset classes. Dr. Sherwood left Access Global Partners to pursue a Senior Portfolio Manager position at The Schonfeld Group, before obtaining the Chief Strategist role at Ivy Strategy, and now he is the Director of Public Markets Investments at MMBB Financial Services.

Sherwood graduated Summa Cum Laude from the Honors Program at Liberty University. He went on to graduate with honors from his Master of Business Administration, where he studied Finance and Economics. Sherwood studied business quantitative methods and economic theory on the doctoral level and obtained his Doctor of Philosophy in Business Administration from Northcentral University. Sherwood is an appointed Fellow in Business and Finance and an adjunct faculty member at The King's College, and a guest lecturer at Columbia University, where he lectures on ESG Investing and Derivatives.

Sherwood is also an Investment Committee Member and Head of the ESG/SRI Working Group for the Plan Sponsor Council of America (PSCA). Sherwood has also been a featured speaker on ESG investing for investment industry conferences, such as the CIO Summit, Agecroft, AIMSE, Connex, Pensions & Investments, and Institutional Investor. Sherwood has been retained as an Expert Witness in multi-billion dollar litigation for his expertise in equity valuation and corporate governance.

Julia Pollard

Ms. Julia Pollard has a Finance degree with a concentration in International Investments from The King's College. Pollard's career focus is in asset management. Pollard has a research focus in Environmental, Social, Governance (ESG) investing and has a specific interest in integrating ESG strategies within institutional portfolios.

Contributors

We would like to acknowledge the following contributors:

1. Dr. Robert Eccles, *Visiting Professor of Management Practice*, Said Business School, Oxford University (England)
2. Dr. Gregory Norris, *Professor*, Harvard College (USA)
3. Dr. Jason Jay, *Professor of Sustainability*, Massachusetts Institute of Technology's Sloan School (USA)
4. Dr. Lloyd Kurtz, *Lecturer*, University of California, Berkeley Haas School of Business and *Head of Social Impact* at Wells Fargo Private Bank (USA)
5. Aniket Shah, *Head of Sustainable Investing*, OppenheimerFunds, Inc. and *Chairman*, Amnesty International (USA)
6. Hanna Kaskela, *Director of Responsible Investment*, Varma (Finland)
7. Wim Van Hyfte, *Global Head of Responsible Investments & Research* and Keith Dixson, *Head of Institutional Development*, Candriam Investors Group (Luxembourg)
8. Matt Craig, *European Content Director*, Institutional Investor and Ole Buhl, *Head of ESG* at ATP (Denmark)
9. Faith Word, *Chief Responsible Investing Officer* and Judy Darley, *Communications Manager*, Brunel Pension Partners (England)
10. Eoin Fahy, *Head of Responsible Investing* and William Boardman, *Senior Vice President*, KBI Global Investors (Ireland)
11. Melissa Chase, *Marketing Specialist*, Sustainalytics (Canada)
12. Heidi Welsh, *Executive Director*, Sustainable Investments Institute (USA)
13. Dan Hanson, *Lecturer*, University of California, Berkeley Haas School of Business and *Head of Impact Investing*, JANA Partners (USA)
14. Lawler Kang, *Chief Executive Officer and Co-Founder*, League of Allies (USA)
15. Tony O'Toole, *Chief Financial Officer and Chief Investment Officer*, Truth Initiative (USA)
16. Usman Ali, *Consultant*
17. Jason Mitchell, *Sustainability Strategist and Chair of the United Nations (UN) PRI Advisory Committee*, Man Group (United Kingdom)
18. Mark E Bateman, *Director of ESG/SRI Research*, Aperio (USA)
19. Anthony Waskiewicz, *Chief Investment Officer* and Elizabeth Jordan, *Deputy Chief Investment Officer*, at Mercy Health (USA)
20. Josh Zimmer, *Chief Executive Officer* and Susana McDermott, *Director of Communications*, at the Interfaith Center on Corporate Responsibility (ICCR) (USA)
21. Branka Nikci, *Executive Director, Co-head of Investment Capabilities working group — Sustainable Investment Leadership Team* and Peter Kocubinski, *Managing Director, Co-head of Investment Capabilities working group — Sustainable Investment Leadership Team*, J.P. Morgan Asset Management (USA)
22. Rob Fernandez, *Head of ESG Research* and Tim Coffin, *Senior Vice President*, Breckinridge Capital Advisors (USA)
23. Tom Pollihan, *Principal* and Michael Lauer, *Consultant*, Summit Strategies Group (USA)
24. Alex Monk, *Sustainability Investments Analyst*, Schroders (England)
25. Lisa Hayles, *Vice President, Institutional Investment Services*, Boston Common Asset Management (USA)

26. Hannah G. Commoss, *Partner*, Spruceview Partners (USA)
27. Rev. Fletcher Harper, *Executive Director*, GreenFaith (USA)
28. Nicolas Vuignier, *Chief Investment Officer*, CIEPP (Switzerland)
29. Thomas Schmidt Christenson, CFA, *Senior Quantitative Analyst for Global Core Equity* and Peter Mullineux, *Director of Equity Business Development*, AllianceBernstein (Benmar)
30. Oliver Garrett, *Analyst*, The King's College (USA)
31. Sonya Hetrick, *Sector Analyst*, Sustainable Accounting Standards Board (SASB) (USA)

Preface

The authors wrote this book to serve as an industry handbook and academic textbook for the field of ESG investing. The authors are both investment practitioners and academic experts of ESG investing. This book is necessary as it establishes standardization of terminology based on the thought leadership and scholarly literature in the field. This book provides a clear explanation of the theory and practical considerations of ESG investing, and all the many facets of responsible investment research, risk, and analysis. An empirically supported framework of the approaches, methodologies, and investment strategy within the field is presented. Furthermore, this book will serve as a guide for the introductory learning of the subject matter and a foundation for further study.

Acknowledgments

We would like to thank the academics and investment professionals who paved the way for the field of ESG investing. A special thanks to our families and friends for their support during the research and writing process of this book.

Chapter 1

Introduction

Environmental, social, and governance factors are tools of great power. The measurement of these three factors provides the insight which grants quantitative authority for regulation and control by governments, corporations, investors, and consumers. This regulation and control has been shown to materially impact corporate action.

This chapter is an introduction to ESG investing terminology and to the scope of this textbook. As ESG investing is notorious for vague terminology and undefined nomenclature, this chapter brings clarity by outlining the assumptions about terminology made by the authors. Based on a wide range of sources, Environmental, Social, and Governance (ESG) investing will the overarching term under which impact investing, sustainable investing, socially responsible investing (SRI), and mission-related investing (MRI) will exist. This decision reflects current trends in vocabulary regarding this investment strategy. This chapter also discusses practical uses of the textbook, and includes brief mentions of useful features for students.

1.1 Assumptions for this textbook

Within sustainable investing there exists a few distinctions which are important to master before going further. The first distinction is between investing **strategies**. Investment strategies involve a set of rules, beliefs, or assumptions that govern an investor's investment decisions. These rules, beliefs, or assumptions are based on technical and fundamental analysis of the potential investments. Within traditional investments, the reader may be familiar with investment strategies such as value investing, growth investing, and momentum trading. Within ESG investing, strategies include impact investing, ESG tilt strategies, ESG momentum strategies, green investing, and best-of-class (as well as many others that continue to develop as the concept gains traction).

Within these **strategies** are a variety of **methodologies**. These methodologies are the investor's techniques and investing decisions made to accomplish the underlying strategy. Within traditional investing, these methodologies might include decisions based on the market capitalization, liquidity, or stock beta. Within ESG investing, these methods include ESG inclusion, ESG integration, ESG engagement, and ESG screening. Chapter 4 will provide an in-depth analysis of each of these methodologies. For now, suffice it to say that each strategy is implemented using specific methodologies. This textbook will broadly refer to all sustainable strategies as "ESG investing strategies," and refer to each methodology by its specific strategy.

Learning objectives

- Discuss trends within ESG investing nomenclature
- Define ESG investment parameters
- Compare terminology used in Europe and North America to discuss ESG investing strategies

After this chapter, readers should have a basic understanding of ESG terminology, and an ability to discuss assumptions made by the authors about current trends in ESG investing nomenclature.

The role of Environmental, Social, and Governance (ESG) research-based investment strategies has been an important topic of discussion and study amongst investors for the past 30 years. To understand the different dimensions and facets of ESG investing, it is useful to first investigate the development of relevant terminology.

1.2 Terminology

One major criticism of ESG investing strategies, per academics and investors alike, is its lack of standardization of terminology and defined nomenclature. Russell Sparkes, in an article entitled "Ethical Investment: Whose Ethics, Which Investment?", described the problem thus: "Surely here is an area characterized by at best loose terminology, at worst by a conceptual confusion that would benefit from the rigor of academic analysis" (2001). Sparkes's criticism was in regards to the collection of vaguely defined terms surrounding socially responsible investing, which only became more extensive as the concept popularized amongst investors as the investment strategy grew. Many of the phrases critical to understanding ESG-relative investment strategy are without standardized definitions with which to identify them.

The investment industry may elect to use their own terms and phrases for their reinvestment practices. Institutional investors, asset managers, service providers, and consultants generally use the terms and definitions for ESG investing that are chosen by their governing boards, or at the request of the clients they serve. In practice, such ESG-related terminology is often interchangeable in implementation and intended meaning. Nevertheless, differences in terms, particularly in ESG approaches and methodologies, which span a broad spectrum of the field as ESG investing, are representative of a broad category with many underlying subcategories of research, risk, and financial analysis.

Many academics have attempted to identify trends in terminology that would help to define the concepts. These academics have made some progress in recent years by standardizing definitions for different relevant concepts. Below are certain definitions which have been widely accepted as accurate identifiers of certain ESG-related practices and ideas:

Impact investing: Impact investments are investments made into companies, organizations, and funds with the intention to generate social and environmental impact alongside a financial return. (Global Impact Investing Network definition).

Socially responsible investing (SRI): Sustainable, responsible, and impact investing (SRI) is an investment discipline that considers environmental, social, and corporate governance (ESG) criteria to generate long-term competitive financial returns and positive societal impact. (The Forum for Sustainable and Responsible Investment, USSIF definition).

Responsible investing (RI): Responsible investment is an approach to investing that aims to incorporate environmental, social, and governance (ESG) factors into investment decisions, to better manage risk and generate sustainable, long-term returns. (UNPRI definition).

These definitions will continue to evolve as ESG investing rapidly gains traction and study within academia. Though the terminology for socially responsible investing strategies is often vague and undefined, a widely accepted definition is:

ESG investing is the research and investment strategy framework that evaluates environmental, social, and governance factors as non-financial dimensions of a security's valuation, performance, and risk profile.

This definition will serve as a broad scope for this book.

1.3 Useful features for students

This textbook will include several useful features for students and professors, to assist with presenting new ideas and fostering helpful discussions on the topics.

Learning objectives and discussion questions: the learning objectives, presented at the beginning of each chapter, serve to present the main ideas of a chapter in a way that prepares the reader for major takeaways and concepts to focus on. Discussion questions, presented at the end of each chapter, will correspond with the various learning objectives and will allow the reader to engage with the main concepts of the text.

Case studies: Case studies are "real-life" examples of the concepts presented in each chapter. These case studies were drafted by investment managers, policy makers, nonprofits, data service providers, independent consultants, members of the UN, and various other groups who engage daily with ESG issues. These case studies provide students with practical examples of how the topics and definitions offered in the text play out for various academics and practitioners. They offer a broad range of opinions and options for students to consider.

Learning perspectives: Learning perspectives are academic approaches to the concepts described in the text. They are more technical in nature than many of the case studies, and are designed to present a deeper dive into various topics than case studies. Learning perspectives were drafted by academics or practitioners who have spent years studying ESG investing or relevant related topics.

This textbook has been compiled first with the intent to document the history and status of ESG investment strategies in the global marketplace. To do this, this textbook discusses motivators for ESG investment strategies, potential hindrances to its growth on the global stage, and how current trends may lead to future implementation in various capacities. To that end, this textbook should be viewed as a high-level overview of the factors at place in the ESG sphere, and is most useful as an introduction for those who seek to gain a well-rounded perspective on the themes at play.

Discussion questions

1) Provide a definition of ESG investing (LO1)
2) Discuss the definitional differences between: impact investing, ESG integration, and exclusion (negative screening) (LO3)

Chapter 2

A historical survey of ESG investing

In this chapter, we will consider some of the major historical, political, social, and cultural factors which have led to the growth of ESG (Environmental, Societal, Governance) investing. Insight into the relationship between financial performance and emerging ESG strategies will be presented. Special consideration will be made of the influence that Corporate Social Responsibility (CSR) has had in the development and adoption of ESG strategies. We will view the development of ESG investing regionally and discuss modern investment practices that originated in ESG strategies, such as impact investing, micro-finance, and social venture. This chapter will specifically highlight the different types of institutions (boutique firms, large institutional investors, private investors, etc.) that have contributed to ESG investing's growth. We note investment trends based on the investor demographics of those who have been historically attracted to ESG investing strategies and discuss the expansion of ESG investing in a variety of investment sectors and asset classes. In summary, this chapter should provide a helpful summary of the environment in which ESG investment trends developed – a historical foundation upon which the rest of this book depends, and a tool through which readers can use historical trends to predict the future of ESG Investing.

Learning objectives

- Name and discuss historical, political, social, and cultural events contributing to the growth of ESG investment strategies
- Examine major causal factors which have and will affect the development of ESG investing
- Identify facets of the relationship between financial performance and ESG investment strategies
- Distinguish between the varying levels of ESG investment integration in different markets such as the United States, Europe, Asia, and emerging markets
- Use financial tools to analyze potential future trends in ESG investing

2.1 Progression of investing theories: neo-classical economics encounters human nature

Historically, economists and investors alike operated on the notion that investment behavior need be influenced by only two factors: financial return and risk. This notion emerged from the neo-classical economics school of thought, which holds three main tenants:

1   Individuals have rational preferences regarding purposes
2   Individuals maximize utility and firms maximize profits
3   Individuals act independently based on complete and relevant information (Roy Weintraub, 2002; Marinescu, 2016)

Understanding the "Homo oeconomicus" (the "economic man") is key to unlocking neo-classical economics. The term refers to the economic individual characterized by the following traits: rational, self-interested, insatiable, and utilitarian.

The perception of mankind's prevailing self-interest has not changed since Adam Smith published *The Wealth of Nations* in 1776. In "Homo Oeconomicus and Behavioral Economics," Justyna Brzezicka and Radoslaw Wisniewski described "The classical homo oeconomicus" as "like a cyborg calculating costs and profits: he lacks passion, does not give into temptations, and is not greedy nor altruistic."

In his study "The Rational Choice Generalization of Neoclassical Economics Reconsidered: Any Theoretical Legitimation for Economic Imperialism?", Milan Zafirovski described *homo oeconomicus* as:

> Atomistic individuals free from complex interdependencies, the pursuit of pure self-interest (construed as happiness), farsighted rationality and accurate cost-benefit calculation, market equilibrium and/or (the Pareto) optimum, parametric individual preferences/values, technologies, social institutions and cultures, consistent maximization of profit (producers) and utility (consumers), free and perfect competition, a laissez-faire government, full knowledge and complete information.

Theories such as the **rational choice theory** were based on the idea that in the same situation, every individual would make the same decision to maximize his own self-interest (Marinescu, 2016). However, this *homo oeconomicus* was a dissatisfying model for many who argued the advantage of incorporating psychology within economic analysis. **Behavioral economic theory** began to gain a foothold in the early to mid-1900s, supported by those who were unable to reconcile the cold and calculating *homo oeconomicus* with the behaviors and tendencies of their own experience. Behavioral economics attempted to restore psychological analysis of human behavior to economic thought and practice through experimentally testing the relationship between rational choice and the unpredictable nature of human psychology which compete in decision-making. Through these tests, advocates for behavioral economics empirically demonstrated the effect of human nature in the economic sphere, further questioning either the assumption that one makes rational decisions based solely on self-interest, or the assumption that an individual's self-interest is fixed in his or her person. In other words, the experiments and tests of behavioral economics have demonstrated one of two things: either one is not primarily rationally self-interested, or one considers self-interest to include a wider sphere than just his or her person. In either case, scholars in the mid-1900s publicly and academically introduced economics to human nature in a way that ushered in the acknowledgement of qualitative impacts on market movement.

2.2 Socially responsible investing's historical beginnings: religious and corporate development (1800s–1950s)

Apart from these economic theories, a more primal investment framework had long been established (Schueth, 2003; Epstein, 1987; Renneboog, Horst, and Zhang, 2008). People of faith had influenced investing based on qualitative criteria for thousands of years. From early biblical times until today, Jewish directives offered in the Mosaic Law specifically mandated methods for ethical investing. More recently, in the Christian era, Methodists, Quakers, and various other religious faith-based investors consciously avoided investing in stocks that they labeled "sin stocks," which included a range of industries such as the alcohol, gambling, tobacco, and war-related materials industries (Schueth, 2003; Brimble, 2013; Waring and Lewer, 2004; Renneboog, Ter Horst, and Zhang, 2008), echoing those directives in the Jewish culture. These decisions emanated not from a desire to maximize economic profitability or utility alone, per the neo-classical economic school of thought, but instead were based on a desire to conform to a set of values that transcended personal economic gain. This framework provided an experiential foundation for exploring ways to value other environmental, social, and governance objectives in investing.

Christian investing

John Wesley's 1872 sermon, "The Use of Money," outlined the basic tenants of what became known as **socially responsible investing**. Wesley instructed his parish to use and invest money only in ways that did not hinder or damage the opportunities of other men. He stated:

> We are . . . to gain all we can without hurting our neighbor. But this we may not, cannot do, if we love our neighbor as ourselves. We cannot, if we love everyone as ourselves, hurt anyone *in his substance*. We cannot devour the increase of his lands, and perhaps the lands and houses themselves, by gaming, by overgrown bills (whether on account of physic, or law, or anything else,) or by requiring or taking such interest as even the laws of our country forbid. Hereby all pawn-broking is excluded: Seeing, whatever good we might do thereby, all unprejudiced men see with grief to be abundantly overbalanced by the evil. And if it were otherwise, yet we are not allowed to "do evil that good may come." We cannot, consistent with brotherly love, sell our goods below the market price; we cannot study to ruin our neighbor's trade, in order to advance our own; much less can we entice away or receive any of his servants or workmen whom he has need of. None can gain by swallowing up his neighbor's substance, without gaining the damnation of hell![1]

This sermon grew to be the foundation of socially responsible investing practices for the Methodists. The Quakers in the 18th century acted upon these principles and boycotted investments which supported the slave trade using **issue-specific screening strategies**. This went directly against the wisdom of the day, which insisted that slavery made up the necessary building blocks of Southern culture and profitability.

Islamic investing

Interpretations of the Koran likewise influenced investing practices, developing into what is now known as Islamic investing. This manner of investing avoids companies involved with undesirable industries ranging from pork to gambling. Islamic investing, otherwise referred to as **sharia-compliant investing**, follows a few basic rules, including the screening of investments in companies involved with alcohol, tobacco, pork-related products, conventional finance, defense, weapons, gambling, casinos, music, hotels, cinema, and adult entertainment. More broadly, sharia-compliant investing screens for the following criteria:

1   Business of the investee company should be halal (permissible per Islamic law)
2   Interest-bearing debt should be less than 40% of total assets
3   Non-sharia-compliant investments should be smaller than 33% of total assets
4   Non-compliant income should be less than 5% of the total revenue of the investee company

5   The quotient of illiquid assets and total assets should be greater than 20%
6   The market price per share should be higher than the net liquid asset per share (Lobe, Röble, and Walkshäusl, 2012)

These rudimentary investment screening processes developed by Christian and Islamic investment strategies continued to be refined throughout the 1800s and into the early 1900s.

The awakening of corporate social responsibility

As these religious groups continued to develop issue-specific screens to exclude undesirable investments, the concept of **corporate social responsibility** and the role of private business in the public sphere also began to develop. This era (1890–1900) brought the realization for many investors that the role of corporations effecting positive social change might be relevant to portfolio construction and capital allocation (Schueth, 2003; Epstein, 1987; Waring and Lewer, 2004; Gilbert, 2010; Renneboog, Ter Horst, and Zhang, 2008). The 1900s brought an increased interest in the effects of business ethics and corporate social responsibility on financial performance. These topics began to make their way into academic literature during this period as well. Albion W. Small published his study "Private Business Is a Public Trust" in the *Journal of Sociology* (1895), joining his fellows within the **behavioral economic** field in asserting the inseparable relationship between economics, psychology, and sociology. Small famously stated:

> In back of all formal contracts or statutes or institutions, therefore, is this unwritten law of civilization that every citizen shall be a public servant. The cycles of social growth, arrest, decay, have always illustrated in turn observance, neglect, and violation of this law. Men and institutions have begun by serving their day and generation in a socially meaningful way. They have sometimes ended by making their day and generation serve them in a socially harmful way. Then has come social condemnation, rejection, substitution . . . every class, occupation, and institution, past or present, is a specific application or perversion of this unwritten law of reciprocal human agency. The presumption behind our political, industrial, civil, educational, and ecclesiastical order is that it is the best arrangement at present practicable to secure from each member of society the quality and quantity of work which each is best fitted to render, in return for the services of society as a whole.
>
> (Small, 1895, 285)

In this groundbreaking study, Small asserted that it was a fundamental responsibility of all private business to be a servant of the larger society. This statement profoundly changed the expectations for public businesses. Berle and Means, in their 1932 publication "Modern Corporation and Private Property" further supported Small's argument by declaring corporations to be more than simply "legal devices," but "a 'corporate system' – as there was once a feudal system. This recognition entitled corporations to a similar degree of prominence, causing them to be dealt with as a major social institutions" (548). They detailed clearly how public corporations had their earliest foundations in undertakings involving "a direct public interest," such as "the construction of turnpikes, bridges and canals, the operation of banks and insurance companies, and the creation of fire brigades." They argue that corporations, having been founded with the public interest as a primary focus, have a duty both in philanthropic efforts and in conscientious day-to-day business practices. Andrew Carnegie famously exemplified this behavior and provided evidence for Berle and Means's conclusions in his many publications and speeches. In his 1899 book *The Gospel of Wealth*, Carnegie contended that wealthy individuals and businesses alike had a steward-like obligation to their communities, caring for the privileges granted them, including property, influence, and opportunities. Carnegie's influence spread throughout the early 20th century, and combined with Berle and Means's work, began to impact the direction of the roles of corporations in society. J.D. Rockefeller, influenced by Carnegie's example, donated $183 million to start the Rockefeller foundation in 1913. Rockefeller continued this interest in **corporate social responsibility** well into the 1900s, supporting academic works such as "Social Responsibilities of Business Corporations," a survey conducted to study the multiple objectives of a modern corporation in 1968 (Paul and Hall, 1995). This subsidized publication motivated many prominent business leaders to begin speaking publicly about the importance of incorporating social responsibility into corporate decision-making. Henry Ford, founder of Ford Motors, likewise came to see his role as more than simply to earn a profit. Ford famously stated, "A business that makes nothing but money is a poor type of business" (Wulfson, 2001), and was famous for providing abundantly for his employees, beyond any corporations of his time. The Great Depression and World War II continued to popularize the process of considering extra-financial factors within company policy. It is perhaps only natural that the weight of social responsibility should spread from corporations to shareholders. Investors and consumers became increasingly educated through academic publications and through raised awareness from philanthropists and prominent members of society such as Rockefeller, Carnegie, and Ford until corporations were positively contributing to society. Particularly during the Great Depression, investors were inspired in a large measure by general concern over the rapidly growing economic, political, and social power of large business organizations. Consequently, there were numerous attempts to render these corporate giants formally accountable to public authority, primarily through the legal process. The result of this concern, combined with increased insight into company impact and founded upon the **investment screening processes** of the Quakers and Methodists, introduced the widespread implementation of **filtering investments through non-financial screens**, bringing elements of socially responsibility into mainstream portfolio theory (Hill, 2006; Epstein, 1987).

In 1953, Howard Bowen's *Social Responsibilities of the Businessman* ushered in the second era of socially responsible investing: the development era.

2.3 Development era: key milestones in the development of SRI investing (1950s–1990s)

The intense cultural development of the 1950s–1990s increased a national emphasis on individual social responsibility (Schueth, 2003). The SRI development era built upon the foundation of changing economic theories, religious practices, and business ethics, with increasing attention to social responsibility. A number of significant historical events and trends in the 1950s through the 1980s contributed to the enabling environment wherein SRI investing flourished. Schueth (2003), in his article "Socially Responsible Investing in the United States," described the impassioned political climate of the 1960s as the beginning of this era with thematic movements such as the anti-Vietnam war protests, civil and women's rights activities, and concerns about the Cold War. Schueth (2003) argues that these political themes escalated the individual's sensitivity to social accountability.

Protests and social change initiatives brought to the attention of the public during the turmoil of the 1950s and 1960s renewed interest in the social implications of business practices and investments (Hill, 2006; Schueth, 2003). The culture inspired by the aftermath of World War II, the Cold War, and the Civil Rights Movement further emphasized the importance of social responsibility to investors and businessmen (Renneboog, Ter Horst, and Zhang, 2008; Gilbert, 2010; Schueth, 2003).

In the decades following World War II, conversation about socially responsible investing shifted from questions about the necessity of socially responsible investment opportunities **to** questions about methods for integrating non-financial information into investment theory (Schueth, 2003). During the 1970s, investors and businessmen began to reconsider the traditional view of social responsibility, broadening it from a peripheral concern to a primary focus (Epstein, 1987; Schueth, 2003; Berry and Junkus, 2012; Hill, 2006), and moving SRI from a niche market strategy to a common investment philosophy (Revelli, 2016; Epstein, 1987; Schueth, 2003).

CASE STUDY 2A: Pilgrims Fund Board

Lembaga Tabung Haji (Pilgrims Fund Board) – TH – was established as a premier economic-based Islamic financial institution. The institution's goal was to provide investment services and opportunities while managing pilgrimage activities for the Malaysian Muslim community.

TH was intended for a bigger social role. In addition to managing pilgrimage activities, it operates as an alternative institutional body providing investment opportunities for Islamic depositors to save and invest in accordance to Islamic principles. Depositors' money is invested in selected investment establishments spread across a diverse range of investment portfolios based strictly on Sharia principles to preserve the purity and integrity of profits derived, which is free from "riba" elements and to avoid trading in prohibited "haram" products.

The fund board was established in 1962 as a modest proposal to aid the Malayan rural economy and to enable the Muslims to perform "Hajj," one of the tenets of their faith. Today TH is one of the greatest cooperative success stories in Malaysia. Its basic principles, structured by the Royal Professor Ungku Aziz (an economic lecturer who later became the Vice Chancellor of the University Malaya) remain unchanged, but the institution has developed beyond imagination.

In the early days, the Islamic community in Malaysia resorted to rather unsystematic and traditional methods to save money for the holy pilgrimage. Most believed that money kept under the pillow at home was a guaranteed way to preserve its integrity and keep it free of "riba" practices.

Another critical focus relates to the selling off their land and property for the same purpose. Such unsafe and imprudent ways hinder the growth of the nation's economic resiliency. Pilgrims returning home suffer economic instability with the loss of their vital assets in life such as houses and breeding animals which had either been sold or mortgaged in order to enable them to go perform their hajj.

To overcome this problem, a working paper on "A Plan to Improve the Economic Position of Potential Pilgrims" was presented to the government by the Royal Professor Ungku Aziz in 1959 with the objective of setting up a "riba-free" financial institution operating on a profit basis in line with Islamic principles. The proposal was fully endorsed and praised by Sheikh Muhammad al-Shaltout, the Grand Mufti of Egypt who visited Malaysia at that time.

Following this, in August 1962 the Malayan Pilgrim Savings Corporation was given "quasi" status gazette in November of the same year. The incorporation was launched on September 30, 1963 and six years later merged with the Pilgrims Control Office based in Penang since 1951, giving birth to Lembaga Urusan dan Tabung Haji (Pilgrims Management and Fund Board). In 1995, a study was made to expand the operating framework of TH. As a result, the new Tabung Haji Act 1995 was approved and enacted by the Parliament and Act 8 of Lembaga Urusan Tabung Haji Act 1969 was repealed by Act 535 of the Laws of Malaysia.

With the new Act, TH is able to extend its business networking globally.

Regional examples of historical SRI investing

Malaysia — In 1962, the Lembaga Tabung Haji (the Pilgrim's Fund Board) was created in South-east Asia as the first Islamic Investing fund. This fund had a dual purpose: to provide investment opportunities and services to help Muslims save money for the holy pilgrimage, and to manage pilgrim activities for the Malaysian Muslim community. The Pilgrim's Fund Board invested depositors' money in a wide range of investment portfolios, all of which were consistent with Sharia principles (Siddiqui, 2007).

Sweden — Aktie Ansvar Myrberg, a Swedish responsible investing fund, was founded in 1965 by the Frikyrko and Recreation Movement and intentionally avoided investments in companies concerned with arms, tobacco, distribution of pornography, or alcohol.

United Methodist Church — The Pax World Fund, the first modern SRI fund, was founded shortly after in 1971 by Luther Tyson and Jack Corbett, employees of the United Methodist Church. Tyson and Corbett saw the opportunity to create a mutual fund that allowed investors to easily align their investments with their personal convictions. It embodied the new investment philosophy of the 1960s and 1970s and was catalyzed by the events of the Vietnam War, the Cold War, and the impassioned political climate of the day. These two men responded by providing an innovative method for investors to incorporate non-financial information into their investment decisions. This mutual fund was launched on August 10, 1971 with $101,000 in assets and with the expressed mandate to invest in companies with no military business. It was the first mutual fund in America to implement non-financial screens within investment portfolio construction (Pax World Fund, 2017).

South Africa and the Sullivan Principles — Around this same time, awareness of and dismay at the policies of Apartheid in South Africa caused Americans to demand action at the public and private level. Beyond sanctions and public confrontations, the American people employed private actions to incite public change in South Africa. Most notably, in 1971, Reverend Leon Sullivan constructed the famous "Sullivan Principles" which were intended to guide business practices in South Africa, and which assisted in the development of exclusion and screening principles worldwide (MacLean, 2012; Stewart, 2011). These six principles were:

1   Non-segregation of the races in all eating, comfort, and work facilities
2   Equal and fair employment practices for all employees
3   Equal pay for all employees doing equal or comparable work for the same time period
4   Initiation and development of training programs that will prepare, in substantial numbers, blacks and other nonwhites for supervisory, administrative, clerical, and technical jobs
5   An increase in the number of blacks and other nonwhites in management and supervisory positions, and
6   Improvement in the quality of employees' lives outside the work environment in such areas as housing, transportation, schooling, recreation, and health facilities

These principles became a model for protesting Apartheid and began to define the vague policies of socially responsible investing. At the time, socially responsible investing suffered from a severe lack of defined reasoning or terminology, causing many businesspeople and investors to distain the practices, as Langbein and Posner did in their 1980 article "Social Investing and the Law of Trusts." Langbein and Posner stated,

> It is not easy to specify the portfolio adjustments that an investor committed to social investing would have to make, because the social principles are poorly specified. There is no consensus about which social principles to pursue and about which investments are consistent or inconsistent with those principles.

(1)

They argued that this inconsistency would result in an ill-diversified portfolio with higher risk and lower return potential than a "non-social" investment strategy might yield. Leon Sullivan's principles began to break the superficial surface of socially responsible investing, providing more depth with which investors could investigate and qualitatively measure corporations.

In 1978, following the publication of the Sullivan Principles, the *Wall Street Journal* published an article detailing the Longshoremen and Warehouse Union's decision to avoid investing their pension fund in South African stocks to protest Apartheid. This decision was one of the first documented cases of "**negative screening**," sometimes referred to as "**exclusion**" in a large-scale investment portfolio (Waring and Lewer, 2004). In October 1979, the United Auto Workers followed suit and insisted that their labor contract with Chrysler Corporation mandated that up to 10% of new pension contributions be invested in "socially desirable projects" that benefited the community such as schools, nursing homes, and other like public projects. Perhaps more powerfully, the labor agreement also gave the United Auto Workers the right to reject up to five companies that conducted business in South Africa as a way of protesting Apartheid (Langbein and Posner, 1980).

Domini 400 Social Index – As investors became increasingly aware of social and environmental issues, research began to circulate about potential strategies for ethical and responsible investing (Berry and Junkus, 2012; Hill, 2006). Amy Domini, a retail stockbroker in Boston, noted this trend towards ethical and responsible investing and published *Ethical Investing* in 1984. She wrote about the practical considerations involved in incorporating exclusion and positive screening strategies within portfolio construction. The concepts of ethical and responsible investing appealed to investors on a social and corporate level. Domini's work was instrumental in incorporating concerns about the potential impact of responsible investing on portfolio returns. Domini's work suggested that metrics used for traditional investment strategies could be tailored to more accurately measure the effectiveness of responsible investing strategies. In response to the growing interest, Amy Domini, Peter Kinder, and Steven Lydenberg introduced the **Domini 400 Social Index** in 1990. This index tracked 400 large-cap companies specifically selected for their "positive social and environmental track records" (Gilbert, 2010; Sauer, 1997; Harjoto, 2011). They created the index to be comparable to the Dow Jones Industrial Average or the Standard & Poor's 500 and to be used to determine the financial benefits of investing with social, environmental, and governance factors incorporated into portfolio construction. This index became the backbone of a financial movement, which sought to demonstrate that socially responsible investing could provide equal or superior returns to traditional investment strategies (Gilbert, 2010; Duuren et al. 2015; Revelli and Viviani, 2014).

The Ecumenical Council for Corporate Responsibility (ECCR) – As these ideas developed, events like the Affordable Housing Act, the Chernobyl disaster in 1986, and the Exxon spill in 1989 made supplementing traditional investment strategies with responsible investing factors more attractive. The concept of exclusion became popular, particularly amongst those religious or socially conscious investors who, like those Jewish, Methodists, Quakers, Islamists and other religious investors before them, sought to avoid investing in certain industries or companies they perceived as antithetical to their values (Schueth, 2003; Brimble, 2013; Waring and Lewer, 2004; Renneboog, Ter Horst, and Zhang, 2008). In 1984, the former Quaker UK Life Office Friends Provident launched the Friends Provident Stewardship fund, which approached investing with three goals:

1 Support companies that have a positive impact on society
2 Avoid companies that have a negative impact on society, and
3 Encourage companies to behave more "ethically" or "responsibly"

These three goals are incredibly significant, as they demonstrate the development of responsible factors into portfolio construction. While in the 1800s, responsible investing was exclusively incorporated through "**negative screening**," here it is evident that new strategies such as "**positive** screening" and "engagement" were seen as opportunities to enhance the investor's risk profile and return potential. These new strategies would continue to develop until the present. (Chapter 4 will critically assess the extent to which these strategies and others are currently incorporated into the broader field of ESG investing.) In 1989, the Ecumenical Council for Corporate Responsibility was founded in the UK. This council was comprised of British industrial chaplains who had learned about unethical practices being implemented at a UK company headquartered in the Philippines. These chaplains sought to establish what a "good" company looked like, and what the definition of corporate responsibility should be in practice. From there, the ECCR began to actively engage with companies and countries who sought to improve their shareholder resolutions or corporate responsibility standards.

2.4 The modern era: 1990s–today

The creation of the Domini 400 Social Index, now known as the MSCI KLD 400 Social Index, in combination with the creation of the ECCR, heralded the modern era of socially responsible investing.

Seven Pillars of Corporate Social Performance and Responsibility (CSP/CSR) – After the creation of the Domini 400 Social Index in 1990, Kinder, Lydenberg, and Domini formed KLD, State Street Corp., which began offering SRI mutual funds (Gilbert, 2010), and Jantzi Research Associate, Inc. was established by Michael Jantzi in 1992 (Gilbert, 2010). Michael Jantzi went on to develop the corporate social performance (often referred to as CSP/CSR) as a measure built from **seven pillars**, including:

1   Community issues
2   Diverse workplace
3   Employee relations
4   Environmental performance
5   International
6   Product and business practice, and
7   "Other" (including compensation, proxy voting, ownership in other companies, etc.)

ESG rating system and asset returns – These seven pillars were established in the following years as foundational to the qualitative measurement of sustainability practices within corporations, as well as the development of quantitative metrics which were useful in portfolio construction. Within Michael **Jantzi's model**, companies were assessed on a −2 to +2 scale (−2 indicating severe concern, +2 indicating major success), within the bounds of each of the seven pillars (Fauzi, 2009). This system was the beginning of the **ESG rating system**, which has simultaneously provided cross-sectional data aiding in the prediction of the return distribution of assets in variety of asset classes. His model has also allowed companies to measure the extent to which their behaviors are deemed responsible by a variety of third-party agents who performed in-depth, quantitative, and unbiased analysis of a myriad of corporate issues. The ESG rating system, which will be discussed in Chapter 3, provided an opportunity for companies and private investors alike to integrate environmental, social, and governance preferences into their investment policy, which provided increased insight into previously unrecognized risks within those investments. Around the same time that Jantzi Research Associates developed in 1992, Eugene Fama and Kenneth French published their groundbreaking study "The Cross-Section of Expected Stock Returns," which developed the first asset pricing model to weigh a collection of specifically identified risks to attempt to predict the return distribution of an asset. A large part of Fama and French's conclusion was that cross-sectional data on the risks they identified as material to returns truly allowed investors to more accurately predict asset returns. This same cross-sectional data was developing in the ESG space at the time that Fama and French first published their asset pricing model. Until this time, the foundation was simply being laid for the cautious acceptance of the possibility that ESG integration could provide investors more opportunities to pursue returns in a saturated market.

United Nation's Principles for Responsible Investment (PRI) – The development of this cross-sectional global data was supported in large part by European legislation that required businesses to disclose environmental and social practices. This legislation is best displayed by the 2002 High Level Group of Company Law Experts Report, which was one of the first to implement government policy changes because of the rising interest in responsible investing. This report specifically focused on improving corporate disclosure requirements, shareholders' rights and proxy voting, board regulations, and the broader responsibilities of institutional investors. This set the tone for the 2003 Corporate Governance Action Plan, which supported the 2002 High Level Group of Company Law Experts Report, and further established the regulation of corporate disclosure and shareholders' rights, particularly in the context of transparency within boards of directors. Perhaps the most significant report to date within the sphere of responsible investing is the 2004 Environmental Programme Finance Initiative Report, published by the United Nations, which first coined the phrase "Environmental, Social, Corporate Governance analysis" to describe the categories of analysis in socially responsible investing (Gilbert, 2010). This phrase was later shortened to ESG investing (Gilbert, 2010). The United Nations further established the Principles for Responsible Investment, which was released in 2006 (Gilbert, 2010; Himick, 2011; United Nations, 2006). These principles have served the purpose of setting standards by which companies can set their policies. **The Principles for Responsible Investment (PRI)** declare six basic principles:

1   We will incorporate ESG issues into investment analysis and decision-making processes
2   We will be active owners and incorporate ESG issues into our ownership policies and practices
3   We will seek appropriate disclosure on ESG issues by the entities in which we invest
4   We will promote acceptance and implementation of the principles within the investment industry
5   We will work together to enhance our effectiveness in implementing the principles
6   We will each report on our activities and progress towards implementing the principles (United Nations, N/A)

The PRI currently have over 1,600 signatories, globally and industry-wide.

Impact investing – Soon after, Deutsche Asset Management established the first thematic mutual fund, which focused on climate change (Gilbert, 2010). Thematic portfolio construction quickly developed into a common investment strategy known as "impact investing" (Gilbert, 2010; Domanska-Szaruga and Wysokinska-Senkus, 2013; Combs, 2014). Green Investing became a common impact-investing model, wherein portfolios were constructed with the goal of reducing environmental risk (Domanska-Szaruga and Wysokinska-Senkus, 2013; Lesser, Lobe, and Walkshausl, 2014). This was especially made visible by the 2015 conference of parties at the United Nations Climate Change Conference (also referred to as COP21). Multiple countries made public commitments to reduce greenhouse gas emissions through greenhouse gas reduction goals.

Government initiatives support ESG investing – Since the 1990s many studies have sought to quantify the value of research-based ESG integration by measuring returns, volatility, overall portfolio performance, and other quantitative investment metrics, as well as measuring the extent to which ESG-based investment strategies have been integrated into institutional investment portfolios (Dorfleitner, Halbitter, and Nguye, 2015; Banerjee and Orzano, 2010; Chelawat and Trivedi, 2013; Duuren et al. 2015; Himick, 2011; Meziani, 2014; Odell and Ali, 2016). The United Nations and the US Department of Labor, as well as many independent national regulatory bodies, have encouraged investors to integrate ESG-based strategies into investment portfolios (United Nations, 2006; Department of Labor, 2015; European Commission, 2014; Ioannou and Serafeim, 2011). The US

Department of Labor issued new guidance in 2015 on **Economically Targeted Investments** within retirement plans. The Department of Labor defined ETIs as "investments that are selected for the benefits they create in addition to the investment return to the employee benefit plan investor." In this new issue, the US Secretary of Labor, Thomas E. Perez, stated:

> Investing in the best interest of a retirement plan and in the growth of a community can go hand in hand. We have heard from stakeholders that a 2008 department interpretation has unduly discouraged plan fiduciaries from considering economically targeted investments. Changes in the financial markets since that time, particularly improved metrics and tools allowing for better analysis of investments, make this the right time to clarify our position.

This new issue specifically confirms that

> the department's long-standing view that fiduciaries may not accept lower expected returns or take on greater risks to secure collateral benefits but may take such benefits into account as tiebreakers when investments are otherwise equal with respect to their economic and financial characteristics. The guidance also acknowledges that environmental, social and governance factors may have a direct relationship to the economic and financial value of an investment. When they do, these factors are more than just tiebreakers, but rather are proper components of the fiduciary's analysis of the economic and financial merits of competing investment factors.
>
> (Department of Labor, 2015, 1)

This ruling did much to change the general attitude by large pension funds towards ETIs and ESG research-based strategies within portfolio construction. Due to the influence of these regulatory bodies, ESG-based investing strategies have become more commonly integrated, not only in developed nations such as the United States and Western Europe, but also increasingly within emerging market nations such as parts of Asia and Latin America (Odell and Ali, 2016; Passant et al. 2016).

Figure 2.1 details the breakdown by region of socially responsible investments (as of end of year 2016).

Table 2.1 details the proportion of SRI assets relative to total managed assets within each region, demonstrating the significance in weighting towards responsible investing strategies for each region.

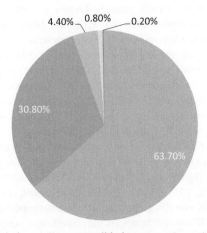

Figure 2.1 Proportion of global socially responsible investment assets by region

Table 2.1 Proportion of socially responsible investments relative to total managed assets[2]

Region	Proportion of SRI assets relative to total managed assets
Europe	52.60%
United States	21.60%
Canada	37.80%
Australia/New Zealand	50.60%
Asia	0.80%
Japan	3.40%
Global	26.30%

It is imperative to note that though the United States accounts for approximately 38.1% of global SRI assets, SRI assets only make up 21.6% of its total managed assets. Interestingly, though Canada only makes up 4.7% of global SRI assets, its socially responsible investments account for 37.8% of Canadian total managed assets. This is extremely significant, as it supports the notion that SRI assets are an opportunity for arbitrage within regions. This conclusion is founded in the idea that regions such as the United States have failed to thus far incorporate SRI assets into its investment strategies to the extent that Canada and parts of Europe have done, indicating that an interesting development will take place in the next few years to demonstrate whether incorporating ESG strategies such as screening (both positive and negative), ESG integration, and ESG engagement will prove themselves to provide higher returns than investments without such information incorporated.

Figure 2.2 shows the breakdown between institutional and retail investments within responsible investing.

The data provided by the GSIA 2016 Annual Report demonstrates the rapid growth of ESG investments, and the influence of social, environmental, and governance-based ideals on both retail and institutional investors.

Today, the major indices measuring the aggregate performance of ESG-rated companies are the MSCI Inc. ESG indices, the Dow Jones Sustainability Index, and the Sustainalytics STOXX ESG Leaders indices. Chapters 3 and 7 will discuss the implications that these indices have on the performance effect of incorporating ESG factors within portfolio construction and management.

The development of ESG investing throughout the centuries has been one founded fundamentally on the relationship between financial return and social, environmental, and governance-based convictions. Religious investors originally introduced the thought that their beliefs should influence their investment practices. From there, other investors increasingly became convinced that their investment decisions could influence cultural events, and began to develop the idea that responsible investing factors could be helpful indicators of a company's long-term financial performance. This combination of basic business sense and investor sentiment led to the introduction of ESG-integrated funds, ESG best-in-class investments, ESG screened funds, and thematic funds. These funds have grown in popularity especially over the past few years, and have been shown to outperform their benchmarks over a long-term time frame (this will be discussed further in Chapters 3 and 7). ESG-incorporated investments are growing within the institutional and retail investment fields in all regions, as demonstrated by the data from the Global Sustainable Investment Review (2016). With this growth comes new opportunities for investors and academics to investigate the extent to which ESG-factor incorporation within investment strategies is demonstrated by stock prices. As this is still such a relatively new field to be measured and studied, it will be interesting to investigate in the next few years what the opportunities are for yielding higher financial performance from ESG-incorporated investments globally.

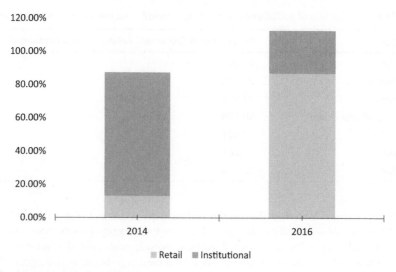

Figure 2.2 Institutional/retail SRI assets

Data sourced from the GSIA 2016 Annual Report

CASE STUDY 2B: African Investing for Impact Barometer (2016)

The African Investing for Impact Barometer is compiled from publicly available information sourced from fund manager disclosures, and seeks to provide insight into the impact investing market in Africa, and specifically within Eastern, Western, and Southern Africa. It specifically focuses on the three largest economies in Eastern, Western, and Southern Africa: Nigeria, Kenya, and South Africa, respectively. As of 2016, Sothern Africa has reported $325.9 billion invested in strategies with at least one sustainable investing strategy, such as ESG screening, ESG integration, ESG engagement, sustainability-themed investing, or impact investing. Eastern Africa reported a total of $15.4 billion invested with at least one of those strategies, and Western Africa reported $12.6 billion invested with at least one of those strategies. Though the leading ESG strategy in Southern Europe was reported to be ESG integration (attracting a total of $307.7 billion), sustainability-themed investing leads the ESG strategies in Eastern and Western Africa, attracting a total of $11.7 billion and $9.8 billion in assets under management respectively.

The IFI strategy gaining great momentum amongst African fund managers is sustainability-themed investment, most notably in East Africa and West Africa. Prominent sustainability themes receiving allocations of assets include agriculture, SMEs, energy, health, inclusive financial services, and substantial allocations to infrastructure investments. This is encouraging for the achievement of the United Nations Sustainable Development goals (SDGs), which will require private capital to be achieved. However, investments in other key sustainability themes for the SDGs, such as education or water and sanitation, are not as prominent (in fund manager portfolios). Education is in 9th position in Southern Africa whereas in East and West Africa, education stands at the 6th position. In Southern Africa, water and sanitation is the 12th most prominent sustainability theme funded. The water and sanitation sustainability theme is in 7th and 9th position respectively in East and West Africa.

Today, many investors have accepted the advantages of ESG research-based integration into portfolio allocation (Roselle, 2016). As the result of increased research, retail investors and wealth managers are adopting ESG research-based investment integration at some level into their investment portfolios (Roselle, 2016). According to the 2016 Global Sustainable Investment Alliance report, a total of $22.89 trillion (as of December 2016) is invested globally in socially responsible investments (see The Global Sustainable Investment Review, 2016).

Footprints and handprints

Chapter 3 will provide detail on ESG investment research and risk, and Chapter 4 will discuss the mainstream ESG investment approaches. The evolution of ESG investing has transformed the practice to no longer being limited to excluding certain securities or only focusing on an investor's footprints. Now, investors structure their investments, as well as measure investment performance, through the lens of "footprints" and "handprints." "Footprints" are the intangible costs or negative implications of our actions and existence. This encompasses everything from the pollution our cars create, to the inadvertent social and environmental consequences of our choices as a consumer. While a footprint is combination of the negative impacts one's investments have on the environment or society, a handprint is all of the positive things one does to affect their footprint. "Handprints" are the contributions or positive implications that are created by an investor's investments and investment decisions. This includes reductions an investor brings about in their own footprints, reductions an investor may bring about in the footprints of others, and actions that have a positive effect on the world and its population. A handprint of a product can be created either by preventing or avoiding negative impacts (footprints) that would otherwise have occurred, or by creating positive benefits that would not have occurred.

LEARNING PERSPECTIVE 1: handprinting: driving positive impacts

Gregory A. Norris, Ph.D., in addition to teaching life cycle assessment at Harvard School of Public Health, is also co-director of SHINE (Sustainability and Health Initiative for Net-positive Enterprise). SHINE is an initiative of the Harvard School of Public Health's Center for Health and the Global Environment. It helps corporations across all sectors measure and accelerate the ways in which they help the world become a healthier, more sustainable place, by connecting business leadership with pioneering research to advance corporate responsibility, sustainability, and health and well-being practices across the globe.

Norris also founded New Earth, a nonprofit institute developing and deploying technologies that enable people around the world to drive sustainable development from the bottom up. Its projects include Earthster, an open-source platform for product-level sustainability assessment; Handprinter, which helps people take actions at home and at work to compensate for their environmental and social footprints; and the Social Hot Spots Database, a transparent data source on supply chain impacts and opportunities for improving human rights, working conditions, and community. In 1996, Norris founded Sylvatica, an international life cycle assessment institute that has consulted on LCA to the UN, governments in the US and abroad, a variety of Fortune 500 companies as well as smaller companies, industrial associations, and the nonprofit sector.

Norris was a member of the Royal Government of Bhutan's International Expert Working Group, comprised of 60 experts from around the world. The WG was engaged to draft a new

*global development paradigm to promote human flourishing as a global goal through effective
and pragmatic international public policies. He is an editor for the International Journal of
LCA, the Journal of Industrial Ecology, and Greenhouse Gas Measurement and Management.*

Part 1: introduction to handprints

What are handprints?

The concept of "handprinting" – causing changes, ideally positive ones, relative to business as usual – is gaining visibility within sustainability assessment and reporting in
recent years. This comes as part of an increased interest in encouraging actors at all
levels to pursue the creation of positive impacts with greater intent, *and* at greater scale.
The increased interest is evidenced in part by:

- The rise of publications and meetings on the topic of accounting for "avoided
  emissions";
- The rise in activity under the heading of "net positive" sustainability, including several
  multi-stakeholder initiatives on this topic at both national and international scales; and
- The rise of public commitments, by more than a few companies, to not only continually reduce their footprints but also to increase their creation of positive impacts.
  Some of these commitments go further still by declaring the pursuit of net positivity,
  conceptualized as creating positive impacts (e.g., handprints) greater than the company's footprints, on some or all material footprint impact categories.

Now, there is certainly nothing new about companies claiming that they provide positive
impacts or benefits in the world, nor in setting out to increase them. But what makes
the recent action on positive sustainability impacts notable is that the positive impacts
are *meant to occur in relation to the same impact categories for which footprints are being
reduced*. And it is this sameness of impact category that drove handprinting methods to be
intentionally built on the same foundation as are footprinting methods: life cycle assessment (LCA). For more on the origins of handprinting, see "Handprinting origins."

A recently approved Annex to the ISO 14044 standards for LCA provides the definition for footprint as "Metric(s) used to report life cycle assessment results addressing an
area of concern." In turn, area of concern is defined in this same Annex as an "Aspect of
the natural environment, human health or resources of interest to society." Given these
definitions, the definition of a handprint can be explicitly connected to the LCA-based definition of footprints, as follows:

Handprints are positive changes that we bring about, in relation to an area of concern, relative to business as usual; they are reported using the same metrics used to
report footprints.

Handprinting origins

I've been practicing and teaching life cycle assessment (LCA) since the mid-1990s. LCA
can be considered the art and science of footprint assessment. This of course includes
providing guidance to all kinds of decision makers about how they – we – can reduce our
footprints. So, it can feel like a worthwhile and meaningful pursuit.

But it didn't take me too many years of LCA practice to realize that no matter how
much I might help clients reduce the footprints of their goods and services, they would not
be able to bring these footprints to zero. And I immediately connected this back to my life:

I'm using products and services every day. No matter how much responsible consumption I pursue – biking to work, eating less meat, insulating my home, etc. – I'll still have a footprint. Strictly speaking, in footprint terms, the planet would be better off without me.

I remember it was around 2,000 when this realization hit home. And I immediately asked myself how I might go about changing this fact. Could I live my life in a way that meant there were somehow *less* pollution and *more resources available* as a result of my presence? As an LCA consultant, the natural place for me to look was via *creating change*. I reasoned that if I could help a client such as a Fortune 100 company make major reductions in the footprints of their products that they wouldn't make without my help, then maybe the net result of me living my life this year could be beneficial: positive changes (handprints!) greater than the "cost" of supporting my life that year (my footprint). And I realized that this potential to create positive change rested with every person, not just LCA consultants. Each of us, all of us, can help our neighbors reduce their footprints and can help organizations in our communities reduce their footprints. We can do this by sharing good ideas, coming up with new ones, providing funding or labor to projects that reduce footprints and create positive social and environmental impacts.

I started sharing this message with some corporations, and with students at the end of my semester-long course in LCA at Harvard. The students in particular found it motivating, and many told me so. This led me to make handprinting the center of the course. But the big change came in 2011 when Dan Goleman and the Mind and Life Institute invited me to present footprints and LCA to His Holiness the Dalai Lama in India. I developed and shared an explanation of handprints to the organizing committee for that wonderful meeting. That exercise, and the reception of all present at the meeting – including of course His Holiness! – encouraged me to make further development and testing of handprinting methods and actions the focus of my work. That in turn led to the creation of the handprinter app and website, and to the launching of the Sustainability and Health Initiative for Net-Positive Enterprise (SHINE) at Harvard, in which we engage with companies to advance and implement handprinting methods. It also led to an opportunity to integrate handprinting into the "Living Product Challenge" of the International Living Future Institute, and to the co-launching with BSR and FFF of the Net Positive Project. As I've told Dan Goleman more than once, his handprints are all over handprinting! My work with colleagues worldwide on handprinting continues to be a ripple effect of that meeting in Dharamsala, India, in 2011.

What value can handprints bring?
A fair and important question is whether the world needs a new concept or term "handprints" when we are already working well with the concept of footprints. And if handprints are just "changes in footprints" then why don't we just speak about "changes in footprints" and leave it at that, avoiding needless new jargon?

The first key point is that handprints and footprints measure truly different things, even if they are measured in the same units, and even if both are based on LCA. This is true as follows.

- First, handprints and footprints are assessed in relation to different baselines.

  o Footprints (of a product or of a person or of an organization) are assessed in relation to "vanishing without replacement." That is, we assess the footprint for example of an organization relative to a hypothetical scenario from which the organization and its activities all vanished and were not replaced. This baseline for footprints is implicit and in fact is often not even recognized.

- ○ Handprints (of any actor) are assessed in relation to "business as usual" (BAU) for that actor, using intentionally simple and straightforward definitions for BAU. Business as usual for a company is responding to this year's demand with last year's products and processes. BAU for a person is even simpler: a repeat of last year's footprint.

- Second, handprints and footprints address different scopes of influence.

  - ○ Footprints of a product span the full life cycles of the product. Footprints of an organization are given by existing standards for footprint assessment, and generally include the impacts of the activities directly owned and operated by the organization, plus the impacts of the organization's supply chain, plus relevant downstream impacts of the organization's products.
  - ○ Handprints of a given actor include *any* changes brought by the actor in relation to an area of concern (impact category), *both inside and outside the scope of the actor's footprint*. They can include three "handprint scopes":
    - ▪ Internal handprints are changes brought within the footprint of the actor; they are *changes to* the footprint of the actor.
    - ▪ External handprints include changes brought to the footprints of other actors, outside the scope of the footprint of the handprinting actor in question.
    - ▪ External handprints may also include changes that are not footprint changes for any actor, but nevertheless produce changes reportable using the same metrics as are used for footprints, and relevant to the same areas of concern.

The second key point is that handprint assessment is offered as something to add to, and be used in conjunction with, footprint assessment. There is no intent to replace footprint assessment with handprint assessment. Indeed, there is an explicit intent to *retain focus on footprints while attention to handprints is added*. Handprints are to be assessed in relation to, in the context of, footprints. Thus, the addition of handprints is not an attempt to "change the subject," but rather one to broaden the discussion. Handprints leave fully in place the perspective of responsibility that comes with attention to one's own footprints; they further add a sense of opportunity if not further responsibility, to pursue reductions in the footprint of other actors, and of humanity in general, beyond the scope of one's own footprint.

Third, since handprinting has a wider scope of potential influence, and opens many new avenues for action, it frees the actor from a dynamic of "diminishing returns" as the actor's own footprint is increasingly reduced. When the focus is strictly the reduction of one's own footprint, the scope of potential change to bring in subsequent years shrinks along with the actor's footprint. But the scope of handprint potential remains virtually unbounded, at least as long as humanity itself has detrimental impacts in relation to areas of concern.

Fourth, when the focus is strictly the reduction of one's own footprint, we inevitably arrive at the discouraging realization that the goal of zero footprint is unattainable, meaning that we must remain "net negative," a net cost to society in relation to the areas of protection being considered. However, when the focus is expanded to include handprints, this opens the possibility that we can become "net beneficial," having a net positive impact on balance, if we are able to sufficiently shrink our footprint while simultaneously sufficiently growing our handprint. This realization turns out to be transformative to the self-concept of the people involved, and to their notion of the purpose or nature of the organization in question. This shift in self-concept has been seen to unleash higher levels of energy and commitment to the pursuit of sustainability-related goals. The goal of "net positive" is not only inspiring but also ambitious, which has been seen to increase levels of innovation.

Fifth, when the focus is expanded beyond strictly reducing one's own footprint, this promotes collaboration, the sharing of innovation, and designing actions with the expressed intent to maximize their positive "ripple effects," or indirect, secondary/tertiary impacts. The scaling potential brought by ripple effects in turn can help to increase the motivation to consider taking actions that, on an individual level, reduce total impacts by a very small amount, but when scaled can bring benefits that are significant from a macro perspective.

In summary, handprints are, in relation to the focus on reducing one's own footprint:

- Different
- Additional
- Motivational
- Collaboration-promoting
- Unbounded
- Even serving to drive increased attention to actions that reduce one's own footprint, in the context of simultaneous design for intentional ripple effects

Part 2: ways to pursue friendly handprinting activism

Summary of definitions and concepts
To recap: the footprints of an actor, whether a person, organization, or group of such actors, are the negative impacts associated with provision, use, and end-of-life management of the goods and services used by that actor to sustain itself during a year. There are carbon footprints, water footprints, health footprints, biodiversity footprints, even slavery footprints and child labor footprints.

And handprints are changes (in footprint-related impacts) with respect to business as usual, where business as usual (BAU) for an organization performing net positive assessment is defined as: operating in next year's economy with this year's products and processes.

We have also identified three ways to create handprints:

- Be a cause of reductions in your footprint relative to BAU
- Be a cause of reductions in some other actors' footprint relative to BAU
- Create positive impacts which are measurable in footprint units

An actor can be net positive for a given impact category if its handprint for that impact category is greater than its footprint, for a given year. "Handprint larger than footprint" means that the benefits of an actor's presence exceed the burdens of its presence.

While handprints are about change, there is also an important role in the pursuit of Net Positive for Appreciation Analysis, which assesses and quantifies:

- Contributions of a company's existing products relative to those products vanishing without replacement
- Contributions of a company's existing products relative to those products being replaced by the most likely alternative

Appreciation analysis highlights promising business-positive ways to create handprints. A company that makes products whose contribution relative to vanishing exceeds the footprint of creating the product can move towards net positive by increasing demand for such products. A company that makes products whose contribution relative to their most likely alternative exceeds the footprint of creating the product can move towards net positive by increasing their market share for these products.

Another way to move towards net positive – shrinking its footprint and growing its handprint – is through constructive supply chain engagement. For example, a company which transfers technology to its suppliers in order to reduce their carbon footprint will shrink its own footprint (by reducing the footprint of what the actor purchases from their supplier) and further grow its handprint by reducing the footprint of the supplier's other customers.

Process indicators and impacts

As noted above, handprints are changes measurable in footprint units; and they are measures of impact. Much sustainability-related reporting in frameworks such as the GRI relate to impact measures. Handprinting is based on footprinting, which in turn is based on methods of environmental and social life cycle assessment (LCA) which in turn estimates environmental and social impacts of products and services across their life cycle.

In addition to impact measures, much sustainability ranking and assessment of organizations also relates to process indicators. These include characteristics of the company: e.g., levels of gender diversity in leadership positions, presence of an ISO 14000 certified environmental management system, and so on. Process indicators are valued largely because they tend to correlate with impacts of interest.

Many sustainability reporting, ranking, and scoring systems for companies (DJSI, RobecoSAM, FTSE4Good, GRI, etc.) combine process indicators and impact measures. And some process indicators are so salient to stakeholders that a shift in such an indicator can be considered a positive outcome (if not impact). Increasing gender diversity on a board of directors is a good example.

Handprints have been defined so far in relation to impacts, and this is because handprints were developed to be compared directly with footprints. Because of the salience of process indicators for stakeholders, and because of their correlation with material impacts, it will be valuable for friendly handprint activism to develop a second category of positive change indicators (yet to be named, but I'm reluctant to call them handprints) which measure positive movement (change) on process indicators for the company, and perhaps also change on process indicators for portions of its value chain.

Handprint creation examples

There are literally an infinite number of ways to create handprints. The addition of handprint creation into the pursuit of sustainability adds a wide set of "spheres of influence" which were not present when sustainability was primarily about footprint reduction (see Figure 2.3 below).

I provide examples of handprint creating actions for each of the spheres of influence illustrated in the figure. I provide examples of both environmental and social handprints, with several different impact categories in each of these two impact types.

The white portions represent activities in the organization's value chain; they are the spheres of influence for footprint reduction as well.

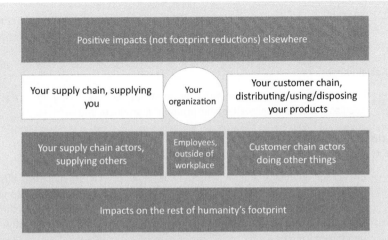

Figure 2.3 Handprinting spheres of influence

Handprint examples by sphere-of-influence segment

Your organization
- Climate handprints

  ○ Pursue energy efficiency in your operations
  ○ Install onsite renewables

- Social Handprints

  ○ Provide right to collective bargaining to employees

Your supply chain (both selling to you, and selling to others)
- Water handprints

  ○ Pursue water use efficiency, or energy efficiency (which brings water footprint reduction benefits) in your suppliers' operations and their supply chains. This will reduce your own footprint by reducing the impacts of what they sell you. Assuming that they also sell to other customers, the "spillover effects" of your engagement will reduce the footprints of their other customers, further growing your handprint.

- Social handprints

  ○ Reduce the risk of child labor at your suppliers. This can be done most effectively by addressing root causes, one of which is poverty wages paid to adults. Thus, raise wages at your supplier, which will reduce the risk of child labor at not only your supplier, but at all businesses in the region. If this is done in a way that puts positive wage pressure on other businesses in the region, this further amplifies the child labor risk handprint.

Your customer chain, distributing, using, disposing your products
- Energy and water and environmental health handprints

  ○ Make your product more energy efficient during the use phase. This reduces your customers' footprint.

- ○ Encourage or engage your customers to use your product in more eco-efficient ways. For example: Levi's encouraging customers to wash in cold water, wash less frequently, and line-dry rather than machine dry their Levi's.
- Social handprints
  - ○ Increase demand for products that bring social benefits during the use phase, such as educational or well-being-promoting products and services.

Your customer chain actors, doing other things
- Energy and water and environmental health handprints
  - ○ Encourage or engage your customers to use *other* products in more eco-efficient ways. For example: when Levi's encourages customers to wash in cold water, wash less frequently, and line-dry rather than machine dry their Levi's, this will likely bring behavior change to their washing and drying of other clothes not purchased from Levi's.

Employees, outside of workplace
- Energy and water and environmental health handprints
  - ○ Engage employees in handprint creation, using the Handprinter.org platform. This enables them to:
    - Take actions and register that they took them, providing quantified estimates of the environmental benefits by impact category
    - Engage their friends, family, neighbors, and others in handprinting, further growing their handprint
    - Propose new actions, which when added to the database and taken by others, further grows their handprint
  - ○ Social handprints
    - Provide volunteering opportunities to employees

Impacts on the rest of humanity's footprint
- Energy and water and environmental health handprints
  - ○ Share handprint action ideas usable by citizens and/or by other organizations; technology transfer to other businesses in your region, etc.
  - ○ Join forces with other companies and other organizations to push for changes in environment-related regulations, such as building codes, zoning ordinances, efficiency standards, etc.
  - ○ Join forces with other companies and other organizations to co-fund research to develop and demonstrate healthier materials, cleaner technologies, etc. Adopt the new technologies first to gain competitive advantage, and disseminate the technologies widely to build long-term brand value.
- Social handprints
  - ○ Join forces with other companies and other organizations to push for changes in socially related regulations, such as minimum wage ordinances.

Positive impacts (not footprint reductions) elsewhere
- Energy and water and environmental health handprints
  - Plant trees, clean up rivers and beaches, etc.
- Social handprints
  - Launch programs supporting local schools, youth groups, etc.

Implementation

Companies can make shifts in process indicators without changing corporate strategy and vision. Companies can likewise bring about footprint reductions, and the creation of some handprints, without such fundamental change. These shifts in process indicators, footprints, and handprints represent positive, value-creating movement that a company can pursue over short and medium time frames. In some cases, such positive shifts represent "low hanging fruit" that can bring upward movement in sustainability rankings and assessment in rapid fashion.

In my experience working with companies pioneering in the net positive sustainability movement, a deeper kind of change is also possible: alignment of the business strategy with the pursuit of net positive outcomes on sustainability impact categories that are material for the company. This shift calls on businesses to perform:

- A materiality assessment, engaging external stakeholders to identify the categories of material adverse impact (footprint) for the company, environmentally and socially
- A footprint assessment, addressing at least all material impact categories, and ideally using environmental and social LCA to double-check and augment input from external stakeholders
- Appreciation analysis: identifying ways that the company's products deliver social value as part of BAU, with respect to vanishing or replacement or both
- Identification of specific ways and examples of how the organization's culture and values align with the net positive aspiration to be a positive contributing member of society, to do more good than harm
- Product innovation around handprint creation
- Promotion of existing net positive products

Companies who pursue net positive in these ways report the following benefits:

- Increased rates of innovation
- Increased employee engagement, recruiting, and retention
- Integration of what had been diverse and even scattered sustainability-related initiatives and goals into a single, simple, coherent, and compelling narrative
- Lifting the company's sustainability case from the level of individual products to the brand as a whole
- Increased profitability among product portfolios with net positive attributes and credentials
- Increased brand value, stakeholder relationships, and license to operate

Discussion questions

1) In your personal assessment of the chronological evolution of ESG investing, when do you feel ESG investing was recognized as investment philosophy, and why was this moment significant to the practice? (LO1)
2) Name:

   a   Two political events contributing to the growth of ESG investing (LO2)
   b   Two social events contributing to the growth of ESG investing (LO2)
   c   Two cultural events contributing to the growth of ESG investing (LO2)

3) Discuss various ways that ESG investing might impact investment returns (LO4)
4) Describe how views on ESG investing differ between regions, culture, and population groups (LO5)
5) Discuss how ESG investing might be considered an expansion of traditional investing principles (LO6)

Notes

1   www.umcmission.org/Find-Resources/John-Wesley-Sermons/Sermon-50-The-Use-of-Money
2   Asia figure includes Japan in 2014, but excludes Japan in 2016. Eurosif used a narrower definition of SRI in 2016 than in 2014. (See Appendix 1 of Global Sustainable Investment Review, 2016, for details.)

References

"About the Pri." About the PRI | Principles for Responsible Investment. www.unpri.org/about. Accessed September 5, 2017.

Banerjee, Alka A., and Michael Orzano. 2010. "Performance Analysis of Two Indian Equity Indices. S&P Indices." S&P Dow Jones Indices, March, 2010. https://us. spindices.com/documents/research/PerformanceAnalysis of Two Indian Equity Indices 2010Mar.pdf. Accessed November, 2016.

Berle, Adolf A., and Gardiner Coit Means.*The Modern Corporation and Private Property*. New York: Harcourt, Brace & World, 1969.

Berry, Thomas C., and Joan C. Junkus. "Socially Responsible Investing: An Investor Perspective." *Journal of Business Ethics* 112, no. 4 (2012): 707–20. doi:10.1007/s10551-012-1567-0.

Brimble, Mark, and Ciorstan Smark. "Financial Planning and Financial Instruments: 2013 in Review, 2014 in Prospect." *Australasian Accounting, Business and Finance Journal* 7, no. 3 (2013): 1–4.

Brzezicka, Justyna, and Wiśniewski, Radosław. "Homo Oeconomicus and Behavioral Economics." *Contemporary Economics* 8, no. 4 (December 28, 2014): 353–64. Available at SSRN: https://ssrn.com/abstract=2548414

Chelawat, Hemlata, and Trivedi, I. V. "Impact of Ethical Screening on Investment Performance in India." *IUP Journal of Financial Risk Management* 10, no. 4 (2013): 16–34.

Combs, K. "More Than Just a Trend: The Importance of Impact Investing." *Corporate Finance Review*, 18, no. 6 (2014): 12–18. https://tkc.idm.oclc.org/login?qurl=?url=http://search.proquest.com/docview/1548696618?accountid=11861

Cortez, Maria Ceu, Florinda Silva, and Nelson Areal. "Socially Responsible Investing in the Global Market: The Performance of US and European Funds." *International Journal of Finance and Economics* 17, no. 3 (2012): 254–71.

Department of Labor. "Interpretive Bulletin Relating to the Fiduciary Standard under ERISA in Considering Economically Targeted Investments." *Department of Labor*, October, 2015. https://dol.gov/opa/media/press/ebsa/ebsa20152045.htm. Accessed November, 2016.

Domańska-Szaruga, B., and Wysokińska-Senkus, A. "Green Investing – Investing Based on Environmental Protection Criteria from the Eastern Europe Perspective." Proceedings of the International Scientific Conference: Rural Development, 2013, 6118–24.

Domini, Amy L., and Peter D. Kinder. *Ethical Investing*. Reading, MA: Addison-Wesley Publ. Co., 1990.

Duuren, Emiel Van, Auke Plantinga, and Bert Scholtens. "ESG Integration and the Investment Management Process: Fundamental Investing Reinvented." *Journal of Business Ethics* 138, no. 3 (2015): 525–33.

Eccles, N. S., and S. Viviers. "The Origins and Meanings of Names Describing Investment Practices that Integrate a Consideration of ESG Issues in the Academic Literature." *Journal of Business Ethics* 104, no. 3 (2011): 389–402.

Epstein, Edwin. "The Corporate Social Policy Process and the Process of Corporate Governance." *American Business Law Journal* 25, no. 3 (1987): 361.

European Commission. "Improving Corporate Governance: Europe's Largest Companies Will Have to Be More Transparent About How They Operate." *European Commission*. 2014. http://europa.eu/rapid/press-release_STATEMENT-14-124_en.htm. Accessed October, 2016.

Eurosif. *European SRI Study*. Brussels: Eurosif, 2014. www.eurosif.org/wp-content/uploads/2014/09/Eurosif-SRI-Study-20142.pdf. Accessed October 1, 2016.

Fauzi, H. "Corporate Social and Financial Performance: Empirical Evidence from American Companies." *Globsyn Management Journal* [Serial online] 3, no. 1 (January 2009): 25–34. Available from: Business Source Complete, Ipswich, MA. Accessed August 25, 2017.

Gilbert, Katie. "The Managers: Money from Trees Asset Managers Are Finding an Unlikely New Source of Alpha: Responsible Investing." *Institutional investor* 44 no. 9 (2010): 42.

Harjoto, Maretno A., and Hoje Jo. "Corporate Governance and CSR Nexus." *Journal of Business Ethics* 100, no. 1 (2011): 45–67.

Heald, Morrell. *The Social Responsibilities of Business: Company and Community, 1900–1960*. New Brunswick, NJ: Transaction Publications, 2005.

Hill, Ronald Paul, Thomas Ainscough, Todd Shank, and Daryl Manullang. "Corporate Social Responsibility and Socially Responsible Investing: A Global Perspective." *Journal of Business Ethics* 70, no. 2 (2006): 165–74.

Himick, Darlene. "Relative Performance Evaluation and Pension Investment Management: A Challenge for ESG Investing." *Critical Perspectives on Accounting* 22, no. 2 (2011): 158–71.

"History." *Pax World Funds*. http://paxworld.com/about/history/. Accessed September 5, 2017.

Ioannou, Ioannis, and George Serafeim. "Executive Summary: The Power of Transparency." *Business Strategy Review* 22, no. 3 (2011): 76. doi:10.1111/j.1467-8616.2011.00780.x.

Langbein, John H., and Richard A. Posner. "Social Investing and the Law of Trusts." *Michigan Law Review* 79, no. 1 (1980): 72. doi:10.2307/1288337.

Lesser, Kathrin, Sebastian Lobe, and Christian Walkshäusl. "Green and Socially Responsible Investing in International Markets." *Journal of Asset Management* 15, no. 5 (2014): 317–31.

Lobe, S., Röble, F., and Walkshäusl, C. "The Price of Faith: Performance, Bull and Bear Markets, and Screening Effects of Islamic Investing Around the Globe." *Journal of Investing* [Serial online] 21, no. 4 (Winter 2012):153–64. Available from: Business Source Complete, Ipswich, MA. Accessed August 7, 2017.

Lydenberg, Steven. "Universal Investors and Socially Responsible Investors: A Tale of Emerging Affinities." *Corporate Governance: An International Review* 15, no. 3 (2007): 467–77.

Maclean, Richard. "ESG Comes of Age." *Environmental Quality Management* 22, no. 1 (2012): 99–108.

Marinescu, Ada. "Axiomatical Examination of the Neoclassical Economic Model: Logical Assessment of the Assumptions of Neoclassical Economic Model." *Theoretical & Applied Economics* 23, no. 2 (2016): 47–64.

Meziani, A. Seddik. "Investing with Environmental, Social, and Governance Issues in Mind: From the Back to the Fore of Style Investing." *The Journal of Investing* 23, no. 3 (2014): 115–24. doi:10.3905/joi.2014.23.3.115.

Odell, Jamieson, and Usman Ali. "ESG Investing in Emerging and Frontier Markets." *Journal of Applied Corporate Finance* 28, no. 2 (2016): 96–101.

Passant, Francois, Jessica Robinson, Lisa Woll, Deb Abbey, and Simon O'Connor. "2016 Global Sustainable Investment Review." *GSI Alliance*, 2016. www.gsi-alliance.org/wp-content/uploads/2015/02/GSIA_Review_download.pdf. Accessed October 6, 2016.

Paul, K., and Hall, P. "The Influence of the JDR 3rd Fund on 'Business and Society': Incorporating Corporate Social Responsibility in the Business Curriculum." *Journal of Business Ethics* [Serial online] 14, no. 9 (September 1995): 769–79. Available from: Business Source Complete, Ipswich, MA. Accessed August 11, 2017.

Renneboog, Luc, Jenke Ter Horst, and Chendi Zhang. "Socially Responsible Investments: Institutional Aspects, Performance, and Investor Behavior." *Journal of Banking & Finance* 32, no. 9 (2008): 1723–42.

Revelli, Christophe, and Jean-Laurent Viviani. "Financial Performance of Socially Responsible Investing (SRI): What Have We Learned? A Meta-Analysis." *Business Ethics: A European Review* 24, no. 2 (2014): 158–85.

Revelli, Christophe. "Re-Embedding Financial Stakes within Ethical and Social Values in Socially Responsible Investing (SRI)." *Research in International Business and Finance* 38 (2016): 1–5.

Roselle, Peter. "The Evolution of Integrating ESG Analysis into Wealth Management Decisions." *Journal of Applied Corporate Finance* 28 no. 2 (2016): 75–9.

Roy Weintraub, E. "Neoclassical Economics." The Concise Encyclopedia of Economics. David R. Henderson, ed. Originally published as The Fortune Encyclopedia of Economics, Warner Books, 2002. Library of Economics and Liberty [Online]. www.econlib.org/library/Enc1/NeoclassicalEconomics.html. Accessed September 5, 2017; Internet.

Sauer, David A. "The Impact of Social-Responsibility Screens on Investment Performance: Evidence from the Domini 400 Social Index and Domini Equity Mutual Fund." *Review of Financial Economics* 6, no. 2 (1997): 137–49.

Schnepp, Gerald J., and Howard R. Bowen. "Social Responsibilities of the Businessman." *The American Catholic Sociological Review* 15, no. 1 (1954): 42.

Schueth, Steven. "Socially Responsible Investing in the United States." *Journal of Business Ethics* 43, no. 3 (2003): 189–94.

Siddiqui, R. "Shari'ah Compliance, Performance, and Conversion: The Case of the Dow Jones Islamic Market Index^sup SM^*." *Chicago Journal of International Law* 7, no. 2 (2007): 495–519.

SIF, U. "The Forum for Sustainable and Responsible Investment." 2016. www.ussif.org/performance. Accessed October 6, 2016.

Small, Albion W. "Private Business Is a Public Trust." *American Journal of Sociology* 1, no. 3 (1895): 276–89. www.jstor.org/stable/2761559.

Smith, Timothy. "Institutional and Social Investors Find Common Ground." *The Journal of Investing* 14, no. 3 (2005): 57–65.

Sparkes, Russell. "Ethical Investment: Whose Ethics, Which Investment?" *Business Ethics: A European Review* 10, no. 3 (2001): 194–205. doi:10.1111/1467-8608.00233.

Statman, Meir, and Denys Glushkov. "The Wages of Social Responsibility." *Financial Analysts Journal* 65, no. 4 (2009): 33–46.

Stewart, James B. "Amandla! The Sullivan Principles and the Battle to End Apartheid in South Africa, 1975–1987." *The Journal of African American History* 96, no. 1 (2011): 62.

United Nations. "Principles for Responsible Investment." 2006. www.unpri.org. Accessed October 6, 2016.

Waring, Peter, and John Lewer. "The Impact of Socially Responsible Investment on Human Resource Management: A Conceptual Framework." *Journal of Business Ethics* 52, no. 1 (2004): 99–108.

Wulfson, M. "The Ethics of Corporate Social Responsibility and Philanthropic Ventures." *Journal of Business Ethics* [Serial online] 29, no. 1/2 (January 2001): 135–45. Available from: Business Source Complete, Ipswich, MA. Accessed August 11, 2017.

Zafirovski, M. "The Rational Choice Generalization of Neoclassical Economics Reconsidered: Any Theoretical Legitimation for Economic Imperialism?" *Sociological Theory* [Serial Online]. 18, no. 3 (November 2000): 448. Available from: SocINDEX with Full Text, Ipswich, MA. Accessed August 6, 2017.

Chapter 3

The development of ESG risk and the ESG rating system

After this chapter, readers should have a broad understanding of how and why ESG risks developed, how companies are rated through third-party rating agencies, and the advantages and disadvantages of rating agency processes. This chapter will provide a foundation for Chapter 8, which will discuss the creation of a new quantitative model incorporating ESG ratings.

Learning objectives

- Define the concept of risk premia
- Describe common risk premia presented by value, momentum, carry, liquidity, and volatility
- Define the concept of ESG risk and distinguish ESG risk from other recognized risk premia, such as value, carry, momentum, liquidity, size, etc.
- Evaluate the potential for risk premia through ESG investing strategies
- Describe the concept of ESG rating systems and compare major ESG rating methods
- Appraise the usefulness of the different ESG rating methods

3.1 Introduction to ESG risks

The term **ESG risks** encapsulates a wide range of environmental, social, and governance risks that are relevant based on investor's objectives, fiduciary duties, and policies. These risks are integral to the argument for ESG integration, as they provide defined fields of analysis for investors to measure the performance effect of considering ESG factors as part of portfolio construction. In this way, ESG risks may even serve as a driver for an investor to adopt an ESG methodology for performance reasons, rather than as a moral choice. As this chapter is meant to serve as an introduction to ESG risks, only the three main ESG risks are described in this section: namely **policy risks**, **headline risks**, and **performance risks**.

3.2 Policy risk

Investment managers and asset managers, particularly on the institutional level, are often guided by **investment policies** that are constructed to adhere to the needs or objectives of their clients, plan participants, governing bodies, or counterparties. As these policies are constructed based on the specific constituency to which that investor is accountable, these policies can vary greatly. **Policy**

risk, or **ESG-based policy risk**, represents the risk that an investment will violate the policies to which investors are accountable.

Investment managers represent a broad category of investors who manage investments on behalf of an organization, such as a pension fund, university endowment, or foundation, but can also represent a collective group of investors, such as financial advising or private wealth management. It is common practice for investment managers to allocate capital to external products, such as hedge funds or mutual funds. Wealth managers and financial advisors may manage money for individual or family clients, and thus view ESG policy risks as a factor of their client's principles, their own personal standards, and their client's instructions. Investment managers may be subject to ESG-based policy risk because of institutional by-laws, beneficiaries' desires, interest of investors, board of trustees' beliefs, or plan participants.

Asset managers, likewise, may encounter ESG-based policy risk through alignment of an investor's guidelines, board of directors or executive team's mandate, or counterparty requirements.

Institutional investors

Pension funds are institutional investors that manage money on behalf of others, or structure retirement plans for individuals to invest within; such as members, participants, and employees. **Pension funds** may serve public employees, and are commonly managed by the governing body of the employees, or may be private, such as a corporation or nonprofit organization. These funds have what is known as a **fiduciary responsibility** to their plan participants. This fiduciary responsibility is a legal designation that requires pension funds to objectively act in the best interest of their plan participants, and causes pension funds to face ESG policy risk because the funds have a legal duty to represent a group or a combination of groups that are, generally, bound by common interests. Pension funds implement **investment policies** to ensure that they are fulfilling their fiduciary responsibility to their participants.

Public Retirement Funds representing teachers are required to reflect the policies of the school district board in investment portfolio construction. The pension plan may be careful to conduct **proxy voting** for gender diversity, equal composition of teachers, and gender equality in the workplace on invested companies' board of directors if the teachers' union has such a policy for the school district board. In this manner, the public pension investment policy may encounter ESG risk if the investments, investment decision-making process, and investment officials are not aligned with the plan's participants. In the same way, it would be appropriate for a State Parks and Wildlife Conservation retirement plan to avoid investing in companies that profit from business activity that harm the environment. This retirement plan would benefit from an ESG policy which directs the plan in accordance with the interests of the plan participants. See Case study 3A for how a Danish pension fund integrates ESG factors to mitigate policy risks.

CASE STUDY 3A: ATP

Matthew Craig, European Content Director at Institutional Investor, and Ole Buhl, Head of ESG at ATP.

ATP is a mandatory pension scheme for Danish workers and a supplement to the Danish tax-financed old-age state pension. ATP currently has 4.9 million members of which 950,000 are pensioners. For 50% of Danish pensioners, ATP pension is their only source of pension income other than their old-age state pension. ATP is one of Europe's largest pension plans with net assets of €94 billion. The average yearly return has been 10.5% over the last ten years. ATP's investment strategy is fundamentally built around the objective of producing stable future pension cash flow streams. All ATP's liabilities are fully hedged against interest rate risk and ATP currently has a funded status of 115%. ATP has divided its portfolio into a hedging portfolio (composed of long-dated fixed income instruments and real assets) and a return-seeking portfolio (composed of a highly diversified risk parity portfolio). Eighty-five percent of assets are managed internally (mainly in fixed income, listed equities, real estate, and special situation direct investments) with external mandates mainly in the areas of private equity, specialized credit funds, and infrastructure.

ATP's work with ESG is based on the guidelines set down by our board which states that the objective of the guidelines is to safeguard the value of ATP's investments and to be instrumental in obtaining the lowest possible capital costs for the companies through a focus on and respect for social responsibility. Furthermore, companies shall respect the rule of law in the countries in which they operate; and secondly, they shall respect the rules, norms, and standards that ensue from conventions and other international agreements ratified by Denmark – this applies irrespective of whether the country in which the company operates has ratified those agreements.

ATP's activities in ESG are coordinated by a special internal Committee for Social Responsibility, chaired by the CEO of ATP. The Committee convenes four times a year, supplemented by ad hoc sessions. The day-to-day responsibility lies with the portfolio manager with the ESG team acting as a resource center for the rest of the organization.

ATP had for a number of years been unhappy with the governance of the organization behind the UN-backed Principles for Responsible Investment (PRI) and in December 2013, ATP, along with other Danish pension funds, exited the organization. It is always hard to assess whether one's actions has had a meaningful impact, but they do note that the PRI has taken steps to improve the governance of the organization since their exit.

Private retirement funds also face ESG policy risks. These pension plans represent a company's employees. For example, several pension plans that have an affiliation with the Church Benefits Association (USA) utilize ESG policies, which change based on member demand. The governing administrators of the pension plan align the values of the organization with that of the investment principles through investment policies. A religious organization may implement a policy excluding pornography from their investable universe so that the plan will not be invested in business activity that is against the belief system of the religious institution. Further, if excluding pornography was part of the faith-based retirement plan's investment guidelines, the pension plan would encounter ESG policy risk if they were to invest in the stock of a company whose revenue is derived from pornography.

Retirement plans can also face policy risk at the plan offering level. Whether public or private, retirement plans are structured in several ways. Two of the most common pension plan offerings are defined contribution and defined benefit.

Defined contribution plans are retirement plans that are designed to allow organizations to annually set aside money for employees. Defined contribution plans allow employees to select from various investment options. These investment options are restricted by the employers in a variety of ways, including frequency of trading the investment options, loans, and withdraws without penalties. Defined contribution plans may encounter ESG policy risk if the investment options lack offerings that individuals, or groups of individuals, require for their investment preference or ethics. For example, an employee of a company who holds an environmentalist belief system and a personal commitment to climate change may litigate the defined contribution plan if the plan, as a fiduciary, does not offer any fossil fuel free investment options, in which the investment option has divested from companies that derive revenue from fossil fuels.

Defined benefit plans, unlike defined contribution plans, offer a fixed rate benefit at a specific future date. Defined benefit plans encounter ESG policy risk if the investment pool of assets is not aligned with the collective interests of the employees as represented by the board of trustees or investment committee.

Endowments, particularly those representing education institutions, also face ESG policy risks. University or college endowments manage a pool of assets endowed to the university to benefit the long-term stability, growth, and success of the institution. If the investment manager of the endowment does not invest the endowment funds through ESG parameters aligned with that of the donors, the institution's culture, or the student body, the endowment may be opening themselves to policy risk. This risk may not just be loss of future donation by alumni, but also a loss of federal or state funding support or grants, or a loss of future enrollment. A university or college may consider drafting ESG investment policies that align the interests of the community they operate within, the principles they teach, and the students' interests in order to protect themselves from ESG policy risk.

In April 2016 at Stanford University, students presented a proposal known as "Fossil Free Stanford" (Stanford University, 2017). In response, the Board of Trustees released a Statement of Investment Responsibility. This Statement of Investment Responsibility outlines a specific set of criteria by which the trustees may evaluate whether a company is inflicting social injury in a manner that warrants consideration of divestment. To assist the Board on these matters, the university has established an Advisory Panel on Investment Responsibility and Licensing (APIRL). APIRL is a community panel of students, faculty, staff, and alumni that provides a recommendation to the Board's Special Committee on Investment Responsibility (SCIR), which, in turn, provides a recommendation to the trustees to consider such ESG issues. By producing the Statement of Investment Responsibility, the panel, and special committee, Stanford has created a clearly defined process for ESG policy.

Foundations are a type of institutional investor that manages assets that allow the foundation to operate and further the mission or service of the foundation. A foundation may face risk if the investment policies are not aligned with the ESG investment standard of the donor(s) who contribute funds to the foundation, which could jeopardize the sustainability of the organization and the amount of services or monies offered through the foundation's operation. Foundations can also face ESG policy risk if they make investments that are contrary to the mission and purpose of the assets, which may make a negative impact on the foundation's employees and beneficiaries. Such an event that demonstrates an investment policy that is not aligned with the ESG-related principles of an organization may also be understood through the viewpoint of headline risk. See Case study 3B to learn about how an institutional investor views policy risk and headline risk.

CASE STUDY 3B: ESG risk for an institutional investor

The Truth Initiative (formerly the American Legacy Foundation) is a United States, Washington, DC-based, nonprofit tobacco control foundation with a mission of educating society and developing a culture that is supportive of young adults rejecting tobacco. The Truth Initiative was established in March 1999 as a result of the Master Settlement Agreement between the attorney general of 46 states in the United States, the District of Columbia, five United States territories, and the tobacco industry. Truth Initiative's foundation assets support the nonprofit's operating budget and organizational activities. Such organizational activities include youth smoking prevention campaigns, tobacco control research and policy studies, and other tobacco-free initiatives. As of 2017 the organization has approximately one billion USD in assets and more than 130 employees. For the purposes of this textbook, Tony O'Toole, Chief Financial and Investment Officer of Truth Initiative, was interviewed for the aim of understanding the ESG risks that the Truth Initiative may face.

"Tobacco is the number one cause of preventable death and disease in the U.S.," said Tony O'Toole. "At Truth Initiative, we make a conscious decision not to invest in tobacco because it goes against our mission: to achieve a culture where all youth and young adults reject tobacco." Through this lens, it is observed that investing in a company, through any part of the company's capital structure and regardless of the type of a company's securities offering (e.g. equity or credit), that generates revenue from tobacco would be contrary to investment policy and the mission of the organization. ESG risk for the Truth Initiative may be understood as investing in any securities of companies that manufacture cigarettes, cigars, chewing tobacco, and smokeless tobacco, or supplying key component elements for production, sale, and marketing of tobacco-related products. As this is the policy of the Truth Initiative, it may be considered a policy risk; however, such an ESG risk may also be considered a headline risk.

Investing in the securities of companies who manufacture cigarettes, cigars, chewing tobacco, and smokeless tobacco, or supplying key component elements for production, sale, and marketing of tobacco-related products could be considered a headline risk as the mission of the foundation would not be aligned with the investment principles, which would enable a critical lens to be aimed at the Truth Imitative. Such an event could be negatively construed in the media and put pressure on the Truth Initiative. O'Toole stated, "Tobacco is a bad choice if you're interested in ESG investing and we applaud both individual and institutional investors who are able to achieve strong returns without including companies that make a product that kills 540,000 people a year." If this occurred, the Truth Imitative might experience the loss of support from donors, employees, and volunteers, and the mission of objectively educating society of the risks of tobacco.

The ESG risks for the Truth imitative reach beyond policy and headline risk. O'Toole also addressed the issue of performance risk when he stated, "We have proven that you don't need to invest in tobacco to be financially successful and have maximized our returns without it, even outperforming our benchmarks."

CASE STUDY 3C: gender equality and ESG investing: the Boston Common approach

Lisa Hayles, Vice President of Boston Common Asset Management

Hayles is a Board Member of the Thirty Percent Coalition, which advocates for the inclusion of women on corporate boards and management teams. Hayles is also a Board Member of the Boston Impact Initiative.

Women hold 21% of board seats among the largest listed companies in the US as of 2017 (Catalyst, 2018), and though board-level statistics in Europe have improved (in part due to quotas requiring the appointment of women directors), women are still woefully under-represented in the ranks of senior executives globally. Across the wider economy, though women's labor force participation has increased rapidly in the second half of the 20th century, "large gaps remain between women and men in terms of employment rates, the wages they earn, the jobs they hold, and their overall economic security" (Burke, 2017, 1). These facts are problematic not just for individual women who may struggle to achieve career success but also for the health and well-being of our economy. At Boston Common Asset Management, a sustainable investment firm dedicated to generating competitive financial returns and meaningful improvements in corporate performance, we believe eliminating barriers to the full participation of women in economic life is financially savvy and can pay dividends in the form of higher productivity, expanded markets, and improved work-life balance for all employees. As a women- and minority-led firm, we view equal opportunity and gender equality in our portfolio companies throughout all sectors as a priority and we carefully monitor our portfolio companies according to a robust set of sustainability criteria on environmental, social, and corporate governance (ESG) issues, including gender diversity on boards and equal opportunity policies for employees and suppliers.

Our investment approach on gender equality and inclusion is guided by two core principles:

1   Companies need to attract, develop, retain, and motivate a richer and deeper talent pool – not only half of it – to be successful.
2   The evolving roles of women and men in the workplace and in family life have created new expectations for everyone to live and work differently in the 21st century. Many recent studies support our view. For example, McKinsey found that "companies in the top quartile for gender or racial and ethnic diversity are more likely to have financial returns above their national industry medians" (Hunt, Layton, and Prince, 2015, 1).

Diversity as a lens

Board diversity and women in management have been key themes for both our ESG research and our engagement work since the mid-1990s. As part of our integrated ESG investment approach, we examine women's representation on company boards and in senior management. We seek to understand whether a company has policies and guidelines to encourage equal opportunities and encourage diversity in the workplace, and to understand how those policies are implemented. We then engage with companies to address any gaps in their policies. As a signatory to the Women's Empowerment Principles – a set of seven commitments promoted by the United Nations to support gender equality in business, government, and society – we integrate gender equality into our overall sustainability assessments of companies.

Addressing the gender gap

Though research suggests that companies with women in leadership positions tend to have better-than-average approaches on a range of sustainability issues, few companies excel at addressing the under-representation of women in leadership (American Association of University Women, 2017). As active investors we utilize all the tools at our disposal to influence corporate behavior including:

- Voting at Annual General Meetings (AGMs) and filing shareholder resolutions
- Engaging in dialogue directly on gender equity with our portfolio companies
- Initiating research on corporate practices and publishing benchmarking reports
- Collaborating with other investors internationally to raise this critical issue to companies across multiple sectors
- Participating in public policy advocacy through testimony and public comments we submit to regulators, state and federal agencies

Gender equality, like many of the sustainability issues we are trying to address, cannot be solved on a company-by-company basis. Lasting change requires improvements across the practices of entire sectors. To illustrate our process, we have described specific approaches we have used to encourage companies to improve their performance on gender equality including direct dialogues, collaboration with other investors, and public policy submissions.

Advocate for gender equality with companies directly
One of the most critical platforms investors must communicate their stance on governance issues is through their proxy voting guidelines. Boston Common takes a strong stance on gender diversity on boards across all markets.

In recent years, we have filed shareholder proposals in the US asking companies like Discovery Communications, Cognizant Technologies, and Old Dominion Freight Line to make diversity part of every director search. Resolutions voted on by all shareholders at a company's annual general meeting are a good way to educate other investors and apply public pressure to management. In many cases, we negotiate a withdrawal of the proposal based on the company agreeing to improve their director search process by expanding the networks they use or the qualification criteria employed to identify candidates for the board.

In international markets where filing shareholder proposals is not an option, we have proactively engaged our Japanese holdings on gender equality for almost a decade on how they are creating the infrastructure to support working mothers and a career path for women. Lack of sufficient day care options, flexible work schedules, and nursing facilities have been cited as key barriers to increasing the participation of working mothers in Japan and elsewhere in Asia. We are seeing more Japanese companies join the Women's Empowerment Principles (WEPs) to learn from what their global peers are doing.

In 2017, we launched a dialogue on gender equity focused on eight firms held across our core US strategies: Baxter Pharmaceutical, Crown Castle International, CME Group, Mohawk Industries, Merck, Oracle, Northern Trust, and Zimmer Biomet using the WEPs as a framework. We asked them to disclose how they ensure a robust system for upholding equal opportunities for all employees including:

- **Board level oversight:** is there a board member or committee of the board responsible for monitoring company performance on gender equity?
- **Pay gap:** do they consider, monitor, and measure gender and racial disparities – and are these reflected in total compensation?

- **Goals and metrics:** do they have company-wide initiatives to ensure the health, safety, and well-being of all employees (and do they track quantitative metrics over time on the performance of these initiatives)?
- **Education, training, and mentoring:** what education, training, and professional development opportunities exist for women and other under-represented groups within the firm?
- **WEPs:** would they consider endorsing the CEO Statement of Support for the Women's Empowerment Principles?

We have been pleased with the willingness of firms to share their challenges and successes with us as they pursue a variety of strategies to support gender equity. Our focus in the next phase of our engagement will be on encouraging companies to systematically collect and publish data about their success in meeting their stated targets.

Collaborate with other investors

Boston Common is a board member of the Thirty Percent Coalition, a national nonprofit dedicated to increasing the gender and racial diversity of boards at publicly listed companies. The Coalition is responsible for a multi-year letter-writing campaign directed to the largest publicly listed companies in the US that do not have women represented on their boards. Since the coalition began their "Adopt a Company" campaign in January 2012, over 150 US companies have appointed at least one woman to their boards.

Support gender-friendly government policy and regulation

In 2016, the Government Accountability Office estimated that it would take more than 40 years to achieve gender parity on boards, even if equal numbers of women and men are appointed going forward (US Government Accountability Office, 2016).

We believe policy levers are an essential tool to help increase the urgency among nominating committees at public companies to address the lack of diverse boards and senior management teams. More disclosure from companies on their recruitment processes can help investors benchmark performance and distinguish leaders from laggards. To help address this issue, we submitted letters, independently and collaboratively, to both the EEOC (Equal Employment Opportunity Commission) and the SEC (Securities and Exchange Commission) encouraging improved disclosure on diversity indicators. In places like Japan we have used regulatory guidance put in place in 2015 to establish goals to increase women in management at all levels (management, senior executives, and the board). We sought improved disclosure on the gender and racial composition of their nominees for director; their plans for achieving greater general and racial diversity among their leadership groups; and data about employee earnings and hours by ethnicity, race, gender, and job category.

Closing the gaps

Our approach to gender equality is continually evolving to include emerging issues, as we urge companies to make stronger commitments to equality in the workplace. In North America and other markets, we continue to focus on increasing the number of women leaders at the very top of corporations, alongside creating the enabling environments that support greater participation by women at every level in the economy. The tasks vary depending on the cultural and socio-political context of our investee firms. In our engagement efforts in Asia we have focused on addressing sexual harassment for women, from workers in apparel factories in Bangladesh, to financial services employees in India and chemists working in Japan. As part of our work to promote the UN Guiding Principles for Business and Human Rights, we have asked companies how they are addressing sexual harassment, discrimination, and pay disparity with their suppliers.

Through our work with the Thirty Percent Coalition, we continue to focus on the "demand side" of the equation for women leaders – encouraging companies to expand their candidate pool(s) and to be more deliberate in their approach to seeking potential board members with diverse backgrounds. We will support the coalition's work by launching a survey in 2018 to track the number of investors who use their proxies to vote against all male boards of directors. The survey will also track how many investors make an explicit commitment to supporting racial or ethnic diversity at the board level in addition to gender diversity.

At Boston Common, we believe advancing gender equality is an issue that everyone – men and women – should want to address. Research by the World Bank suggests that eliminating discrimination against female workers could boost productivity by up to 40% globally (Cuberes, David, and Mark Teignier-Baque, 2011), an outcome that is good for workers, companies, and investors. As a global investor with investments spanning a multitude of countries, cultures, and languages, we are committed to fostering a diverse and inclusive work environment. We believe promoting diversity is aligned with our sustainable investing approach and is consistent with our goal to be a responsible business and crucial for achieving positive environmental, social, and governance improvements in our investee firms. By engaging in dialogue with companies, using our proxy votes, filing shareholder resolutions, and working collaboratively with other investors, Boston Common continues to encourage companies to enhance transparency on gender equality and to proactively identify and address structural barriers to women's participation.

To modify an old proverb, advancing women's work is never done.

The information in this document should not be considered a recommendation to buy or sell any security. All investments involve risk, including the risk of losing principal.

3.3 Headline risk

Headline risk can be understood as any risk to the **reputation**, and subsequently the **sustainability** and **profitability**, of an organization. This risk is a major factor particularly for all investors managing money for others. It is also a major risk component within ESG risk. Investors might consider ESG-based investing in order to mitigate negative news coverage events. The above section on policy risks illustrated how various institutional investors might be at risk if their policy conflicts with their investments. Headline risk builds on policy risk, as it presents first the side effects of a policy lapse (the negative news coverage that results from a breach of policy), and second the potential for reaping the negative consequences of poor environmental, social, or governance decisions made by underlying companies within their investment portfolio.

Institutional investors view ESG factors as an increasingly viable method for predicting and avoiding headline risk. Asset managers may also align their money management philosophy with ESG investing as negative news coverage could lead to the perception of inability or instability.

CASE STUDY 3D: Mercy Health and exclusion-based ESG investing

Anthony Waskiewicz, *Chief Investment Officer,* **and Elizabeth Jordan,** *Deputy Chief Investment Officer*

Mercy Health's mission began 190 years ago, when the Sisters of Mercy built a house on Baggot Street in Dublin, Ireland in response to the needs of the poor.

Mercy Health of Saint Louis was established by the Sisters of Mercy in 1986. Today, Mercy Health has 44 hospitals and hundreds of outpatient facilities, and provides care to thousands every year across four states in the Midwest and outreach services in three additional states. As Mercy has grown and a larger focus has been put on the investment portfolio, the system has dedicated more resources to responsibly investing its $2.7B investment portfolio and ensuring the portfolio aligns with our values.

In 2016, Mercy Health established a new portfolio governance structure; setting up a dedicated Investment Committee and re-writing the Investment Policy Statement to reflect the health systems' evolving risk tolerances and goals. Following this process, Mercy determined that a new, more comprehensive Socially Responsible Investment Policy was the next priority, as the policy had not been reevaluated in ten years. The SRI policy prior to the re-write was very limited, and only had a restriction on owning securities issued by companies with tobacco revenues of 10% or more. The investment team met with two sisters involved with the health system to determine the issues most aligned with Mercy's mission and values. Mercy's current SRI policy focuses on four critical concerns important to Mercy Health:

- Human dignity (human trafficking, dignity of human life, empowerment of women and children)
- Non-violence
- Stewarding the Earth's resources (climate, water)
- Advancing quality healthcare and healthcare innovation

These focuses were formally approved by Mercy's Investment Committee in December of 2016. At the same time, the Investment Committee created a Socially Responsible Investing task force to monitor and govern Mercy's responsible investment efforts. This task force is composed of two investment committee members, a doctor from the health system, a Sister of Mercy, a member from the Mission and Ethics department, and Mercy's CFO. The task force meets quarterly, and the approved recommendations from this SRI committee must be brought to the Investment Committee for a final vote to be implemented.

The investment team has flexibility in determining the most effective ways to address each of the four critical concerns of Mercy's SRI policy, while also prioritizing the importance of financial stewardship to allow the ministry's mission to continue in perpetuity. Mercy's policy states that the investment team will have discretion on how to apply the policy across all assets classes. It is likely that application of the policy will differ depending on the asset type. The dimensions of implementation encouraged include: negative screening, ESG factor integration, and impact investment. This allows the team to be selective in making sure an investment has an effective socially responsible impact, while also considering the impact that will make on total return.

Today, Mercy currently uses ISS to vote proxies in accordance with Catholic standards (based on guidance from the United States Conference of Catholic Bishops), and MSCI to screen long-only traditional equity and fixed-income separate accounts. The negative screen is applied to almost 30% of the portfolio, using to a detailed negative screening criteria based on the four critical concerns. This negative screen addresses tobacco, abortion and contraceptives, embryonic stem cell research, adult entertainment, and defense and weapons. The screen uses revenue thresholds to determine issuers that cannot be held by the portfolio. According to Mercy's analysis, this will have a minimal impact on performance – most managers reported it would affect less than 5% of the portfolio they manage.

Jared Bryson, Mercy's vice president of mission, said: "It is our expectation the portfolio will continue to evolve over time as we seek excellence across many socially responsible investment initiatives."

3.4 Performance risk

Performance risk is the risk of underperforming **benchmarks, peer groups**, and **investment mandates**. Investors may utilize ESG investment policies if they believe that ESG investing methodology will benefit the performance of their investments. As discussed in the previous chapter on the history of ESG, integrating environmental, social, and governance factors into portfolio construction was long viewed as a detractor to performance. This viewpoint was held by investors when ESG investing was understood solely as socially responsible investing (SRI), which traditionally involved moral screens in investment portfolios against firearms, alcohol, pornography, etc. However, today investors at the personal and institutional level view ESG investment policies as performance enhancers, since quantitative data continues to show the superior long-term performance of ESG-integrated portfolios over traditional portfolios. For example, screening out a tobacco company as their product has a negative impact on their consumer's health. ESG investing has evolved in the 21st century as many investors consider ESG research a form of fundamental research that is measurable through factors that have impact on securities' performance. ESG performance risks could arise when investors choose to not consider, or ignore, such ESG factors.

Empirically, research continues to be produced on the correlation between ESG integration, the underlying companies in a portfolio, and the financial performance of that portfolio. This research provides insight into the extent to which ESG factors influence quantitative performance, and further the argument for performance risk mitigation through ESG factor analysis. For instance, Clark, Feiner, and Viehs (2015) reviewed 41 papers on sustainability and its relation to financial market performance. According to them, superior sustainability quality is valued by the stock market: more sustainable firms generally outperform less sustainable firms. Clark, Feiner, and Viehs (2015) summarized from all reviewed papers that 33 (80%) of total papers document a positive correlation between superior sustainability and superior financial market performance. In that same vein, Orlitzky and Benjamin (2001) conducted a meta-analytic review on the association between corporate social performance and firm risk covering 18 US-based primary studies. Most reviewed studies found evidence that higher corporate social performance leads to lower financial risk. Further, the stakeholder theory, which is discussed in detail later in this book, suggests that better corporate social performance leads to fewer financial risks and therefore to a lower degree of market risk and a lower likelihood of downside risk (Oikonomou, Brooks, and Pavelin, 2012).

3.5 Introduction to risk premia

Many have undertaken to identify the measurable factors behind return compensation in investments. The prevailing view has been that excess returns can be predicted by the analysis of observable exogenous fundamentals such as cash flow, financial ratios, and market events (Kurz and Motolese, 2010). However, Fama and French (1992, 1993) introduced the concept of **risk premia**: the idea that investors are compensated not for their asset allocations per se, but for the risk that they undertake in each investment. Fama and French (1992, 1993), Carhart (1997), and others, acting on the assumption that even the most experienced investors might be miscalculating the investment risk, empirically documented factors termed "risk premia" that include value, size, momentum, and liquidity. These risk premia were deemed to provide excess returns consistently across geographies and time frames, and were both intuitively and measurably independent from each other.

This concept comes back to the basic idea that an investor is compensated for the risk that he or she assumes. The riskier the investment, the higher the performance potential must be in order to incentivize the investor. The safer the investment, the ostensibly lower the return potential. "Risk premia" is the performance premia that incentivizes investors to assume investment risks. Academics and investors have dedicated themselves to refining the analysis of risk premia, breaking down the different risk factors which have independent and quantitative impact on the **return distribution** of an asset. Empirical research by Fama and French, Carhart, and others provided a foundation for the study of risk premia and factor analysis, and serves as a lens for research conducted to establish ESG risk premia as an alternative risk premia (Sherwood, Pollard, and Klobus, 2018).

Identifying risk premia factors and how those factors might interact with each other is a continuously evolving area for investors and researchers. For the purposes of better understanding risk premia, the risk premia factors of market, size, value, profitability, investment, and ESG are discussed below.

Market risk premium – risk premia can also be calculated in terms of asset class beta or asset class risk characteristic. Equity, also known as market, risk premium is the differential between the market yield and the risk-free rate, and is commonly understood as the premium investors take for accessing the higher risks associated with investing in equities as compared to a low risk asset class, such as government bonds. Investment risk premium was calculated as the average return of two conservative investment portfolios minus the average return of two aggressive portfolios.

Size risk premium – is commonly understood as the premium gained over time through investment in a specific size market capitalization. Size risk premium is in favor when the specific market capitalization selected outperforms the relative market over time. For example, the growth of investment return of small-cap equities over large-cap equities can be identified as size risk premium.

Value risk premium – is the premium provided to an investor for investing in securities of companies that demonstrated the financial characteristic of value, most often observed through the price-to-book measure in equities. For the equity market, the lowest third book-to-market equities are considered value stocks, whereas the top third, highest, book-to-market stocks are considered growth stocks. In other words, value risk premium represents the premium gained from investing in value stocks over growth stocks, or vice versa.

Profitability risk premium – is the return premium gained from investing in companies that have a more robust operation that yields measured and consistent profits. Those interested in profitability risk premium might seek to invest in companies focused on generating current profits for the shareholders, rather than growth companies that re-invest revenue into business growth plans and new developments for the future.

Investment risk premium – this is the return premium gained from investing in conservative vs. aggressive investment portfolios. This is calculated as the average return of two conservative investment portfolios minus the average return of two aggressive portfolios.

As the study of risk premia becomes more popular, new risk premia factors are being added to the list in academia and practice.

Historical risk premia

In 2014, Eugene Fama and Kenneth French, more than 20 years after their initial research, presented a study entitled "A Five Factor Asset Pricing Model," measuring the extent to which investment risk premium, market risk premium, size risk premium, profitability risk premium, and value risk premium explain the probability distributions in average stock returns. Fama and French conclude that this five-factor model effectively explains return distributions, by quantifying and organizing cross-sectional data. Pástor and Stambaugh (2003) added to the list of established risk premia in their quantitative study entitled "Liquidity Risk and Expected Stock Returns," in which they investigated the relationship between asset pricing and market-wide liquidity, using cross-sectional data relating the sensitivities of returns to fluctuations in aggregate liquidity. In doing so, Pástor and Stambaugh establish liquidity as a risk premium by demonstrating its efficiency in predicting the probability distribution of returns for an asset. Ya-Wen Lai supports the empirical validity of the Fama and French (2015) five-factor analysis model and further risk premia models for identifying risk premia, and affirms the practical implications of cross-sectional data at fostering informational insight on risk premia in a 2017 quantitative study entitled "Macroeconomic Factors and Index Option Returns" (Ya-Wen Lai, 2017). Lai's study established the existence of a correlation between stock returns and the existence of risk premia. Jennifer Bender, Hammond, and William Mok (2013) analyzed the extent to which risk premia incorporated in portfolio construction process impacts the portfolio performance, in a quantitative study entitled "Can Alpha Be Captured by Risk Premia?" The results of this research indicated that 80% of alpha generated from an equity portfolio are directly attributable to factors of risk premia. These findings illustrate the impact that risk premia have on generating alpha in equity investments, and emphasize the fact that no single risk premia can exist as a constant through time. Furthermore, the results of this study indicate that additional risk premia may exist outside of currently established risk premia. It is important to note that risk premia may fall in and out of favor throughout the market cycle and climate.

ESG risk premia

Investors use risk premia to **analyze risk factors** in order to determine the overall risk profile of a portfolio and the subsequent return distribution to be expected. This advantages the investor in two ways: it gives the investor a better understanding of the quantitative risk profile of an investment, and it allows the investor to structure their portfolio in order to balance their risk exposure and maximize the risk-return correlation.

In addition to the accepted risk premia discussed by Fama and French, there are alternative risk premia which are in the process of using Fama and French's methodology to be established. Investors are increasingly looking to ESG investing as an opportunity to outperform benchmarks, peer groups, and investment mandates. The use of **ESG factor analysis** (otherwise known as ESG investing) allows investors to identify and utilize ESG risk premium. In establishing the existence of risk premia, Fama and French provide a modern, empirically tested base model that can be modified to use to assess the validity of ESG risk premium and other alternative risk premia, by analytically testing the consistency in correlation between the factor and a long-term average expected return distribution, regardless of geography or time. ESG risk premia was most notably asserted in the study "Establishing ESG Risk Premia" by Pollard, Sherwood, and Klobus (2018). The authors asserted that the professional forecasting displayed through ESG research and cross-sectional ratings yield significant insight into the probability distribution of long-term risk-adjusted equity returns, establishing ESG as independent risk premia. Fama and French's methodology provided the theoretical framework for the efficacy of ESG as risk premia (Pollard, Sherwood, and Klobus, 2018). In one notable quantitative comparative entitled "Do Social Investment Policies Add or Destroy European Stock Portfolio Value?" Benjamin Auer (2016) compared ESG company ratings listed on the European stock market with the corresponding financial performance of those companies in order to measure the correlation between fluctuations in financial performance and fluctuations in the ESG ratings of equities over time within a diversified equity investment portfolio. In this way, Auer was able to test the effectiveness with which ESG ratings predict stock return distributions and risk. The results from Auer's study indicated that a diversified European equity portfolio of highly ESG-rated equities outperforms an associated benchmark portfolio of similar diversified equities, and a negatively ESG-rated diversified equity portfolio underperforms the same benchmark. These results suggest that ESG provides risk premia, and that ESG company ratings can provide effective cross-sectional data for ESG risk premia to exist longitudinally. It is important to note that the populating of data allows for greater efficiency of cross-sectional data as the cross-sectional information expands exponentially as a result of the growth and acceptance of the data. When considering risk premia, the growth of cross-sectional data may help in the identification, analysis, and efficacy of the risk premia (Fama and French, 2014).

ESG risk premium is the difference in returns between strategies which integrate environmental, social, and governance factors and strategies which ignore these factors. ESG integration in global equity portfolios provides higher risk-adjusted returns than non-ESG-integrated portfolios selected from the same pool of equities (Pollard, Sherwood, and Klobus, 2018). Pollard, Sherwood, and Klobus (2018) analyzed sample portfolios that integrated stock turnover on a quarterly time period based on ESG ratings' changes. The study displayed statistically significant evidence of the persistence of ESG risk premia throughout time and geographies. Simply stated, ESG risk premia was established through the analysis of integrating favorable changes in ESG ratings (Pollard, Sherwood, and Klobus, 2018). Only increased research into ESG risk premium will uncover the potential correlations to other known risk premia, such as those discussed above. Much research will continue to develop in this field, building upon that mentioned above and many others.

Implementing ESG risk premium

Analysts and third-party administrators are constantly updating company ESG ratings based on their research. This causes a **latency effect** in the data derived from ESG risk premium, meaning that the data reflects events and research from a period before the present. On the other hand, it also takes a period of time for the profitability and return distribution of a corporation to reflect the effect of non-traditional metrics, such as those measured by ESG factors. For this reason, the cross-section of ESG ratings may provide a forward-looking probability distribution, despite the latency effect of the data. As data continues to populate, several aspects of risk premia will have a material impact in the effect of ESG data on predicting the future return distribution of a corporation.

1   ESG analysts, third-party rating agencies, and money spent on ESG data will continue to grow, as investors, corporations, and governments are educated on the qualitative and quantitative effects of ESG ratings data

2   Corporations will be incentivized to report on ESG factors within their balance sheets, which
    will further encourage attention towards the environmental, social, and governance elements
    of the corporation

The above aspects create a cycle, in which more data encourages more corporate attention on ESG
issues, which in turn produces more data to be analyzed.

3.6 ESG identification and the ESG rating system

Identifying, measuring, and rating ESG factors has been an area of development within the field of
ESG investing since the early 1990s. Asset managers and providers of structured products (e.g. ETFs,
Index Funds, etc.) utilize third-party ratings agencies to provide data on the environmental, social,
and governance factors within public and private corporations. These organizations focus on ESG
factors that affect social impact, accounting standards, water pollution, air pollution, land pollution,
accounting standards, brand reputation, sustainability practices, corporate social responsibility,
board and management team diversity, climate conditions, labor practices, and more. Institutions
use this ESG data to measure risk, predict future returns, and remain within the bounds of investment policy statements.

CASE STUDY 3E: MSCI ESG ratings

MSCI uses a clearly defined process for creating their ESG Ratings. MSCI analysts score
companies based on a research process built on four main value pillars. The first pillar is
referred to as the MSCI ESG Intangible Value Assessment (ESG Ratings). Here, analysts
first identify major industry-specific factors related to the specific company being rated
that may affect investor sentiment or financial performance. This is done using the Global
Industry Classification Standard, a taxonomy developed by MSCI Inc. and Standard and
Poor's in order to categorize industries for further analysis. Analysts next evaluate the
degree to which the individual company is exposed to those industry-related risks (ESG
risks) and further assign ratings to the companies based on any unmanaged ESG risk.
The second pillar is referred to at the MSCI Impact Monitor, and builds upon the first pillar by assigning company-specific ratings based on relevant ESG-related controversies
resulting from unmanaged ESG risk. The third pillar is the MSCI ESG Business Involvement Screening Research, which quantifies to what extent the individual company has
incorporated ESG portfolio screening and supported ESG-related company actions. The
fourth pillar is referred to as the MSCI ESG Government Rating. This final pillar assesses
overall government-related ESG risk exposure and risk management practices, beyond
the individual company (MSCI, 2014).

These four pillars of ESG research are synthesized into three separate rating values: one
aggregate value for all environmental concerns, one aggregate value for all social concerns, and one aggregate value for all governance concerns. These aggregate values are
presented on a scale of one to ten, with ten being the highest rating available. To present
these three values in a consistent manner for each rated company, environmental, social,
and governance ratings are weighted by industry, based heavily on the first pillar of ESG

research: MSCI ESG Intangible Value Assessment (ESG Ratings) and the key industry issues which have been identified. These scores are updated monthly by MSCI analysts, based on the second pillar of ESG research, which measures the impact of ESG-related controversies on individual companies (MSCI, 2016).

The MSCI ESG database has been frequently used to examine the effect of ESG integration on investment returns, specifically by Hillman and Keim (2001); Mattingly and Berman (2006); Dorfleitner, Gerhard, and Nguyen (2015); Singal (2014); and Sherwood and Pollard (2017), amongst others.

CASE STUDY 3F: Sustainalytics

Melissa Chase, *Marketing Specialist*

The evolution of ESG research and data

As a global leader in corporate environmental, social, and governance (ESG) research, rating and analysis, Sustainalytics supports hundreds of the world's leading institutional investors. However, when Sustainalytics was founded in the early 1990s, socially responsible investing (SRI) was still a niche part of the investment landscape. SRI investors wanted to align their investments with their values or ensure their investments did not harm the environment or society. Money managers, responding to the demands of their SRI clients, started to look beyond financial performance at companies' sustainability profiles.

As SRI investment approaches evolved, so too did the data required by investors to make truly informed decision. Sustainalytics and other ratings organizations, along with our clients and other SRI investors, have created demand for greater transparency from companies on sustainability issues and their impact on society. As the integration of ESG and corporate governance data into the investment process swiftly moves into the mainstream, the reporting, gathering, and assessment of this data will become ever more systematic and ingrained for both companies and their shareholders.

The early days of sustainability research

Twenty-five years ago, very few companies produced sustainability and CSR reports. The governance and measurement of ESG factors was generally considered "extra-financial" and not baked into the corporate outlook. Most investment managers also did not consider corporate sustainability material to the financial performance of a stock, and thus were not demanding companies disclose this type of information. Company annual reporting was focused on financial performance, and sustainability/ESG information was not readily available. To formulate an assessment of corporate sustainability performance, investors and research firms relied on printed copies of company annual reports, government databases, and other publicly available filings, company interviews and engagement, and news and non-governmental organization reports to track major controversies. At that time, Sustainalytics' assessments of corporate sustainability were constrained by the lack of ESG data and metrics, and highlighted specific areas of sustainability strength or concern for each company.

Sustainalytics' early assessments supported a negative screening strategy, which was a popular approach among SRI investors. Using ESG data as an overlay, stocks were eliminated from investment universes based on their business activities (i.e., the production of alcohol, gambling, or tobacco), or their failure to meet some other ESG criteria. While Sustainalytics' corporate sustainability assessments were sufficient to address investors immediate needs at the time, it realized these reports had to evolve to support more sophisticated investment approaches.

Investors demand sustainability transparency
By the early 2000s, SRI investors were looking more deeply at companies' sustainability profiles. Some adopted a more nuanced investment approach, wanting to understand the financial materiality of ESG issues. While negative screening strategies continued to be common, many aimed to identify and integrate the risks E, S, and G issues could pose to a company.

Within the mainstream investment community, momentum was also slowly shifting towards greater consideration of ESG factors in the investment process. The 2005 Freshfields report on fiduciary responsibility (Freshfields, Brukhaus, and Deringer, 2005) stated integrating ESG considerations was permissible and arguably required in all jurisdictions. In 2006, the UN-supported Principles for Responsible Investment (PRI) launched with the goal to "understand the investment implications of ESG factors" and to support investors incorporating these factors into their investment and ownership decisions.

With the growing realization of the materiality of ESG issues, investors of all stripes were demanding greater amounts of detailed, quantitative information on corporate ESG activities. They were also searching for ways to more easily determine corporate sustainability performance. Sustainalytics' transition from binary assessments to a weighted score-card research methodology and company sustainability scores provided that detail. Investors now had more flexibility in how they could use the assessments. For instance, companies could be ranked within a sector making leaders and laggards easy to identify; or investors could easily set screening thresholds when selecting stocks for their portfolios. The inclusion of company scores and more quantitative metrics also allowed for better integration of ESG data into traditional financial analysis.

As investors sought greater transparency and more disclosure of corporate ESG information, organizations like the Global Reporting Initiative and CDP (formerly known as the Carbon Disclosure Project) in the late 1990s and 2000s, and the Sustainability Accounting Standards Board and International Integrated Reporting Council more recently, provided frameworks to support companies with their sustainability reporting. As these frameworks have become more widely adopted, the number of corporate sustainability reports published by listed companies has increased and their quality has improved. Progress toward standardization in the reporting of ESG metrics has enabled Sustainalytics to develop tools and methodologies to more reliably assess companies within and across industries. The scope of the information tracked also expanded, allowing Sustainalytics to provide more holistic assessments of companies ESG performance and to calculate more meaningful company ratings and rankings.

As we look to the future . . .
Investors continue to develop new investment products and strategies to capitalize on growing client demand – such as impact investing and ESG-themed smart beta offerings. Changes in the asset management world, such as the ongoing shift from active to passive management, the move from fundamental to data-driven strategies, and the increasing use of machine learning and artificial intelligence, could fundamentally change the way ESG information is used in investment decision-making and corporate engagement. These changes are likely to place new demands on ESG research and data, and raise expectations for product innovation and sophistication.

ESG assessments are just one of several inputs used in the investment decision-making process by a growing number of investors globally. The consideration and incorporation of ESG data has become mainstream, and tremendous progress has been made in the number of meaningful metrics reported. However, the types and amount of information available is still far from perfect for many investors. Tracking the metrics of material ESG issues down the entire supply chain – for a true assessment of a company's ESG impact and risk – is a systemic challenge that will not easily be solved. But, as they did 25 years ago, investors will likely continue to demand more and better ESG disclosure, and the market will move to ensure they have the right data to make truly informed decisions.

ESG ratings providers include (but are not limited to) Institutional Shareholder Services (ISS), IW Financial, Sustainalytics, MSCI, and Barra. These data providers may differ in the way they classify securities and identify industry criteria. For example, simply identifying companies within the gambling industry may not be appropriate for an institutional investor who has a policy mandate to exclude companies who generate revenue from any gambling activity. Technology companies, hotels, and financial companies are not traditionally considered to be in the gambling industry, but may generate revenue through gambling-associated activities. The differences between ratings agencies provides cross-sectional data which allows investors to view multiple different aspects of a company's ESG factors. As ESG analysts and ratings agencies continue to multiply, data will become more comprehensive and will provide more information into the future returns distribution of a company. For this reason, it is common for investors to use multiple service providers for the identification and classification of securities, to ensure the validity and wholeness of information.

Practical example: screening for fossil fuels

An investor wishing to exclude companies generating revenue from fossil fuels might utilize multiple data providers in order to assure that all fossil fuels related business activities are thoroughly excluded per their investment objective. Such an exclusion of all fossil fuels related business activities might use a combination of multiple classification tools, in which the following grouping of six classification datasets might be aggregated together in an overlapping, comprehensive manner:

1. Fracking (provided by IW financial)

This dataset criteria seeks to classify companies known to be involved in hydraulic fracturing as a method for recovering oil and natural gas. Examples of fracking companies include Anadarko Petroleum Corporation and Apache Corporation.

2. Tar sands (provided by IW financial)

This dataset criteria seeks to classify companies identified by non-governmental organizations (NGOs) such as the Rainforest Action Network as having tar sands operations. Examples of tar sands companies include Chevron Corporation and ConocoPhillips.

3. Carbon reserves (provided by MSCI)

This dataset criteria seeks to classify all companies with disclosed fossil fuel reserves in oil, natural gas, or coal. The companies in this set, some of which are multi-industry conglomerates with subsidiaries in the fossil fuel industry, come from industries including: consumer discretionary, consumer staples, energy, industrials, materials, and utilities. Note: there may be companies that do not have disclosed fossil fuel reserves that are categorized as in the oil, gas, and consumable fuels industry.

4. Oil, gas, and consumable fuels (provided by GICS industry from Barra)

This dataset criteria seeks to classify companies defined within the industry of oil, gas, and consumable fuels. This option does not include oil and gas drilling or oil and gas equipment and services sub-industries. Please note that an oil, gas, and consumable fuels exclusion will include the coal companies exclusion.

5. Coal companies (provided by GICS industry from Barra)

This dataset criteria seeks to classify companies defined within the sub-industry of coal and consumable fuels. This dataset only addresses the production of coal; it does not include coal-powered utilities. To identify coal-powered utilities, an investor might consider a sub-industry dataset of electric utilities.

6. Energy equipment and services (GICS industry from Barra)

This dataset criteria seeks to classify companies engaged in the manufacture of equipment, including drilling rigs and equipment, and providers of supplies and services to companies involved in the drilling, evaluation, and completion of oil and gas wells. Examples of such companies would be Halliburton Company and National Oilwell Varco Inc.

ESG research can become extremely granular, as investors vary greatly in the types of ESG issues that relate to their investment principles or mandates. The nonprofit organization GreenFaith is an example of an organization which applies ESG ratings data to a specific subset of investors. GreenFaith produces research on how religious-affiliated investors, such as church endowments or ministry-based retirement funds, should be considering the impact their investments make on the environment. See Case study 8A to learn more about GreenFaith.

ESG analysis: overview of the "Major Players"

Notable organizations that produce ESG research include (but are far from limited to) Equator Principles, Eurosif, US SIF, Global Impacting Investing Network, Global Initiative for Investment Ratings, Global Thinkers Forum, Greenhouse Gas Protocol, Interfaith Center on Corporate Responsibility (ICCR), Intentional Corporate Governance Network (ICGN), Overseas Private Investment Corporation (OPIC), Sustainable Investment Research Initiative Library, Responsible Investor, MSCI Inc., Sustainalytics, The Conference Board Center for Corporate Citizenship and Sustainability, The European Center for Corporate Engagement (ECCE), United Nations Global Compact, United Nations Principles for Responsible Investing (UNPRI), World Business Council for Sustainable Development, yourSRI, and many more. Each of these organizations target ESG-related research specific to their mission statements and specializations, resulting in ESG research being produced across issues, themes, industries, and investment sectors. In 2017, over 650 organizations produce

ESG-related research, with about 150 of those organizations producing ESG ratings (Mercer, 2017). Although several consultant organizations and asset management companies produce ratings, the independent ESG rating service providers have gained the most significant attention from investors.

CASE STUDY 3G: Interfaith Center on Corporate Responsibility

Nearly every faith tradition has investment guidelines calling for a more thoughtful alignment of money and mission. As some of the earliest practitioners of socially responsible investing, faith organizations recognized how invested capital can be used as a catalyst for social change both through the funding of solutions and opportunities or through the withdrawal or withholding of capital to discourage destructive practices and policies.

In 1971, the faith-based institutions that founded the Interfaith Center on Corporate Responsibility discovered a more nuanced and potentially more powerful investment strategy designed to help shape corporate practices on core environmental, social, and governance concerns: shareholder advocacy through the annual proxy process and via ongoing dialogues with management. The catalyzing issue during ICCR's genesis was the racist system of Apartheid in South Africa, and the first resolution citing a social justice concern was filed by the Episcopal Church at General Motors requesting that the company withdraw its business operations from South Africa until Apartheid was abolished.

Nearly five decades after its founding, ICCR continues to attract global investors eager to employ this more direct shareholder advocacy model and work in coalition with like-minded investors on some of the world's most intransigent social and environmental issues. Among the ranks of ICCR's 300-plus member institutions are a broad spectrum of faith-based organizations, socially responsible asset management companies, unions, foundations, and other responsible investors that collectively represent well over $400 billion in managed assets. ICCR's engagement strategies are built on the expertise of both staff and members who use their access as investors to champion change from the inside, while partnering with extensive networks of NGOs and community groups that apply pressure from the outside. When there is a clear investor case, members are also engaged in grassroots policy advocacy.

ICCR members file close to 300 shareholder resolutions each proxy season and, if they are not withdrawn as a result of a corporate commitment, the majority of these proposals are voted on by all shareholders at company annual meetings. In addition, members convene regular in-person or telephone dialogues with hundreds of these same companies, often addressing a variety of investor concerns, and if engagements become stalled, ICCR may convene industry roundtables inviting relevant companies and stakeholders to achieve broader consensus that accelerates progress.

Utilizing ESG ratings data

ESG ratings may be utilized for various purposes by the investment community. For example, a structured or financially engineered product, such as an ESG-focused equity index or index fund may utilize ESG ratings to positively or negatively screen for quality. An institutional investor may use underlying ratings data for ESG reporting. ESG ratings provide a granular depiction of a portfolio's ESG quality composition. ESG ratings are the underlying source of heat mapping and other technological-enabled portfolio holdings measurement for ESG impact reports. ESG ratings data can be interpreted as another fundamental factor that can be utilized in the valuation of a company's securities. An investor may also view the ESG ratings marketplace as a cross-section of ESG sentiment (Wu, Liu, and Chen, 2016). Asset managers and hedge funds may look to ESG ratings for insight into risk premia harvesting opportunities.

3.7 The impact of ESG risk on portfolio management

ESG investing continues to grow in acceptance and adoption within investment methodology and practice. As this happens, an entire spectrum of ESG risks will continue to be measured and integrated into investment portfolios in much the same way as fundamental or macroeconomic risks are measured and calculated, varied based on the investor's mandate or objective. Companies research and identify ESG factors to improve their business model, operational productivity and workflow, and growth potential. Similarly, investors (both institutional and private) use ESG research in portfolio management to prevent future unforeseen risks, manage and mitigate current risk, and cultivate the ability to achieve higher risk-adjusted returns.

Institutional investors

Institutional investors are the most powerful type of investor, as they are asset owners governing the largest capital pools, and can thus have a material impact on asset pricing. Thus, the perception of ESG risks by institutional investors can have a significant impact on the market pricing of assets. By nature, and due to an institution's structural deep-rootedness, institutional investors have a long-time horizon for their investment return objectives. This extended time horizon allows the institutional investor to make measured decisions on portfolio turnover with relatively low frequency when compared to other investors. Given this time horizon, and the ability to have low turnover, institutional investors will often devise frameworks, mandates, and guidelines for how portfolios should be managed internally, by investment team members, and externally by money managers. Institutional investors identify ESG risks and construct frameworks, mandates, and guidelines for portfolio management policy. Such ESG frameworks, mandates, and guidelines have both a direct and indirect impact on portfolio management. Directly, such frameworks, mandates, and guidelines can impact how asset-liability projections are made, the asset allocation of the portfolio, the performance benchmarks used, and the calculation of volatility risk. Indirectly, the ESG risks incorporated in such frameworks, mandates, and guidelines impact the way in which an external money manager may manage a portfolio of capital allocated from the institutional investor.

Active management

Money managers, such as asset managers and hedge funds, are impacted by ESG risks in various ways. One such way is through their portfolio management strategy. With the growth of ESG research and ratings, active money managers can more easily access third-party research to help in their evaluation of securities. Further, asset managers incorporate ESG research and risk assessment internally in order to avoid proven performance risk associated with ESG factors. Examining information that is not easily visible in a company's financials, such as ESG research and ESG factors, are important as the synthesis of ESG risks add value to the portfolio management and risk management of active money management. Such money managers may also view these ESG risks as informational insight on potential idiosyncratic risks within their portfolio. For example, if an asset manager manages a portfolio of equities and learns of negative environmental actions or procedures by a company that they are invested in through the discovery of ESG research, they may consider exiting the position from their portfolio to avoid future risks to the stock price due to potential environmental disaster or regulatory action.

As institutional investors alter their frameworks, mandates, and guidelines to account for ESG risks, and thus, increase external allocation to ESG-mindful asset managers, asset managers will continue to evolve their portfolio management processes to serve institutional demand. Not only is the growth in ESG within the investment community an opportunity for asset managers to gather additional assets, but it is also a threat to asset managers who do not assess ESG risks within their portfolio management as they might lose invested capital to competitors. The concept of ESG risk premia has had a tremendous impact on portfolio management for anyone actively managing money. Avoiding policy violations, headline risks, and the proven performance risks associated with ESG factors are all incentives for active asset managers to integrate ESG factors into portfolio construction.

Passive management

Passively managed portfolios, such as index funds, exchange-traded funds, and sector swaps have also been impacted by ESG risks. Institutional and retail demand continues to increase for ESG-related products. Structuring a passively managed product is a fast and efficient way for the asset management and investment banking community to bring an ESG product to the market. The financial engineering and structuring of passive products, such as systematic or quantitatively derived index funds, exchange-traded funds, or sector swaps, are being encouraged by investors and governments to consider accounting for ESG risks at the inception of such funds, or through indices that a fund or separate account is tracking. These passive index funds may be structured out of best interest of the investor to track an ESG-related index. A plethora of ESG-related indices exist in the marketplace from an array of index providers. MSCI alone has more than 600 ESG indices (MSCI, 2016). Since passively managed products are generally static or fixed in terms of turnover and rebalancing, the management of passive products by the issuer is relatively seamless once created. Furthermore, it is easier for an issuer of such passively managed products to integrate ESG factors.

Wealth management (financial advisors)

The wealth management industry has also shifted towards ESG consciousness. Financial advisors have a fiduciary duty to ensure that their clients' investment guidelines are being met. They are also sensitive to headline risks associated with investing in corporations with negative press, and are held responsible for underperformance. Each of these mandates demonstrate areas where financial advisors can utilize ESG factors to understand and mitigate risk. Wealth managers, such as retail financial advisory offices and robot-advisory platforms are forced to develop a range of available ESG-based investment products in order to meet the demands of current clients and prospective clients. Developing a variety of ESG-based investment offerings impacts the way in which wealth managers manage a portfolio as additional time and energy must be deployed in the due diligence and education on such products. Further, the education of these products is not solely for the wealth manager, as the wealth manager must have a broad enough understanding to educate their client base and any prospective clients. As retail investors continue to learn more about ESG investing, they continue to require more information on the ESG factors and risks associated with each investment. Clients look to their wealth managers to be accountable for adopting and implementing ESG practices to prevent and mitigate ESG risks. This demand for accountability requires wealth managers to integrate new processes, such as the use of GICS, ESG ratings, and ESG portfolio impact monitoring.

Retail investor

The retail investor, such as an individual managing a personal online brokerage account or an individual retirement account, is also impacted in the way they manage a portfolio because of ESG risks. As the development of ESG strategies has led to the creation of more investment products by index providers, asset managers, and hedge funds, the retail investor faces these research and educational hurdles. The retail investor identifies which investment products properly consider ESG risks.

Environmental, social, and governance risks have been shown to have a material long-term impact on the financial performance of a corporation. Incorporating ESG factors into portfolio management in a similar way to fundamental and technical analysis is the best way to analyze the policy, headline, and performance risks associated with an investment. As ESG ratings data continues to proliferate, investors and corporations will continue to implement environmental, social, and governance factors into their portfolio management and corporate policy.

CASE STUDY 3H: Brunel Pension Partnership

Faith Ward, Chief Responsible Investment Officer, Brunel Pension Partnership

Being a **responsible investor** is primarily a mindset, in that it acknowledges that the investment decisions we make often on behalf of others, and in the case of pension funds tens of thousands of others, can be impacted by a whole host of factors that fall outside traditional financial analysis.

The responsible investor understands that every company or asset we invest in operates interdependently with the economy, civil society, and the physical environment. Considering whether these interdependencies create **financially material risks or opportunities** for the investments is a core part of responsible investment (RI). But it is wider than looking at individual investments; it's about the beliefs and principles of the investor themselves, and using this to guide their strategic thinking and embedding it in all that they do. It is vital to reemphasize that the purpose of doing this is to **better manage risk** and **generate sustainable, long-term returns**. All actions are predicated on fulfilling our core legal financial duties, also known as "**fiduciary duties,**" to the end beneficiaries.

Brunel Pension Partnership was formed in July 2017 and oversees the investment of the pension assets (around $40bn) of ten (Avon, Buckinghamshire, Corwall, Decon, Dorset, Environment Agency, Gloucestershire, Oxfordshire, Somerset, and Wiltshire Funds) Local Government Pensions Scheme funds in the UK. We use the name "**Brunel**" to refer to the company and its approach to responsible investment.

Brunel believes the only way to truly fulfill one's fiduciary duty is to be a responsible investor from the top-down and the bottom-up. This case study draws out the ways in which it has developed this approach and in practical terms goes about being a responsible investor.

Brunel's organizational values
- We believe in making long-term sustainable investments supported by robust and transparent process
- We are here to protect the interests of our clients and their members
- In collaboration with all our stakeholders we are forging better futures by investing for a world worth living in

These values are underpinned by a set of investment principles that were agreed collabora-tively across the partnership. Although **responsible investment** and **responsible steward-ship** (the policies and actions you take on the assets once invested) are singled out separately, all the principles are intertwined with each other. For example, "long term," "full risk evalua-tion," and "innovation" all easily fit with being a responsible investor and vice versa.

Brunel Pension Partnership investment principles
- Long-term investors
- Responsible investors
- Best-practice governance
- Decisions informed through experts and knowledgeable officers and committees
- Evidence and research at the heart of investments
- Leadership and innovation
- Right risk for right return
- Full risk evaluation
- Responsible stewardship
- Cost-effective solutions
- Transparent and accountable
- Collaboration

Drilling down into the practicalities, Brunel outlines its approach to **Responsible Invest-ment Strategy**, which is summarized in its publicly available **Responsible Investment Policy**. The aim of the strategy is *"to deliver stronger investment returns over the long term, protecting our clients' interests and contributing to deliver a more sustainable and resilient financial system, which supports sustainable economic growth and a thriving society."* The approach has three pillars: to integrate, to collaborate, and to be transparent.

To integrate
As a top-level heading of our strategy, we use the term integration to capture a whole variety of actions, not just the process of integrating environmental, social, and gover-nance factors into the portfolio construction (see Chapter 4).

Every member of staff has objectives relating to responsible investment, tailored to their area of work and reflecting the **expected behaviors of staff** – from corporate culture, policies on diversity, and inclusion to individuals' travel choices – as an organization we need to "**walk the talk**" and "**practice what we preach**."

The integration commitment includes the range of **investment opportunities** provided to ensure those funds who want more explicit sustainability criteria, e.g. low-carbon or impact investing, have those choices.

However, where it matters most to Brunel as an organization is embedding responsible investment into our core purpose, which is the **selection and monitoring of managers**. This is not just about how the manager looks at ESG on their potential investments and what ESG data sources they use, but also the philosophy and policies the managers have themselves. When you select a fund manager you are often buying the skills of an individ-ual or team – how the company manages its people, the broader culture, and alignment of incentives are all critical RI or ESG factors that fall outside of the investment process itself, but done badly directly damage financial performance.

It is important to stress that Brunel integrates RI into all asset classes. How this manifest itself varies and the approach is tailored so it is fit for purpose and ensures that we **focus on material financial risks always**.

To help remember all the factors we take into account, we can group six Ps:

- **P**hilosophy (investment, corporate culture, board-level leadership)
- **P**olicies (commitment, policy framework, pricing, and transparency)
- **P**eople (numbers, retention, cognitive diversity)
- **P**rocesses (investment process, performance, reporting, stewardship)
- **P**articipation (thought leadership, innovation, contribution to investment industry)
- **P**artnership (in it together, are we a cultural fit?)

Whilst we do look broadly at the same set of factors, the relative importance varies depending on the particular mandate at the more detailed due diligence. Asset class, geography, and risk objectives will have a bearing on which RI and ESG risks are most essential to focus on when making an appointment. Integrating RI into the **mandate design** and **risk appraisal** process prior to going out to search for a manager is therefore critical in ensuring that we focus on the right things.

More information about the selection and monitoring of managers is on our website.

To collaborate
We aim to provide useful **feedback** to all managers following a selection exercise as well as on an ongoing basis, which we have found very productive in seeing improvements of the management of ESG risks and approaches to RI by the industry.

In addition to asset managers, we work collaboratively with other pension funds, policy makers, and regulators, as well as industry bodies and NGOs (non-governmental organizations). The aim is to **amplify** the **impact and outcomes** of our actions as well as to support each other and share best practice.

One of the areas where this has proved very effective is in **collaborative engagement and proxy voting** with corporations. Groups of investors can speak with one voice, providing clarity to the company being engaged with as to the areas of concern to its shareholders. More information on our partnerships, affiliations, engagements, and voting are on our website.

To be transparent
Brunel demands high standards of transparency of the companies and organizations it works with, so likewise places a high priority in being transparent itself and providing high standards of reporting and communication.

Communication builds trust, which is vital in all parts of the finance industry. Particular areas of focus for Brunel include transparency on costs, tax, and climate change. Brunel is also committed to reporting on the positive impacts the investment makes. The UN Global Goals provide a useful framework to translate the positive outcomes of the investments we make and the impacts these have on real-world issues.

Discussion questions

1) Define and discuss:

   a   Risk premia (LO1)
   b   Examples of risk premia, and investment strategies investors use to harvest various risk premia opportunities (LO2)

2) Define ESG Risk (LO3)
3) In your own analysis, how has the use of ESG factors in investing become a risk premia opportunity set? (LO4)
4) Discuss the role of research and rating agencies in the investors' practice of using ESG factors in their responsible investing process and/or policy (LO5)

References

American Association of University Women (AAUW). "Barriers and Bias: The Status of Women in Leadership." www.aauw.org/files/2017/03/barriersbias-one-pager-nsa.pdf March, 2017.

Baule, Rainer, Olaf Korn, and Sven Saßning. "Which Beta Is Best? On the Information Content of Option-implied Betas." *European Financial Management* 22, no. 3 (2016): 450–83. *Business Source Complete*, EBSCO*host*. Accessed February 20, 2017.

Bender, Jennifer, Hammond, Paul Brett, and Mok, William. "Can Alpha Be Captured by Risk Premia?" (May 30, 2013). Available at SSRN: https://ssrn.com/abstract=2543987 or http://dx.doi.org/10.2139/ssrn.2543987.

Burke, Allison. "10 Facts about American Women in the Workforce." Brookings Institute: Brookings Now. (December 5, 2017). https:// brookings.edu/blog/brookings-now/2017/12/05/10-facts-about-american-women-in-the-workforce/.

Carhart, Mark. "On Persistence in Mutual Fund Performance." *The Journal of Finance* 52, no. 1 (1997): 57–82.

Catalyst, Pyramid: Women in S&P 500 Companies. 2018. http:// catalyst.org/knowledge/women-sp-500-companies (updated February 2, 2018).

Clark, G., A. Feiner, and M. Viehs. "From the Stockholder to the Stakeholder: How Sustainability Can Drive Financial Outperformance." (March 5, 2015). doi:10.2139/ssrn.2508281. Available at SSRN: https://ssrn.com/abstract=2508281 or http://dx.doi.org/10.2139/ssrn.2508281.

Colacito, Riccardo, Eric Ghysels, Meng Jinghan, and Wasin Siwasarit. "Skewness in Expected Macro Fundamentals and the Predictability of Equity Returns: Evidence and Theory." *Review of Financial Studies* 29, no. 8 (2016): 2069–109. *Business Source Complete*, EBSCO*host*. Accessed February 20, 2017.

Cuberes, David and Mark Teignier-Baque. "Gender Equality and Economic Growth World Development Report 2012: Gender Equality and Development 2011: The World Bank Group." http://siteresources.worldbank.org/INTWDR2012/Resources/7778105-1299699968583/7786210-1322671773271/cuberes.pdf

David, Joel M., and Ina Simonovska. "Correlated Beliefs, Returns, and Stock Market Volatility." *Journal of International Economics* 99 (March 2, 2016): S58–S77. *Business Source Complete*, EBSCO*host*. Accessed February 20, 2017.

Dawson, Julia, Richard Kersley, and Stefano Natella. "CS Gender 3000: Women in Senior Management." Credit Suisse Research Institute, 2014. https://publications.creditsuisse.com/tasks/render/file/index.cfm?fileid=8128F3C0-99BC-22E6-838E2A5B1E4366DF. Accessed May 19, 2018.

Dorfleitner, Gregor, Gerhard Halbritter, and Mai Nguyen. "Measuring the Level and Risk of Corporate Responsibility – An Empirical Comparison of Different ESG Rating Approaches." *Journal of Asset Management* 16, no. 7 (2015): 450–66. doi:10.1057/jam.2015.31.

Fama, Eugene, F., and French, K. "The Cross-Section of Expected Stock Returns." *The Journal of Finance* 47, no. 2 (1992): 427–65.

Fama, Eugene, F., and French, K. "Common Risk Factors in the Returns on Stocks and Bonds." *Journal of Financial Economics* 33 (1993) 3–56.

Fama, Eugene F., and Kenneth R. French. "A Five Factor Asset Pricing Model." *Journal of Financial Economics* 116 (2014): 1–22.

Freshfields Brukhaus Deringer. "A Legal Framework for the Integration of Environmental, Social and Governance Issues into Institutional Investment." 2005. www.unepfi.org/fileadmin/docu ments/freshfields_legal_resp_20051123.pdf

Galai, Dan, Haim Kedar-Levy, and Ben Z. Schreiber. "Volatility-Decay Risk Premia." *Journal of Derivatives* 22, no. 1 (Fall 2014): 57–70. http://search.proquest.com.proxy1.ncu.edu/ docview/1564423013?accountid=28180. Accessed February 10, 2017.

Hillman, Amy J., and Gerald D. Keim. "Shareholder Value, Stakeholder Management, and Social Issues: What's the Bottom Line?" *Strategic Management Journal* 22, no. 2 (2001): 125–39. doi:10.1002/1097-0266(200101)22:2<125::aid-smj150>3.0.co;2-h.

Hunt, Vivian, Denis Layton, and Sarah Prince. "Diversity Matters." *McKinsey & Company*, 2015. https://assets.mckinsey.com/~/media/857F440109AA4D13A54D9C496D86ED58.ashx. Accessed May 19, 2018.

Julia L. Pollard, Matthew W. Sherwood, and Ryan Grad Klobus. "Establishing ESG as Risk Premia." *Journal of Investment Management* 16, no. 1 (2018): 1–12.

Kotsantonis, Sakis, Chris Pinney, and George Serafeim. "ESG Integration in Investment Management: Myths and Realities." *Journal of Applied Corporate Finance* 28, no. 2 (2016): 10–16. *Business Source Complete*, EBSCOhost. Accessed February 20, 2017.

Kurz, Mordecai, and Maurizio Motolese. "Diverse Beliefs and Time Variability of Risk Premia." *Economic Theory*, vol. 47, no. 2–3, 2010, pp. 293–335., doi:10.1007/s00199-010-0550-1.

Lai, Ya-Wen. "Macroeconomic Factors and Index Option Returns." *International Review of Economics & Finance* 48, no. C (2017): 452–77.

Li, Junye. "Option-Implied Volatility Factors and the Cross-Section of Market Risk Premia." *Journal of Banking & Finance* 36, no. 1 (2012): 249–60. *Business Source Complete*, EBSCOhost. Accessed February 20, 2017.

Lydenberg, Steve. "Integrating Systemic Risk into Modern Portfolio Theory and Practice." *Journal of Applied Corporate Finance* 28, no. 2 (Spring 2016): 56–61. *Business Source Complete*, EBSCOhost. Accessed March 3, 2017.

Lubos Pastor, and Robert F. Stambaugh. "Liquidity Risk and Expected Stock Returns." *The Journal of Political Economy* 111, no. 3 (June 2003): 642. ABI/INFORM Global.

Mattingly, J. E., and Shawn L. Berman. "Measurement of Corporate Social Action: Discovering Taxonomy in the Kinder Lydenburg Domini Ratings Data." *Business & Society* 45, no. 1 (2006): 20–46. doi:10.1177/0007650305281939.

"Mercer's ESG Ratings." Mercer, www.mercer.com/our-thinking/mercer-esg-ratings.html.

MSCI Inc. "MSCI ESG Research." MSCI Inc., 2014. https://msci.com/documents/10199/40f512f3-f89d-40b5-8c41-248fae4305bf. Accessed October 25, 2016.

MSCI Inc. "MSCI ESG Research [Brochure]." MSCI Inc., 2016. https:// msci.com/documents/ 10199/40f512f3-f89d-40b5-8c41-248fae4305bf. Accessed October, 2016.

Oikonomou, I., C. Brooks, and S. Pavelin. "The Impact of Corporate Social Performance on Financial Risk and Utility: A Longitudinal Analysis." *Financial Management* 41 (2012): 483–515.

Orlitzky, M., and J. D. Benjamin. "Corporate Social Performance and Firm Risk: A Meta-Analytic Review." *Business & Society* 40 (2001): 369–96.

PWC's. "Annual Corporate Directors Survey." 2017. www.pwc.com/acds2017/

Singal, Manisha. "The Link between Firm Financial Performance and Investment in Sustainability Initiatives." *Cornell Hospitality Quarterly* 55, no. 1 (2014): 19–30. doi:10.1177/1938965513505700.

Stanford University. "Stanford and Climate Change: A Statement of the Board of Trustees." *Stanford News*. June 9, 2017. https://news.stanford.edu/2016/04/25/stanford-climate-change-state ment-board-trustees/. Accessed March 30, 2018.

Te-Feng, Chen, Chung San-Lin, and Tsai Wei-Che. "Option-Implied Equity Risk and the Cross Sec-
    tion of Stock Returns." *Financial Analysts Journal* 72, no. 6 (2016): 42–55. *Business Source Com-
    plete*, EBSCO*host*. Accessed February 20, 2017.
"U.S. Government Accountability Office Corporate Boards: 'Strategies to address Representation of
    Women include disclosure requirements'." January 2016. www.gao.gov/products/GAO-16-30
Wu, Po-Chin, Shiao-Yen Liu, and Che-Ying Chen. "Re-Examining Risk Premiums in the Fama –
    French Model: The Role of Investor Sentiment." *North American Journal of Economics & Finance*
    36 (2016): 154–71. *Business Source Complete*, EBSCO*host*. Accessed March 4, 2017.

Chapter 4

Common methods for incorporating ESG investments into portfolio management

This chapter investigates the four most common methods investors use to incorporate ESG investing strategies into portfolio construction and management. This chapter identifies the pathways used for ESG investing because of the reasons discussed in Chapter 5 and 7, including those reasons that investors avoid committing to ESG investing strategies, and the investment theories discussed in Chapter 6 that have bearing on portfolio management. This chapter segments the incorporation of ESG investing strategies into four sections: integration-based ESG investing, exclusion-based ESG investing, and impact- and engagement-based ESG investing. This chapter is structured as an introduction, attempting to give the reader a basic understanding of how the combination of the reasons for concern regarding ESG investing, the current level of incorporation of ESG investing, and the influence of common investment theories have lent themselves to the methods through which ESG investing is incorporated.

Learning objectives

- Define and explain:
  - Integration-based ESG investing as a method of incorporating ESG investing strategies into investment portfolios
  - Exclusion-based ESG investing as a method of incorporating ESG investing strategies into investment portfolios
  - Impact-based and engagement-based ESG investing as methods of incorporating ESG investing strategies into investment portfolios
- Compare the four most common investor methods of incorporating ESG investing strategies into investment portfolios
- Assess the benefits and downfalls of each common investor method in the context of different markets, asset classes, and investment sectors

After this chapter, readers should have a foundation of some of the practical factors used by investors deciding how to incorporate ESG investing strategies into portfolio management.

4.1 Exclusion-based ESG investing

Exclusion-based ESG investing, also referred to as **negative screening**, is an ESG investing methodology for portfolio management. As discussed in Chapter 2, ESG investing began with exclusionary investing (Caplan et al., 2013). Institutional investors in particular would strive to align investments with the interests of their constituents. Practically, this involved creating investment policy statements that excluded investments in financial instruments and securities conflicting with the mission and policy of the constituents (see Chapter 3 for a discussion of investment policy statements).

Exclusion is still at the forefront of ESG investing implementation methodologies for many institutional investors worldwide (see Chapter 5 for a discussion of the current implementation levels of different ESG investment implementation methodologies). When an investor excludes certain investments from a portfolio that were previously included in the investment portfolio, this is referred to as **divestment**.

Exclusion-based ESG investing was first publicly implemented by faith-based institutional investors. These institutional investors coined the term "sin stocks," referring to equities that generate a percentage of their revenue from industries that conflict with the religious convictions of the faith-based organization, such as weapons, alcohol, pornography, child labor, or gambling. As discussed in Chapter 2, the Quaker and Methodist Christian denominations are recognized as some of the first religious groups to exclude firearms and other "sin stocks" from their investment portfolios. In recent years, many of these faith-based institutional investors extend exclusionary screening beyond equities and into other asset classes such as credit and hedge funds.

More recently, some Catholic-based archdioceses' endowment and retirement investment managers refrain from investing in sovereign bonds of governments that are not directly aligned with their mission. This policy might exclude Myanmar (formerly Burma) bonds because of the country's association with child labor practices or the United States treasury bonds because of the heavy military-based weapons manufacturing.

One of the early cases of large-scale exclusion-based ESG investing was the divestment from South African assets during Apartheid. This was a mainstream example of how institutional investors from various organizations, representing sovereign wealth funds, public and private pension funds, endowments, and foundations, implemented exclusionary policies on South African investments. Exclusions of South African assets were not simply limited to equities, but extended to investments in credit and governmental bonds as well. Some economists suggest that the deliberate lack of foreign investment in South African infrastructure, particularly in the development of railroad systems, contributed to the end of Apartheid.

Exclusion requires company-specific research and analysis. An investor uses publicly disclosed information to assess whether a corporation operates in accordance with the investor's beliefs, policies, or inclusion criteria. Depending on the outcome of the investor's analysis, the investment is either included or excluded from the investment. For example, an investor may wish to exclude a company's securities if the investor determines that the corporate board has a history of poor practices of social responsibility within a community that the company operates within (Lokuwaduge and Heenetigala, 2017).

As noted in Chapter 3, investors may leverage the use of third-party classification systems and codes, such as GICS, to identify and classify such securities. Investors may also use screening tools provided by research firms, such as MSCI's Low Carbon Screen. Some institutional investors may decide to create their own analytical measurement tools to determine the identification and classification of such securities. Retail investors may decide on exclusionary criteria based on personal choice or preference, whereas an asset manager may enact exclusions under the investment guidelines provided by their client or, perhaps, by the instructions of the executive team or board.

Institutional investors have an added complexity in determining their exclusionary policy, because they represent a broader population. Institutional investors are challenged with the task of aligning their exclusionary policy with that of the population they represent. The exclusionary policy is a list of the guidelines mandated to exclude certain securities or securities' classifications from the investment universe, and it is often a part of the institution's investment policy. This challenge may be faced in various ways. Some instructions may have, or create, lines of communication to the population, or a sample of the population, that they represent. In this manner, these institutions may inquire and measure the topics or issues that they might consider relevant to the requests and collective desires of the population. For example, a retirement plan that represents a workers' union might consider gathering information from the union members through the union voting process. Other institutions might consider drafting their exclusionary policy based on a board of directors or a management team's exclusionary choices. As the board of directors, advisory board, investment committee, or investment team are fiduciaries to the population that the institution represents, it may be appropriate for this governing body to decide on what the exclusionary policy should be on behalf of the population they serve. A corporate pension plan may execute exclusionary policy based on the governance of the board of directors, who may be the most appropriate members to weigh the principles of the organization with that of what is best for their employees. Other institutions may find an external resource, or resources, best to determine what should be excluded from investments. In this way, an institutional investor that manages a retirement plan for a network of churches' employees might engage the hierarchy, or leadership, of the church to identify what exclusions might best be aligned with the plan's participants. Other institutional investors might have a hybrid approach.

Exclusion-based ESG investing implementation is generally stringent, and black and white, in nature. Regardless whether an investor uses proprietary classification systems, identification criteria provided by a broker-dealer, or third-party screening resources, it is extremely important that the investor can report on the efficacy of the exclusions and measure the consistency of the investments included within the total portfolio. Reporting is a key element to the exclusion-based ESG investing, as reporting on what investments are within an investment fund or portfolio allows the board of directors, advisory board, investment committee, investment officers, or membership population to understand that their interests, guidelines, or policy is being executed with accuracy. Reporting on what investments are included within the investments allows the investor to identify, and react to, any risks that to the exclusion criteria of the investor.

CASE STUDY 4A: Schroders Asset Management

Alex Monk, Sustainability Investments Analyst
Demystifying negative screens: the full implications of ESG exclusions

Screening out investments that do not meet environmental, social, or governance (ESG) criteria is superficially simple but fraught with practical challenges. Understanding the complexities and biases screens created before they are implemented and appropriately assessing performance afterward is crucial for investors. In this paper, we investigate the pitfalls when implementing different screens.

Executive summary

Negative screens that sieve investments on environmental, social, and governance grounds remain critical to many investors, with close to one-fifth of all professionally managed assets subject to some form of exclusion (GSIA, 2017). Of course, negative screening is only one aspect of sustainable investment, and serves a different purpose to activities such as integration and engagement. While the last two are designed to help investors reach better investment outcomes, exclusion policies reflect investors' choices to avoid activities they consider unpalatable. But even if decisions on screens are taken separately from investment analysis, it is vital to understand their effect on investment goals.

Typically, this is discussed in terms of the impact of screening on historical performance, a rear-view focus that distracts from more important questions. History tells us there is no reason to expect exclusions to systematically reduce long-term returns. But by increasing volatility and inhibiting investment styles, choices over how exclusions are applied and defined can make it significantly harder for managers to execute certain strategies. Implementing screens may be mechanical, but assessing their impact on portfolios is a complex task.

This paper explores the role of screening, the activities typically targeted, the different ways that exclusions are defined, and their effects on investment strategies. The aim is to help both those investors with exclusion policies already in place and those considering them to understand the options available and the full implications of their choices.

Screening remains very popular but some screens are more popular than others
As suggested, over 20% of globally invested assets exclude companies involved in controversial activities, a statistic that comes from the most recent Global Sustainable Investment Review (Figure 4.1) (GSIA, 2017). And the role of screening continues to grow, with the global value of assets adopting screens rising at an annual rate of 16% for the last

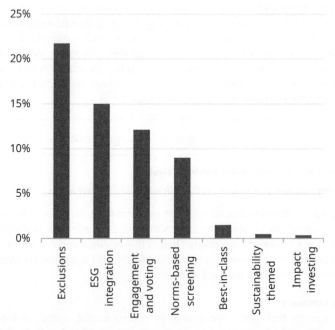

Figure 4.1 Exclusions remain the most popular sustainable investment policy . . .

Globally managed assets subject to sustainable investment policies (percentage of assets) (Schroders, 2017)

Source: Global Sustainable Investment Alliance (GSIA), 2017.

four years and the value of European excluded assets more than doubling since 2011 (Figure 4.2) (Eurosif, 2016). While integration, engagement, and other sustainable investment policies are quickly catching up, it is clear that negative screening remains a popular investor choice.

Most screens typically focus on traditional "sin" industries, such as tobacco, gambling, alcohol, pornography, or those involved in the manufacture and sale of weapons (Figure 4.3). Yet exclusions are generally specific to individual clients and their values. For instance, Sharia-compliant funds exclude businesses selling or producing pork or those involved in lending. Similarly, attitudes toward nuclear power, animal testing, and genetically modified organisms vary from strong support to high resistance. These opinions differ both regionally and nationally and are often reflected in the screens applied in different countries (Figure 4.4).

Changing attitudes towards negative screens
Many see divestment as a mechanism to drive change in business strategies, activities and practices. But while starving companies of capital may appear to be a powerful lever, divestment offers only limited leverage as few of the industries targeted rely on equity capital to fund growth. Indeed, typically, they return a significant share of their earnings to investors. As a result, selling (or not buying) shares in the secondary market has limited impact on their funding, which is largely organic (Ansar, Caldecott, and Tilbury, 2013). Other investors view – or justify – divestment on investment grounds. This is probably the least powerful reason to divest: while several industries targeted for exclusion have

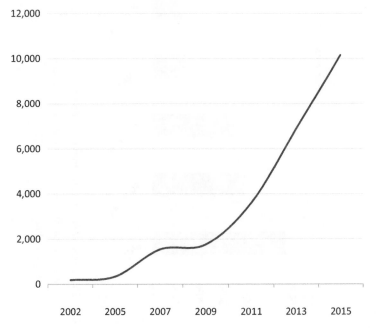

Figure 4.2 . . . which is reflected in the growth of assets subject to negative screening
European assets with screens (US$bn)
Source: Eurosif, 2016.

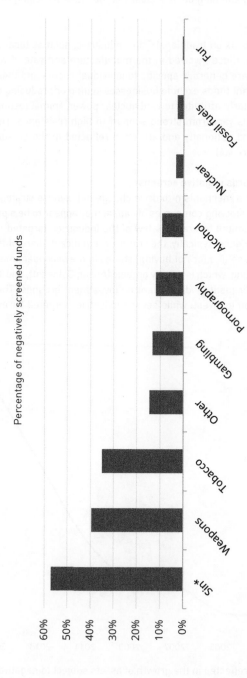

Figure 4.3 "Sin" stocks and weapons dominate the screens Schroders apply for clients . . . .

*Sin stocks include tobacco, alcohol, gambling, and pornography.

Source: Schroders, 2017. Data as at June 30, 2017.

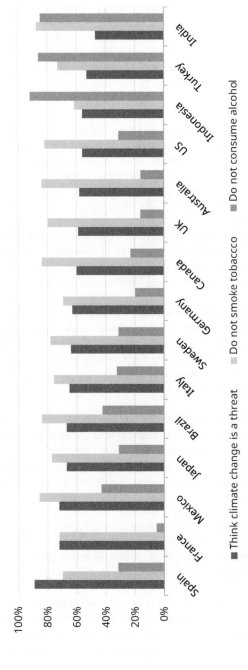

Figure 4.4 . . . but consumer views and practices vary by country

Sources: Leading Global Security Threats, Pew Research Center, 2017; Global Health Observatory Indicator Views, World Health Organization, 2017; and Schroders, 2017.

long-term structural liabilities, these are typically well understood and recognized in valuations.

Despite these shifting attitudes, it is clear that opposition to particular business practices on ethical grounds and therefore an unwillingness to benefit financially from these activities remains the principal driver of negative screens. This sort of pressure to divest is only going to grow. Change.org, the nonprofit-making online campaign platform, currently has 31 petitions on oil, gas, and coal divestment seeking signatures. Google searches for divestment terms continue to rise, with interest in fossil fuels and tobacco particularly high (Figure 4.5).

While fossil fuel exclusions are currently small, high interest in this option means the value of screened assets is growing quickly from a low base. Rising concerns over climate change have driven dramatic divestment in oil, gas, and coal, with globally screened assets more than doubling from $2.6 trillion to $5.4 trillion over the last two years and sizeable asset owners implementing restrictions alongside universities and local governments (Figures 4.6 and 4.7).

Tobacco divestment has been a longer-term trend, but has similarly grown in recent years with a number of insurers, plus a range of sovereign wealth funds and certain pure fund managers all choosing to divest. In total, around $4 billion of previously held positions have been divested from tobacco companies in the last four years (Ralph, 2017).

Focusing narrowly on returns can be deeply misleading
The performance costs of screening tobacco have received a lot of attention recently. According to the London Business School and Credit Suisse, tobacco companies outperformed the wider US and UK markets by more than 3% annually between 1900 and 2014 (Keating and Natella, 2015). Anecdotal evidence like this is, however, not the best way to assess the performance of screens.

Looked at in a wider context, exclusions do not have a huge impact on returns. For example, although tobacco companies have outperformed the MSCI World global benchmark by 87% over the last ten years, because the sector accounts for just 1.7% of the index, the difference between the standard and tobacco-free index is negligible. Across the spectrum of common exclusions, screening makes only a small difference to long-run returns (Figure 4.8).

Importantly, while the long-term performance impact of exclusions is usually minimal, more substantial variation can exist over short periods of time. Different screens can exhibit periods of materially stronger or weaker performance relative to the standard benchmark, depending on the market environment (Figure 4.9).

The effects of screens on short-term performance reflect their sensitivity to the macroeconomic factors which drive returns. The chart in Figure 4.10 statistically models the expected influence of a variety of market factors on the performance of the MSCI World Index with a number of popular screens applied. Screens that remove more of the investible universe generally exhibit bigger performance effects. For example, strong energy

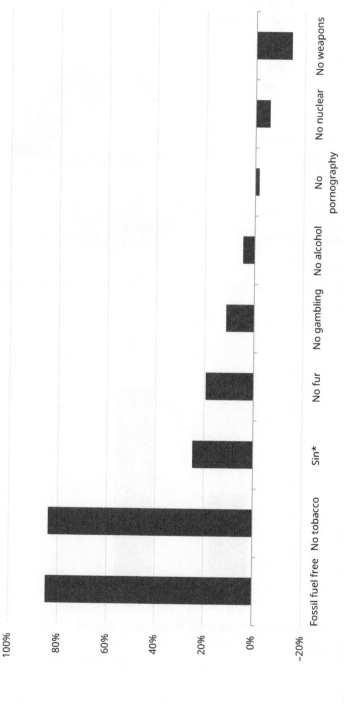

Figure 4.5 Fossil fuels and tobacco seem to be the main preoccupations for divestment searchers on Google

*The sin search takes the average of the tobacco, alcohol, gambling, and pornography searches.

Google search interest represents the yearly average search interest relative to the highest point for the given region and time.

Sources: Google; Schroders, 2017.

sector returns will, not surprisingly, lead funds that exclude fossil fuels to underperform, but, less obviously, higher bond yields are associated with underperformance by funds which screen out "sin" stocks. These influences typically have limited persistent impact, but in the short-term they can be significant.

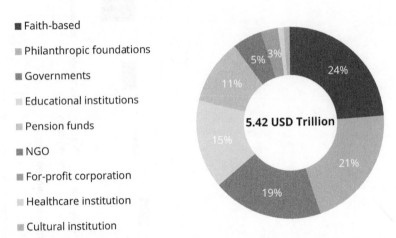

Figure 4.6 Religious, charitable, and government investors have led the way in fossil fuel divestment . . .

*Global fossil fuel divestment by asset owner (US$trn)

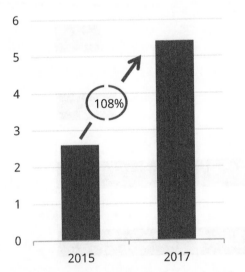

Figure 4.7 . . . helping to double the amount of investment rejected

Change in fossil fuel divestment (US$trn)

*The figures shown are based on the value of institutions' assets under management (AUM) that have made full or partial divestment commitments.

Source: Fossil Free Divestment Commitments. Data from September 2015 and August 2017.

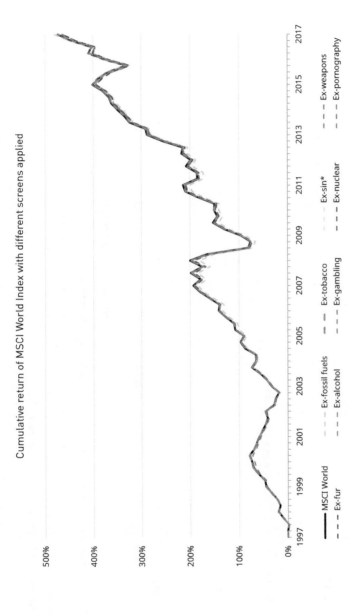

Cumulative return of MSCI World Index with different screens applied

| MSCI World | Ex-fossil fuels | Ex-tobacco | Ex-sin* | Ex-weapons |
| Ex-fur | Ex-alcohol | Ex-gambling | Ex-nuclear | Ex-pornography |

Figure 4.8 Screens make only a minimal difference to long-run index performance....

*Sin stocks include tobacco, alcohol, gambling, and pornography.

Exclusions for fossil fuels and all sin stocks are based on 10% revenue cut off, as defined by MSCI. Exclusions for weapons, fur, and nuclear are based on business involvement, as defined by MSCI. Index returns calculated using quarterly rebalancing of the MSCI World Index over the last 20 years, resulting in slight differences from the true performance of the index.

Source: Datastream and Schroders, 2017, as at June 30, 2017.

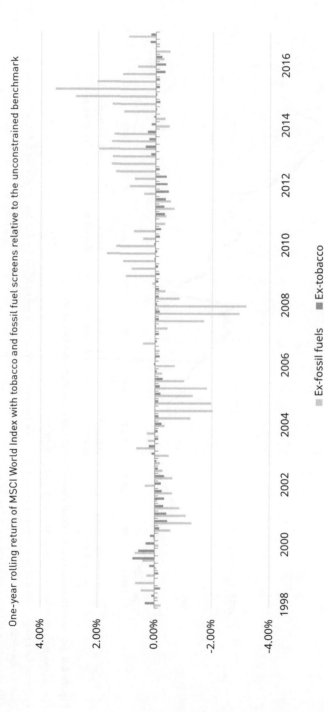

One-year rolling return of MSCI World Index with tobacco and fossil fuel screens relative to the unconstrained benchmark

■ Ex-fossil fuels   ■ Ex-tobacco

Figure 4.9 . . . but can have a substantial impact over shorter periods of time

Exclusions for fossil fuels and tobacco are based on 10% revenue cut off, as defined by MSCI. Index returns calculated using quarterly snapshots of the MSCI World Index over the last 20 years, resulting in slight differences from the true performance of the index.

Source: Datastream and Schroders, 2017, as at June 30, 2017.

Predicted return of screened MSCI World Index after a one standard deviation move in the listed factors, relative to the unconstrained MSCI World Index

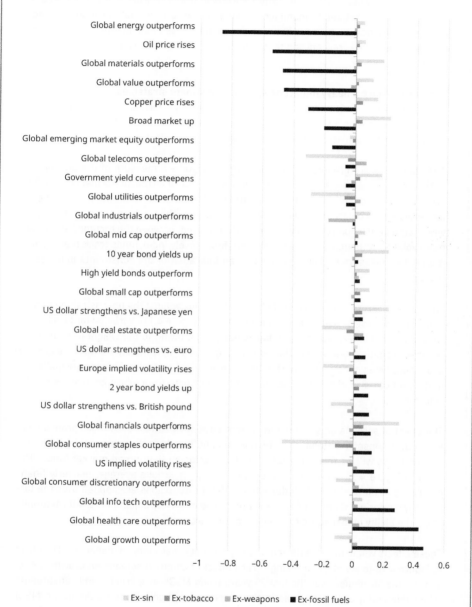

Figure 4.10 Different market factors affect the screened universe in very different ways

*Sin stocks include tobacco, alcohol, gambling, and pornography.

Exclusions for fossil fuels and all sin stocks are based on 10% revenue cut off, as defined by MSCI. Exclusions for weapons, fur, and nuclear are based on business involvement, as defined by MSCI.

Source: Schroders, as at June 30, 2017.

This potential for short-term variation means it is vital to dissect portfolio performance into those elements attributable to the shrunken universe from which securities are drawn, and those related to managers' skills in drawing from that universe. If screens result in a significant difference between the performance of the investible universe and the fund benchmark, recognizing that impact is especially important in assessing managers' performance.

Screens can have a heavy impact on specific investment strategies
Although most screens have little impact on long-term performance, they can still place severe constraints on investors' ability to execute their investment strategies. This challenge applies to both active strategies and passive factor strategies.

The difficulties are greatest where the tracking error – a measure of the discrepancy between the benchmark performance and screened universe performance (tracking error is calculated as the standard deviation of the differences between the screened universe and unconstrained index returns) – is largest. The tracking error is typically big when large proportions of the benchmark are removed, or when the excluded stocks are more volatile. Although often used to gauge how closely index funds track their benchmarks, this measure can also be used as an indication of the constraints imposed on managers.

The tracking errors of the screened MSCI World Index against the unconstrained benchmark over the last 20 years show large differences (Figure 4.11). Variation for fossil fuels, weapons, and nuclear screens are particularly high, owing to the weight of companies removed from the benchmark. Higher tracking errors imply managers will face greater challenges when constructing portfolios and executing strategies. This is principally due to the reduced size of the available investment universe from which companies can be selected.

The effect of screens on specific investment strategies can be even more pronounced. For example, insofar as tobacco companies and utilities typically pay sizeable dividends, income funds will be more disrupted by their exclusion than broad market funds. The chart in Figure 4.12 shows the percentage change in various average quarterly financial ratios of the MSCI World Index when different exclusions are applied over the latest 15-year period. Compounded over time, these quarterly adjustments will materially affect the ability of managers to achieve certain targets.

These effects will in turn create actual and potential constraints on managers. The chart in Figure 4.13 looks at the tracking error impact of common screens on growth, value, and income strategies over the last 20 years using MSCI-style criteria and constituents (The value and growth strategies in the chart included only those stocks in the MSCI Global Value or Growth Indexes, respectively, while the income strategy included only those stocks with a dividend yield greater than 4%. Screens were then applied to each of these indexes to examine the relative effects of exclusions on each strategy). Individual managers have different approaches to each of these styles that may vary significantly from MSCIs, but this a reasonable reflection of many investors' views of style exposures. Higher tracking error impacts reflect greater constraints on managers' abilities to execute their chosen strategy.

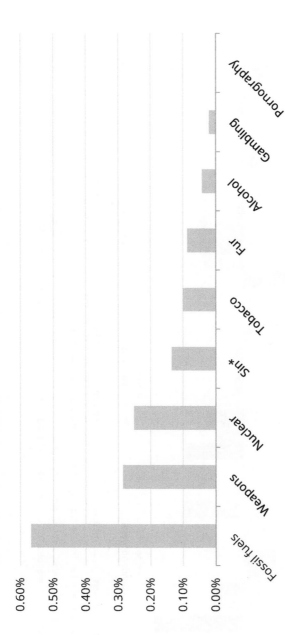

Tracking error of screened MSCI World Index relative to the unconstrained benchmark over the last 20 years

Figure 4.11 The performance of a screened universe can differ substantially from the benchmark

*Sin stocks include tobacco, alcohol, gambling, and pornography. Exclusions for fossil fuels and all sin stocks are based on 10% revenue cut off, as defined by MSCI. Exclusions for weapons, fur, and nuclear are based on business involvement, as defined by MSCI. Index returns calculated using quarterly rebalancing of the MSCI World Index over the last 20 years, resulting in slight differences from the true performance of the index.

Source: Datastream and Schroders, as at June 30, 2017.

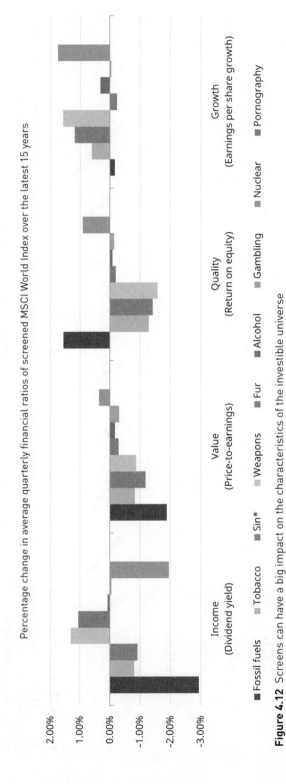

Percentage change in average quarterly financial ratios of screened MSCI World Index over the latest 15 years

Figure 4.12 Screens can have a big impact on the characteristics of the investible universe

*Sin stocks include tobacco, alcohol, gambling, and pornography. Exclusions for fossil fuels and all sin stocks are based on 10% revenue cut off, as defined by MSCI. Exclusions for weapons, fur, and nuclear are based on business involvement, as defined by MSCI.

Source: Datastream and Schroders, as at June 30, 2017.

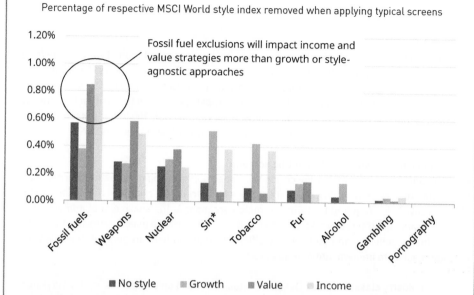

Percentage of respective MSCI World style index removed when applying typical screens

Fossil fuel exclusions will impact income and value strategies more than growth or style-agnostic approaches

■ No style   ■ Growth   ■ Value   ■ Income

Figure 4.13 Different screens can have very different impacts on different investment strategies

Tracking error of screened MSCI World style indices relative to the unconstrained MSCI World style indices over last 20 years

Table 4.1 Growth of investment screens

Strategy	Fossil fuels	Weapons	Nuclear	Sin*	Tobacco	Fur	Alcohol	Gambling	Pornography
No style	8.90%	7.10%	7.60%	3.60%	1.70%	3.00%	1.20%	0.40%	0.00%
Growth	1.70%	3.50%	2.70%	2.50%	0.90%	2.50%	1.00%	0.30%	0.00%
Value	6.30%	3.10%	4.40%	0.90%	0.70%	0.50%	0.10%	0.10%	0.00%
Income	2.40%	0.40%	1.10%	0.70%	0.50%	0.10%	0.10%	0.10%	0.00%

*Sin stocks include tobacco, alcohol, gambling, and pornography.

Exclusions for fossil fuels and all sin stocks are based on 10% revenue cut off, as defined by MSCI. Exclusions for weapons, fur, and nuclear are based on business involvement, as defined by MSCI. Style index based on MSCI-style criteria and constituents. Index returns calculated using quarterly rebalancing of the MSCI World Index over the last 20 years, resulting in slight differences from the true performance of the index. Percentage of index removed based on index as at June 30, 2017.

Source: Datastream and Schroders, as at June 30, 2017.

The analysis highlights the markedly different effects of screens on different investment styles. For example, the tracking error impact of fossil fuel screening is twice as large on value strategies as on growth, reflecting the relatively low multiples on which much of the fossil fuel sector currently trades. Similar variation in tracking error impact – and the associated strategy execution constraints – can be seen across the range of screens examined.

Geographic boundaries also have important implications. The broad MSCI World Index is used in this analysis, reflecting the impact of screens on global markets. Applying exclusions to narrower, local markets can exacerbate the effects. For example, large-cap UK strategies are limited to around 100 stocks. Companies exposed to fossil fuels represent 14% of that market, but 28% of the income stocks in the FTSE 100 Index, presenting sizeable challenges to UK income managers applying fossil fuel restrictions.

Details matter when implementing screens
The analysis in this report describes the impacts of screening in abstract terms using standard criteria. In reality, there are many ways to translate exclusion principles into the objective rules required for rigorous implementation. At the sharp end of implementing and maintaining screens discrepancies in the specific criteria used for apparently similar exclusion policies can result in very different exclusion lists. In general, there are two approaches to implementing exclusions:

1 **Industry classification** – Defining exclusions based on companies' sector classification provides a comprehensive, consistent, and straightforward approach, but lacks flexibility and can miss companies with diverse business portfolios.
2 **Company exposures** – Focusing on companies' actual exposures to specific activities, using share of revenues for instance, provides a more granular view but puts a heavy reliance on third-party organizations. Decisions over how to treat companies with only a marginal exposure to an activity or those that are indirectly exposed through associated industries (such as retailers of harmful products) create a long list of choices and outcomes. For example, pornography screens can reject nearly all telecommunication companies due to their fractional income from streaming. Higher thresholds militate against unintended outcomes, but also dilute the strength of the exclusions. Exposure levels of around 5–10% of sales are typically viewed as being appropriate, although the final level must ultimately reflect investors' own inclinations.

These definitional decisions are not trivial. They can significantly alter the size and nature of any exclusion list. An MSCI tobacco screen that excludes companies with any tie to the sector removes 111 companies from the MSCI World Index, whereas a screen based on a Global Industry Classification Standard (GICS) classification expels just six.

Screen definition decisions can significantly alter exclusion lists and investment results.

Just as different screens affect the ability of mangers to execute strategies in varying ways, so too do different screen definitions. For example, while the average quarterly dividend yield for the MSCI World Index over the last 15 years reduces 3.5% when excluding companies exposed to any revenue from fossil fuels, it reduces just 0.15% when only restricting companies with revenues from coal.

The chart in Figure 4.14 shows the range of tracking error impacts on strategies as a result of different screen definitions. The wider the range of tracking errors, the more sensitive the screen is to definitional choice.

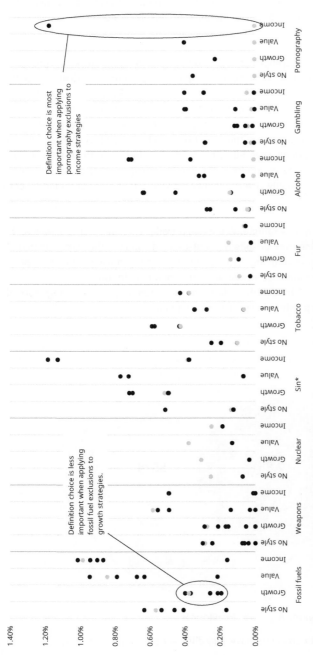

Figure 4.14 The sensitivity of definition choice depends on the screen and strategy adopted

*Sin stocks include tobacco, alcohol, gambling, and pornography.

Typical screens for fossil fuels and all sin stocks are based on 10% revenue cut off, as defined by MSCI. Typical screens for weapons, fur, and nuclear are based on business involvement, as defined by MSCI. The alternative screen definitions used are shown in the appendix. Style indices based on MSCI-style criteria and constituents. Index returns calculated using quarterly rebalancing of the MSCI World Index over the last 20 years, resulting in slight differences from the true performance of the index.

Source: Datastream and Schroders, as at June 30, 2017.

Range of 20-year tracking errors of MSCI World style indices resulting from different screen definitions relative to the unconstrained benchmarks

Different data providers can produce very different exclusion lists

Screening relies heavily on a handful of information sources from independent firms. It is important to recognize differences in the assessments made by these organizations. The charts below show how, for a number of identical or closely related criteria, two widely used ESG data providers offer very different exclusion lists.

A large proportion of this difference can be explained by coverage, with certain providers offering data and analysis on a wider set of companies than others. In Figure 4.15, the universe covered by Provider A is 3,300 companies, whereas Provider B covers 8,425. But even allowing for the fact that much of the variation in exclusion lists is caused by differences in the number of companies covered by each provider, there were often large disparities among the precise companies excluded by each when only considering the 2,851 companies commonly covered by both. This is reflected in the exclusion consistency of the different screens (Figure 4.16). Exclusion consistency reflects the percentage of companies commonly covered by two providers that were excluded by both providers.

Fur exposure provides a good example. While one provider excludes 120 companies, the other excludes just 47. Moreover, despite the well-defined nature of the screen, with both providers aiming to exclude companies involved in the manufacture or sale of fur products, only 28% of all companies screened were common to both. One provider excludes Walmart, the other eBay. Although the criteria for a screen may be concretely worded, the "answers" each firm provides invariably rely on judgment.

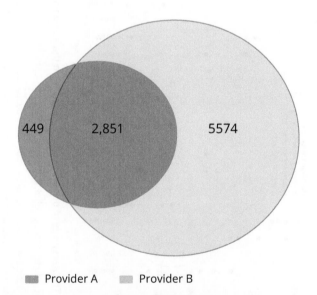

■ Provider A   ■ Provider B

Figure 4.15 Different data providers have very different company coverages...

Total universe of companies covered by two different data providers

Sources: anonymous data providers and Schroders, as at November 17, 2017.

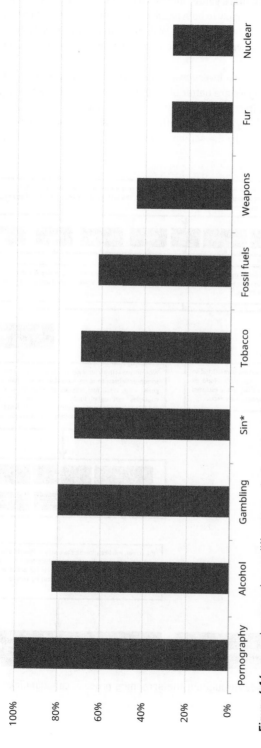

Figure 4.16 . . . and can reach very different conclusions about the companies they commonly cover

Percentage of commonly covered companies excluded by both providers for different screens

*Sin stocks include tobacco, alcohol, gambling, and pornography. Exclusions for fossil fuels and all sin stocks are based on 10% revenue cut off. Exclusions for weapons, fur, and nuclear are based on business involvement.

Sources: anonymous data providers and Schroders, as at November 17, 2017.

Active management can add more value than passive when applying screens

The issues raised in this report apply to both passive index and factor strategies, on the one hand, and actively managed funds, on the other. With the former a screen will alter the index; with the latter, the investible universe from which managers make selections is curtailed.

While passive strategies have no levers available to them to mitigate the impact of a chosen screen, active managers are better able to adapt (Figure 4.17). Passive products cannot offset the negative effects of exclusions on specific portfolio targets. Active managers have more flexibility. They can look for other stocks with similar financial profiles to mitigate the biases introduced by the screen. Active managers are also better placed to

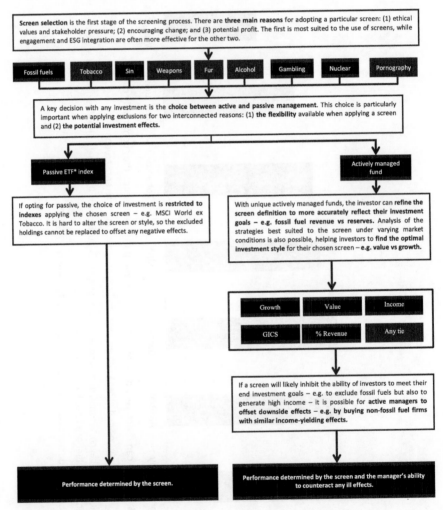

Figure 4.17 Decisions made throughout the screening process can significantly impact investment outcomes

*Exchange-traded fund.

Source: Schroders, 2017.

refine screening criteria to more accurately reflect investors' goals – for example, the choice between fossil fuels and reserves.

Screening is superficially simple, but fraught with practical challenges that can have a significant impact on managers' abilities to execute the specific strategies for which they are selected. Understanding the complexities and biases screens create for wider investment goals before they are implemented and appropriately assessing performance afterwards is critical.

Appendix: a close look at different screening options

Alcohol

Alcohol screens can be defined by sector classification, industry involvement, or revenue exposure. Sector classification typically uses the Brewers and Distillers & Vintners GICS classifications. While these classification screens exclude most companies involved with alcohol, they often fail to exclude more diversified beverage manufacturers. The screen can capture any activity or only those companies involved in production or supply. The "any activity" screen will exclude diversified retailers, but revenue thresholds can be set to avoid this result.

Table 4.2 Selected asset owners adopting screen

Asset owner	AUM (USD billion)*
Kuwait Investment Authority	592
Malaysian Employee Provident Fund	165
Wespath Investment Management	21

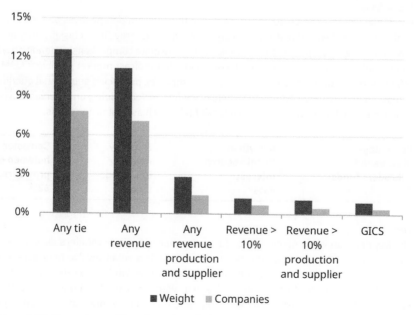

Figure 4.18 Percentage of benchmark excluded by different definitions

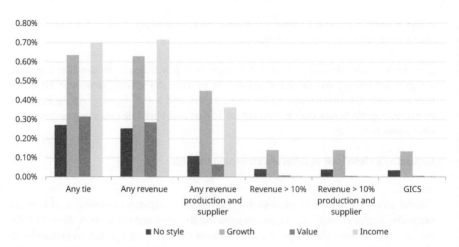

Figure 4.19 Style tracking error

*Assets under management (AUM) shown represent the total AUM of asset owners as at year end 2016. Asset owners may have divested fully or partially, and positions may have subsequently changed. Definitions based on widely applied exclusions and as defined by MSCI.

Source: Datastream and Schroders, as at June 30, 2017.

Percentage of screened Schroders funds: 9%	Growth in Google search interest: 5%	Strategy most impacted: growth	Consistency between data providers: 83%

Fossil fuels

Fossil fuel screens can be quite diverse due to the different perspectives on the industry. At the broadest level, investors can screen using the Energy GICS classification or any involvement by a company in the business. These are quite comprehensive definitions, but will exclude oil and gas service companies and other indirect market participants. More refined screens aiming to capture only those companies producing substantial quantities of fossil fuels can use a revenue threshold of 20–50% or focus solely on reserves. Screens can also be applied to exclude certain fossil fuels, such as coal or tar sands.

Percentage of screened Schroders funds: 3%	Growth in Google search interest: 83%	Strategy most impacted: income	Consistency between data providers: 62%

Fur

The key decision when screening for fur is whether to exclude retailers as well as producers. This is important as the result is not trivial: a retail involvement screen will exclude large retailers such as Amazon.com and eBay, while a screen for producers will not. Company disclosures on involvement with fur are often limited. As a result, providers of screens must often make a judgment as to how much involvement should be critical.

Table 4.3 Selected asset owners adopting screen

Asset owner	AUM (USD billion)*
AXA	1,265
Government Pension Fund Norway	893
Aviva	556
CalPERS	306

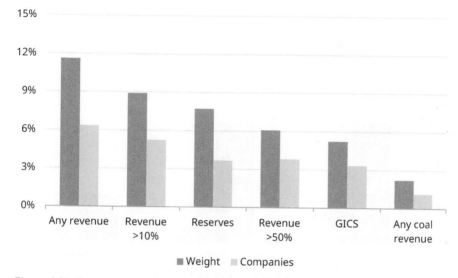

Figure 4.20 Percentage of benchmark excluded by different definitions

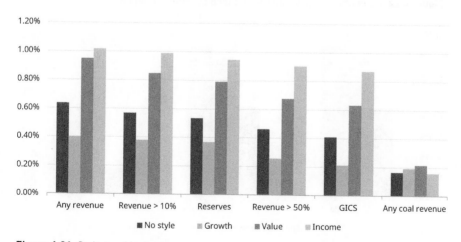

Figure 4.21 Style tracking error

*Assets under management (AUM) shown represent the total AUM of asset owners as at year end 2016. Asset owners may have divested fully or partially, and positions may have subsequently changed. Definitions based on widely applied exclusions and as defined by MSCI.

Source: Datastream and Schroders, as at June 30, 2017.

Percentage of screened Schroders funds: 1%	Growth in Google search interest: 19%	Strategy most impacted: growth	Consistency between data providers: 28%

Table 4.4 Selected asset owners adopting screen

Asset owner	AUM (USD billion)*
ABN AMRO	339
Triodos Bank	3
RSPCA	<1

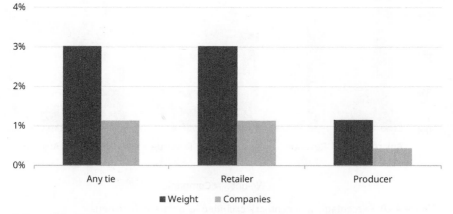

Figure 4.22 Percentage of benchmark excluded by different definitions

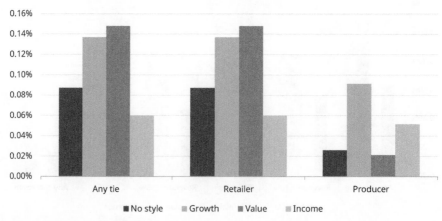

Figure 4.23 Style tracking error

*Assets under management (AUM) shown represent the total AUM of asset owners as at year end 2016. Asset owners may have divested fully or partially, and positions may have subsequently changed. Definitions based on widely applied exclusions and as defined by MSCI.

Source: Datastream and Schroders, as at June 30, 2017.

Gambling

Gambling screens can be defined by sector classification, industry involvement, or revenue exposure. Sector classification typically uses the gaming and casinos GICS classification. While these exclude most companies, it may fail to exclude more diversified entertainment and leisure companies, such as hotels. The screen can capture any activity or only those companies that are involved in operations and licensing to avoid excluding diversified service providers. Revenue thresholds can be set to avoid excluding these diversified providers.

Percentage of screened Schroders funds: 13%	Growth in Google search interest: 11%	Strategy most impacted: impact	Consistency between data providers: 80%

Table 4.5 Selected asset owners adopting screen

Asset owner	AUM (USD billion)*
Kuwait Investment Authority	592
Malaysian Employee Provident Fund	165
TPT Retirement Solutions	11

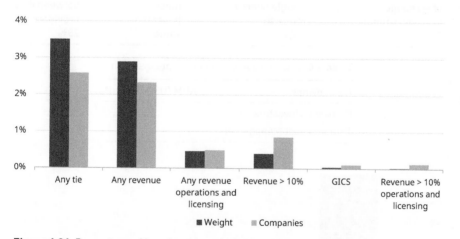

Figure 4.24 Percentage of benchmark excluded by different definitions

Nuclear

Nuclear exclusions are focused on nuclear power as opposed to weapons. The main decision here concerns whether any involvement or a revenue threshold is used. A higher threshold will ensure diversified utilities are still investible. A threshold based on any revenue or a simple involvement tie would exclude a significantly larger number of power companies.

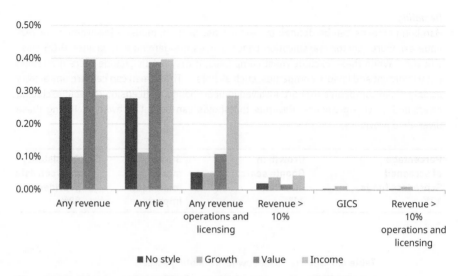

Figure 4.25 Style tracking error

*Assets under management (AUM) shown represent the total AUM of asset owners as at year end 2016. Asset owners may have divested fully or partially, and positions may have subsequently changed. Definitions based on widely applied exclusions and as defined by MSCI.

Source: Datastream and Schroders, as at June 30, 2017.

Percentage of screened Schroders funds: 3%	Growth in Google search interest: –6%	Strategy most impacted: value	Consistency between data providers: 28%

Table 4.6 Selected asset owners adopting screen

Asset owner	AUM (USD billion)*
Parnassus Investments	24
Trillium Asset Management	2

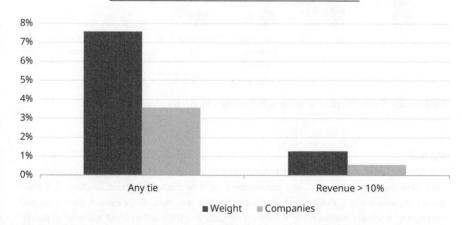

Figure 4.26 Percentage of benchmark excluded by different definitions

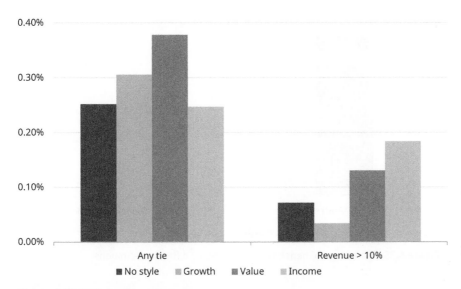

Figure 4.27 Style tracking error

*Assets under management (AUM) shown represent the total AUM of asset owners as at year end 2016. Asset owners may have divested fully or partially, and positions may have subsequently changed. Definitions based on widely applied exclusions and as defined by MSCI.

Source: Datastream and Schroders, as at June 30, 2017.

Pornography

Pornography screens are typically defined by revenue threshold. This threshold is commonly set at between 5% and 10% of turnover. If the definition is set to exclude companies with any revenue exposure, the screen will often catch the telecommunications sector owing to the marginal revenues that it generates from this activity.

Percentage of screened Schroders funds: 12%	Growth in Google search interest: −2%	Strategy most impacted: income	Consistency between data providers: 100%

Sin

Sin screens capture companies exposed to alcohol, gambling, pornography, and tobacco. The encompassing nature of this screen means that various approaches exist, like those for the individual screens. The key challenge arises when screening is based on

Table 4.7 Selected asset owners adopting screen

Asset owner	AUM (USD billion)*
Malaysian Employee Provident Fund	165
Wespath Investment Management	21
Tridios Bank	3

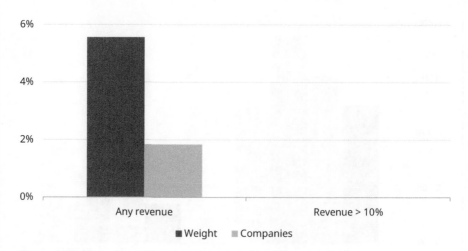

Figure 4.28 Percentage of benchmark excluded by different definitions

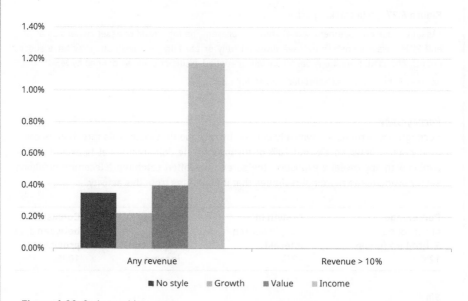

Figure 4.29 Style tracking error

*Assets under management (AUM) shown represent the total AUM of asset owner as at year end 2016. Asset owners may have divested fully or partially, and positions may have subsequently changed. Definitions based on widely applied exclusions and as defined by MSCI.

Source: Datastream and Schroders, as at June 30, 2017.

revenues. Here investors must choose whether to exclude on total exposure – thus where a company generates, say, 2% of revenues from each activity, 8% overall, it is omitted – or based on an individual element – say, where a company generates at least 5% of revenue from any one of the activities screened.

Percentage of screened Schroders funds: 57%	Growth in Google search interest: 25%	Strategy most impacted: growth	Consistency between data providers: 72%

Table 4.8 Selected asset owners adopting screen

Asset owner	AUM (USD billion)*
Malaysian Employee Provident Fund	165
Wespath Investment Management	21
Tridios Bank	3

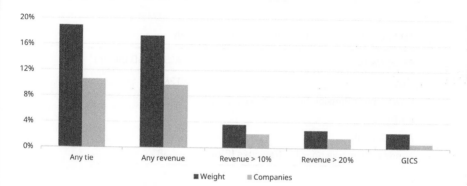

Figure 4.30 Percentage of benchmark excluded by different definitions

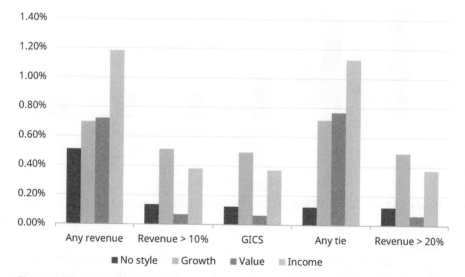

Figure 4.31 Style tracking error

*Assets under management (AUM) shown represent the total AUM of asset owners as at year end 2016. Asset owners may have divested fully or partially, and positions may have subsequently changed. Definitions based on widely applied exclusions and as defined by MSCI.

Source: Datastream and Schroders, as at June 30, 2017.

Tobacco

Tobacco screens can be defined by sector classification, industry involvement, or revenue exposure. Exclusion by GICS sector is the most common, with most tobacco companies focused on tobacco production alone. Industry involvement can be defined as any company with tobacco-related activity or only those companies involved in production or supply. The latter screen will avoid excluding retailers. Revenue thresholds can also be set at appropriate levels to avoid excluding retailers.

Percentage of screened Schroders funds: 35%	Growth in Google search interest: 84%	Strategy most impacted: growth	Consistency between data providers: 70%

Table 4.9 Selected asset owners adopting screen

Asset owner	AUM (USD billion)*
AXA	1265
Government Pension Fund Norway	893
CalPERS	306
AMP Capital	168
Fonds de Reserve pour les Retraités (FRR)	38

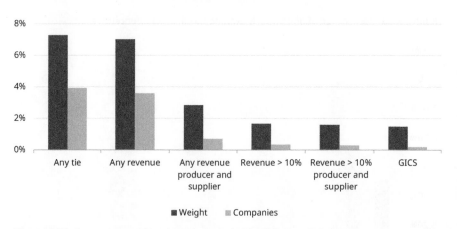

Figure 4.32 Percentage of benchmark excluded by different definitions

Weapons

Weapons screens can vary substantially according to different views of the industry. Controversial weapons (such as cluster munitions and biological and chemical weapons) and nuclear weapons are the most commonly screened. Broader weapons screens are also applied, but these can exclude companies like auto manufacturers due to their role in providing military engines. Screens can also distinguish between companies that manufacture weapons and those that sell them.

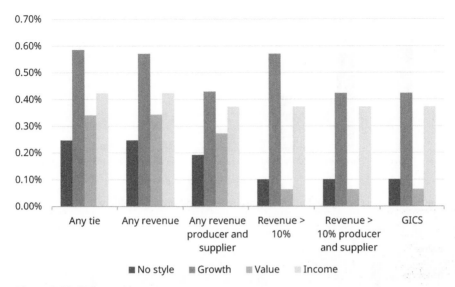

Figure 4.33 Style tracking error

*Assets under management (AUM) shown represent the total AUM of asset owners as at year end 2016. Asset owners may have divested fully or partially, and positions may have subsequently changed. Definitions based on widely applied exclusions and as defined by MSCI.

Source: Datastream and Schroders, as at June 30, 2017.

Percentage of screened Schroders funds: 40%	Growth in Google search interest: –15%	Strategy most impacted: income	Consistency between data providers: 44%

Table 4.10 Selected asset owners adopting screen

Asset owner	AUM (USD billion)*
Allianz	1968
Nordea	340
Wespath Investment Management	21
Spoorwegpensioenfonds	16

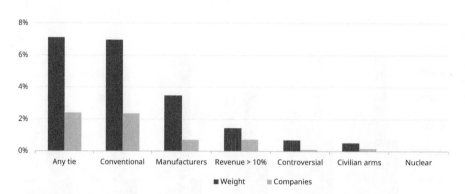

Figure 4.34 Percentage of benchmark excluded by different definitions

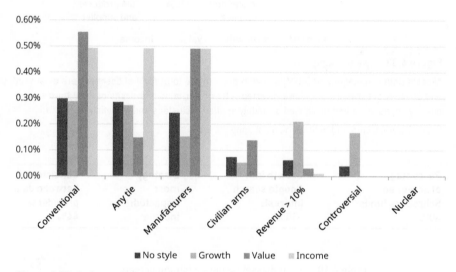

Figure 4.35 Style tracking error

*Assets under management (AUM) shown represent the total AUM of asset owners as at year end 2016. Asset owners may have divested fully or partially, and positions may have subsequently changed. Definitions based on widely applied exclusions and as defined by MSCI.

Source: Datastream and Schroders, as at June 30, 2017.

Information herein is believed to be reliable but Schroders does not warrant its completeness or accuracy. Reliance should not be placed on the views and information in this document when taking individual investment and/or strategic decisions. Past performance is not a reliable indicator of future results, prices of shares, and the income from them may fall as well as rise and investors may not get back the amount originally invested. The opinions included in this document include some forecasted views. We believe that we are basing our expectations and believes on reasonable assumptions within the bounds of what we currently know. However, there is no guarantee that any forecasts or opinions will be realized. The stocks and sectors mentioned above are for illustrative purposes only and are not a recommendation to buy

4.2 Integration-based ESG investing

Integration-based ESG investing, also known as ESG integration, is more complex in nature than exclusion-based ESG investing. While exclusion-based ESG investing explicitly identifies and screens out securities conflicting with policy mandates, ESG integration is the explicit inclusion of securities based on factors of ESG risks and opportunities (Eurosif, 2014). ESG integration is the practice of integrating ESG factors, research, or data within an investment portfolio. Investors often implement ESG integration strategies or policies to mitigate risk and/or to help generate alpha. Whereas exclusion-based ESG investing has a primary objective of adhering to a specific policy mandate or guidelines, ESG integration is a method of ESG investing that is used with the intention to add quantifiable value to the investment process. The added value that ESG integration targets is aimed at either reducing portfolio risks or volatility, increasing returns, or adding value to the portfolio's effect on society or the environment.

Excluding certain securities or assets may be a practical component of ESG integration. This is common when the integration of certain ESG factors calls for the exclusion of securities or segments of the capital markets in conjunction with the integration of other factors. For example, an ESG integration strategy that seeks to maximize the long-term sustainability of energy equities might consider excluding coal mining and oil exploration equities and, instead, allocate to natural gas exploration equities.

Although exclusionary elements can be incorporated within integration-based ESG investing, investors generally choose ESG integration for its flexibility in implementation. Whereas exclusionary investing is fundamentally grounded on prohibiting securities, ESG integration does not restrain an investor, whether an investment manager or asset manager, in such a "black and white" fashion. ESG integration is a methodology that focuses on incorporating insights on environmental, social, governance, and other related non-financial performance factors in order to optimize an investor's risk-and-return profile without restraining an investor by policy or investment guidelines.

Investors practice integration-based ESG investing by analyzing ESG factors that may affect the securities of a company that they are considering investing in, or already own. ESG factors cover a vast range of topics and issues such as (but not limited to) board or management diversity, cyber security, accounting standards, financial reporting, waste management, carbon emissions management, energy efficiency, carbon footprint management, raw materials use, water use, water pollution, climate change risk management, labor management, workplace safety, human capital development, supply chain labor management, chemical safety, privacy and financial product security, and corporate governance. Researching and analyzing these ESG factors allow investors to measure a company's securities based on key metrics not found within a company's financials or traditional valuation metrics. Further, assessing companies through ESG factors allows an investor to discover any risks to the company and provides a pathway for companies to be measured against their peer group, sector, industry, and broader market.

There are several ways in which investors practice ESG integration. Practitioners often debate the optimal implementation of ESG integration. To better understand the practical implementations of ESG investing, it is helpful to examine some of the mainstream approaches for ESG integration. Fundamental research-based ESG integration and systematically implemented ESG integration are two mainstream approaches for implementing integration-based ESG investing.

Fundamental ESG integration can be implemented through fundamental research methodologies. Fundamental ESG integration is like traditional fundamental investment strategy. In fact, asset managers often integrate ESG factors holistically within their fundamental analysis process (van Duuren, Plantinga, and Scholtens, 2016). In this methodology, an investor will analyze specific ESG factors as criteria for their ESG integration. ESG factors may be analyzed in collective groupings through general qualitative research or are analyzed at the specific ESG factor level. Investors may use research reports on ESG factors produced by ESG research firms, financial institutions, or academics, or they may conduct their own proprietary research based on their own standards and processes. Generally, this approach to analyzing ESG factors is more qualitative in nature and requires careful examination of both direct and indirect data. ESG integration through fundamental ESG integration may also incorporate the analysis of macro-thematic ESG factors that may affect the industry a company operates within or that affect the company specifically. Fundamental ESG integration allows investors to draw insight from research reports, news, and information discovery.

Investors may incorporate their own system for weighting and evaluating the insight gained through fundamental ESG integration. As investors value ESG factors differently, they also measure the insight gained from ESG research differently in the way they practice fundamental ESG integration. For example, one investor may value, and prioritize, the issue of gender diversity of a company's management team much higher than other ESG factors, whereas a different investor may weigh the ESG factors of pollution much more than gender diversity for the same company. The differences between an investor's prioritization of ESG factors are not only driven by the investor's personal belief or policy, but also by a determination of what factors the investor considers risky or valuable. Fundamental ESG integration may be focused on mitigating risk or focused on increasing returns, or both. It is a continual process of evaluating ESG factors and their effect on risk and return projections.

Systematic ESG integration is the quantitative application of integrating ESG factor analysis in an investor's decision-making process. ESG factors can be measured quantitatively, and thus assigned set values for monetarization and systematic analysis. Systematic ESG integration incorporates assigned ESG-classification, ESG factor ratings, or security-level ESG quantification within an investor's investment process in a formulaic process. These preset quantitative criteria are integrated into the investment portfolio rather than qualitatively deriving ESG insight for integration.

Positive screening is one method for systematic ESG integration. Negative screening was discussed in the above exclusion-based ESG investing section. Investors may also choose to systematically integrate ESG factors through positive screening: a method for filtering a universe of securities in order to integrate securities with favorable ratings on ESG factors into a portfolio. This is often implemented using ESG ratings produced by a research firm or ESG ratings agency. An investor may screen the universe to only include securities of a certain rating hurdle (e.g. securities rated A or higher) as part of the investment process (MSCI, Inc. 2014). For example, an investor might conduct positive screening to integrate only securities rated AA or AAA into an investment portfolio as part of their systematic ESG integration process. Further, an investor may use the positive screening to narrow their investable universe. The positive screening ESG integration approach is also referred to as **tilting** as an investor is essentially tilting their portfolio towards a criterion of ESG ratings quality.

An investor might also systematically use ESG ratings as a component of other factors, such as integrating the ESG ratings scores as a principal component of other factor analysis metrics in a multi-factor analysis strategy. For example, ESG may be utilized as a factor in conjunction with factors such as quality, value, and profitability in a systematic portfolio construction approach.

Another systematic ESG integration implementation strategy that uses ESG ratings is ESG rating momentum. Relative to a long-only portfolio of securities, an investor might integrate securities that display momentum in the rating, or scoring, of the security's ESG factors. For example, an equity investor may use quantitative measurements over a time series of ESG ratings to systematically integrate equities of companies that have ratings improvement momentum during a set time period (MSCI, Inc. 2014).

Integration-based ESG investing can be conducted in a variety of approaches. The choice of fundamental, systematic, or hybrid ESG integration is largely driven by investor preference. Investors will naturally use the integration-based ESG investing approach that they believe adds the most value to their investment process and investment objectives. Investors might also consider using an ESG integration approach that is beneficial to their results measurement and ESG investment reporting requirements.

Investors often choose to utilize integration-based ESG investing approaches for the less restrictive nature. Investors may come to use ESG integration for various reasons, such as risk aversion and mitigation or for alpha generation. Further, although integration-based ESG investors may hold different perspectives on the use of ESG, ESG factor analysis, and the practical implications of ESG integration strategies, common ground exists in the belief that ESG integration adds value to the investment process.

CASE STUDY 4B: ESG integration at J.P. Morgan Asset Management

J.P. Morgan Asset Management (JPMAM) is a global asset management firm with over 1,200 investment professionals providing clients with strategies that span the asset classes, including equity, fixed income, cash liquidity, currency, real estate, hedge funds, and private equity.

The firm has been a signatory to the United Nations-supported Principles for Responsible Investment (PRI) since 2007, a year after the initiative was formed, and as such, is committed to the six PRI principles:

1   Incorporate ESG issues into investment analysis and decision-making processes
2   Be active owners and incorporate ESG issues into our ownership policies and practices
3   Seek appropriate disclosure on ESG issues from the entities in which we invest
4   Promote acceptance and implementation of the Principles within the investment industry
5   Work together to enhance our effectiveness in implementing the Principles
6   Report on our activities and progress towards implementing the Principles

As one of the firm's senior portfolio managers put it, there are three simple reasons that his team needs to think about ESG: "It is our responsibility to consider the broader consequences of our investment choices; incorporating ESG is important to many of our clients; and it is entirely consistent with our long-term approach to investing."

In line with this commitment, the firm stepped up its efforts in 2016 and embarked on a journey to integrate ESG into the investing process. While many investment teams already had a long-standing commitment to incorporating ESG factors into their investment practices where it is material and relevant, the firm lacked a common definition and an internal minimum standard. The Sustainable Investment Leadership Team (SILT) was formed to fill that gap by developing and implementing a coordinated strategy for sustainable investing across asset classes and investment offerings.

SILT defined ESG integration as "a systematic and explicit consideration of ESG factors in the investment decision-making process." SILT also established an internal minimum standard that would be required for an investment strategy to be considered "ESG integrated." The standard is meant to ensure that investing teams capture both the risks and the opportunities associated with ESG factors, without limiting their respective investment universe or targeting specific ESG tilts.

To uphold the integrity of the new definition of ESG integration, SILT developed a three-step framework called "Commit/Implement/Demonstrate" to keep the investment teams systematic and explicit in their ESG assessment of companies, from research to portfolio construction.

J.P. Morgan Asset Management's Sustainable Investment Leadership Team "commit/ implement/demonstrate" framework

- **Commit**: An investment head or chief investment officer commits to dedicating resources to ESG integration by nominating an ESG champion.
- **Implement**: ESG champions engage with SILT to learn best practices and leverage them with stakeholders on their investment teams, to help them develop a project plan for ESG integration. The ESG champions are encouraged to think about embedding ESG considerations throughout the investment process. This includes identifying appropriate sources for ESG data and research, elevating ESG expertise among the firm's analysts and portfolio managers, determining the materiality of ESG factors and embedding ESG analysis into research and risk systems.
- **Demonstrate:** The investment team must present to SILT how it is considering ESG factors at various stages of the investment process. They are asked to note the metrics in use, and to include specific examples to validate that ESG factors are being integrated into investment decisions – quantifying their impact, where possible. These presentations give SILT members an opportunity to ask questions, raise concerns, and ultimately validate whether the team has integrated ESG considerations according to SILT's established definition. Those that receive SILT's approval are considered ESG-integrated.

Investment teams follow a structured, three-step process to gain ESG-integrated status:

1 **Commit:** Dedicate resources and set goals
2 **Implement:** Develop and execute at each step of the investment process
3 **Demonstrate:** Articulate process to SILT for formal sign-off to qualify for ESG integration

Since J.P. Morgan investment teams each have their own well-established philosophies and methods, they have the discretion to choose the most appropriate ways to integrate

ESG so it will be authentic and meaningful within their existing investment process (examples are outlined below.)

To measure progress and success, J.P. Morgan Asset Management documents and tracks investment teams and strategies across the various stages of their journey to ESG integration. The effort is voluntary and aspirational. Teams have an opportunity to share best practices and help each other reach the end goal, although they don't all do it at the same time. There is a shared understanding that this effort is an ongoing process and every team can incorporate ESG to some extent, but the SILT framework ensures that becoming approved as "ESG integrated" is a high bar and a clearly defined standard.

Examples of ESG integration in various asset classes
Developed market fundamental equities

J.P. Morgan Asset Management's research-driven equity strategies, which follow a common investment philosophy focused on long-term fundamental company research, are all ESG-integrated. These strategies draw on research analyst, directors of research and governance specialists in the US, Europe, and Asia. These teams collaborate globally to identify negative ESG outliers, focusing on the potential impact on the sustainability and redeployment of cash flows. Specifically, the teams consistently consider six areas to help identify negative outliers (Figure 4.36).

Research analysts or directors of research identify companies as ESG outliers in a proprietary ESG outlier research database, the same location where analysts record their earnings estimates. At least quarterly, ESG outliers are discussed among the analysts, portfolio managers, and regional and global directors of research at sector reviews. Portfolio managers review companies flagged as negative outliers when they consider the position sizes they hold, or might hold, in that company.

Equity governance specialists work closely with portfolio managers and research analysts as they engage with portfolio companies on substantial ESG issues. When the company has been identified as an ESG outlier in the proprietary database, the engagement focuses on the issues specified there. These engagements are an ongoing effort. J.P. Morgan Asset Management may seek more public disclosure from the issuer, urge management to adopt best industry practices and will monitor the company's progress. The governance teams' engagement efforts are shared with portfolio managers, who may also participate in these meetings. Periodically, the governance specialists will also identify thematic ESG issues that are likely to become more significant in the future, and where the firm needs to develop internal understanding by engaging with multiple companies on that issue.

Proprietary research and risk management tools are supplemented by third-party ESG data to further inform the teams' insight. The list of ESG outliers is fluid and updated in real time when an event or newly emerging issue causes additional companies to be flagged.

Emerging market fundamental equities

The Global Emerging Market (EM) Fundamental Equity team strongly believes that ESG considerations, particularly governance, need to be a foundation of any investment process supporting long-term investing, and that corporate policies at odds with

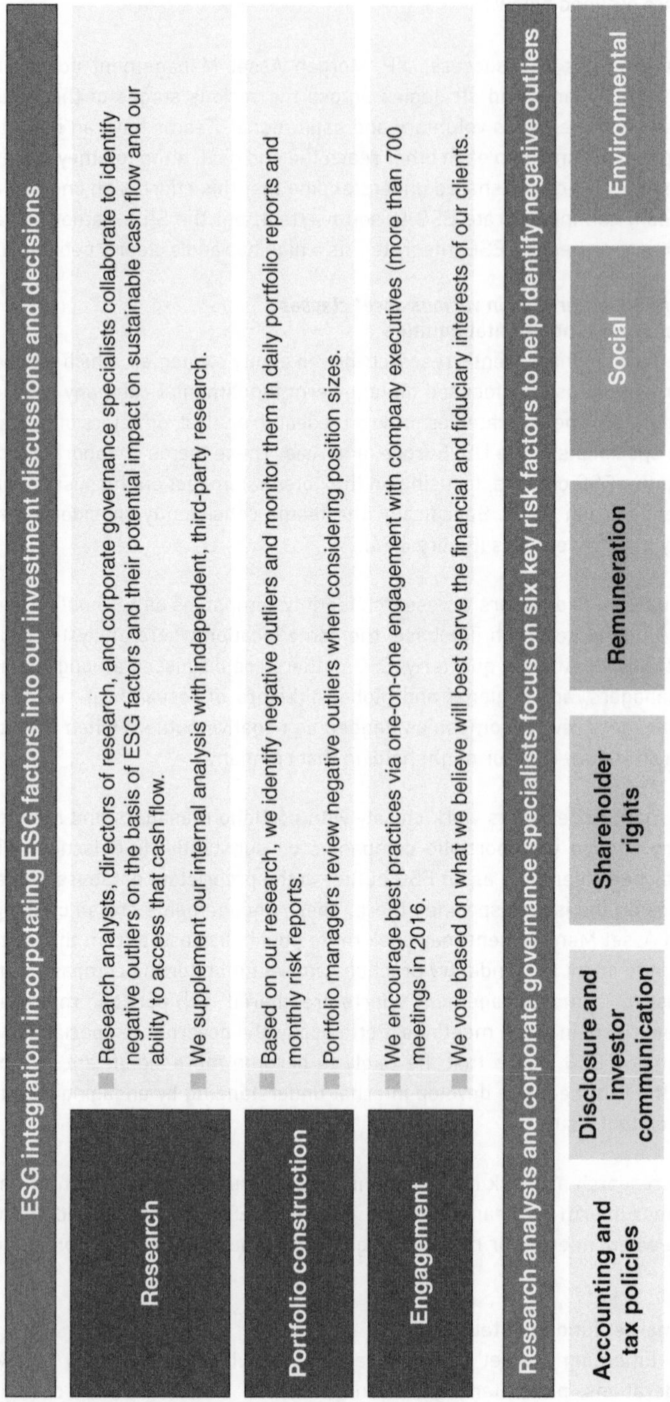

ESG integration: incorpotating ESG factors into our investment discussions and decisions

Research

- Research analysts, directors of research, and corporate governance specialists collaborate to identify negative outliers on the basis of ESG factors and their potential impact on sustainable cash flow and our ability to access that cash flow.
- We supplement our internal analysis with independent, third-party research.

Portfolio construction

- Based on our research, we identify negative outliers and monitor them in daily portfolio reports and monthly risk reports.
- Portfolio managers review negative outliers when considering position sizes.

Engagement

- We encourage best practices via one-on-one engagement with company executives (more than 700 meetings in 2016.
- We vote based on what we believe will best serve the financial and fiduciary interests of our clients.

Research analysts and corporate governance specialists focus on six key risk factors to help identify negative outliers

| Accounting and tax policies | Disclosure and investor communication | Shareholder rights | Remuneration | Social | Environmental |

Figure 4.36 Developed market fundamental equities areas of ESG consideration

environmental and social issues are not sustainable. Integration of ESG factors is critical to successful investing across emerging markets. While the J.P. Morgan Global EM Fundamental Equity Team does not explicitly exclude individual stocks based on social, environmental, or ethical criteria, ESG factors could affect the degree of conviction the team has, and impact a stock's position sizing during portfolio construction.

The team's fundamental analysis of any company examines its economics, sustainability, and governance, resulting in what the team calls a "Strategic Classification." Environmental and social issues are important considerations within this analysis; a business isn't thinking about its long-term future if it's destroying the environment or abusing the community in which it operates, and it will eventually pay a price for this. So, the team needs to consider these areas when thinking about future cash flows. In this respect, an ESG concern is no different from any other factor that could have the same effect, whether competition, innovation, or regulation. They are all part of a broad consideration of the sustainability of corporate value.

All analysts are tasked with completing and maintaining a proprietary "Risk Profile questionnaire" for companies they cover. The majority of the questionnaire focuses on governance and specific ESG issues. These risk assessments inform our Strategic Classification of companies, which helps us gauge a business's potential for long-term value creation. The team categorizes companies as Premium, Quality, or Trading.

Portfolio position sizing, and whether the team takes an ownership stake, is informed by our Strategic Classification framework and Risk Profile. The team targets companies rated Premium or Quality. Businesses classified as Premium and Quality tend to have strong governance and few red flags and outperform over time, while businesses classified as Trading tend to have numerous red flags and underperform over time.

Investment grade corporate debt

The Global Investment Grade Corporate Debt team systematically considers ESG risks as part of the bottom-up, fundamental analysis of corporate bond issuers. Credit analysts examine all aspects of a company, including how ESG risks and opportunities are currently affecting cash flows, and how these ESG risks may affect cash flows in the future. If the team's analysts believe that the ESG factors are material and could impact the company's cash flow profile in the future, they will reflect that in their credit opinions and proprietary issuer rankings. Credit analysts' proprietary fundamental research is supplemented with third-party ESG data and research reports. Analysts' research communication has an "ESG Comments" section where they explain the role, if any, that ESG risks play in a particular issuer view.

Portfolio managers have access to the proprietary analyst issuer rankings, third-party ESG rankings and inputs from the firm's fixed income quantitative research group. Portfolio managers identify both negative and positive ESG outliers in their portfolios through monthly ESG risk reporting, on an industry-adjusted basis. Portfolio managers take this information into account when they assess the fundamental, quantitative, and technical factors in the marketplace to arrive at an investment decision. In addition, at quarterly meetings, portfolio managers review and discuss their holdings with low and high ESG scores, to identify risks and opportunities associated with these ESG factors.

Fixed income analysts have access to equity research and may attend management meetings with their equity counterparts, and highlight in discussions with management any ESG factors that could represent a significant credit consideration to an issuer and/ or a sector.

Private equity group (PEG)

The objective of the J.P. Morgan Asset Management Private Equity Group is to identify and select attractive investments for its clients from across a broad spectrum of private equity investment opportunities. Sustainable investing is an important component of PEG's investment diligence process. Prior to making an investment, PEG assesses the ESG behaviors and practices of the companies, and of the underlying third-party private equity managers with which we invest.

PEG's standard investment process includes due diligence on sustainability, a written investment memorandum, and ongoing discussion with the portfolio managers of PEG about sustainability issues. This process includes clarification and assessment of material risk factors of sustainability, including ESG factors. When investing in a third-party manager, PEG encourages it to carefully consider these factors in their own investment due diligence, as well. Sustainability considerations are an important component of both PEG's initial due diligence and screening process and its ongoing investment monitoring.

Consistent with PEG's ultimate objective of providing attractive risk-adjusted returns, it does not exclude specific companies and investment managers, or types of companies or managers, from client portfolios solely based on ESG criteria. However, PEG views sustainability issues, based on over 35 years of investing, as important factors likely to impact performance. PEG believes that sustainability considerations should be reviewed holistically, to account both for material risks and potential opportunities that may make companies, or funds, more or less attractive for investment.

PEG encourages the portfolio companies, and the fund managers with which it invests, to advance the principles of sustainable investing in a practical manner, consistent with return objectives and fiduciary duties.

PEG itself seeks to integrate ESG considerations into the investment process in a practical manner, to ensure that the investment process is clear and consistent with the portfolio's investment objectives. This includes developing guidelines and an approach adaptable to market conditions, portfolio construction, and investment opportunities.

Infrastructure investing

The J.P. Morgan Asset Management infrastructure group integrates ESG factors through the investment and asset management life cycles. As an asset class, infrastructure is intrinsically aligned with ESG priorities because its investments are long-lived assets integral to the communities they serve. Accordingly, the infrastructure group believes a formalized, systematic focus on material ESG matters both identifies opportunities and results in effective risk management. Well-managed companies operating in an environmentally sustainable and socially responsible way significantly de-risk their business model, and therefore deliver better performance and achieve greater cost efficiencies and profitability. As such, ESG assessment and integration is important to the design of, and ongoing decision-making process for, infrastructure investments. It is part of due diligence procedures, investment decision-making, and ongoing asset management.

ESG factors are integrated into the investment decision-making process at several stages: during due diligence, underwriting, and transition plans. Areas of focus include (to the extent they are material) governance framework, environmental impacts of and on the company, cyber security and data protection, health and safety, corruption, catastrophe resilience, stakeholder engagement, and community impact reviews. ESG matters are a distinct topic within investment committee memoranda, to ensure that committee members are informed of these considerations prior to voting on any proposed investments.

Once a company is acquired, the group uses its active asset management practices, working with portfolio company boards and executive management teams to engage with the companies around their approach to ESG issues in a number of ways:

- Requiring transparent reporting by our portfolio companies on ESG initiatives on an ad hoc, quarterly, and annual basis
- Working with our portfolio companies to address emerging ESG issues
- Striving to share and adopt a best-practice approach in the practical implementation of decision-making across our portfolio companies
- Onboarding new portfolio companies and boards with ESG trainings and encouraging continual improvement in ESG performance
- Aligning executive team compensation to include consideration of ESG matters

J.P. Morgan Asset Management has embarked on a continuously evolving journey to ESG integration. What the firm has learned so far is that ESG factors contain relevant, material information that can be used to better manage risks and opportunities in clients' portfolios, and which may potentially add value to performance. It has also learned that to truly embrace ESG integration, it must be made authentic to the organization and its investment teams – not be a forced or box-ticking exercise. A bottom-up ESG-integration movement can begin with finding believers who are well-respected within the organization and who are willing and ready to lead by sharing best ideas and supporting their colleagues.

4.3 Impact-based ESG investing

ESG investing that is designed to produce a positive impact on a specific issue as part of the investment process is referred to as **impact investing**. Impact investing is generally cause-based and mission-oriented. In impact investing, investors will invest in companies, or practice specific investment strategies, that combine both social and financial returns (Mahn, 2016). An investor might prefer impact-based ESG investing methodology for a variety of reasons, but the two most significant reasons are 1) to meet the social or environmental objective of the asset owner(s), or the investor's belief system, or 2) to yield the best risk-adjusted return compared to other investment choices.

Impact-based ESG investing examines business processes and activities of companies in order to measure the impact that investing in, or owning, those companies would have on certain issues.

Impact-based ESG investors might consider how investing in companies with sustainable business policies can benefit the environment, while providing a long-term advantage to return potential. Impact investing often focuses on the cause and effect relationship of investing in order to measure the true impact (i.e. financial and non-financial) of the investment.

Impact investing can be thematic in nature. Themes may be aligned to general impacts or can be isolated to a specific cause or issue. Themes may be global, regional, country-specific, or targeted to specific local population. Themes can also be targeted to impact a certain culture, socioeconomic status, or population group. Impact investing can differ in investment liquidity, geography, asset class, and the type of environmental or social theme that the impact is directed towards, but impact-based ESG investing is consistent in the cause-effect embodiment. An example of an impact-based ESG investing theme can be observed through the lens of an investor who desires to reduce carbon emissions as part of their investment process may implement an investment strategy that is designed to proactively impact carbon emissions. This investor may dually invest in companies that have business models that feature technologies that are carbon-reduction technologies, as well as construct portfolios that are more aware of their carbon footprint within their equities. This investor might strive to develop a portfolio of companies that have management teams and boards that are active in carbon emissions reduction. In this example, the investor might utilize elements of exclusion and integration, but have a core focus on the impact of carbon footprint reduction.

Historically impact investing has been associated with sustainability practices. Today, sustainability practices are incorporated across the spectrum of ESG investing methodologies. The association of impact-based ESG investing with sustainability practices may be because impact investing is often associated with environmental impact topics and issues. Impact-based ESG investors have long questioned how an investment influences the practices of corporate management teams and company policies on issues such as stranded fossil fuel assets and carbon emissions, water usage, and food waste.

Asset managers may have product offerings centered around impact investing or produce strategies that are designed to demonstrate an impact through their investment strategy and process. Asset managers, although having a mission centering around a positive impact within a specific realm, such as an environmental or social cause, use impact investing as a manner that can produce attractive returns, in order to obtain capital investment from institutional or retail investors. Asset managers who are practicing impact investing will often structure investments and take risk in opportunity sets that align their impact goals with the ability to generate desired objective returns. For example, a private credit firm that aims to develop a clean water drinking system in a third-world country where credit yields are high (e.g. 17% per annum), may be able to both deliver an attractive double-digit net-of-fees return to their investors and make a positive impact on the region's environment and society, while doing so at a lower cost than would be possible for a local group or organization. Asset managers also, as their businesses depend on investors' capital in order to collect fees from the assets under management, may use the impact they are trying to make as a marketing construct to gain business from institutional investors who practice impact-based ESG investing.

Institutional investors approach impact-based ESG investing in various ways. Investment managers may access impact investing as a source of alpha if they hold the view that the investment offers higher returns when also associated with making impacts outside of pure financial return incentive. Investment managers may practice impact-based ESG investing if they feel the risk profile is more attractive than a non-impact-based investment given the sustainable nature of an impact-based investment. Investment managers may approach an impact-based ESG investment as a source of diversification to their existing portfolio as impact-based investments, often by design, naturally have a unique return distribution or revenue stream source, which generally differs from traditional investment strategies.

Investment managers might also access impact-based ESG investing as a means to align their institutional mission with their investment decision-making process. Institutional investors might practice impact-based ESG investing because of the same policy risks identified in Chapter 3. These managers may also implement impact-based ESG investing to prevent headline risk, and access positive headline visibility for their contribution to making an impact through their investing.

It is important to understand the necessity of measuring the impact of one's investment process as part of their impact-based ESG investing approach. Using the previous example of carbon emission reduction, it is important to quantitatively understand the degree of the impact, which requires proper analytical measurement. Investors may utilize a proprietary internal model for calculating such measurement, or use an independent resource for providing the analysis, such as Sustainalytics, MSCI, or Trucost. Such analytic service providers offer analytics that gauge the impact of a specific, or general, theme(s) within a portfolio. For the investor seeking an impact on carbon pollution, independent analytics-based service providers quantify the measurement of the investor's carbon footprint through carbon-metrics measurement. Reporting is important for asset managers to validate their efforts to their investors and for investment managers to illustrate the impact-based investment measurement to their clients or membership population. Reporting is also a key element of justification of an impact investment, as well as the addressing of the "effect" component of the cause for implementing the cause-driven impact objective.

CASE STUDY 4C: impact investing at JANA Partners

Dan Hanson, CFA – Head of Impact Investing at JANA Partners

Dan Hanson, CFA, *is Head of Impact Investing at JANA Partners. Mr. Hanson is on the faculty at UC Berkeley Haas and serves as a judge for the Moskowitz Prize. He was a founding member of the board of directors of the Sustainable Accounting Standards Board (SASB) and serves as Vice-Chair of the Canadian Coalition for Good Governance (CCGG) E&S committee. Prior to joining JANA, Dan was Partner with Jarislowsky Fraser Global Investment Management, where he served in roles including Head of US Equities, Co-Manager of Global Equities, and Co-Chair of the Investment Strategy Committee. Previously, Dan spent ten years at Black-Rock as Managing Director, Portfolio Manager, and Head of Fundamental Research for $30B AUM. As manager of the BlackRock Socially Responsible Equity portfolio, Dan delivered top-decile performance for more than five years. He earned a BA from Middlebury College, and an MBA degree in analytical finance and accounting from the University of Chicago.*

Impact investing[1]

"All investing is impact investing."
– Clara Miller, President *Emerita* of the Heron Foundation

Impact investing has captured the spirit of the times. In the following pages I will explore: 1) definitions of impact investing, 2) a brief history of impact investing, and 3) impact measurement. From there, I will explore the broader issues of 4) why now?, and 5) all investing is impact investing. I offer perspectives and frameworks on impact investing from the vantage point of a public markets investor who has been investing in businesses with positive impact while seeking above market returns since before the term "impact investing" was coined in 2007.[2]

1. Impact investing defined: fundamental active investing for deliberate impact

At its core, impact investing is an engaged ownership approach to fundamental active investing which acknowledges the impact and linkages that capital allocation actions have to the real economy, including what classic economics labels "externalities" – such as society and the environment. Those externalities can range from very company-specific and geographically localized, to systematic.[3]

Business practices undeniably have an impact on society and the real economy – both positive and negative, direct and residual, intentional and unintentional, and impacts which are measured and unmeasured. Impact investors seek to specifically identify and measure positive and negative impacts, and further, to drive specific and deliberate incremental positive impact through engagement and capital flows. Concessionary impact investors are willing to sacrifice returns for positive societal impact, whereas non-concessionary (market) impact investors identify opportunity to drive positive impact while achieving market and better-than-market returns. The proverbial "have your cake and eat it too" – which is eminently achievable as demonstrated by practitioners and theoretical study alike.[4]

Impact is a natural complement to ESG, where the impact objective is made explicit, additional, intentional, and measured.[5] There are a range of approaches to impact investing, across full range of the capital structure (debt, preferred, and equity), and ranging from highly concessionary to pure market return and alpha seeking. As for any investment discipline, specific philosophies, processes, and records matter. Practitioner implementation is key.

The Global Impact Investing Network (GIIN) has stated the following definition: impact investments are investments made in companies, organizations, and funds with the intention to generate measurable social and environmental impact alongside a financial return.

The financial return may range from concessionary, for philanthropic initiatives (including traditional nonprofits and social entrepreneurs), to market rate (which include double and triple bottom line), and above market in cases where an incremental positive impact is also contributing to underlying business value. As with any form of active investing, in impact investing there are many different philosophies and processes. Disciplined underwriting and implementation are key to delivering alpha.

2. A brief history of impact investing
The origins of modern impact investing lie in the communities of philanthropic foundations and social entrepreneurs, who were inspired to unleash entrepreneurial market-driven energies to solve for market failures. Many of the frameworks of impact investing have been fostered and developed by nonprofits and non-governmental organizations (NGOs). It is noteworthy that, in contrast to nonprofits and NGOs which are labeled by what they are "not," impact investing is an affirmation of positive intention and action.

In the context of philanthropy, non-concessionary socially motivated investments are often called mission-related investments (MRIs), and are distinguished from program-related investments (PRIs), which are concessionary (and specifically defined as such a matter of US tax code). Under US tax law foundations are required to spend 5% of their assets per year, leaving 95% to be invested in market return vehicles, typically managed for long-term total return and appreciation of capital in perpetuity.

The modern model of concessionary impact investing in the United States can be traced back to 1968, when the Ford Foundation began making below market rate (i.e. concessionary) charitable loans to its grantees. The Tax Reform Act of 1969 subsequently codified PRIs, and PRIs became broadly used by major foundations as means to fulfill their charitable program objectives (5% spending).

Just as the practice of "ESG" analysis of investment risks and opportunities predates the acronym (by many decades),[6] the practice of impact investing predates the label by a number of years. The term "impact investing" was coined at a Rockefeller Foundation convening in 2007. While the term was coined then, impact investing had already been in practice around the world for a number of years in a number of frameworks, so what was already happening finally got a name that "stuck."

By identifying and measuring impact, capitalism has the potential to drive much more meaningful impact than charitable and government funded initiatives. The World Bank International Finance Corporation has long had a program of investing with specific measurable social outcomes in concert with financial targets. The MacArthur foundation in the US made innovative steps to align its program and investment activities in the 1990s. Concessionary approaches by the likes of the Acumen Fund in the US and Bridges in the UK paved the way via thought leadership, capital allocation, and demonstrated impact. The "Bottom of the Pyramid" concept ("BOP") popularized by *The Fortune at the Bottom of the Pyramid* by CK Prahalad in 2004 helped to popularize the notion of positive social impact via profit motives.[7]

Foundations have played a leadership role into designing and popularizing returns to impact. Any list would be incomplete but Rockefeller, Ford, Omidyar, MacArthur, Case, and Heron have all played leadership roles, as have global NGOs. Market return approaches such as DBL Ventures backing Tesla at the venture stage with the support of the Ford Foundation delivered a double bottom line of both financial returns and impact (through local production jobs), and also a highly visible case study in success.

In practice, the more visible impact investment initiatives have been philanthropic and concessionary, as implemented by mission-driven foundations. However a greater amount of capital is at work in non-concessionary market returns, also expressed as the idea of a double bottom line – financial plus social or environmental impact, and triple bottom line – financial, social, and environmental impact, and blended value, are other ways to frame what is now called "impact investing." According to a Global Impact Investing Network (GIIN) survey of over $114 billion in assets, 66% of the impact investing market is pursuing risk-adjusted market returns, with 18% pursuing concessionary strategies "closer to market rate," and 16% pursuing concessionary strategies "closer to capital preservation."[8]

Impact investing is practiced across the capital structure, from pure debt instruments, to private equity, to public equity. It includes a range of return characteristics, from market-based returns to concessionary returns in which investors willingly receive lower financial returns due to an expectation of a positive social or environmental impact. The notion of concessionary returns has sparked the concept that impact investing would be more properly labeled "impact finance," with the further notion that deliberately seeking out concessionary returns may be a fraught approach, given the scarcity of PRI assets. A label of "impact philanthropy" could fairly describe "concessionary impact investing"; either label is unambiguous – capital is being deployed with objectives of impact and lower than market returns.

3. Impact measurement

In my experience, sound investing is as much an art as it is a science. Likewise sound impact investing cannot be reduced to a scientific set of processes or measurements.[9] By analogy, classic value investors do not simply look at accounting book value, accounting cash flow, or stated balance sheets; they dig deep to understand the basis for these numbers and whether these metrics are aggressive or conservative, i.e. a combination of art and science come in to play.

As another analogy, consider the role of credit ratings in bond investing. For a traditional credit investor or lender, the ratings agency framework from the likes of S&P and Moody's is a helpful part of the process. For credit investors, it is invaluable to understand the basis for rating agency assessments. However, that is the start and not the end of a credit analysis process. A credit analyst will add value by going above and beyond any third-party rating agency framework through deeper and bespoke analysis. Likewise, there are limitations to the roles that third-party entities can play for analysis of impact KPIs and ESG ratings.

With impact investing, the measurement challenge is even more daunting. Identifying points of impact and ways to measure and monitor that impact is necessarily nuanced; there are no equivalents to GAAP financial statements for impact. So while fellow impact educators have shared that students are dismayed to learn that while there is no "magic" metric for impact, practitioners know that judgment is vital in underwriting and appraising impact.

Yet identifying and measuring impact objectives is important – to paraphrase Peter Drucker, you cannot manage what you cannot measure. As for any business process, experienced managers know that there is a tension between measurement disciplines, the tactics of effective execution, and the strategy of achieving key objectives. In the extreme, Management by Objective (MBO) and Key Performance Indicators (KPIs) used without context can have negative consequences. Goodhart's Law states that "When a measure becomes a target, it ceases to be a good measure" and highlights the dangers of metric centricity in isolation. A prominent example of unintended consequences and failure of a KPI is the Wells Fargo fake account opening scandal. A powerful alternative to MBO and KPIs is provided in the discipline known as Objectives and Key Results (OKRs), pioneered by Andy Grove at Intel.[10] An OKRs approach recognizes both the value and limitations of process and metrics.

OKRs have proven to be highly effective management tools for driving impact at organizations ranging from the Gates Foundation, Bono's ONE Campaign, to Google and Intel. As John Doerr writes,

> Objectives and key results are the yin and yang of goal setting – principal and practice, vision and execution. Objectives are the stuff of inspiration and far horizons. Key results

are more earthbound and metric-driven . . . objectives must be *significant*. OKRs are neither a catchall wish list nor the sum of . . . mundane tasks. They're a set of stringently
curated goals.[11]

Myriad impact rubrics have been developed by various organizations and managers,
which has created a formidable challenge in the ability to translate these various frameworks, standards and measurement approaches. There is a veritable cottage industry of
efforts to improve and harmonize impact measurement. These efforts are in many cases
are thoughtful, dense, and complex. This exhibit is from a detailed report by the G8 Social
Impact Investment Task Force, "Measuring Impact."[12]

More recently, *Investor's Impact Matrix* is a significant collaborative effort by 1,000+ practitioners to improve definition around measurement of impact investing. The initiative is
in the process of developing conventions for defining a multiple dimensions of impact,
impact goals, and investor contributions.[13] *Investor's Impact Matrix* is a proposed con-
vention for communicating impact expectations and linking to different frameworks,
standards and measurement approaches, such as ESG and CSR data, and the Impact
Reporting and Investment Standards (IRIS).[14]

An area which measurement rubrics focus on includes Enterprise Impact, which is comprised of both Product and Operational Impacts.[15] Product Impact relates to the impact
of the goods or services that the business produces, for example health, education, or
energy efficiency. As an example of positive product impact, Borg Warner manufactures
products (turbo chargers) which improve engine fuel efficiency. Operational Impact
relates to business practices – such as labor and community relations. As an example of
positive operational impact, the Fortune 100 "Best Places to Work" identifies employers
with positive labor relations.

Additional considerations relate to inputs, intended output, and intended outcome. Outputs may not be directly linked to outcomes. What to measure, what the measurements
mean, and whether metrics are available and validated, are all complexities unique to
each investment.

CSR data can be a source of impact of measurement information. Public company ESG
data availability has exploded in the past decade, with a ten-fold increase in GRI annual
reports (over 6,000 per year), a five-fold increase in combined mandatory and voluntary reporting instruments (383 across 71 countries and regions), and over 900 KPIs now
available on the Bloomberg terminal.[16] SASB and the GRI are among the organizations
which have helped to drive harmonization of issues and metrics, however the data is still
highly idiosyncratic. Third-party ESG scoring services have also proliferated, however
in many ways share the same attributes, both positives and negatives, as credit ratings
(described above).[17] NGOs are a useful source of insight and metrics.[18]

In sum, the broad range of guidelines and matrices promulgated by various organizations
suggests that there is no single way to approach impact measurement. We think the
true north for fundamental impact investors is to use measurement disciplines that are
appropriately attuned to management and impact objectives, which may be on a bespoke
basis.

Having said that, there is a robust and growing set of KPIs and tools to support improved measurement and accountability. The key is in implementation, and discipline in monitoring ex ante objectives as compared to ex post results. An OKRs framework can provide the flexibility to be custom tailored and focused on key issues.

4. Why now?

Walk across a college campus, survey a group of millennials, or run a Google Trends survey, and it is undeniable: impact investing – as well as social entrepreneurship and sustainable investing – is the zeitgeist of the day. People are "all in on impact"; it's not just the thought leading foundations, but equally at the grassroots level. Students and millennials are drawn to impact investing, and the institutional ecosystem has developed to support the rising demand. There are multiple drivers, both demand and supply driven.

The demand is in part from new generations with new attitudes. Prior generations lived with strong institutions of government, life-long corporate employers, religion, and the fourth estate of the press. Each of these four institutions has a greatly diminished standing as compared to prior generations. Confidence in the role of the capital markets was undermined by the Great Financial Crisis (GFC) as reflected in the Occupy movement in 2011. Income inequality is growing, in part as a function of the structure of an asset-light economy. Disillusionment by millennials with regard to traditional institutions may be contributing to a dissonance which needs to be solved.

With these shifts, some of the great enthusiasm and confidence in free enterprise has also shifted to become directed in new ways, including social entrepreneurship and purpose-driven ventures. Many of the leading supporters and innovators in impact investing, in fact, come from the technology sector where wealth generation has been tremendous as a function of some of the above structural changes.

On the supply side is a flourishing ecosystem of newly developed models and tool kits for impact investing, which have evolved from the old models of nonprofit philanthropy. Foundation support in particular has paved a vital role, as a recent example the Rockefeller Foundation and Ford Foundation supported the first Global Faculty Convening on Impact Investing for graduate business school faculty, hosted by Northwestern University Kellogg School of Management in June 2017. Grassroots interest has spawned the development of a large number of impact investing curriculums at leading universities globally. Curriculum is still emergent, as academics are trading notes and evolving best practices alongside practitioners.

Intangibles dominate market valuation

The four largest companies by market value [Apple, Amazon, Google, and Facebook] don't need any net tangible assets. They're not like AT&T, GM or ExxonMobil requiring lots of capital to produce earnings. American industry is much more profitable in aggregate over the last twenty years. Earnings on tangible net worth growth is due to fact that we have become an asset-light economy.[19]

– Warren Buffett, 2018 Shareholder Meeting

Increasingly, market value and future earnings streams are derived from intangible assets rather than physical assets. In 2015 public market valuations were comprised of

84% intangible assets and only 16% tangible assets, a complete reversal from 1975 when the mix was 17% and 83% respectively.[20]

The phenomenal growth of asset-light businesses in the past decade is the result of technology-enabled businesses in many cases reliant on intangibles such as a powerful network-effect of a broad-ubiquitous user base or ecosystem. This transition in the structure of business is reflected in writings such as "The Capitalist's Dilemma" by Clayton Christensen and Derek van Bever[21] and *The End of Accounting and the Path Forward for Investors and Managers* by Baruch Lev and Feng Gu.

Businesses like Apple, Amazon, Google, and Facebook all fit a general paradigm of growth unconstrained by high capital investment requirements. And as a result, asset-intensive accounting and measurements paint an incomplete picture of the business. Investors and corporate managers need to be attenuated to issues of social license to operate, impact, and ESG.

Hyman Minsky describes a transition from the post-WWII era of "Managerial Capitalism," where entrenched professional management take a "statesmanship" approach to running businesses for the long term – neither attenuated to stock prices nor responsive to disperse individual shareholders – in contrast to the current era of "money manager capitalism"[22] where professional money managers are the dominant shareholders and promulgate short-termism by corporate managers. Impact investors play an important role in solving for the void created by a diminished role of traditional institutions. Impact investing stands to address market failures with massively more scale than is capable from traditional philanthropic or governmental capital. The enthusiasm around the UN Strategic Development Goals (SDGs) and FSB Task Force on Climate-related Financial Disclosures (TCFD) is reflective of this aspiration for systematic impact.[23]

5. All investing is impact investing

We agree with Clara Miller, President *Emerita* of the Heron Foundation, who has helped to popularize the notion that "All investing is impact investing." In 2012, the Heron Foundation put that belief into practice by committing its endowment to be invested 100% into investments that satisfied the foundation's impact objectives, thereby eliminating the dissonance of an investment operation that could include negative-impact activities funding the foundation's mission-oriented programs. In recent years a number of prominent foundations have likewise proclaimed that in furthering their mission objectives, endowment assets will be investing for impact and mission.[24]

The notion that all investing has impact is self-evident. The only debate should be as to whether the impacts are actively managed – deliberate or unintentional, positive or negative. The measurements may be codified[25] or bespoke. A company may have an impact mission core to its purpose, or an impact mission may be a part of the fabric of a company's culture. A company may have an explicit set of impact objectives (for example, reduce energy consumption, reduce waste production, increase employee health and well-being, increase customer satisfaction). Engaged investors who drive actions on impact objectives which complement a company's core franchise can contribute to the sustainability of a company's competitive advantage. This fits in well with a non-concessionary approach to positive impact if combined with an investment discipline which does not overpay to invest in those businesses.

The tools and frameworks of impact investing and ESG in many cases are one in the same. There is frequently confusion in language around impact, ESG, SRI, MBI, RI, VBI, to name but a few acronyms.[26] Businesses which have a favorable ESG profile are the same businesses that have historically delivered positive impacts, and businesses which have positive ESG momentum are those businesses which are improving their business practices and thereby driving incremental positive impact.

Businesses very often are deliberately managed to be viewed as having high-quality business practices which have positive impacts on society and environment. This supports their social license to operate. As a general matter, high-quality business practices can provide businesses with the potential to gain a competitive advantage – for example by being viewed as an attractive employer capable of recruiting top talent, or being welcomed as a new entrant to a community, being favored as a partner of choice or attractive acquirer of businesses or innovators which may have multiple suitors. These are all examples of how an impact framework can help illuminate attractive investment opportunities.

By contrast a poorly managed or inwardly focused corporation which may operate within the limits of the law but is viewed as a drain on its community will be competitively disadvantaged and may lose its social license to operate. Evidence clearly shows that negative ESG momentum can translate to negative stock performance. An asset owner who invests capital in businesses with negative business practices, in an unengaged manner, will be contributing to a negative impact. Impact – whether positive or negative – is a necessary result of an engaged ESG investing approach.

Conclusion
In closing, the "impact investing movement," including the ecosystem of tools of measurement, engagement, and accountability, is bringing significant private capital to address unmet societal needs and market failures. The power of private capital and industry to catalyze positive impact is unmatched by philanthropic or governmental resources. Furthermore we are encouraged that a long-term stewardship approach to managing businesses is a sustainable way to catalyze positive change.

An important role for impact investing in society is entirely consistent with a careful reading of the framework provided in Milton Friedman's well-known rejoinder regarding the social responsibility of business.

> There is one and only one social responsibility of business – to use its resources and engage in activities designed to increase its profits so long as it stays within the rules of the game, which is to say, engages in open and free competition without deception or fraud.[27]

Embedded within Friedman's famous quote, and within his larger article, is the acknowledgement that the "rules of the game" matter. And in today's society, leading businesses can and are being held to an ever higher bar. Uber, Valiant Pharmaceuticals, and Wells Fargo offer three vivid examples of the high costs that can be imposed by society on businesses that are not managed in a way that is mindful of broader societal impact. Friedman's passage may not have anticipated the extent to which traditional institutions have evolved, but the simple fact is that the "rules of the game" today include social norms and instant accountability via social media in a way that can promote positive corporate behavior and impact.[28]

We have provided some definitions of impact investing, a brief history and the context behind the evolution of impact investing, a discussion of the current heightened interest and enthusiasm around impact investing, and perspectives on both the importance of and limitations of measurement around impact.

At its core, impact investing is about the linkage between the allocation of capital by investors, and the impact on the real economy and society. The growing impact investment ecosystem is playing a vital role in evolving our capital markets to address market failures and to effect positive change at a powerful level in terms of scale and ultimate impact. In this manner we see impact investing paving the way to a more sustainable financial market ecosystem. This, then would be the ultimate "impact."

4.4 Engagement-based ESG investing

Engagement-based ESG investing is the fourth and final approach to ESG investing. **Engagement** is the act of communicating and collaborating with a company that is a current or prospective investment. Engaging with companies allows investors to increase the weight of investors' demands in the eyes of corporate management (Piani and Gond, 2014). Investors choose engagement-based ESG investing so that they may communicate their beliefs or views on a particular issue or topic in order to serve as a catalyst for change. Institutional investors may engage with companies as part of their investment policy statements, in reaction to negative headlines, or as a part of client demand.

The tone of engagement can vary greatly in the engagement-based ESG investing spectrum. In some cases, the engagement process is collaborative. Other times, the engagement process can be hostile, as investors maximize pressure on a corporation to effect change. In either case, engagement can grant the investor the opportunity to make a material impact in corporate policy.

Collaborative engagement is the method of engagement where investors attempt to work alongside the company in a supportive manner. An example of a collaborative engagement-based ESG investment action could be observed through the lens of a hedge fund that contacts a **mid-size market capitalization** ("mid cap") company through a private letter to the board of directors explaining governance issues, the need for gender and minority diversity at the senior management and executive suite level, and a pathway to create greater shareholder value, along with an offer to commit time and energy in assisting the company in accomplishing the suggested objectives. See Case Study 4B for an example of collaborative engagement.

CASE STUDY 4D: Wellington Asset Management

Wellington Management Company LLP is a Boston, Massachusetts, United States-based asset management company. Wellington serves both retail and institutional investors through various asset classes and strategies. Wellington provides a good example of how an asset manager might collaboratively engage with a company for promoting gender diversity on its publicly traded board of directors.

Wellington believes that boards create shareholder value by appointing qualified directors with a wide range of perspectives, and who can counsel management teams on major strategic decisions. Wellington's position was that they believe diverse boardrooms are essential as companies are navigating increasingly complex issues (e.g., geopolitical changes, regulatory intricacies, disruptive technologies, activism, etc.). In Wellington's role as fund sponsor of commingled vehicles, they sent a letter in September 2017 to mid- or large-cap companies that Wellington owned at the time that did not have any women on their boards. The letter asked companies to engage with Wellington so that Wellington can understand the company's overall approach to boardroom diversity. Wellington acknowledges that gender is just one of many facets of diversity, but, at the time the letter was distributed, they had not identified good datasets that would let them pull a list of companies that lack diversity in other forms (e.g., disability, race, nationality). In this example of engagement, Wellington used gender as the start of a conversation with companies on this issue, and not as the only aspect of diversity that they are interested in.

Below is the text of the letter that Wellington sent to companies in September of 2017. It was signed by Brendan Swords, CEO and Managing Partner of Wellington.

Wellington Management Company LLP is an investment adviser that manages approximately $1 trillion in assets on behalf of our clients worldwide. We have investment discretion for clients who hold [Number] shares of [Company Name] common stock. Of the [Number] shares over which we have investment discretion, we have voting discretion with respect to approximately [Number] of such shares.

We are writing to encourage you to address the issue of diversity on your company's board. While gender is just one of many aspects of diversity, your company has come to our attention because your boardroom does not include a single female director.

In our view, businesses create shareholder value by appointing boards that thoughtfully debate company strategy and direction. Such debate is enhanced when boards elect highly qualified and diverse directors who contribute insights from a range of perspectives.

We encourage you to consider the widest possible pool of skilled candidates. We do not presume to know the variety of views that each director currently brings to your board meetings, but from a shareholder's perspective, the absence of women on your board is noticeable. No boardroom should be comprised of directors from a single industry. Consequently, while some industries have a relatively small number of women in senior roles, we are generally unpersuaded by the contention that a board cannot find qualified female directors.

We hope you will carefully reexamine the diversity of your board and, if you conclude that change is unnecessary, engage with us so that we can better understand your evaluation. To schedule an engagement, please send an email to [Wellington E-Mail Address].

Sincerely,
Brendan Swords

If the companies that received the letter do not engage with Wellington on this topic nor add diverse members to their Board, Wellington has stated that they are reserving the right to vote against them at their next annual meeting.

Hostile engagement, on the other hand, is the act of engaging with a company in an aggressive manner to use the investor's position to forcefully be a catalyst for change. Although the effects of collaborative engagement can be positive or negative, hostile engagement is more likely to cause a conflict within the company, deter other investors from investing, or reflect negatively in the eyes of the company's consumer or client. That said, hostile engagement can be successful at creating shareholder value. Using the same mid-cap company example, a hostile engagement practice by a hedge fund might be to leverage their position as a stakeholder by campaigning for a board seat(s) amongst other shareholders and publicly discussing the company's governance issues in attempt to gain greater control of the company's management team. Hostile engagement might also engage other decision makers at the company through their new, potential, position on the company's board of directors in the effort to forcefully effect change (Piani and Gond, 2014).

Asset managers, as fiduciaries, will often act on behalf of their investors in engagement practices. Asset managers demonstrate dedication to ESG issues through their alignment to ESG mandates and corporate engagement (Piani and Gond, 2014). The approach, or strategy, for engagement can vary greatly in practice. As discussed above, engagement can be private or public.

Private engagement may include confidential communications on constructive ESG issues, intellectual capital and strategy sharing, and research and development. Regardless how engagement-based ESG investing is practiced, the core focus is to be a catalyst, or contributor, for change relative to an ESG issue or risk in order to create greater shareholder value.

Public engagement may entail open letters, use of media platforms and social media channels to communicate desired engagement and goals for change. Engagement may also come in the form of activism, which may be collaborative or hostile in nature. Investors buy large amounts of a public company's stock and then attempt to obtain seats on the company's board with the goal of creating a major change in the company (Becht et al. 2010).

A 2018 empirical study titled "ESG Shareholder Engagement and Downside Risk" written by Andreas Hoepner, Ioannis Oikonomou, Zacharias Sautner, Laura Starks, and Xiaoyan Zhou analyzed the engagement of companies by a $200 billion pension fund. The study quantitatively examined the effect of institutional investor engagement on the publicly traded companies' securities. The results of the study found that companies targeted through ESG engagement displayed less downside risk (measured by partial movements and value-at-risk analysis). Further, the authors showed that engagement targets are statistically more optimal at downside risk than non-engaged companies. The study also pointed out that higher standards of corporate ESG practice serve as protection against harmful, risk-inducing events such as regulatory, legislative, or consumer action taken against firms.

Proxy voting is a mainstream example of a basic engagement strategy. Investors have the option to vote on shareholder resolutions proposed, particularly those that are relevant to environmental, social, and governance factors. See the Learning perspective at the end of this chapter for recent examples of a granular synthesis of shareholder resolutions. Investors, both retail and institutional, engage with companies through their decision-making practices relative to proxy voting. Institutional investors, who might own equities directly or own equities and have a money manager managing within a separately managed account (SMA), may vote based on their own guidelines or ask the money manager to vote in accordance with their guidelines. Asset managers who offer mutual funds, index funds, exchange-traded funds (ETFs), collective investment trusts (CITs), and other co-mingled vehicles will often vote in a process that is in accordance with their fiduciary nature, aligned with their own business principles, and what will be best for shareholder value.

Institutional investors will often write language in their investment policy or guidelines for managers to follow that can be explicit on various topics and issues. See Case study 4E to learn how Switzerland-based pension fund, Caisse Inter-Entreprises de Prévoyance Professionnelle (CIEPP), engages companies through proxy voting.

CASE STUDY 4E: CIEPP and engagement through proxy voting

A 7 billion CHF Switzerland-based Pension Fund, Caisse Inter-Entreprises de Prévoyance Professionnelle (CIEPP) practices ESG engagement through their proxy voting. CIEPP is led by a Board of Directors made up of heads of member firms, representative of their staff and retirees. The Board is responsible for all administrative and investment decisions. An investment committee led by the Board's President and Vice President and made up of internal and outside investment professionals advise the Board on investment decisions and execute the investment strategy. The pension fund management team performs the pension fund activities and manage the assets on a day-to-day basis. Assets are held at a custodian bank responsible for safekeeping, administering, and performing accounting.

As part of CIEPP's investment management process, the Board has established a voting policy for proxy voting. CIEPP exercises its voting rights systematically on domestic equities and European shares held in its portfolio. The Board has adopted voting principles to guide the Pension Fund Investment Head in his or her voting. Systematically voting proxies in adherence to the voting principles guide allows CIEPP to properly execute decisions on ESG issues that are in the best interest of their pension fund's participants. Further, independent outside analysis is also purchased to guide voting. In this manner, CIEPP leverages proper research and analysis on voting proxies in order to engage the company with their view on a particular issue, such as a public company's Board of Directors' composition. Such votes are transmitted to an independent proxy chosen by the company's Board and accepted by a shareholder's vote. CIEPP's use of proxy voting, and their policy around their voting principles guide, is an example of the mainstream ESG engagement technique of proxy voting.

A pension plan may use general language in the investment guidelines provided to an external equity manager that reads, "Manager shall vote proxies of companies held in the portfolio in the best economic interests of the plan participants." However, a pension plan may explicitly provide predefined directives on issues, like "Manager shall recognize that Client is sensitive to gender diversity on corporate boards of directors and agrees to advance that interest when considering whether to vote for or against a company's proposed slate of directors." Gender diversity on corporate boards is a common engagement issue conducted by investment and asset managers.

The reasons for engaging may differ depending on the investor. Investors that practice engagement-based ESG investing hold to the rationale that a company's value management system is based not only on economic profit maximization, but also on ESG value maximization, which can be achieved through stakeholder engagement, if such engagement is implemented in the management system of the company (Martirosyan and Vashakmadze, 2013). Engaging with a company allows investors to advocate for positive change on an issue, or issues, within the company.

LEARNING PERSPECTIVE 2: ESG proxy voting

Heidi Welsh is the founding Executive Director of the Sustainable Investments Institute (Si2). Welsh has analyzed and written about corporate responsibility issues since the late 1980s. She oversees Si2's operations and research. Welsh was the lead author of Si2's two studies about the corporate governance of political spending in the S&P 500 (US Equity Index), published in 2010 and 2011 with the IRRC Institute. Previously, Welsh helped author seasonal and annual reports on proxy voting trends starting in 1987 at the Investor Responsibility Research Center (IRRC), closely followed social and environmental shareholders resolutions and their results, and for 16 years ran the monitoring program examining corporate compliance with the Mac-Bride principles for fair employment in Northern Ireland. She co-authored the Carbon Disclosure Project's 2007 report on S&P 500 companies and set up a global sustainability metrics project for RiskMetrics analyzing 1,800 of the world's biggest companies. Welsh also served on the Global Reporting Initiative's Electric Utility Sector Working Group in 2008–2009 and participated in an Oxford University assessment of Northern Ireland's affirmative action legislation. Welsh received her bachelor's degree in political science, cum laude, with a concentration in science, technology and public policy, from Carleton College. She holds a master's degree from the Institute for Conflict Analysis and Resolution at George Mason University.

This Learning perspective features Welsh's 2017 mid-year review on proxy voting.

Proxy season review: social, environmental, and sustainable governance shareholder proposals in 2017
By Heidi Welsh
October 2017
(*Revised*)

Executive summary

The 2017 spring proxy season ended with a bang, with long awaited success for investor activists bolstered by mainstream investors, tempered by legal peril for the entire shareholder resolution process. By far the most significant vote was the 62% result for a climate risk proposal at **ExxonMobil**'s May 31 annual meeting – which occurred after the mutual fund giant BlackRock decided for the first time to lend its support. Exxon has considered shareholder resolutions for many years and has been a high-profile focus for activists but the highest vote until now was 38.1% for a climate strategy resolution last year. The new vote at Exxon was not the only unusually high climate tally of the season, as other large funds reportedly reversed course to support the proposals for the first time.

But the ink on celebratory press releases had was hardly dry when the House of Representatives approved the Financial CHOICE Act, which would gut the shareholder proposal process. The measure, which also would walk back many of the Obama-era financial reforms, is not expected to pass the Senate, but sets out long-held aspirations of those who see shareholder resolutions as a pesky nuisance. Efforts to significantly scale back the ability of investors to file and resubmit proposals may make their way into a Securities and Exchange Commission (SEC) rulemaking, but the shape of any such rule remains to be seen as of late October 2017.

After a dip last year, the total number of environmental and social policy shareholder resolutions filed in 2017 rose substantially, reaching a record of at least 488 as of mid-August – compared with 432 in 2016 and 462 the year before. By late October, the total had reached 495, with 229 having gone to votes and eight more results pending before the end of the year. The marked increase this year came not from environmental resolutions, but rather from social policy issues – specifically a raft about equitable pay. In all, there have been six majority votes. Last year's dip in the proposal withdrawal rate reversed itself, while more companies persuaded the SEC that they could omit resolutions – also reversing last year's result. The total number of votes now seems likely to be 237, slightly less than the record number of 243 in 2016. (See list, Table 4.11, for all proposals at companies with annual meetings after July 31.)

Table 4.11 2017 Resolutions

High scoring 2017 resolutions			
Company	Proposal	Proponent	Vote (%)
Hudson Pacific Properties	Report on board diversity	CalSTRS	84.8
Occidental Petroleum	Report on climate change strategy	N. Cummings Foundation	67.3
Cognex	Adopt board diversity policy	Philadelphia PERS	62.8
ExxonMobil	Report on climate change	NYSCRF	62.1
PPL	Report on climate change strategy	NYSCRF	56.8
Pioneer Natural Resources	Publish sustainability report	NYSCRF	52.1
PNM Resources	Report on climate change strategy	Levinson Fndn	49.9
Dominion Energy	Report on climate change strategy	NYSCRF	47.8
Ameren	Report on climate change strategy	Mercy Inv.	47.5
	Report on coal ash risks	Midwest CRI	46.4
Duke Energy	Report on climate change strategy	NYSCRF	46.4
Occidental Petroleum	Report on methane emissions/ targets	Arjuna Capital	45.8
Southern	Report on climate change strategy	Srs., St. Dominic-Caldwell	45.7
DTE Energy	Report on climate change strategy	NYSCRF	45
Middleby	Publish sustainability report	Trillium Asset	44.6
FirstEnergy	Report on climate change strategy	As You Sow	43.4
	Report on lobbying	N. Cummings Fndn	41.5
Devon Energy	Report on climate change	Gund Fndn	41.4
NextEra Energy	Review/report on political spending	NYSCRF	41.2
Marathon Petroleum	Report on climate change strategy	Mercy Inv.	40.9
Kinder Morgan	Report on methane emissions/ targets	Miller/Howard Inv.	40.6
Emerson Electric	Review/report on political spending	Trillium Asset	40.3
AES	Report on climate change	Mercy Inv.	40.1
Emerson Electric	Report on lobbying	Zevin Asset Mgt	40.1

Average overall support was 21.2%, up from 21.1% in 2016 to 20% in 2015. As noted, last year's very low withdrawal and omission rates appear to be an aberration. Fully 16% of those filed were omitted from proxy statements after company challenges, the highest proportion since 2011. The withdrawal rate of 34% is still below the decadal high of 40% reached in 2014.

Investors cast majority votes in favor of board diversity with wide margins at the real estate firm **Hudson Pacific Properties** (84.8%) and the scientific instrument firm **Cognex**

(62.8%). But climate change also seems to have come into its own this year, reflecting the global scientific consensus about its risks that many on Wall Street seem to have taken to heart: shareholders gave climate risk reporting proposals 67.3% at **Occidental Petroleum**, 62.1% at **ExxonMobil**, and 56.8% at the utility **PPL**. The final majority vote of 52.1% was for a sustainability reporting proposition at **Pioneer Natural Resources**, another oil and gas firm. (There were eight majorities in 2016 for proposals opposed by management, as well.)

Company action that usually involves more disclosure as well as shifts in policy are the prime objective of shareholder proponents and this year they have withdrawn 170 resolutions so far, nearly always because of negotiations. In volume, this is below the all-time high of 181 withdrawals back in 2014 but a bump-up, as noted, from last year's 139 tally.

In major 2017 subject categories, proponents were far and away most likely to withdraw board diversity resolutions (fully 73% of filings). They also withdrew half the resolutions on workplace diversity and nearly the same proportion (46%) of those on-board oversight issues. In what may not be surprising in this age of political discord, proponents withdrew just 17% of resolutions they filed asking for more corporate political spending transparency; the majority of these dealt with lobbying.

High scoring proposals: In addition to the majority votes, another 18 earned between 40% and 49% (Table 4.11). As with last year, more of the top-scorers related in some way to the environment and sustainability (14) than any other categories; three more concerned election spending or lobbying.

2017 In review

This section describes the main topics raised in proxy season, highlighting new issues, continued big campaign and significant results. Twenty-five resolutions were submitted at companies with meetings after July 31; as of late October, seven votes had yet to be tabulated (see shaded entries on Table 4.12).

Environment

This report discusses environmental issues in the categories of climate change, environmental management (mostly recycling), toxics, and industrial agriculture (including pesticides and animal welfare). A separate section on sustainable governance covers proposals that encompass elements of environmental issues as well as social impacts and related corporate governance, looking at board diversity, board oversight, and disclosure and management.

Climate change

The proxy season produced several unprecedented votes on climate change, including three of the seven majority votes and 13 more above 40%. A total of 90 resolutions focused specifically on climate change (additional sustainability reporting proposals also invoked climate-related subjects).

Impacts and strategies

Twenty-seven resolutions took up different aspects of climate risk and the ways in which companies are grappling – or not – with these challenges, including potentially stranded assets. Proponents went to nine fossil fuel producers and 12 utilities; investors responded across the board with high levels of support for more disclosure. Fifteen of the 22 proposals were resubmissions. Unprecedented majorities occurred at **ExxonMobil** (62.1%) and **Occidental Petroleum** (67.3%), as investors agreed the companies need to explain in more detail about long-term portfolio impacts from action by governments to curb global

Table 4.12 Late season proposals

Company	Issue	Proponent	Status
Alliance One Intl	Report on OECD human rights mediation	AFL-CIO	Not presented*
Altaba	Report on human rights policy	Jing Zhao	Oct. 24 mtg
CACI International	Report on board diversity	Episcopal Church	Withdrawn
Cardinal Health	Report on lethal injection drug policy	NYSCRF	Omitted (i-7)
Cisco Systems	Disclose workforce breakdown in Israel-Palestine	Holy Land Principles	Withdrawn
	Report on lobbying	Unitarian Universalists	Pending (Dec. 11)
Coach	Report on animal welfare issues	HSUS	Pending (Nov. 9)
	Report on GHG emissions targets	Jantz Management	
ConAgra Brands	Report on supply chain deforestation impacts	Green Century	Withdrawn
Darden Restaurants	Phase out antibiotic use in animal feed	Green Century	0.128
FedEx	Report on anti-gay law impacts	NorthStar Asset Mgt	0.026
	Report on lobbying	Teamsters	0.25
	Review/report on political spending	Newground Social Inv.	Not in proxy
Hain Celestial	Publish sustainability report	As You Sow	Withdrawn
J.M. Smucker	Report on climate change	Trillium Asset Mgt	Withdrawn
	Report on pesticide monitoring	Trillium Asset Mgt	Withdrawn
	Report on renewable energy goals	Trillium Asset Mgt	0.275
Lam Research	Disclose EEO-1 data	NYC pension funds	Pending (Nov. 8)
NetApp	Disclose EEO-1 data	NYC pension funds	0.281
NIKE	Review/report on political spending	Investor Voice	0.201
Oracle	Report on female pay disparity	Pax World Funds	Pending (Nov. 15)
	Review/report on political spending	NYSCRF	

Company	Issue	Proponent	Status
Palo Alto Networks	Disclose EEO-1 data	Trillium Asset Mgt	Pending (Dec. 8)
Procter & Gamble	Implement Holy Land Principles	Holy Land Principles	Withdrawn*
	Report on anti-gay law impacts	NorthStar Asset Mgt	0.067
	Report on conflict zone operations	Heartland Initiative	0.076
Universal	Report on OECD human rights mediation	AFL-CIO	Not presented*
Xilinx	Report on board diversity	Trillium Asset Mgt	Withdrawn

*Appeared in proxy statement

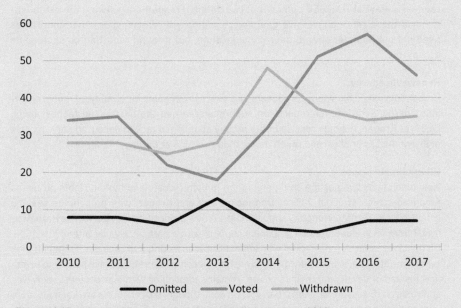

Figure 4.37 Climate change shareholder resolutions since 2010

warming in line with the Paris climate treaty. A new resolution to **Marathon Petroleum** went even further, asking about impacts from a business plan that would cut warming to well below the treaty's two-degree aim; it earned 40.9%. The utility votes were especially high, with a 56.8% majority at **PPL** and seven more proposals over 45%.

Proponents withdrew when **Anadarko Petroleum** and **Chevron** agreed to provide more climate risk projections, while **NRG Energy**, **Southern**, and **Xcel Energy** also saw withdrawals when they agreed to provide more risk management information. The SEC turned back arguments from companies that contended current reporting made more disclosure moot.

Shale energy

Investor attention to shale energy sharpened to focus more particularly on methane emissions and leaks. High votes included 40.6% at **Kinder Morgan** and 45.8% at **Occidental** on requests for reduction goals. (The Occidental vote rose from 33% last year.)

After a majority vote in 2016, the California State Teachers' Retirement System (CalSTRS) reached an agreement this year with **WPX Energy**, which will provide more information. Three other utilities – **Sempra**, **Southern**, and **WGL Energy** – also agreed on more disclosure and prompted withdrawals.

Carbon accounting

A big new push on greenhouse gas (GHG) emissions accounting was the proposition that companies should set targets to achieve net-zero emissions, but these earned far less than more general and familiar proposals to set goals and report on them. Four votes for the latter "traditional" carbon accounting resolutions were in the 30% decile, with the highest being 36.7% at **Fluor**. Amalgamated Bank and Jantz Management proposed the net-zero resolutions, the highest of which resulted in 23.9% for a report request at **PayPal**. The SEC opined that two detailed resolutions seeking the establishment of these more aggressive goals were ordinary business issues that companies need not put forth for shareholder consideration, but it found reporting on such goals acceptable.

Renewable energy

Proponents asked big energy producers and users to set goals for employing more renewable energy. Requests for reports on such goals earned the most – the highest being 24.8% at **Kroger**. A single reprise of the mostly abandoned tack to encourage greater use of distributed energy earned much more, though – 35% at **Entergy**.

Other climate issues

New resolutions tying action on deforestation to both climate and human rights problems produced scores of about 23% at **Domino's Pizza** and **Kroger**, with proponents seeking action in these firms' commodity supply chains. A new proposition that **Berkshire Hathaway** divest from fossil-fuel related companies came in with a particularly low vote of just 1.3%. On the other hand, Arjuna Capital won 26% at **Chevron** asking it to consider selling off high carbon assets. The "climate dividend" idea, that oil companies should give money to investors instead of developing their reserves, remains unpopular with shareholders, however, and votes on this issue were less than 4%. On coal, though, shareholders are keen for more information about coal combustion residuals from **Ameren**, where the vote was 46.4%.

Environmental management

Almost all proposals about dealing with environmental concerns outside the direct climate arena were on recycling, as in the past. The highest vote was 32% at **McDonald's** on cutting the use of styrofoam cups. On a closely related angle, both **Amazon.com** and **Target** agreed to curb foam packing. Food waste is also an emerging concern and a repeat resolution asking for details at **Whole Foods Market** attracted 30.4% support.

Toxics

There were no votes, since the SEC decided a new proposal seeking company help to educate the public about lead risks was ordinary business at **Lowe's**, although **Home Depot** agreed to work on it and prompted a withdrawal from Arjuna Capital.

Industrial agriculture

Eighteen filings yielded a mixed bag of 11 votes and seven withdrawals.

Antibiotics

In the realm of food production, a recurrent push from the Interfaith Center on Corporate Responsibility to get companies to restrict antibiotic use in the meat supply chain continued and attracted its highest support of 31.5% at **Sanderson Farms**, which contests the science connecting agricultural use of drugs with growing antibiotic resistant illnesses. At **McDonald's**, a resolution seeking an extension of the company's ban on antibiotics for chicken to beef and pork also earned 31%. Such an extension is more difficult since beef and pork production is less vertically integrated than chicken farming, but going forward attention to the issue is likely to continue given the threat to human health.

Pesticides

Otherwise, regarding pesticides, As You Sow raised the new issue of pre-harvest glyphosate treatment in a resolution it withdrew at **Kellogg**, which has agreed to explore how often this occurs among its suppliers as part of its focus on sustainable agriculture. Investors also gave significant support of 31.6% at **Dr Pepper Snapple Group** for a report on how it can cut pesticide use by its suppliers to protect pollinators that appear to be hurt by the use of neonicotinoids.

Animal welfare

The highest scoring of just four resolutions on animal welfare was 24.3% on a proposal to cereal company **Post Holding**, seeking a report on brand risks connected to caged egg production. Egg products make up 28% of the company's net sales and Post says it is committed to a transition to cage-free housing.

A new proposal at **Tyson Foods** combined climate concerns with animal welfare, but Green Century Capital Management ended up withdrawing that request for evaluation of the potential impact on Tyson of more vegetarians when it learned the company had acquired Beyond Meat, a meatless protein firm.

Social issues

Animal welfare

Investors put to bed a resubmission of last year's proposal from People for the Ethical Treatment of Animals (PETA) on how a Texas monkey farm owned by **Laboratory Corp. of America** might become a vector for the spread of the Zika virus, giving it just over 4% and not enough for resubmission. Shareholders also gave scant support (2.6%) for a **Charles River Labs** resolution on banning business with primate dealers and labs that have violated the Animal Welfare Act. But the proposal highlighted the Trump administration's move early in the year to yank animal use reports from the US Department of Agriculture website. That has prompted a spate of Freedom of Information Act requests since.

Corporate political activity

Shareholder proponents continued their push for more disclosure from companies about their spending on lobbying and elections, with the focus most intense on lobbying. Lobbying proposals votes drew even this year (about 27% on average) with those about election spending (which also averaged about 27% this year, down from about 33% two years ago at their apex). The withdrawal rate for both types overall is relatively low, just 19% of those

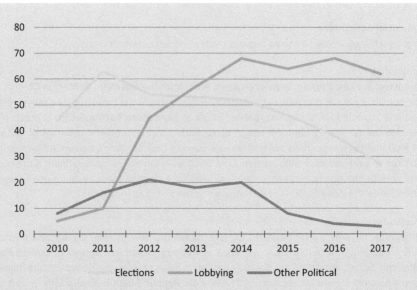

Figure 4.38 Resolutions filed on corporate political activity

filed, showing the limits of agreement between activists and companies. There will be 68 votes in 2017, with 18 withdrawals and five omissions; still pending as of late October are resolutions at **Cisco Systems** and **Oracle**.

A coming flashpoint may be a highly contentious proposal from President Trump to remove restrictions on political giving by 501(c)3 charities, including churches, but this would require legislation that has yet to be proposed. Another open question is whether big mutual funds will extend their proxy voting to political spending proposals, as they have with climate change this year. Such a move is being sought by the Corporate Reform Coalition and its allies that include both corporate governance and good government advocates, although the funds have yet to respond.

Proponents encountered a new problem that arose at **Anthem** when it successfully challenged a lobbying proposal that the SEC agreed was like earlier election spending proposals since both mentioned trade group spending, which encompasses both lobbying and election activity. Careful drafting in the future could solve the problem and allow both subjects to be raised at a single company.

Lobbying
Votes above 40% occurred at **FirstEnergy** and **Emerson Electric**, while four more were in the high 30% range at **AT&T**, **Honeywell International**, **Travelers**, and **Walt Disney**.

A notable withdrawal occurred at **Pinnacle West**, where the company has come under fire for its efforts to influence the Arizona public utilities commission; the utility agreed to provide more information on both lobbying and contributions to nonprofit charities, social welfare groups, and political committees – a key point of contention.

Election spending
The overall average for Center for Political Accountability (CPA) proposals fell, as noted, as did the number filed, although there were several high votes – just above 41% at both **Emerson Electric** and **NextEra Energy**. The average this year fell from earlier results given tallies in the low teens at **Alphabet**, **Berkshire Hathaway**, and **Expedia**, and just

under 8% at **Occidental Petroleum.** (Next year the CPA and its allies intend to increase the number of their filings.)

Three of the seven withdrawals to date came at companies with previous high votes – **Fluor** (61.9% last year), **McKesson** (44.4% in 2016) and **NiSource** (50.3% in 2016). All three agreed to the CPA-defined oversight and disclosure approach.

Other political issues

Six of seven additional filings on political money went to votes. Investors gave the most support to the AFL-CIO's proposition that companies end premature vesting of equity awards when employees leave for government jobs – what the union terms "government service golden parachutes." This earned 35.5% at **Citigroup** but less at **JPMorgan Chase** (26.8%) and **Morgan Stanley** (17.7%).

Decent work

The big surge that started last year with pay equity proposals increased further in 2017, with a total of 53 filings on this plus labor standards and working conditions more broadly. Votes were not high – in the teens – but proponents withdrew half of the pay equity resolutions after agreements for more reporting by companies. The highest vote was 18% for a report on gender pay equity at **Travelers**. Just four proposals that addressed pay equality more generally went to votes but earned little support – the highest was 7.4% at **CVS**.

Resolutions on working conditions produced higher support, with 28.1% for an accident prevention resolution at **Du Pont**, down from 30% last year. Companies promised more reporting on supply chain labor standards in response to the New York State Common Retirement Fund (NYSCRF) and it withdrew five proposals; one was omitted on ordinary business grounds, however.

Diversity in the workplace

Resolutions on workplace diversity and more opportunity for women and minorities complemented the pay equity proposals with a call to end discriminatory practices beyond compensation, but also addressed LGBT rights. While the pay equity resolutions focused

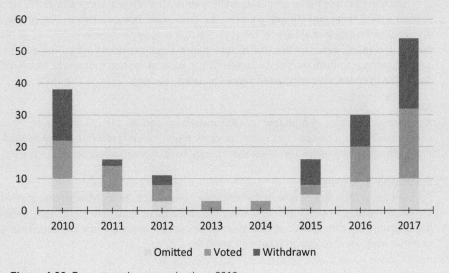

Figure 4.39 Decent work proposals since 2010

for the most part only on women, the workplace diversity slate included race, reflecting the national conversation. Four votes were over 30% at financial firms: **First Republic Bank** (32.9%), **T. Rowe Price** (36.8%), and **Travelers** (36.4%), as well as for the long-time resolution at **Home Depot** (33.6%). Given agreements to adopt LGBT policies, no proposals went to votes out of seven filings. One new angle came up in a proposal to **Amazon.com** about potentially discriminatory use of background checks in hiring, but it earned just 7.3%.

A notable SEC decision occurred at **Cato**, where the commission staff agreed that a proposal to include LGBT protections in the company policy was moot given putative federal protections. The company argued court decisions ensure the federal protections, but no law is in place to that effect. The company's policy also does not explicitly protect LGBT workers.

Human rights
Half of the human rights resolutions were about the Israeli-Palestinian conflict while the rest addressed a variety of mostly long-standing issues.

Conflict zones
Despite the high volume of filings, resolutions about conflict zones got very low votes. The campaign for the Holy Land Principles about fair employment continues to attract little traction; eight votes missed resubmission thresholds and the SEC turned back an attempt by the Holy Land Principles organization for a second type of resolution (following missed resubmission thresholds on the main proposal) asking for a breakdown of Arab and non-Arab employees. More successful was a resolution from the Heartland Initiative at **Merck**, which earned 23.6%. It was a detailed request for information on the company's approach to doing business in "situations of belligerent occupation" – including but not limited to the Middle East.

Other issues
New proposals addressed the *rights of indigenous peoples* and earned the highest support of 35.3% at **Marathon Petroleum**. Companies appeared somewhat willing to negotiate and **Goldman Sachs** prompted a withdrawal after it agreed to report, as did **Morgan Stanley** and **Phillips 66**.

Few other human rights proposals went to votes. The highest score was 29.1% for a request asking **Newmont Mining** to provide a *human rights risk assessment*. But proposals about *technology and privacy* all fell (again) to the ordinary business exclusion, as did resolutions on the *penal system* that included ones about execution drugs. Resolutions seeking corporate affirmation of the *human right to water* all were withdrawn by NorthStar Asset Management after companies agreed to policy changes.

Media
A new resolution asking **Alphabet** and **Facebook** to report on the risks posed by "fake news" touched on a key point of public contention but investors did not appear to think much of it; since votes were 1% or less the proposal failed to earn enough for resubmission.

Sustainable governance
Proponents increasingly have added a corporate governance flavor to their requests that companies reform how they handle a wide range of social and environmental risks, seeking to change the composition of boards, to ensure proper oversight of sustainability, and to report using commonly agreed upon standards.

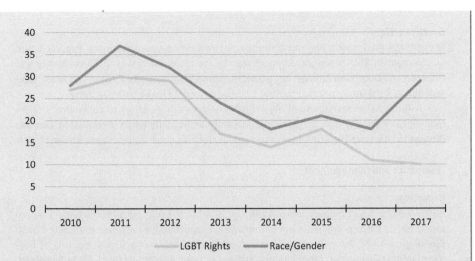

Figure 4.40 Workplace diversity proposals since 2010

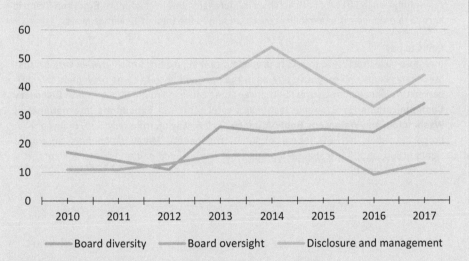

Figure 4.41 Proposals on sustainable governance since 2010

Board diversity
Proposals seeking greater diversity on corporate boards have always attracted lots of support from investors at large, but this year there were spectacularly high scores – 62.8%
at **Cognex** and 84.8% at **Hudson Pacific Properties**, with just eight votes overall and 24
withdrawals after companies agreed to change their board recruitment policies to include
more women and minorities. A new feature introduced this year was the "Rooney Rule"
idea borrowed from the National Football League, that at least one candidate should be a
woman or minority. Also new was a focus by the UAW Retirees' Medical Benefits Trust on
smaller companies in the Midwest.

Board oversight

Proponents filed about the same number of resolutions seeking more explicit board involvement in ESG oversight. Support was in the teens for resubmitted resolutions to **Chevron** and **Dominion Energy**, but activists logged what they see as a big win when **ExxonMobil** elected atmospheric scientist Dr. Susan Avery to its board in January.

Trillium Asset Management also reports success in its effort to concentrate pharmaceutical company boards' attention on safety and quality when it convinced **Zimmer Biomet** to add more explicit board responsibility for this issue and increase its disclosure.

Disclosure and management

Reporting

Sustainability reporting proposals peaked in 2014 but the number of votes has not fallen precipitously since proponents are withdrawing proportionally far fewer than in the past. (See Figure 4.42.) Votes were again substantial and there was a 52.1% majority at **Pioneer Natural Resources**, where its disclosure lags peers, followed by 44.6% at **Middleby**. While resolutions asked for more reporting on many social and environmental issues, the most common requests were about climate change. In a notable withdrawal, after annual resolutions since 2011 that attracted ever-increasing levels of support, **Emerson Electric** agreed to produce a sustainability report, adding to the total of 12 withdrawals.

Links to pay

Investors gave mostly low marks to proposals seeking explicit links between various sustainability issues and executive pay, as in the past and despite some movement by companies to adopt such measures. Still, three votes came in around 20% or more: **Discovery Communications** (19%, double last year's vote), 21.8% at **Expeditor's International of Washington**, and **Walgreens Boots Alliance** (23.1%, way up from only 5.7% last year.) Yet proposals asking for ESG links from some proponents – Mercy for Animals, an animal rights group, and the Heartland Initiative that has focused on the Arab-Israeli conflict – each earned less than 5%.

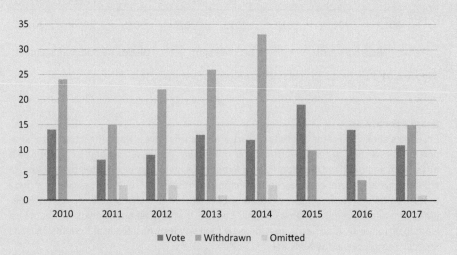

Figure 4.42 Sustainability reporting resolutions since 2010

Proxy voting

The decision by mutual fund giant **BlackRock** to support at least some climate change resolutions proved to be a game changer this year and will substantially affect votes in the future, shifting the landscape dramatically. BlackRock's move came after proponents asked it and a handful of other asset managers to stop voting in lockstep with management, as they have until now. Nonetheless, three other votes were less than 10% this year. An additional new wrinkle at BlackRock came in a proposal about supporting LGBT non-discrimination proposals; Trillium withdrew after the fund agreed to address the subject as part of its discussions about human capital management with its portfolio companies.

Fair finance

Just one resolution about ethics and lending occurred in 2017 – a proposal to **Wells Fargo** asking for a report on the "root causes" behind its business practices that prompted regulatory scrutiny last year. It earned 21.9%.

Conservatives

Political conservatives – mostly the National Center for Public Policy Research (NCPPR), a Washington, DC-based group – kept up efforts to recruit companies to adopt right-wing ideas. But NCPPR received no more affirmation than in the past from investors, with most proposals omitted and votes below 3% for those that made it onto proxy statements. New this year were two ideas – that companies face risks from advertising in the mainstream media given its putatively inherent bias, and that corporate support for LGBT rights violates religious freedom rights. The SEC said both were ordinary business affairs and blocked any votes.

About Si2

The Sustainable Investments Institute (Si2) is a nonprofit organization which helps its institutional investor subscribers make informed, independent voting decisions on social

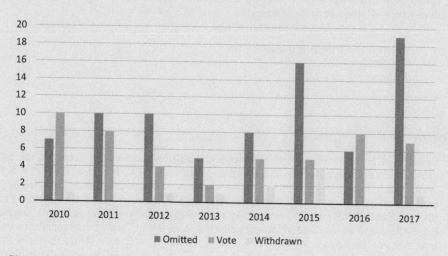

Figure 4.43 Conservative proposals filed since 2010

and environmental shareholder proposals. Si2 also researches related efforts to influence corporate policies, explaining what investor reformers want and how companies respond. Primary support comes from annual fees paid by the largest US college and university endowments and the largest North American pension funds. Si2 also has received significant grants from the Investor Responsibility Research Center Institute.

For this report, Si2 is grateful for the generous cooperation of shareholder proponents, especially for their explanations about what happened when resolutions did not go to votes. This report aims to provide a compilation of all social policy shareholder activism for the record, alongside the more visible votes and efforts by companies to challenge the admissibility of proposals at the Securities and Exchange Commission. Such information provides a critical measure of shareholder "success" but negotiations often occur privately. Valuable editing from Carolyn Mathiasen improved this report.

Discussion questions

1) Discuss:

    a   Ways that integration-based ESG investing might be additive to risk management (LO1)
    b   Ways that integration-based strategy might enable an investor to recognize idiosyncratic risks within the portfolio (LO1)

2) Develop and discuss an impact-based ESG investing set of criteria for an investor who manages a portfolio of public equities, who wants to reduce the carbon footprint. Assume that the investor has a viewpoint that companies that are negatively affecting climate change will suffer financial performance over the long term because of an aware consumer mindset, a depletion of resources, regulation, and operational accidents that might harm the environment and then be negatively affected by stock price. (LO3)

3) Assume the role of an activist investor, representing a Hedge Fund with a 15% equity stake in XYZ Corporation, who can influence XYZ Corporation as a Board of Director and stakeholder. How might you engage with XYZ Corporation? Provide an environmental, social, and governance-related example of engagement-based ESG investing. (LO4)

4) List the pros and cons of the four common ESG integration methods in the context of:

    a   Developed and emerging markets (LO6)
    b   Asset classes (LO6)
    c   Investment sectors (LO6)

Notes

1 Based on a presentation entitled "Impact Investing" delivered by the author at the Social Ethics & Entrepreneurship (SEE) Conference, Washington DC, March 4, 2018. The author would like to express appreciation and acknowledge the benefit of insightful conversations with numerous authorities including Matthew Bishop (Rockefeller Foundation), Robert Eccles (Oxford), Edward Freeman (University of Virginia), Robert Gertner (Chicago Booth), Stephanie Gripne (Impact Finance Center), Meeta Kothare (University of Texas, Social Innovation Initiative), Susan MacCormac (Morrison & Foerster), William F. McCalpin (Athena), Nancy Pfund (DBL Partners), Fran Seegull (The U.S. Impact Investing Alliance), Brian Trelstad (Bridges Fund Management), Matthew Weatherley-White (Caprock).

2   The term was coined in 2007 at a Rockefeller Foundation convening. Since the 1990s there had been an increased enthusiasm around the idea of using for-profit mechanisms to address social needs and market failures. *Impact Investing*, Antony Bugg-Levine, Jed Emerson, 2011.

3   By contrast much of finance today is "post modern" financial engineering paper shuffling, which impacts the real economy, but often in a disintermediated, knock-on, and unintended manner, which can lead to negative impacts as highlighted by figures ranging from Warren Buffett to Pope Francis: www.bloomberg.com/news/articles/2018-05-17/pope-goes-off-on-cds-market-calls-derivatives-ticking-time-bomb

4   For example see Khan, Mozaffar N., George Serafeim, and Aaron Yoon. "Corporate Sustainability: First Evidence on Materiality." Harvard Business School Working Paper, No. 15–073, March 2015; and "How ESG Affects Equity Valuation, Risk and Performance", MSCI 2018: www.msci.com/www/research-paper/foundations-of-esg-investing/0795306949

5   Unpacking the Impact in Impact Investing, Paul Brest and Kelly Born, Stanford Social Innovation Review (SSIR), August 14, 2013: https://ssir.org/articles/entry/unpacking_the_impact_in_impact_investing

6   Hanson, Dan, ESG Investing in Graham & Doddsville (Summer 2013). *Journal of Applied Corporate Finance*, Vol. 25, Issue 3, pp. 20–31, 2013. Available at SSRN: https://ssrn.com/abstract=2371473 or http://dx.doi.org/10.1111/jacf.12024

7   Prahalad, C. K. *The Fortune at the Bottom of the Pyramid: Eradicating Poverty through Profits*. Upper Saddle River, N.J. :Wharton School Pub., 2010.

8   GIIN 2017 Annual Impact Investor Survey: https://thegiin.org/assets/2017%20Survey%201%20Pager.pdf

9   "The "Science" and "Art" of High Quality Investing", Dan Hanson, Rohan Dhanuka, *Journal of Applied Corporate Finance*, Spring 2015: https://irrcinstitute.org/reports/the-science-and-art-of-high-quality-investing/

10 John Doerr, *Measure What Matters: How Bono, the Gates Foundation, and Google Rock the World with OKRs* (Portfolio/Penguin 2018).

11 John Doerr, *Measure What Matters: How Bono, the Gates Foundation, and Google Rock the World with OKRs* (Portfolio/Penguin 2018), page 50.

12 G8 Social Impact Investment Task Force, "Measuring Impact," 2014, page 16: www.socialimpactinvestment.org/reports/Measuring%20Impact%20WG%20paper%20FINAL.pdf

13 The Impact Management Project has developed *Investor's Impact Matrix*: www.impactmanagementproject.com/

14 Why IRIS?, Stanford Social Innovation Review (SSIR), 2012 https://ssir.org/articles/entry/why_iris; https://iris.thegiin.org/

15 A Short Guide to Impact Investing, The Case Foundation: https://casefoundation.org/resource/short-guide-impact-investing/

16 GRI: www.globalreporting.org/

17 KPIs and ESG "scores" must be used with care. In some cases disclosures and metrics can have the opposite of the intended outcome – for example, research indicates that a greater number of CSR policies predicts both higher (better) ESG scores yet higher (worse) future negative controversies: "A Pitfall in Ethical Investing: ESG Disclosures Reflect Vulnerabilities, Not Virtues", Gerald T. Garvey, Joshua Kazdin, Ryan LaFond, Joanna Nash and Hussein Safa, *The Journal of Investment Management* (*JOIM*), Volume 15, Number 2, 2017.

18 Putting the 'S' in ESG: Measuring Human Rights Performance for Investors, NYU Stern Center for Business and Human Rights, 2017: www.stern.nyu.edu/experience-stern/global/putting-s-esg-measuring-human-rights-performance-investors

19 Warren Buffett comment at 2018 Berkshire Hathaway annual meeting: www.valuewalk.com/wp-content/uploads/2018/05/Adam-Blum-notes-from-2018-Berkshire-Hathaway-annual-meeting-May-5-2018.pdf

20 Ocean Tomo, *Ocean Tomo's Intangible Asset Market Value Study*, September 2017.

21 The Capitalist's Dilemma, Clayton M. Christensen and Derek van Bever, *Harvard Business Review*, June 2014.

22 Financial Crises and the Evolution of Capitalism: The Crash of '87: What Does It Mean? Hyman P. Minsky Ph.D. https://digitalcommons.bard.edu/cgi/viewcontent.cgi?article=1462&context=hm_archive

23 An encouraging vision of a path forward to a more sustainable financial markets ecosystem and the potential leadership role for asset owners to drive long-term thinking, was provided by pension expert Keith Ambachtsheer at the request of UK's ShareAction in his "Gateways" lecture to the House of Parliament. *The Future of Pension Management: Integrating Design, Governance, and Investing*, Keith P. Ambachtsheer, 2016, p. 3–10.

24 Ford Foundation Is an Unlikely Convert to 'Impact' Investing, James B. Stewart, April 13, 2017 www.nytimes.com/2017/04/13/business/ford-foundation-mission-investment.html

25 Numerous industry and academic initiatives, including the likes of The GIIN/IRIS, iPar, SASB, GRI, IIRC. See Supplemental Resources.

26 Hanson, Dan, ESG Investing in Graham & Doddsville (Summer 2013). Journal of Applied Corporate Finance, Vol. 25, Issue 3, pp. 20–31, 2013. Available at SSRN: https://ssrn.com/abstract=2371473 or http://dx.doi.org/10.1111/jacf.12024

27 Milton Friedman, "The Social Responsibility of Business Is to Increase Its Profits", *The New York Times Magazine*, September 13, 1970

28 Social license to operate is not limited to actions taken by judges or lawmakers. Market accountability outside of governmental action is a bit of a salve or counterpoint to Reich's view that

there is no free market in nature. The free market is really a set of rules created and enforced by government. Elected officials, agency heads, and judges make the rules. . . . The real issue is who the rules benefit, who they hurt, and who has the most influence over making them.

Economics in Wonderland, Robert Reich (Fantagraphics Books, 2017)

References

Ansar, Antif, Ben Caldecott, and James Tilbury. "Stranded Assets and the Fossil Fuel Divestment Campaign: What Does Divestment Mean for the Valuation of Fossil Fuel Assets?" In *Stranded Assets Programme, University of Oxford, Smith School of Enterprise and the Environment*, 2013. http://smithschool.ox.ac.uk/publications/reports/SAP-divestment-report-final.pdf.

Becht, M., J. Franks, C. Mayer, and S. Rossi. "Returns to Shareholder Activism: Evidence from a Clinical Study of the Hermes UK Focus Fund." *Review of Financial Studies* 23 (2010): 3093–129.

Caplan, L., J. S. Griswold, W. F. Jarvis, and I. Commonfund. "From SRI to ESG: The Changing World of Responsible Investing." 2013. https://files.eric.ed.gov/fulltext/ED559300.pdf

Eurosif. *European SRI Study*. Brussels: Eurosif, 2014.

Eurosif. *European SRI Study*. Brussels: Eurosif, 2016.

Global Health Observatory Indicator. " Global Health Observatory." 2017. http://who.int/gho/en/.

Global Sustainable Investment Review. "2016 Global Sustainable Investment Review." 2017. www.gsi-alliance.org/wp-content/uploads/2017/03/GSIR_Review2016.F.pdf.

Hoepner, Andreas G. F., Ioannis Oikonomou, Zacharias Sautner, Laura T. Starks, and Xiaoyan Zhou. "ESG Shareholder Engagement and Downside Risk." (2016).

Keating, Giles, and Stefano Natella. "Credit Suisse Global Investment Returns Yearbook 2015." *Credit Suisse*, 2015.

Lokuwaduge, Chitra Sriyani De Silva, and Kumudini Heenetigala. *Integrating Environmental, Social and Governance (ESG) Disclosure for a Sustainable Development: An Australian Study*. Provider: John Wiley & Sons, Ltd, 2017. http://dx.doi.org/10.1002/bse.192710.1002/bse.1927

Mahn, K. D. "The Impact of Sustainable Investment Strategies." *Journal of Investing* 25, no. 2 (2016): 96–102.

Martirosyan, E., and T. Vashakmadze. "Introducing Stakeholder-Based Frameworks for Post-Merger Integration (PMI) Success." *Journal of Modern Accounting and Auditing* 9, no. 10 (2013): 1376–81.

"MSCI Momentum Indexes Methodology." *MSCI, Inc.*, September 2014. www.msci.com/eqb/meth odology/meth_docs/MSCI_Momentum_Indexes_Methodology_Sep2014.pdf.

Piani, V., and J. Gond. "Facilitating Investor Engagement on ESG Issues: The PRI Initiative in Action." *Rotman International Journal of Pension Management* 7, no. 1 (2014): 14–22. doi:10.3138/ripjm.7.1.14

Ralph, Oliver. "Insurers Join Pension Plans in Filtering Out Tobacco Stocks." *The Financial Times*, 2017.

Reich, Robert B. *Economics in Wonderland: A Cartoon Guide to a Political World Gone Mad and Mean*. Seattle, WA: Fantagraphics Books, 2017.

Schroders. "An Overview of the Different Sustainable Investment Activities and Terms Is Provided in Our Report: Understanding Sustainable Investment and ESG Terms." *Schroders*, 2017. www.schroders.com/getfunddocument?oid=1.9.2760595. Accessed May 19, 2018.

van Duuren, E., A. Plantinga, and B. Scholtens. "ESG Integration and the Investment Management Process: Fundamental Investing Reinvented." *Journal of Business Ethics* 138, no. 3 (2016): 525–33. doi:http://dx.doi.org.ezproxy.liberty.edu/10.1007/s10551-015-2610-8

Chapter 5

The current role of ESG investing in portfolio management

After this chapter, readers should have a comprehensive understanding of the current level of incorporation in ESG investment strategies.

Learning objectives

- Evaluate current ESG investment trends within different markets, asset classes, and investment sectors
- Summarize the role of ESG investments within the context of developed and emerging market investment portfolios
- Theorize about the potential future for ESG investments within:

    ○ Developed markets
    ○ Emerging markets
    ○ Asset classes

- Analyze investor methods used to incorporate ESG investments into major asset classes

Introduction

As discussed in previous chapters, the incorporation of ESG factors within portfolio construction, whether for a social impact, in pursuit of alpha, or as a part of a policy mandate, has been largely affected by geographical location of a company or a company's revenue creation areas, referenced herein as the region. This incorporation of ESG factors includes impact investing, sustainability-themed investing, positive/best-in-class screening, corporate engagement and shareholder action, norms-based screening, traditional ESG integration, and negative/exclusionary screening. Below is Table 5.1 detailing the growth of ESG-integrated assets by region from 2012 to 2016.

The above chart demonstrates clearly how Europe has dominated the sustainable investing realm for the better part of the last decade in terms of total sustainable assets invested. However, it is important to note the enormous growth in regions like Australia/New Zealand, the United States, and Canada. When examining integration levels across regions, one should compare not only total assets under management, but also, more importantly, proportion of ESG investments relative to total managed assets. Table 5.2 compares the growth of socially responsible investments across regions from 2012 to 2016.

Table 5.1 Growth of ESG assets by region 2012–2014 (in millions)

Region	2012	2014	2016	Compound annual growth rate
Europe	8758	10775	12040	0.057
United States	3740	6572	8723	0.152
Canada	589	729	1086	0.22
Australia/New Zealand	134	148	516	0.864
Asia	40	52	526	0.076
Global	13261	18276	22890	0.119

Source: Data presented by GSIA 2014 and 2016 reports.

Table 5.2 Proportion of socially responsible investments (SRI) relative to total managed assets

Region	2014	2016
Europe	59%	53%
United States	18%	22%
Canada	31%	38%
Australia/New Zealand Asia	17%	51%
Asia		1%
Japan	1%	3%
Global	30%	26%

Source: Data provided by GSIA 2014 and 2016 reports.

This table demonstrates the proportion of all investments incorporating environmental, social, and governance factors as material additions to traditional investment strategies. As the data clearly shows, developed Europe, followed by Canada, has led the industry in integration of ESG factors within portfolio management. Though Europe is the clear leader in Tables 5.1 and 5.2, Canada also shows leadership in both in compound annual growth and in proportion of sustainable investments to total managed assets.

The compound annual growth rate for ESG in each of these regions can be attributed to three key factors:

1 The increase in policy mandates relative to responsible investing
2 The competitive pressure of private companies in the wider market
3 The alleged higher performance inherent in investments touted as "responsible" by independent rating agencies

The next few pages will provide a deeper consideration of how these three factors have contributed to the growth rate of ESG investments.

Responsible investing legislation

Broad approaches to regulation

ESG reporting practices have evolved over the past few decades, as the result of pressure from shareholders and stakeholders who demanded that corporations publicly disclose certain extra-financial information. ESG reporting incorporates, but is not the same as, **corporate social responsibility (CSR) reporting**. CSR reporting focuses on the independent efforts of corporations to address primarily social and environmental issues, either as a part of their annual report or as a separate report. However, while corporate social responsibility focuses on the independent efforts of corporations to address certain external issues (such as Coke's partnership with the World Wildlife Foundation to support polar bear welfare), ESG reporting more holistically addresses the internal practices of a corporation. ESG reporting is intended to include CSR reporting, but also discloses decisions made by corporations that span beyond a corporation's social responsibility, and cover issues relative to the corporation's governance structure and the impact of their business practices on the environment. ESG reporting is the reporting on all **material** non-financial performance (NFP) factors. Chapter 6 will discuss what information is classified as material vs. non-material. Because disclosing material ESG-related information is for the most part not enforced at a government level, corporations responded to investor demands for disclosure in a variety of ways. This disparity results in a lack of consistency when it comes to corporate coverage, format, standards, third-party verification, and frequency of updates of ESG-related information.

Non-governmental organization initiatives

To address this, organizations such as the Global Reporting Initiative (GRI), an independent non-governmental organization, have begun to standardize the format and content of ESG reporting. The Organization for Economic Co-operation and Development (OECD) Guidelines for Multi-national Enterprises and the International Integrated Reporting Committee (IIRC) also partner with businesses to provide recommendations to multinational enterprises on business ethics and develop a standard approach to disclosing material financial and extra-financial information (Lu, 2016). The IIRC in particular has been an advocate for integrating traditional and ESG reporting standards and presented a framework for the integration of material financial and extra-financial information to a global audience in 2016, attempting to merge conventional reporting standards with ESG reporting (Mervelskemper, 2016). These approaches have been adopted by a variety of organizations, from government entities to stock exchanges.

Stock exchanges

It has become increasingly common for stock exchanges to regulate the disclosure or reporting of standardized responsible investing metrics. In this practice, regulation can be broken down into three levels: mandatory reporting, mandatory disclosure, and recommended best practices. Mandatory reporting, as present in France, Denmark, India, South Africa, and Malaysia, unequivocally requires the disclosure of a minimum amount of information relevant to responsible investing which every company must disclose. These disclosures are made using a reporting format handed down by the governing authority. The next level down from mandatory reporting is mandatory disclosure, often referred to as the "comply or explain" approach. In this approach, the regulator (stock exchange or government) has set disclosure regulations but offers greater flexibility for the method in which that information is conveyed. In other words, firms have the option under "mandatory disclosure" to provide reasons why it deviates from the required disclosure standards. HKEx, the Hong Kong Stock Exchange, for example, utilizes "mandatory disclosure" standards, and has stated that issuers must consider "their own individual circumstances, the size and complexity of their operations, and the nature of the risks and challenges they face" (Lu, 2016). The third approach, labeled "recommended best practices" is issued by governments or stock exchanges and encourages (but does not require) issuers to disclose certain material non-financial information. This approach is increasingly becoming used as transitionary requirements as firms, stock exchanges, and governments respond to the pressure for more mandatory standards.

Typology of different approaches to regulation

In a study conducted by a partnership with the Principles for Responsible Investing (PRI) and MSCI, Inc., existing regulations on ESG information disclosure were broken into three different types:

1   Pension fund regulations
2   Stewardship codes
3   Corporate disclosures

Pension fund regulations

According to the PRI and MSCI, these are regulations that are established by asset owners demanding ESG incorporation into investment strategies. These demands are then collected and codified into mandates. These types of regulations typically appear either as disclosure requirements (included in a Statement of Investment Principles, Investment Policy Statement, or something thereof), or as regulations targeting state-owned asset owners (e.g. Sovereign Wealth Funds or Public Pension Funds).

Stewardship codes

Stewardship codes are designed to further motivate investors towards engagement with investee companies, aimed towards promoting long-term value creation strategies. This concept has only developed recently, with the first formalized stewardship code developed in 2012 in the United Kingdom. However, the concept was built upon a long history of investor voting and engagement with corporations (see Chapter 2 for a history of corporate engagement).

Corporate disclosures

Corporate disclosures govern the data which corporations must provide on ESG risks and opportunities. These include each of the approaches to ESG reporting regulations referenced above: mandatory reporting, mandatory disclosure, and "recommended best practices." They vary in the issues that they focus on: some regulations focus on a single issue related to ESG factors, while other regulations aim to cover a broader range of a corporation's actions. In this, some regulations specify certain indicators and calculation methodologies, while others provide a general principle which firms are encouraged to incorporate.

CASE STUDY 5A: SASB

Sonya Hetrick, Sector Analyst

Measuring what matters

The Sustainability Accounting Standards Board (SASB) was established in 2011 to address the lack of a market standard for capturing and reporting performance on material environmental, social, and governance (ESG) factors. By fostering consistent, comparable, high-quality disclosure of material sustainability information, the SASB aims to help companies manage key ESG issues more effectively, investors to better understand their impact on risk and return, and markets to efficiently incorporate them into the prices of securities.

The SASB standard-setting process

Although sustainability is often defined in broad macroeconomic terms – e.g., population growth, resource constraints, technological innovation, and globalization – its impacts on a specific organization are microeconomic in nature. For instance, the material business risks related to climate change will vary considerably from one industry to another. An apparel company will want to focus on its ability to source cotton, a crop that is vulnerable to shifting weather patterns; a *commercial bank will be more concerned about the riskiness of its loan portfolio* as carbon-intensive borrowers' own risk exposures threaten their ability to repay or refinance; and an *automaker will more closely manage its development of alternative-fuel vehicles* in response to shifting consumer demand.

Thus, the SASB develops and maintains sustainability accounting standards for 77 industries across 11 sectors. Using a rigorous, multi-step process, the SASB surfaces the ESG factors that are most likely to have material impacts on companies in a given industry.[1] Further, it tailors standardized performance metrics for each of these factors to specific industry circumstances by following an iterative approach that is rooted in evidence, shaped by market input, open to public comment, and subject to independent oversight.

- **Evidence-based:** The SASB performs extensive research to identify and document existing metrics and practices used to account for performance on each of its industry-specific disclosure topics. Whenever possible, the SASB harmonizes its metrics with existing approaches, thereby minimizing duplicative effort. For example, the SASB standards incorporate approaches from more than 200 organizations, including CDP (formerly the Carbon Disclosure Project), the US Environmental Protection Agency (EPA), the US Occupational Safety and Health Administration (OSHA), the Global Reporting Initiative (GRI), the International Petroleum Industry Environmental Conservation Association (IPIECA), and many others. When high-quality performance metrics do not exist, the SASB develops them through technical research and vetting.
- **Market-informed:** Once the SASB has established baseline performance metrics, it vets their quality by soliciting feedback from industry experts and investment analysts. Such feedback is intended to ensure that the SASB standards follow well-established best practices wherever possible and yield data and other information that is decision-useful for investors while also being cost-effective for companies to produce. For example, corporate feedback may help the SASB refine the technical protocol underlying a metric so that it is better suited for incorporation into a robust system of internal control. Likewise, an analyst might help the SASB ensure a metric is verifiable, in accordance with commonly used attestation standards. As an example, in response to a proposed metric for the food retailers and distributors industry, a SASB stakeholder suggested that "to report on the total addressable market would be very difficult as that figure can be very subjective." As a result, SASB modified the metric to address the "total revenue" from certain product lines.
- **Public comment periods:** Before the SASB votes to approve its standards, it welcomes the public to offer feedback on an "exposure draft," typically for a period of 90 days. The SASB encourages public comment to focus on several key outcomes, including the extent to which the proposed performance metrics adhere to the SASB's established Criteria for Accounting Metrics: 1) fair representation, 2) useful, 3) applicable, 4) comparable, 5) complete, 6) verifiable, 7) aligned, 8) neutral, 9) distributive.[2] (See Figure 5.1.)

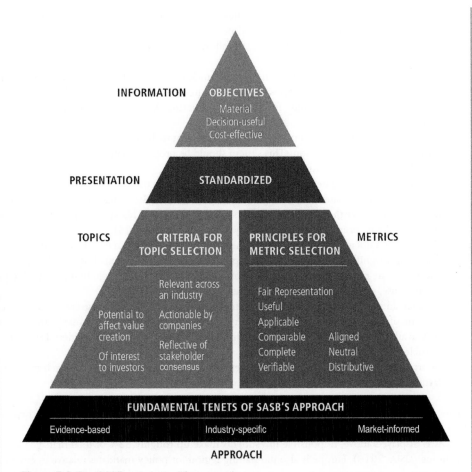

Figure 5.1 The SASB conceptual framework

- **Independent oversight:** Upon completion of the public comment period, the nine members of the SASB undertake a systematic, independent evaluation of a variety of inputs, including their staff's evidence-based research, stakeholder consultation, proposed standards, bases for conclusion, and public comment. In addition to reviewing this material, the SASB judges all standards against the essential concepts of sustainability accounting established in its Conceptual Framework. Finally, the SASB votes on whether to ratify the proposed standards in accordance with its Rules of Procedure.[3]

5.1 ESG investing in developed markets

Responsible investing in Europe

On December 14, 2016, the Institutions for Occupational Retirement Provision (IORP II) Directive were entered in the Official Journal of the European Union, requiring occupational pension providers to evaluate ESG risks and opportunities, and disclose such information to current and prospective scheme members. All occupational pension funds with more than 100 members are subject to this directive, which encompasses the following clauses:

1   Invest in accordance with the Prudent Person Principle. The Directive clarifies that this means acting in the best long-term interests of their members as a whole, and that the Prudent Person Principle does not preclude funds from considering the impact of their investments on ESG factors (Article 19).

2   Hold an effective, transparent system of governance that includes consideration of ESG factors relating to investment decisions. This system should be proportionate to the nature, scale, and complexity of the IORP (Article 21).

3   Establish a risk management function and procedures to identify, monitor, manage, and report risks. ESG risks associated with the investment portfolio and its management are included in the list of risks that the risk management system must cover. This system should be proportionate to the nature, scale, and complexity of the IORP (Article 25).

4   Carry out and document their own risk assessment at least every three years, or without delay following a significant change in the risk profile. This risk assessment should include, where ESG factors are considered, an assessment of new or emerging risks including climate change, resource use, social risks, and stranded assets (Article 28).

5   Produce and review a Statement of Investment Policy Principles at least every three years, or immediately following significant changes to investment policy. This must be made publicly available and explain whether and how the investment policy considers ESG factors (Article 30).

6   Inform prospective scheme members whether and how the investment approach takes ESG factors into account (Article 41).

These directives are both reflective of the growing trend in Europe towards ESG factor incorporation, and predictive of the future levels of ESG investing in Europe.

As is displayed above, responsible investments make up roughly 53% of total managed assets in Europe (GSIA, 2016). Europe is also the leading region for policy mandates relative to environmental, social, and governance disclosure and integration. Figure 5.2 shows the breakdown of how responsible investing is distributed across asset classes in Europe and Canada.

The reader should note the overweight towards sustainable fixed income products within developed Europe as it may pave the way for increased governmental engagement with ESG factors. In mid-December 2016, Poland issued the first government green bond, using a medium term note documentation. This was somewhat of a surprising move, given the country's historic dependence on coal as a major part of its industry. Nevertheless, Poland retained the support of Sustainalytics, a well-respected sustainability research and analysis firm, to verify the green credentials of the five-year euro benchmark bond (Furness, 2016). In March of 2017, the French government issued its first "green bond," and mandated that a large part of the proceeds would be used for tax credits. Demand for the bond far exceeded expectations and was oversubscribed by €23 billion. Stephanie Sfakianos, head of sustainable capital markets at BNP Paribas, made this comment, "There's a lot more private finance in infrastructure now and this deal, which supports subsidies given by the government rather than funding direct public investments in these projects is a good template for the future." Sean Kidney, CEO of the Climate Bonds Initiative, was quoted saying he expects other sovereigns to follow the French example, citing other governments like Nigeria, Morocco, Sweden, and possibly Canada, as having plans for green bonds being issued or in the pipeline (Meager, 2017).

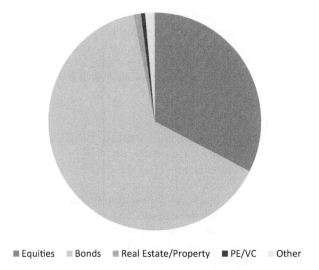

■ Equities   ■ Bonds   ■ Real Estate/Property   ■ PE/VC   ▢ Other

Figure 5.2 SRI asset allocation in Canada and Europe (GSIA, 2017)

Note: Other includes alternatives/hedge funds, monetary deposits, commodities, and infrastructure

Note: Percentages are out of total assets under management in all geographical regions measured by the Global Sustainability Initiative Association, 2016 biennial report

As for equities, Europe currently distributes its ESG investments in the following way:

Table 5.3 2016 distributions of SRI and ESG strategies in Europe (GSIA, 2017)

Strategy	$ (in millions)	(in percentage)
Impact/community investing	107.14	0
Sustainability-themed investing	158.55	1
Positive/best-in-class screening	537.66	2
Norms-based screening	5545.53	22
Corporate engagement and shareholder action	4650.94	19
ESG integration	2882.58	12
Negative/exclusionary screening	11056.93	44
Total (in billions)	24939.33	100

Between 2014 and 2016, ESG equities saw a significant decrease (from 39% in 2014 to 32% in 2016), proportional to a notable rise in ESG bonds (from 49% to 64.4%). This is attributable to the recent popularity of green bonds as a response to increasing environmental concerns. This may also be attributable to the higher yields offered through green bonds as opposed to general obligation government bonds in Europe during the same time period. Integration of ESG strategies into real estate/property remained a small, as did private equity (PE) and venture capital (VC) integration. The largest ESG strategy employed remains negative and exclusionary screening (see Chapter 3 for a more detailed description of the differences between ESG implementation methodology). Norms-based screening trails negative/exclusionary screening as the second most popular ESG implementation method, closely followed by corporate engagement and shareholder action (GSIA, 2017). Though impact/community investing represents only 0.4% of total equity investments, it was the fastest growing strategy (growing 385% since 2014). This growth was consistent with the impact/community investing strategy growth in other regions, referred to below. Retail integration rose from 3% to 22% between 2014 and 2016, though institutional investing continued to dominate the field.

Responsible investing in the United States

Legislation regarding ESG investing in the United States has become increasingly prevalent since the 1990s. This legislation was summed up in a report issued by the Department of Labor in 2015 regarding economically targeted investments (ETIs) and ESG factors. In the new guidance report, the United States Department of Labor (DoL) first defined ESG strategies as any investment that is selected in part for its collateral benefits, apart from investment returns (Department of Labor, 2015). Second, the Department of Labor stated that fiduciaries should not be discouraged from integrating ESG investments into portfolios, as long as the investments were otherwise an appropriate investment in terms of risk levels and expected rate of return (Department of Labor, 2015). Investors commonly refer to this ruling as the "all things being equal" test (Department of Labor, 2015). Similar to legislation in Europe, establishing ESG investing as part of the fiduciary duty of institutional investors was a huge motivator for institutions to increase their integration of ESG factors into investment policies. As such, institutional investing still dominated the ESG space (as opposed to retail investing) through 2016. At the beginning of 2016, ESG investing represented 22% of the total assets under professional management in the United States, rising from 17.9% in 2014.

Of the institutional investors integrating ESG factors into portfolio management, 85% cite client demand as the key factor (GSIA, 2017). The fastest growing ESG methodology in the United States, echoing Europe, was impact investing, though it only represented 1% of total ESG assets under professional management. While in Europe negative/exclusionary screening was by far the most popular ESG strategy (reflected by its assets under management percentage), in the United States the most popular ESG investment method was ESG integration, representing 56% or $10.37 billion in assets by the end of 2016. This is especially significant, as it demonstrates the shift in the United States from corporate engagement and shareholder action (which represented 50.5% of ESG assets in 2014, but only 30.6% of ESG assets in 2016) to ESG integration. This may also reflect the latent effectiveness of corporate engagement and shareholder action, as the ultimate effect of shareholder engagement should naturally be a corporate shift towards the actual implementation of ESG factors within portfolio strategy. To that end, the United States seems to be increasingly willing to accept ESG integration as a key factor for alpha generation within portfolio construction, beyond the more qualitative social or environmental benefits. It is important for institutional investors to acknowledge that as long as a majority of clients demand integration of ESG factors within portfolio management, there is a place for ESG beyond just alpha generation.

As expressed by the Department of Labor's 2015 ruling on ESG factors and ETIs (referenced above), there is a fiduciary duty to integrate these factors, "all things being equal." This "all things being equal" is somewhat of an artificial test, as it implies that ESG factors are a neutral factor: neither adding to the portfolio return positively or negatively. However, many studies have demonstrated the effectiveness of ESG strategies at generating alpha and mitigating risk, especially in emerging markets and sectors and regions where information is not readily prevalent. In those sectors, as well as in developed markets, it has become obvious that all things are not equal when integrating ESG factors into portfolio construction: on the contrary, ESG factors add value that are not attainable without the consideration of ESG information. In the United States, institutional investors are being exposed to the realization that the market has begun valuing ESG metrics, affecting the stock price as both retail investors and institutional investors use the increasing transparency of information (generated by third-party analysts such as MSCI Inc., Sustainalytics, Bloomberg, Thomson Reuters, etc.) to measure ESG risk premia and gain greater insight into the return distribution of their investments. The GSIA 2016 report states,

> Several factors are driving the growth in ESG assets held by money managers. These include: market penetration of SRI products, the development of new products that incorporate ESG criteria, and the incorporation of ESG criteria by numerous large asset managers across wider portions of their holdings. Much of this activity is coming to light because of increased disclosures by signatories to the Principles for Responsible Investment.
>
> (GSIA 2017)

These increased disclosures are encouraged not only by the Principles for Responsible Investing supported by the UN, but also by the positive acceptance by shareholders and by the increasing quality of the data being provided by third-party distributors. As the quality and transparency of the data becomes greater, it is reasonable to assume that the subsequent investments will have greater visibility into the return distribution of the asset, and thus generate higher alpha.

The above-referenced table shows how each ESG strategy is represented across regions. The percentages represent the proportion of total assets in each strategy that are represented in each region. It is interesting to note that the United States makes up at least one-fifth of each of these strategy exposures globally, except for norms-based screening (see Chapter 4 for an overview of the tenants of exclusion-based screening). In contrast, European investments account for 89.3% of norms-based screening. Responsible investing in the United States makes up approximately 22% of total assets under management, as of 2016.

Table 5.4 Representation of ESG strategies across regions (2016) (GSIA, 2017)

Strategy	Europe	United States	Canada	Australia/ New Zealand	Asia	Japan
Negative/exclusionary screening	74%	24%	2%	0%	0%	0%
ESG integration	28%	56%	10%	5%	0%	1%
Corporate engagement and shareholder action	56%	31%	10%	0%	0%	3%
Norms-based screening	89%	0%	10%	0%	0%	1%
Positive/best-in-class screening	52%	24%	21%	0%	0%	2%
Sustainability-themed investing	48%	22%	20%	5%	2%	3%
Impact/community investing	43%	50%	3%	1%	0%	3%

CASE STUDY 5B: Breckinridge Capital Advisors

Introduction

Breckinridge Capital Advisors is an independent fixed income investment manager with over $30 billion in assets under management. The firm manages US dollar-denominated investment grade bond portfolios. Grounded in a mandate to preserve capital, Breckinridge's investment philosophy is to incrementally improve risk adjusted returns through fully integrated bottom-up credit and ESG research, opportunistic trading and the seasoned judgment of the portfolio management team.

With a particular focus on the long term, Breckinridge's resolve is to invest in responsible bond issuers. Over the last decade, a growing body of research has attested to the merits of analyzing environmental, social, and governance (ESG) factors during the investment process. Breckinridge has invested resources into more fully understanding ESG and integrating ESG analysis into their research. One outcome for the firm was the development of multiple systematic sector frameworks for analyzing all the major corporate and municipal bond sectors. Additionally, the firm's investment team actively engages with bond issuers to deepen their dialogue on traditional credit and ESG issues. Through issuer engagement, Breckinridge seeks to gain deeper understanding of the underlying value and risk profile of each investment opportunity over the long term.

Breckinridge invests across investment-grade fixed income sectors in municipal, corporate, securitized, treasury and government agency bonds. In this piece, Breckinridge speaks to its approach to corporate bond investing.

A foundation of fundamental corporate credit analysis

Breckinridge's emphasis on bottom-up fundamental analysis supports the firm's primary investment mandate of preserving capital and building sustainable sources of income while seeking opportunities to increase total return. Accordingly, Breckinridge credit analysts are committed to mitigating credit risk.

The firm's bottom-up research process begins with an assessment of a company's capital sources and operating trends. The review of capital sources focuses on the assessment of key leverage and liquidity metrics, as they are among the most important indicators of default probability and credit health. The review of operating trends focuses on margins and includes an in-depth free cash flow analysis. Credit analysts also assess the strength of a company's business profile, market position, brand, and reputation. This work is summarized in an internal credit rating that is assigned to each corporate borrower.

Why Breckinridge integrates ESG
The changing face of business

Consumer and investor preferences increasingly validate ESG integration, as stakeholder engagement continues to rise, and consumers increasingly favor brands with strong sustainability practices. An increasing number of management teams recognize sustainability as a strategic imperative. Sustainability is driving product line up, manufacturing improvements and recruitment and retention of talent. From the boardroom to the supply chain, companies are exhibiting a growing recognition of the role of business in society and the value creation associated with that responsibility.

There has been a simultaneous evolution in corporate sustainability reporting, which has increasingly served to inform investors and a broad array of stakeholders with more and better *material* ESG information. In 2017 85% of companies in the S&P 500 issued corporate sustainability reports (CSR).[4]

The changing face of risk

Intangible assets, such as brand, reputation, and intellectual capital, have become a critical component of a company's value. For creditors, fundamental credit research that relies on GAAP accounting alone may fail to identify dormant risks or externalities that could negatively impact these intangible values and consequently credit worthiness over the medium to long term.

Since Breckinridge invests in corporate bonds with maturities up to 20 years, a broader assessment of risk, including ESG, may prove a valuable complement to credit ratings alone. ESG integration helps Breckinridge to establish a "check" or a "second opinion" to public or purely fundamental credit ratings. Although the management of certain ESG issues may not have a *short-term* material impact on the credit profile of the company, the stewardship of extra-financial assets and risks may affect the company's ability to repay its debt over the *long term*.

In response, Breckinridge intensified its resolve to focus on the long term. To gain a more holistic, forward-looking assessment of a company's credit profile, the firm made the decision in 2011 to fully integrate the analysis of ESG issues into the fundamental credit-research process. Breckinridge espouses the materiality of ESG factors and maintains that integrating ESG into investment research can help identify symptoms of idiosyncratic risk and provide a more rigorous and comprehensive evaluation of a borrower's ability to repay over the medium to long term.

ESG impact on ratings and relative value assessments

To fully integrate ESG issues into the investment process, Breckinridge built formal and comprehensive frameworks that combine a quantitative assessment of ESG factors alongside a rigorous review of qualitative ESG considerations to derive a composite sustainability rating. Breckinridge generates its own internal credit ratings, and each credit's sustainability rating informs the analysts' overall credit assessments. Importantly, the ESG credit analysis is documented and fully integrated into each analyst's broader relative value, risk, and credit assessment. Note that ESG is not a separate effort for the firm's research team; ESG is fully embedded into the firm's fundamental credit research effort.

- Quantitative sustainability scores are calculated through the firms' proprietary model, which relies on inputs of raw data and of ratings from ESG research firms and third-party providers. Issuers are scored in the environmental, social, governance, and reputation categories.
- Analysts' qualitative assessments include reviews of company reports discussing key ESG and sustainability initiatives; scans of publicly available information; key findings from engagement calls; and sector-level research and analysis pertaining to material ESG factors.

The output from the analysis is a sustainability rating for each borrower, ranging from S1 (lowest ESG risk) to S4 (highest ESG risk). An S1 rating will upgrade the Breckinridge internal credit rating one notch, for example A+ to AA–. An S4 rating will downgrade the internal credit rating one notch, for example A+ to A. This ratings action impacts valuation and trading decisions made by portfolio managers and traders.

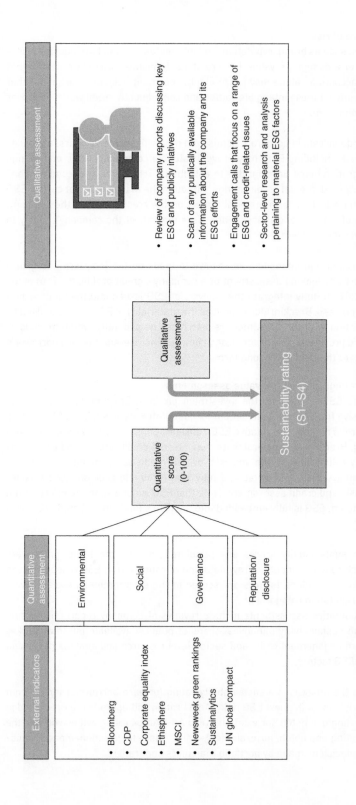

Figure 5.3 ESG integration methodology

Engagement

Knowledge of corporate borrowers is also enhanced through engagement calls, and Breckinridge sees engagement as a critical component of the investment process. The firm's primary engagement objective is to understand the ways issuers are integrating ESG considerations into their strategy and most-important business decisions, the levels of effectiveness of companies' ESG efforts, and the implications of ESG for the issuers' financial performance.

Bondholders play a key role in a firm's capital structure, but – unlike stockholders – bondholders are not provided a formal process such as voting a proxy or filing a resolution to voice their opinion on management. There is no formal venue for bondholders to encourage (for example) issuers to provide transparent reporting on material ESG issues and the management of those risks – especially when issuer disclosure does not satisfy best practices. Breckinridge's formal engagement effort seeks to address this challenge through strategic, direct conversations with management that can benefit both investors and borrowers.

Conclusion

Breckinridge's long-term focus drives forward-looking research, and the firm continuously strives to discover and prioritize the risks and opportunities that will matter most over time. ESG analysis provides a more holistic view by examining policies and practices that are potentially more beneficial to long-term results than to short-term profit.

At the core of their business, Breckinridge is connecting investors and their capital with responsible borrowers to finance essential capital projects and economic growth. As lenders, the firm believes that bond issuers with stronger ESG performance relative to their peers are likely to be better prepared to meet future challenges and to build on new opportunities.

- Strategic significance of ESG
- Quality of ESG management
- Integrated reporting
- Material ESG factors
- Key credit considerations

Figure 5.4 Breckinridge engagement priorities

Responsible investing in Canada

Despite having a smaller market than the United States or Europe, Canada is a major leader in ESG investment practices, both in the institutional and retail space. As of the end of 2016, there were $1.5 trillion in responsible investing assets under management. This represented a 49% increase in the past two years, and increased the representation of responsible investing to 38% of the entire Canadian investment industry (growth from 31% of total Canadian assets under management in 2015). This was especially significant, as (different than in the United States or Europe), personal responsible investing was up 91%. Though pension fund assets remained 75% of growth in the responsible investing industry, this still indicated a significant growth in personal responsible investing. According to the 2016 Canadian Responsible Investment Trends Report, asset managers and owners ranked the following as their top motivators for incorporating ESG factors into investment decisions:

1   To minimize risk over time
2   To improve returns over time
3   To fulfill fiduciary duty

It is imperative to note that this indicates the recognition of Canadian asset managers that ESG investing is not simply as a social statement or an opportunity for a qualitative impact on the environment. Canadian investors have begun to recognize the effect of integrating ESG factors into portfolio management as both a risk-mitigating and alpha-generating tool. According to both the Global Sustainable Investment Review (2016) and the 2016 Canadian Responsible Investment Trends Report, ESG integration has overtaken ESG engagement as the most popular ESG investment strategy. These two strategies are followed by norms-based investment screening. The below chart shows the breakdown of ESG strategies within Canadian asset management, as of 2016:

Figure 5.5 Breakdown of ESG strategies within Canadian asset management (GSIA, 2017)

Note: Figures are in billions

Note: Percentages are out of total assets under management in all geographical regions measured by the Global Sustainability Initiative Association, 2016 biennial report

Starting on January 1, 2016, trustees of all occupational-defined benefit pension plans in Ontario are required to disclose the extent to which environmental, social, and governance factors were incorporated into the pension fund's investment policies and procedures. The policy, under the Pension Benefits Act R.S. 1990 c. P. 8, states:

40. (1) A statement required under subsection 27 (1) of the Act shall contain, as recorded in the records of the administrator, at least . . . a statement that the administrator of the pension plan must establish a statement of investment policies and procedures for the plan that contains, . . . information about whether environmental, social and governance factors are incorporated into

the plan's investment policies and procedures and, if so, how those factors are incorporated. (Law Document, 2015)

This regulation had been pending by Ontario legislators since 2011, was supported by large pension funds such as the Ontario Teachers' Pension Plan (OTPP) and the Ontario Municipal Employees' Retirement System (OMERS). The regulation proved to be a major motivator for pension plans to begin incorporating ESG factors into portfolio strategy (Baert, 2015). This came on the heels of suggestions made by the Financial Stability Board's Task Force on Climate-related Financial Disclosures, which was formed as a response to the Paris climate conference (often referred to as COP 21) in December of 2015. At this conference, Canada joined countries around the world pledging to take actions to limit global warming to below two degrees Celsius above pre-industrial levels. This was particularly significant, as fossil fuels are a major part of the Canadian economy. Following COP 21, Mark Carney (Governor of the Bank of England and former Governor of the Bank of Canada) established the Task Force on Climate-related Financial Disclosures, committed to developing recommendations on standardizing the public information that disclosed by corporations regarding the potential impacts of global warming. This task force, performing similar work to the Sustainable Accounting Standard Board (SASB) in the United States, provided information for investors, lenders, and insurance writers to "appropriately assess and price climate-related risks and opportunities . . . and to develop voluntary, consistent climate-related financial disclosures that would be useful to investors, lenders, and inductance underwriters in understanding material risks." These recommendations were intended to be:

1 Adoptable by all organizations
2 Included in financial filings
3 Designed to solicit decision-useful, forward-looking information on financial impacts
4 Strong focus on risks and opportunities related to transition to lower-carbon economy (TCFD, 2017)

Organizations and task forces such as the Responsible Investing Association and the Task Force on Climate-related Financial Disclosures, have assisted the Canadian investment industry in rapidly providing information and incentivizing the inclusion of responsible investing factors into portfolio management, both on an institutional and retail investment level.

Responsible investing in Asia

Asia has long faced challenges in integrating ESG and responsible investing strategies within their overall assets under management. According to the Global Sustainable Investments Association 2106 report, only $52.1 billion assets under management in Asia (ex Japan) were considered "socially responsible investments." Of that $52.1 billion, ESG integration was the most popular strategy, closely followed by sustainability-themed investing. Approximately $15.9 billion of those sustainable investments are held in Sharia-compliant funds.

However, sustainability-themed investments have begun to gain traction in China, particularly in the face of China's environmental issues. The growing interest in green finance and the reduction of carbon emissions has inspired institutions such as the Institutes of Science and Development, and the Chinese Academy of Sciences. Though access to environmental data is still difficult, organizations such as the Asia Investor Group on Climate Change are attempting to analyze and provide useful data to large institutional investors and smaller retail investors alike.

The above-referenced Asia Investor Group on Climate Change, sponsored by the Investor Group on Climate Change, published a report entitled "Connecting Commodities, Investors, Climate, and the Land: A Toolkit for Institutional Investors." In this report, they established five risk factors which they believed to be integral to the integration of ESG strategies within Asian investments. These five risk factors are:

1   **Operational risk:** Climate change and extreme weather events can jeopardize productivity and result in stranded assets
2   **Regulatory risk:** Unprepared investors may find themselves caught out by regulatory changes
3   **Litigation risk:** Businesses that fail to manage environmental impacts may face litigation, even in the absence of specific environmental regulations
4   **Market risk:** Social and environmental changes can drive price volatility and sourcing constraints
5   **Reputational risk:** Improved transparency and connectivity substantially raise risks to investors seen to be flouting environmental best practices (Asia Investors Group on Climate Change, 2017)

Though these risks are currently applied specifically to the environmental aspect of responsible investing, and the inherent challenges thereof, it could be argued that these risks can easily be broadened and applied to responsible investing overall. As Asia continues to develop its exposure to ESG investing, it is likely that these risks will be increasingly recognized.

According to a 2016 report conducted by CSR Asia, commissioned by the Global Reporting Initiative (GRI) and the Australian Department of Foreign Affairs and Trade (DFAT), established policies and practices exist in the following Asian countries (see Table 5.5):

Table 5.5 Policies and practices established in ASEAN countries

Category	Brunei	Cambodia	Indonesia	Laos	Malaysia	Myanmar	Philippines	Singapore	Thailand	Vietnam
Policy in place			✓	!	✓		✓	✓!	!	✓
Existing Expectations	✓	✓		✓	✓	✓	✓	✓	✓	✓
Incentives to include ESG information			✓		✓					

Source: Data and chart provided by CSR Asia (CSR Asia, 2016)

Policy and regulation: specifically refers to national laws in place in each country, or other forms of mandatory regulation such as stock exchange listing requirements.

Voluntary expectations: refers to reporting and disclosure expectations following non-mandatory guidelines. These could include opportunities to respond to industry authorities or stock exchanges, opportunities to list on sustainability indices, or other guidance or training provided by civil society.

Government incentives: refers to opportunities and benefits subsidized by governments to encourage corporate reporting and disclosure of extra-financial criteria (CSR Asia, 2016).

As far as policy and regulation standards go, Indonesia, Malaysia, the Philippines, Singapore, and Vietnam are the only countries to currently have such legislation established. Bursa Malaysia is currently the only exchange with mandatory CSR disclosures, though the Singapore Exchange is working to instigate mandatory sustainability reporting for all listed companies. Both the Singapore Exchange and the Bursa Malaysia operate on a "comply or explain" basis (discussed above). The Philippines and Thailand stock exchanges likewise have integrated ESG-related legislation within the past few years. The Corporate Governance Guidelines for Listed Companies (PSE CG Guidelines) have implemented an "adopt or explain" basis focused on governance, and the Thailand stock exchange have mandated annual reports for the disclosure of additional information (referred to as Form 56-1) (CSR Asia, 2016). More attention is being drawn to sustainability and sustainable disclosure mandates through sustainability indices such as the Sustainability Index Indonesia Stock Exchange, the FTSE4Good ASEAN 5 Index, and the Channel NewsAsia Sustainability Ranking. According to the GSIA and the CSR Asia report, 58% of ASEAN companies studied are reporting ESG criteria, and 19% of ASEAN companies are applying Global Reporting Initiative Guidelines for sustainable disclosures.

Most sustainable-rating agencies and annual reports on sustainability break out Japan as separate from the rest of Asia, as Japan makes up such a large portion of sustainable assets under management (AUM). Japan has been established as the fastest growing region in sustainable investing by the Global Sustainability Initiative (GSI) between 2014 and 2016. They attribute this rapid growth to greater reporting and sustainable investing activity by Japanese institutional asset owners. The GSIA 2016 annual report also indicated that Japan's primary sustainable investment strategy remains corporate engagement and shareholder action, which indicates that investors can expect continued growth in the sustainable investing options as the trend is being driven primarily by consumer demand (rather than government incentives or legislature).

- Negative/exclusionary screening
- ESG integration
- Corporate engagement and shareholder action
- Norms-based screening
- Positive/best-in-class screening
- Sustainability-themed investing

Figure 5.6 Breakdown of ESG strategies within Japanese asset management (GSIA, 2016)

Note: Figures are in billions

Note: Percentages are out of total assets under management in all geographical regions measured by the Global Sustainability Initiative Association, 2016 biennial report

It is interesting to note also the difference in weightings between ESG investing strategies. Asia ex Japan is dominated almost entirely by sustainability-themed investing, whereas Japan is much more diversified, with higher allocation to norms-based screening.

Responsible investing in Australia/New Zealand

According to the Responsible Investment Association – Australia, 44% of Australia's assets under management are now being invested through some form of responsible investment strategy.

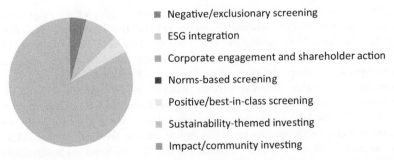

- ■ Negative/exclusionary screening
- ▨ ESG integration
- ■ Corporate engagement and shareholder action
- ■ Norms-based screening
- ▨ Positive/best-in-class screening
- ▨ Sustainability-themed investing
- ■ Impact/community investing

Figure 5.7 Breakdown of ESG strategies within asset management in Asia ex Japan (GSIA, 2016)

Note: Figures are in billions

Note: Percentages are out of total assets under management in all geographical regions measured by the Global Sustainability Initiative Association, 2016 biennial report

- ■ Negative/exclusionary screening
- ▨ ESG integration
- ■ Corporate engagement and shareholder action
- ■ Norms-based screening
- ▨ Positive/best-in-class screening
- ▨ Sustainability-themed investing
- ■ Impact/community investing

Figure 5.8 Breakdown of ESG strategies within asset management in Australia and New Zealand (GSIA, 2017)

Note: Figures are in billions

Note: Percentages are out of total assets under management in all geographical regions measured by the Global Sustainability Initiative Association, 2016 biennial report

Responsible investing in Australia and New Zealand grew 9% from 2015 to 2016, according to the Responsible Investment Association – Australia. This amounted to an increase from $569 billion responsible assets under management in 2015 to $622 billion in 2016. In Australia, as in Europe, positive and negative screening remain the most popular ESG strategies.

Responsible Investment Association – Australia divides responsible investing into two helpful categories – Broad Responsible Investing and Core Responsible Investing. Broad Responsible Investing includes any integration of ESG factors into portfolio construction. This has been labeled "ESG integration" by other organizations (discussed above) and is popular amongst institutional investors who consider ESG factors to be useful for disclosing and measuring traditionally "non-financial" factors as a part of the overall investment process. Core Responsible Investing is a more targeted form of responsible investing, using ESG factors as the most important set of factors in the investment process. Core Responsible Investing can take the form of impact investing, positive, negative, and norms-based screening, community engagement and shareholder action, and sustainability-themed investing.

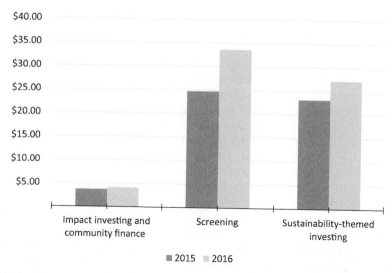

Figure 5.9 Growth of Core Responsible Investing strategies in Australia and New Zealand from 2015 to 2016

Note: Figures are in billions

Source: Responsible Investment Benchmark Report, Australia, 2017.

This breakdown helps to demonstrate that responsible investing in Australia is still dominated by Broad Responsible Investing, utilized most popularly by institutional investors such as pension funds following the ESG integration trends beginning to dominate the industry. However, Figure 5.9 demonstrates the growth of more targeted Core Responsible Investing trends from 2015 to 2016:

Similar to trends in European and Asian Stock Exchanges, the Australian Stock Exchange now requires all listed companies to report on any material exposure to sustainability risks. This was an update to their Corporate Governance Guidelines. The New Zealand Exchange likewise has begun to consider implementing a "comply or explain" policy similar to policies in Asian stock exchanges for listed companies around ESG issues (GSIA, 2016).

5.2 ESG investing in emerging markets

Responsible investing in emerging markets

Currently, opportunities for ESG integration within emerging market equities lag behind developed nations (Passant et al. 2014). Much of this lag is due to regional concerns (Odell and Ali, 2016). Îlhan Meriç, Jie Ding, and Gülser Meriç (2016) conclude that due to high non-diversifiable risk and high correlation with developed markets, investments in most emerging markets no longer easily add the same diversification benefits to global portfolios. Emerging markets had the potential to be a desirable region for diversification (Wenling, 2013; Fernandes, 2005; Sherwood and Pollard, 2017), yet investors are discouraged from committing assets because of the downside volatility and inherent lack of information in emerging markets (Odell and Ali, 2016). However, recent studies suggest that ESG integration might add value for institutional investors who are seeking diversification opportunities in emerging markets. Through ESG research-based investing strategies, institutional investors may be able to mitigate emerging market risks that are due to lack of information and accounting disclosure standards, as well as the unpredictable volatilities resulting from bad governance and social practices. Though many established institutional investors are strategically investing in emerging markets (Fifield, Power, and Sinclair, 2002), their portfolio allocation may result in missing the emerging market alpha (Fifield, Power, and Sinclair, 2002; Wenling, 2013) when emerging markets' equities experience growth.

In a 2016 empirical study measuring the relationship between regulation regarding ESG investing and the investment practices of pension funds in emerging markets, Camila Yamahaki and Jędrzej George Frynas concluded that legislation encourages asset managers' positive attitudes to ESG integration in emerging markets through increased available information and assurance that ESG integration does not violate fiduciary responsibilities (Yamahaki and Frynas, 2016). Because of the current lack of legislation, many companies in emerging markets have no incentive to disclose relevant information for the consideration of ESG factors. However, regulations like Regulation S-K passed by the SEC continue to develop legislation, requiring companies to disclose financial measures and other information that could be useful for measuring ESG factors (Rashty and O'Shaughnessy, 2014; Yamahaki and Frynas, 2016). Though emerging markets traditionally lag developed markets in accounting disclosure standards and information (Siddiqi, 2011), global trends suggest progress towards the increased availability of non-financial information in emerging markets (Stewart, 2015). Organizations like the Sustainability Accounting Standards Board (SASB), the Carbon Disclosure Project (CDP), the Global Reporting Initiative (GRI), the International Integrated Reporting Council (IIRC), CERES, and the UN Principles for Responsible Investment (UNPRI) are all committed to increasing the availability of information relevant to ESG investing (Stewart, 2015; United Nations, 2006). Each of these organizations, and hundreds more smaller organizations, continue to gather material information and investigation tactics that are improving the flow of non-financial information from companies in both emerging and developed markets (Stewart, 2015).

CASE STUDY 5C: hot topic: fossil fuel free (FFF) investment

In 2012, 350.org launched a global campaign to promote fossil fuel divestment, which has since turned into the fastest growing divestment campaign in history. The UN-supported Portfolio Decarbonization Coalition (PDC) was launched in late 2014 as a multi-stakeholder initiative to drive GHG emissions reductions by mobilizing a critical mass of institutional investors committed to gradually decarbonizing their portfolios. The PDC's 27 signatories, representing over US$3 trillion in AUM, include RIA Members Amundi Asset Management and The Atmospheric Fund. The PDC supports the Montréal Pledge, which has reached more than US$100 billion in AUM and includes over 120 investors committed to annually measuring and publicly disclosing the carbon footprint of their investment portfolios.

In Canada, fossil fuel divestment has sparked interest not just on university campuses, but among individual and institutional investors as well, with divestment pledges from the Canadian Medical Association and the United Church of Canada, among others. Leading economists such as Jeff Rubin, a senior fellow at Canada's Centre for International Governance Innovation, are issuing warnings to investors who want to limit their exposure to carbon risk. Against the backdrop of falling fossil fuel prices and global consumption, the business case in favor of fossil fuel free (FFF) investment in Canada has strengthened over the past two years. The benefits of decarbonization include a reduced risk of value impairment because of climate change-related regulation, reduced risk of stranded assets and increased exposure to the companies that are likely to be the beneficiaries of the transition to a low-carbon economy. To address increasing demand, a growing spectrum of FFF investment products and services are emerging in Canada. Current FFF equity funds include the NEI Environmental Leaders Fund, AGF Global Sustainable Growth Equity Fund, BMO Fossil Fuel Free Fund, IA Clarington Inhance Global Equity SRI Fund, RBC Fossil Fuel Free Global Equity Fund, and Genus Capital Management's fossil free funds. Other RI investment managers offer customized FFF solutions, such as Fiera's fossil fuel free filter. Several low-carbon and FFF indices have also emerged in the past two years, such as the MSCI Low Carbon Index, MSCI Global Fossil Fuels Exclusion Index, and S&P/TSX 60 Fossil Fuel Free Index. With oil and gas companies accounting for roughly 20% of the value of the S&P/TSX composite index, some Canadian RI investors still prefer alternatives to FFF investing rather than removing one-fifth of the eligible universe. Investments firms such as NEI Investments, OceanRock Investments, and Addenda Capital pursue shareholder engagement strategies, working directly with the fossil fuel companies in their portfolios to improve their sustainability performance. Shareholder engagement can be a powerful tool to improve a company's ESG performance.

CASE STUDY 5D: SRI investing within hedge funds

Jason Mitchell, Sustainability Strategist

Jason is Man Group's Sustainability Strategist and a member of the Responsible Investment Committee. Besides having managed environmental and sustainability strategies, he speaks and publishes widely on responsible investing. He is also part of Man GLG's ("GLG") European and International Equity team.

He has worked at GLG from 2004 to 2008 and from 2010 to present, taking two years off from 2008 to 2010 to advise the UK government on infrastructure development across Sub-Saharan Africa. He has managed global, long-only sustainability, and environmental strategies from 2010 to 2015, as well as managed a long-short strategy focused on global telecoms and media from 2004 to 2008. Prior to GLG Partners, he was an investment analyst with Pequot Capital and Andor Capital.

Jason has chaired the United Nations-supported Principles for Responsible Investing (PRI) Hedge Fund Advisory Committee since 2014, is a member of the Plastic Disclosure Project Steering Committee and the Tobacco Free Portfolios Working Group. Jason graduated from the London School of Economics with an MSc in International Political Economy and the University of California, Berkeley with a BA in English Literature and Classics. He was named one of Institutional Investor's 2011 Hedge Fund Rising Stars, and is a Fellow of the British American Project.

His articles and comments on sustainable investing have appeared in Institutional Investor, Wall Street Journal, *CNBC* Squawk Box, Aftenposten, Global Times, Responsible

Investor, Ethical Markets, AIMA Journal, *and* Investment Europe. *He has also written widely on the European refugee and migrant crisis, with articles most recently appearing in the* London Review of Books, Christian Science Monitor, *and* Huffington Post. *He is a contributing author in* Sustainable Investing: Revolutions in Theory and Practice (Routledge: 2017) *and Evolutions in* Sustainable Investing: Strategies, Funds and Thought Leadership (Wiley Finance: 2012).

Discuss your thoughts on a standardized practice of integrating ESG factors into portfolio management:

Traditionally, the debate around hedge fund participation in responsible investment has tended to focus on the question: are hedge funds ready for responsible investment? Indeed, cynics wondered if responsible investment was prepared for hedge funds. For some asset owners and investors, the question was almost existential; how could shorting ever be considered a responsible investment practice? For others, the question harbored a deep suspicion that hedge fund involvement in responsible investment and ESG merely reflected their interest in launching new strategies with the ultimate objective of raising assets.

Thankfully, expectations for hedge funds are changing and that hedge funds now recognize that ignoring the existence of responsible investment norms is no longer an option. The debate has evolved to one less ideological and more operationally geared to how hedge funds can embed ESG into their investment and engagement process and reporting function.

Nonetheless, it is important to differentiate between integrating ESG at the firm level and at a strategy level. Hedge funds tend to think reflexively about ESG from a product perspective whereas many asset owners look for evidence of strong RI policies and ESG incorporation at a firm level. In my experience, asset owners are more interested in seeing evidence of a manager's overall commitment to responsible investment which could range from how a responsible investment committee sets policies to how investment teams systematically embedded ESG. The point is that ESG should be ingrained in the culture of the hedge fund manager rather than over represented via a single idiosyncratic ESG fund while its other funds lack integration.

Generically speaking, the investment decision-making process for a fundamental equity long/short fund differs little from that of a fundamental long-only equity fund just as the investment process for a long/short credit fund most likely resembles that of a long-only credit fund. Portfolio construction evolves sequentially by refining a universe of issuers through a process of understanding and managing macro, micro, financial, economic, and political risks ultimately to determine price discovery. The addition of a non-financial ESG lens in many cases already exists informally. And much like long-only funds, hedge funds often work at building a mosaic of contextual financial and non-financial data points to reinforce an investment thesis. This means weighing corporate governance issues and engaging with company management and directors in either a friendly context or a more activist approach.

What differentiates hedge funds from long-only investors is the focus on absolute returns over relative returns and the hedged, or "short-sale" portfolio dimension. As hedge funds are not benchmarked against indices like traditional fund managers, their investment horizon tends to be more sensitive to short-term catalysts impacting security prices. This is not to say that short-termism is endemic in the hedge fund business model. Many hedge fund managers take a longer-term, fundamental investment outlook. And because investment horizons vary much more widely across hedge fund strategies – from fundamental and activist to quant and high-frequency trade strategies – the degrees of ESG integration also differ. It is widely acknowledged that ESG factors become more prominent in company analysis over longer time periods (Figure 5.10).

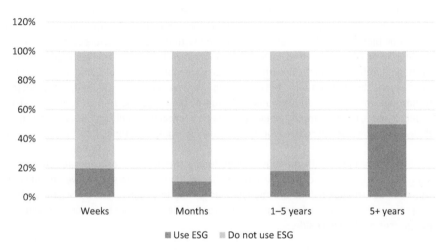

Figure 5.10 Investment time horizons

Source: 2017 Institutional Factor Survey. BofA Merrill Lynch US Equity and US Quant Strategy.

What do hedge fund idiosyncrasies mean in terms of formulating a standardized approach to integrating ESG factors into portfolio management? They provide a strong argument for converging around a standardized reporting and risk assessment approach. However, they also highlight potential risks that can influence a portfolio's factor exposure if not actively managed.

As asset owners and consultants increasingly incorporate ESG considerations in the manager selection process, a common reporting approach to understanding and monitoring ESG risks in manager portfolios will be needed. But reporting ESG exposure poses a number of challenges specifically for hedge funds as no standard or best practice currently exists. For example, how should hedge funds treat the short side of their portfolio when reporting carbon and climate exposure? Should they net out the long and short side of their carbon exposure, or report the decomposed exposure on a gross basis for both long and short sides of a portfolio? Similarly, how should hedge funds report their ESG profile using the scores of a third-party data provider? Should they take a position-weighted average of both long and short sides of the portfolio, or should they report average ESG scores on the long and short side of a portfolio discreetly?

The answers to these hedge fund ESG reporting questions could carry potentially significant implications for portfolio construction and management. In other words, it is important to recognize that a standardized approach applying ESG scores could produce unintended consequences in the form of unwanted factor risk exposure. A growing body of work observes the similarity in characteristics between an ESG factor strategy and a quality factor strategy. In a recent study, *Factor Investing and ESG Integration*, MSCI found that ESG integration increased a portfolio's factor bias towards companies with higher market capitalization, greater earnings quality and stability, lower debt ratios, and lower volatility.

While these would appear to be ideal qualities for any company, they do introduce factor risk. For instance, a portfolio composed of long positions that all demonstrate high ESG scores or high-quality factor and short positions that bear low ESG scores or a low-quality factor will be exposed to factors rotations and changes in investment regime. Strategies with a long-term investment horizon are more capable of riding out these factor rotations, but hedge funds, besides being more performance oriented, are expected to navigate through factor rotations by virtue of their hedges. Hence, it is natural to expect a hedge fund to employ a more pragmatic approach to applying ESG scores rather than a best-in-class approach adopted by many long-only ESG funds.

In another example, multi-manager hedge fund strategies typically operate on a risk-adjusted, market- and factor-neutral basis. Correlation risk exists if all investment silos within a multi-manager fund are managed according to a standardized ESG integration approach that aims to produce high ESG scores for the long side of the portfolio and low ESG scores on the short side.

What is the answer? While it can be argued that asset owners push hedge fund managers to converge around a standardized format towards ESG monitoring and reporting, the application of this ESG data towards portfolio construction and management is a separate issue that should resist a universal prescription.

Describe your experience chairing the PRI Hedge Fund Advisory Committee:
The PRI Hedge Fund Advisory Committee (HFAC) is of one of eight PRI committees governing investment practices. HFAC differs from many of the other committees in that it examines the hedge fund business model and orientation rather than focusing on a specific asset class like equities, fixed income, or private equity.

Since first joining the HFAC in 2012 and chairing the committee since 2014, I have prioritized several areas: better understanding hedge fund involvement in RI/ESG and working towards establishing recommended approaches. We are also examining how systematic hedge fund strategies – "quant funds" – can integrate ESG factors into their investment process. Marisol Hernandez, manager of the PRI HFAC, suggested that "Developing a responsible investment framework will help hedge fund managers not only understand why RI is so important but offer ways to incorporate ESG factors into the investment process and develop metrics to monitor, evaluate and improve their processes."

Asset owners have also played an essential role in advancing the PRI hedge fund work stream, and for continually resetting expectations around manager ESG integration to a higher standard. "With the UN-backed Principles for Responsible Investment having celebrated their 10-year anniversary," according to Edward Mason, Head of Responsible Investment for the Church Commissioners for England and a member of the PRI HFAC, "the Church Commissioners expect all of our asset managers to engage thoughtfully with responsible investment and to incorporate ESG factors and active ownership into their investment practice."

Nonetheless, measuring the degree of activity by hedge funds in responsible investing remains a challenge. Despite a number of resources that now provide a clearer picture of the size and composition of the overall responsible investment market, little information exists for hedge funds. The biennial Global Sustainable Investment Review decomposes responsible investment across several strategies, from negative screening to ESG integration but ignores the hedge fund industry. A 2015 study by Mercer notes that 76% of asset owners incorporate ESG considerations when allocating to alternative asset classes, although the alternative asset definition characterizes a much larger universe that includes private equity and debt, infrastructure, real estate, and natural resources markets.

Resources like PRI's 2017 Reporting Framework Report have begun to offer some understanding behind hedge fund activity in responsible investment. PRI signatories identifying themselves primarily as hedge funds has steadily grown the past decade (Figure 5.11). Signatories – both asset owners and managers – disclosing at least 10% of their AUM managed on a hedge fund basis have also grown (Figure 5.12). It is worth noting that 2016 marked the first year that the number of PRI signatories declined since PRI's inception. This runs counter to PRI's overall trend of rising signatory count and assets under management (AUM), and most likely reflects redemptions and more rigorous reporting and transparency requirements.

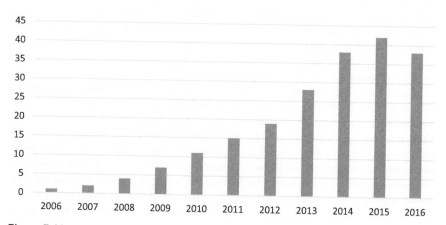

Figure 5.11 Number of hedge fund signatories

The HFAC is working to improve this data and complete a work stream through 2018 that will culminate in the development and inclusion of a hedge fund module in the PRI annual reporting framework. That module will provide a clearer picture of the size and growth of

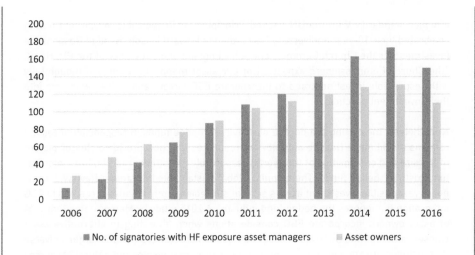

Figure 5.12 Number of signatories

Source: PRI, 2017 Reporting and Assessment Framework.

hedge fund assets in RI/ESG, the RI/ESG strategies they manage, and a baseline for how these evolve in the future.

In 2012, the HFAC published its first formal discussion paper, Responsible Investment and Hedge Funds: A Discussion Paper. The paper focuses on establishing a definitional baseline by explaining the practice of short selling, outlining hedge fund strategies, and summarizing on how hedge fund managers can begin to adopt basic responsible investment policies and reporting practices. The balance between asset owner and investment manager representation on the HFAC is perhaps best illustrated by the paper's dual focus, suggesting actions for managers to implement as well as recommendations for how asset owners can better assess manager integration efforts.

Using the discussion paper as a springboard, the HFAC has achieved progress in terms of formulating and recommending hedge fund-specific standards. In order to create industry standards, we partnered with groups that included the Standards Board for Alternative Investments (SBAI), Alternative Investment Management Association (AIMA), Chartered Alternative Investment Analyst (CAIA), eVestments and the Hedge Fund Review (HFR). This consensus-based effort ultimately ensured a consistent approach when the HFAC developed the Hedge Fund Due Diligence Questionnaire (DDQ). Launched in Spring 2017 in a three-city tour (London, New York, Stockholm), the DDQ provides a toolkit for asset owners and consultants to better assess ESG criteria during the manager selection process across four groups including policy, governance, investment process, and monitoring and reporting.

With the DDQ established as a template for organizations like eVestment, HFR, Bloomberg, AIMA, and SBIA, the HFAC is now turning towards developing a PRI Hedge Fund Guide. This guide will distinguish approaches with the ultimate goal of recommending certain approaches.

Discuss major changes within the industry which you see having
an impact on ESG-integration levels within asset classes:
There are several key trends in the hedge fund industry that will determine the manner and widespread usage in which ESG is integrated and the asset classes that it ultimately pervades.

First, the improving quality and consistency of ESG data will support greater confidence in its integration. Few investment firms have the big data processing resources to evaluate the raw, underlying ESG metrics and key performance indicators. Consequently, much of the investment industry is dependent upon third-party data providers to collect and translate ESG data into composite scores.

ESG composite scores, which are qualitatively produced by analysts compiling underlying data, have demonstrated themselves to have poor predictive power. In fact, a 2014 working paper from the Institute for Research on Labor and Employment found low correlation in ESG scores among six ESG raters, illustrating their subjective nature. This will not always be the case as the market becomes more efficient at quantifying long-term, non-financial risks like climate change.

There is a strong case to be made for hedges recognizing and integrating ESG data and practices in the future. In Europe, regulatory change like Markets in Financial Instruments Directive (MiFID II) legislation debuts in January, 2017. Under MiFID II, financial professionals will now be required to pay for investment research which potentially could mean less reliance on the traditional sell-side research model and greater focus on enhancing in-house research capabilities which could include ESG data.

At the same time, non-traditional approaches to ESG data have begun to produce encouraging results, specifically the identification of patterns in ESG scores. A joint study published last year by the European Centre for Corporate Engagement (ECCE) at Maastricht University and the Dutch firm NN Investment Partners demonstrates that the change in ESG scores, not the scores themselves, can potentially drive outperformance. Research by Barclays has shown that ESG can be a valuable tool in fixed income markets where, for instance, they observation a correlation between governance scores and credit ratings.

Second, the emergence of systematic strategies, otherwise known as quant funds, promises to drive a significant wave of innovation in ESG. Quant funds offer the kind of big data mining capabilities and predictive analytics that will be essential in deciphering raw ESG data to identify statistically significant correlations. Ultimately, this may help establish credible ESG factors alongside other style factors like growth, value, and momentum when managing portfolio risk.

LEARNING PERSPECTIVE 3: MIT Sloan

Jason Jay, Director of Sustainability Initiative at MIT Sloan, has his Ph.D. in organizational behavior, and has been involved with the MIT Sustainability program for the past 12 years. The MIT Sustainability Initiative emphasizes integration and the imbedding of sustainability within MIT Sloan, developing leaders within the broad field of sustainability. This is done through long-term projects, one of which is centered around ESG data and sustainable investing.

From your perspective in the academic world, have you seen interest in ESG investing grow?

Back in 2005–2007, there was no real strength in academia around ESG. Within the last year however, we added a course on sustainability, based on student interest. When we started, with the S-Lab in 2004 (the Sustainable Business Lab, which provides students with a unique opportunity to explore the connection between business, the environment, and society), we did nine projects, with 36 students. Now our new course has been conducting 16 projects per year, with an array of different companies such as GAP, Colgate, JetBlue, and Lockheed, to name a few. At the beginning of our sustainability courses, we were reaching out to companies to feature them in student projects, but now companies are coming to us to be featured in student projects. We've gone from one course on sustainability, to 80% of students from MIT Sloan taking at least one elective in sustainability, and one-third of students taking three or more classes on sustainability. In order to earn the sustainability certificate at MIT Sloan, students are required to take six courses in sustainability over the course of their tenure. This program has grown from 17 to 47. A key approach to sustainability at MIT Sloan has been action learning, including projects with leading companies on sustainability.

Discussion questions

1) Ways that ESG investing differs between regions and countries (LO2)
2) Ways that ESG investing can be useful when investing in companies in the emerging markets (LO3)
3) ESG investing within different asset classes (LO4)
4) Ways that ESG investing might develop within different asset classes (LO5)

Notes

1 Sustainability Accounting Standards Board, SASB's Approach to Materiality for the Purpose of Standards Development (January 2017); available at https://library.sasb.org/materiality_bulletin/.
2 Sustainability Accounting Standards Board, *Conceptual Framework* (February 2017).
3 Sustainability Accounting Standards Board, *Rules of Procedure* (February 2017).
4 Source: Governance & Accountability Institute, Inc.

References

"2014 Global Sustainable Investment Review." *Global Sustainable Investment Review*, 2015. www.gsi-alliance.org/wp-content/uploads/2015/02/GSIA_Review_download.pdf.

"2016 Global Sustainable Investment Review." *Global Sustainable Investment Review*, 2017. www.gsi-alliance.org/wp-content/uploads/2017/03/GSIR_Review2016.F.pdf.

"Asia Investors Group on Climate Change." Connecting Commodities, Investors, Climate, and the Land: A Toolkit for Institutional Investors." 2017. http://aigcc.net/wp-content/uploads/2017/10/IGCC-Sustainable-Land-Use.pdf.

Baert, Rick. "Ontario Requiring All DB Funds to Disclose ESG Data." *Pensions & Investments*. January 9, 2015. www.pionline.com/article/20150109/ONLINE/150109915/ontario-requiring-all-db-funds-to-disclose-esg-data. Accessed March 25, 2018.

CSR Asia, "Sustainability Disclosure in ASEAN." Business Solutions for Global Challenges. 2016. www.globalreporting.org/resourcelibrary/ReportingASEANExtractives2016.pdf.

Department of Labor. "Interpretive Bulletin Relating to the Fiduciary Standard under ERISA in Considering Economically Targeted Investments." *Department of Labor*, October, 2015. https://dol.gov/opa/media/press/ebsa/ebsa20152045.htm. Accessed November, 2016.

Fernandes, Nuno. "Portfolio Disaggregation in Emerging Market Investments: Passive Indexing Strategies Are No Longer Enough." *The Journal of Portfolio Management* 31, no. 2 (2005): 41–9. doi:10.3905/jpm.2005.470577.

Fifield, S., D. M. Power, and C. D. Sinclair. "Emerging Stock Markets: A More Realistic Assessment of the Gains From Diversification." *Applied Financial Economics* 12, no. 3 (2002): 213–29. doi:10.1080/09603100110090082.

"Final Report: Recommendations of the Task Force on Climate-Related Financial Disclosures (June 2017)." *TCFD*. www.fsb-tcfd.org/publications/final-recommendations-report/. Accessed March 25, 2018.

Furness, Virginia. "Poland Stuns Green Market to Become First Sov to Print." *Globalcapital 125*, 2016. Business Source Complete, EBSCOhost. Accessed October 13, 2017.

"Law Document English View." *Ontario.ca*. April 14, 2015. www.ontario.ca/laws/regulation/900909. Accessed March 25, 2018.

Lu, Haitian. "The 'legalization' of Corporate Social Responsibility: Hong Kong Experience on ESG Reporting." *Asia Pacific Law Review* 24, no. 2 (2016): 123–48. doi:10.1080/10192557.2016.1245385

Meager, Lizzie. "Previous Next DEAL: France's First Sovereign Green Bond." *2017 FDI Report: Vietnam | IFLR.com*. http://iflr.com/Article/3658576/DEAL-Frances-first-sovereign-green-bond.html. Accessed July 09, 2018.

Meriç, Ilhan, Jie Ding, and Gülser Meriç. "Global Portfolio Diversification with Emerging Stock Markets." *EMAJ: Emerging Markets Journal* 6, no. 1 (2016): 59–62. doi:10.5195/emaj.2016.88.

Mervelskemper, Laura, and Daniel Streit. "Enhancing Market Valuation of ESG Performance: Is Integrated Reporting Keeping Its Promise?" *Business Strategy and the Environment* 26, no. 4 (2016): 536–49. doi:10.1002/bse.1935.

Odell, Jamieson, and Usman Ali. "ESG Investing in Emerging and Frontier Markets." *Journal of Applied Corporate Finance* 28, no. 2 (2016): 96–101. doi: 10.1111/jacf.12181.

Passant, Francois, Jessica Robinson, Lisa Woll, Deb Abbey, and Simon O'Connor. "Global Sustainable Investment Review." *Global Sustainable Investment Alliance*, 2014. http://gsi-alliance.org/wp-content/uploads/2015/02/GSIA_Review_download.pdf. Accessed October, 2014.

PRI. "Institutions for Occupational Retirement Provision (IORP) Directive – ESG Clauses." [online], 2018. www.unpri.org/policy-makers-and-regulators/institutions-for-occupational-retirement-provision-iorp-directive-esg-clauses/300.article. Accessed May 15, 2018].

Rashty, J. and J. O'Shaughnessy. "Reporting and Disclosures Using Non-GAAP Financial Measures." *CPA Journal* 84, no. 3 (2014): 36–9.

"Responsible Investment Benchmark Report 2017 Australia." Responsible Investment Association Australasia, 2017. https://responsibleinvestment.org/wp-content/uploads/2017/07/Responsible-Investment-Benchmark-Report-Australia-2017.pdf.

Sherwood, M. W. and J. Pollard. "The Risk-Adjusted Return Potential of Integrating ESG Strategies into Emerging Market Equities." *Journal of Sustainable Finance and Investment* (2017): 1–19.

Siddiqi, H. "A Creative Institutional Response to Twin Problems of Liquidity and Information Gaps in Certain Emerging Markets." *International Review Of Finance* 11, no. 4 (2011): 537–52. doi:10.1111/j.1468–2443.2011.01142.x.

Stewart, Levi S. "Growing Demand for ESG Information and Standards: Understanding Corporate Opportunities as Well as Risks." *Journal of Applied Corporate Finance* 27, no. 2 (2015): 58–63. doi: 10.1111/jacf.12118.

United Nations. "Principles for Responsible Investment." *United Nations.* 2006. www.unpri.org. Accessed October 2016.

Wenling, Lin. "Is There Alpha in Institutional Emerging-Market Equity Funds?" *Journal of Portfolio Management* 39, no. 4 (2013): 106–17. doi: 10.3905/jpm.2013.39.4.106.

Yamahaki, Camila, and Jędrzej George Frynas. "Institutional Determinants of Private Shareholder Engagement in Brazil and South Africa: The Role of Regulation." *Corporate Governance: An International Review* 24, no. 5 (2016): 509–27. doi:10.1111/corg.12166.

Chapter 6

The impact of common investment theories on ESG investment trends

This chapter will speak to the impact of several well-known investment strategies on development trends in ESG investing. Investment strategies discussed will be shareholder vs. stakeholder theory, theories about material vs. immaterial information, the universal owners view, and the resource-based view (RBV) vs. Porter's five forces model. This chapter will be structured as a literature review covering a variety of arguments regarding important investment theories that have bearing on investors who are considering incorporating ESG investing into portfolio construction. It will provide insight into the reasons why investors choose to incorporate or exclude ESG investing strategies into portfolio management. This chapter will build upon the current position of ESG investing within developed and developing markets, asset classes (focusing mainly on fixed income and equities), and sectors (discussed in Chapter 4).

Learning objectives

- Describe forward-looking trends within investing relevant to ESG investing
- Thoughtfully assess and critique investor concerns about the performance of ESG investments
- Thoughtfully assess and critique investor concerns about the policies and obligations of investment managers regarding ESG investments
- Thoughtfully assess and critique investor concerns about the availability of material information within different markets, asset classes, and sectors that would affect the accuracy of ESG rating systems
- Thoughtfully assess and critique investor concerns about regions in which ESG investments may be unavailable or severely restricted
- Thoughtfully analyze and critique investor concerns about macro trends which may affect the growth of ESG investment opportunities

After this chapter, readers should have a well-rounded exposure to the common objections to ESG investing, and have a clearer understanding of the reasons behind the current level of incorporation of ESG investing in portfolio construction and management.

ESG investing, regardless of the strategy with which it is implemented, is heavily influenced by several common investment theories. It is important to gain a broad perspective of these theories, in order to facilitate discussion of how ESG methodology can complement existing investment portfolios.

6.1 Shareholder theory vs. stakeholder theory

Stakeholder theory and shareholder theory are studied at length in financial and economic courses across curriculums and courses. These two theories have been, in many ways, formative to debates regarding business ethics and the relationship between corporations and their communities. This section will endeavor to provide a basis for the idea that arguments for both stakeholder theory and its counterpart, shareholder theory, play into the integration of ESG strategies within portfolio construction.

Shareholder theory

Shareholder theory has been the prevalent operational mandate for corporations as long as the concept of owning equity in a company has existed. This is perhaps best exemplified by Milton Friedman in his 1970 New York Times article entitled "The Social Responsibility of Business Is to Increase Its Profits." In this article, Friedman states:

> [I]n my book *Capitalism and Freedom*, I have called [CSR] a "fundamentally subversive doctrine" in a free society, and have said that in such a society, "there is one and only one social responsibility of business – to use its resources and engage in activities designed to increase its profits so long as it stays within the rules of the game, which is to say, engages in open and free competition without deception or fraud."
>
> (Friedman, 1970)

In this way, Milton Friedman strongly objected to the idea that a corporation should have any further aim than the financial profit of its **shareholders**. The term "shareholders" refers to any individual or institution who own shares in the corporation, whether publicly or privately. This idea has become known as the "shareholder theory."

The concept of the **principal-agent relationship** is key to the understanding of the shareholder theory. This relationship emerged from the **agency theory**, which is discussed in the study of business ethics. At its core, agency theory primarily concerns itself with the relationship between a principal and an agent, which arises when **ownership** and the **control of an entity** or an organization is separate. The agent has intrinsic duty to represent the best interests of the principal. This relationship is most clear when corporate leadership plays the role of the agent, and the role of the principal is represented by that corporation's shareholders. In this instance, the corporation (as agent) has the intrinsic duty to represent the interests of the shareholders (the principal entity). Agency theory holds that problems arise through a conflict of interests between the agent and the principals, which can lead to an abuse of power on the part of the agent in his role of representing the principal. Milton Friedman, perhaps the most famous public advocate for the shareholder theory, vehemently argued that those who promoted the "social responsibilities of business" were promoting no more or less than pure socialism. Friedman's argument is based on the principal-agent relationship discussed above. He argued in books and articles that the decision-making executive of a corporation acts as an agent solely responsible to the principals, the owners of the corporation. To that end, the "corporation" (represented by the executives of the corporation) has as its primary responsibility the objectives of the shareholders. Friedman also addresses the potential that the principal has other goals beyond the primary goal of increasing the monetary value of the shares held. He argues that in that case, the corporation is still acting as the agent for the principal. Friedman objects, however, when the corporation takes the role of the principal, operating with its own responsibilities and ambitions beyond those explicitly expressed by shareholders.

With regards to responsible investing, shareholder theory would argue that any goals beyond simply the maximization of share value is antithetical to the purpose of corporations. To that end, shareholder theory would support ESG integration if it was proven to increase share value, through risk mitigation and increased exposure to the return distribution of the investments. However, shareholder theory would not support the notion that it is a corporate duty to act with regard to the environmental, social, and governance aspects of its business any further than shareholders demanded or than was financially profitable. For investors, tenants of shareholder theory would reject impact investing and moral screening, and would support ESG integration and engagement, as long as both were able to demonstrate increased financial profits for shareholders.

The below case study illustrates the emersion of the shareholder vs. stakeholder debate. Henry Ford, founder of Ford Motor Company was sued by John and Horace Dodge in 1916 for using business profits to extend his business, rather than distribute the profits as dividends to shareholders. These articles provide insight into the extent to which shareholder theory protects the interests of the shareholders.

CASE STUDY 6A: *Dodge v. Ford Motor Co.* (Judicial Foundation for Shareholder Theory)

Dodges sue Henry Ford

Stockholders Object to "Reckless Expenditures" of Company's Assets

N.Y. TIMES (1851–2009), Nov. 3, 1916, at 12.

DETROIT, Nov. 2. – John F. and Horace Dodge, automobile manufacturers and stockholders in the Ford Motor Company, obtained a temporary injunction in the Circuit Court here today, restraining Henry Ford from using the assets of the Ford Motor Company to extend the business as planned, instead of distributing profits in dividends.

In their application to the court, the Dodge brothers allege that increased labor costs and unstable business conditions, coming at the end of the war, make "reckless expenditures of the company's assets unwise."

The company's annual statement issued recently, showed profits of several million dollars, which, it was announced, would be put back into the business.

Newspaper specials
WALL ST. J. (1889–1922), Nov. 4, 1916, at 2.

John F. and Horace E. Dodge, owners of the Dodge Bros. Motor Car plant, and holders of 10% of Ford Motor Co. stock have secured a temporary injunction against Henry Ford to restrain the Ford Motor Co. from disbursing and re-investing its surplus earnings in the extension of the business following the declaration by Mr. Ford at the end of the last fiscal year that no special dividends in the future would be declared by the company. Bill recites that $34,000,000 had been distributed from January, 1914, to October, 1915, in addition to regular monthly dividends of 5%. No declaration was made at the end of the last fiscal year, although earnings reached $60,000,000. It is alleged that Mr. Ford owns 58% of the stock of the company and he is contemplating investing millions in iron ore mines in the northern peninsula of Michigan or Minnesota; building ships and establishing steel manufacturing plants. The bill also states that this policy in view of the increased labor and material costs and uncertain business conditions is "reckless in the extreme" and demands that at least 75% of the accumulation of the cash surplus and in the future, all earnings of this company be distributed to stockholders.

Henry Ford Beaten in $60,000,000 suit

Dodge Brothers Win Action for Disbursement of Dividends
  – Ford to Appeal.

N.Y. TIMES (1851–2009), Nov. 1, 1917, at 24.

DETROIT, Mich., Oct. 31. – Minority stockholders of the Ford Motor Company today won the first round of their fight for increased dividends and a more important voice in the transactions of the company's business.

Circuit Judge George S. Hosmer of Detroit handed down a decision for the plaintiff in a suit brought by John F. Dodge and Horace E. Dodge of Detroit against the Ford Motor Company and Henry Ford, to compel Mr. Ford to disburse about $60,000,000 of accumulated dividends to the company's stockholders. The Dodge brothers, who are automobile manufacturers, are also minority stockholders of the Ford Motor Company, in which Henry Ford holds a controlling interest.

Mr. Ford announced some months ago that he hoped to use this money greatly to increase his company's business. One of the features of his plan of expansion was the construction of great blast furnaces on the River Rouge, near Detroit. The Dodge Brothers attempted to obtain an injunction permanently restraining Mr. Ford from starting construction work on these furnaces, but the State Supreme Court allowed him to begin building provided he furnished a bond to protect the company's stockholders from loss in case the Dodge Brothers won their suit.

The bond was furnished and the work at River Rouge was started. Mr. Ford has declared that he would appeal the case to the United States Supreme Court if the lower courts decisions were against him. It was charged by the Dodge Brothers that he was supreme in directing the business of the Ford Motor Company and the minority stockholders had no voice in the affairs of the company. He denied this charge.

Stakeholder theory

The term "stakeholders" refers to entities which are influenced or affected by the behavior of a corporation. Narrowly, this would include employees of the corporation, shareholders, and the community in which the corporation is located. More broadly, this might include the physical environment affected by corporate activities, competitors and the supply chain, and the political sphere. For example, a private paper manufacturing company would traditionally view its stakeholders as its employees, company owners, and the community surrounding the manufacturing headquarters. More broadly, the stakeholders could include the physical location affected by the paper mill, paper manufacturing competitors, and the political decisions made in the small town in which the company is headquartered.

Professor E. Merrick Dodd, in his 1932 Harvard Review article entitled "For Whom are the Corporate Managers Trustees?" summed up **stakeholder theory** by stating,

> Business – which is the economic organization of society – is private property only in a qualified sense, and society may properly demand that it be carried on in such a way as to safeguard the interests of those who deal with it either as employees or consumers even if the proprietary rights of its owners are thereby curtailed.
>
> (Dodd, 1932)

Dodd's theories were heavily influenced by John Maynard Keynes, a highly impactful economist and Dodd's contemporary. In the 1930s, Keynes proposed an increase in the American government's spending aimed at increasing employment. This idea sparked Dodd's theories on the responsibility of corporations to benefit employees and other stakeholders, even at the expense of corporate profitability. Keynes, in his 1928 essay "The End of Laissez Faire," argued that the corporation was increasingly becoming an "integral piece of the social fabric" rather than simply a protective agent for the investor (Elson and Goossen, 2017). Through the lens of the agency theory, Keynes viewed the corporation as the agent, but argued that the principal should encompass more than simply the investor, but should also include employees of the corporation and various other stakeholders (Keynes, 1928). Keynes and Dodd were both heavily influenced by the Great Depression and the country's loss of trust in the traditional roll of corporations within the American social fabric. They called for a dramatic change in the responsibilities to which private corporations were held accountable.

Adolf Berle, H.W. Ballantine, and Gardiner Means, also contemporaries of Dodd and Keynes, elaborated on the expended responsibilities of corporations in their article entitled "The Modern Corporation and Private Property" (1932). They famously stated:

> Corporations have ceased to be merely legal devices through which the private business transactions of individuals must be carried on . . . the corporation has, in fact, become both a method of property tenure and a means of organizing economic life. . . . The corporate system appears only when this type of private or "close" corporation has given way to an essentially different form, the quasi-public corporation: a corporation in which a large-measure of separation of ownership and control has taken place through the multiplication of owners. . . . The economic power in the hands of a few persons who control a giant corporation is a tremendous force which can harm or benefit a multitude of individuals, affect whole districts, shift the currents of trade, bring ruin to one community and prosperity to another. The organizations which they control have passed far beyond the realm of private enterprise – they have become more nearly social institutions.
>
> (Ballantine, Berle and Means, 1932, 24)

The three went on to argue that as the corporate entity is changing and growing, the responsibilities of a corporation to its community, its "stakeholders," should increase in tandem. To state it simply, the essence of stakeholder theory holds that:

> corporations [are] no longer simply economic vehicles to produce shareholder returns, but [have] become vital societal entities that shared interests with multiple groups, including employees, consumers, and the public. Dodd called for a dramatic revision in corporate legal theory that recognized not only investors as the focal point of the enterprise, but suggested that each of these other groups should share equally in the benefits of, and the responsibility for, the operation of the modern corporation.
>
> (Elson and Goossen, 2017)

The concept that corporations have a social responsibility to more than just traditional shareholders gained traction during the Great Depression and the years following. At that time, corporations were widely criticized for hording economic, political, and social power from individuals, while poverty and unemployment were at record highs. The events of World War II continued to popularize the integration of corporate social responsibility within corporate policy. John D. Rockefeller, founder of Standard Oil, Andrew Carnegie, founder of US Steel, and Henry Ford, founder of Ford Motor Company, all publicly backed stakeholder influence of company policy. Notably, John D. Rockefeller Jr., son and heir to John D. Rockefeller Sr., in a radio-broadcasted appeal on behalf of the USO and the National War Fund on July 8, 1941, made a speech which included this famous line, "I believe that every right implies a responsibility; every opportunity, an obligation; every possession, a duty." This statement embodies the essence of stakeholder theory, that the power corporations wield mandates certain responsibilities to those affected by that sphere of authority.

With respect to responsible investing, stakeholder theory would support any business decisions that took into consideration the opinions of stakeholders affected by business decisions, whether or not this affected share value. To that end, tenants of stakeholder theory would likely support impact investing, negative screening, and ESG engagement, if these practices were employed to standardize the consideration of stakeholders in corporate action.

6.2 Material information vs. non-material information

Another concept that has become integral to the adoption of ESG factor acknowledgment and critique by companies and investors, is the theory of **material information**. The United States Securities and Exchange Commission (SEC) defines material information in the following manner:

> The definition of a "material fact" includes a two-part materiality test. A fact is material when it (i) significantly affects the market price or value of a security; or (ii) would reasonably be expected to have a significant effect on the market price or value of a security.

The SEC further mandates that all material information must be disclosed to the general marketplace before it is disclosed to anyone other than in the necessary course of business.

Historically, material information has included information commonly integrated into quantitative or technical analysis, such as information found on financial statements. Only in the past few years has information relevant to environmental, social, and governance factors been considered to potentially have a significant effect on market pricing or the value of a security. Notably, in 2010, the SEC passed regulation mandating the disclosure of certain climate-related information from public companies. See Case study 6B for the explanation on why climate-related information is now considered material information requiring disclosure by the SEC.

CASE STUDY 6B: Securities and Exchange Commission 17 CFR PARTS 211, 231 and 241 [Release Nos. 33–9106; 34–61469; FR-82] Commission guidance regarding disclosure related to climate change

Potential impact of climate change-related matters on public companies

For some companies, the regulatory, legislative, and other developments noted above could have a significant effect on operating and financial decisions, including those involving capital expenditures to reduce emissions and, for companies subject to "cap and trade" laws, expenses related to purchasing allowances where reduction targets cannot be met. Companies that may not be directly affected by such developments could nonetheless be indirectly affected by changing prices for goods or services provided by companies that are directly affected and that seek to reflect some or all their changes in costs of goods in the prices they charge. For example, if a supplier's costs increase, that could have a significant impact on its customers if those costs are passed through, resulting in higher prices for customers. New trading markets for emission credits related to "cap and trade" programs that might be established under pending legislation, if adopted, could present new opportunities for investment. These markets also could allow companies that have more allowances than they need, or that can earn offset credits through their businesses, to raise revenue through selling these instruments into those markets. Some companies might suffer financially if these or similar bills are enacted by the Congress while others could benefit by taking advantage of new business opportunities.

In addition to legislative, regulatory, business, and market impacts related to climate change, there may be significant physical effects of climate change that have the potential to have a material effect on a registrant's business and operations. These effects can impact a registrant's personnel, physical assets, supply chain, and distribution chain. They can include the impact of changes in weather patterns, such as increases in storm intensity, sea-level rise, melting of permafrost and temperature extremes on facilities or operations. Changes in the availability or quality of water, or other natural resources on which the registrant's business depends, or damage to facilities or decreased efficiency of equipment can have material effects on companies. Physical changes associated with climate change can decrease consumer demand for products or services; for example, warmer temperatures could reduce demand for residential and commercial heating fuels, service, and equipment.

The EU passed similar laws in 2013 and 2014, which regulate the disclosure of non-financial and diversity information by large companies. Since the initial laws were formed in 2013, the EU has further introduced directives that mandate sustainable reporting.

Companies in the EU are required to disclose non-financial information such as environmental issues, social issues, human rights, anti-corruption and bribery, leadership diversity, and general business activities. It is significant that both European and North American legislation have publicly acknowledged that information related to environmental, social, and governance issues have a material impact on financial performance in today's marketplace. This will likely have three effects: first it will provide investors with much needed insight into the extra-financial performance of companies, which will empower the investor to make informed choices about the corporations and companies that they choose to support. Secondly it will lead to the propagation of environmental, social, and governance information, further leading to the cross-sectionalizing of data which has been proven to provide greater insight into the return distribution of an investment, further multiplying the impact of ESG factors on stock performance. Third, it will likely encourage corporations to review environmental, social, and governance policies, as the data will be more widely distributed than previously.

6.3 Resource-based view vs. Porter's five forces model

Another key theory which influences environmental, social, and governance factors within corporations is the debate between the resource-based view and the intrinsic view of a corporation.

Resource-based view

The resource-based view became popular in the 1980s and 1990s through three major academic works: "The Resource-Based View of the Firm" (B. Wernerfelt, 1984), "The Core Competence of the Corporation" (Prahalad and Hamel, 1997), and "Firm Resources and Sustainable Competitive Advantage" (J. Barney, 1991). However, its roots stretch back to Edith Penrose's "The Theory of the Growth of the Firm," published in 1959. In this book, Penrose proposed that:

> the resources with which a particular firm is accustomed to working with will shape the pro-
> ductive services its management is capable of rendering. The experience of management will
> affect the productive services that all its other resources are capable of rendering. As manage-
> ment tries to make the best use of the resources available, a "dynamic" interacting process
> occurs which encourage growth but limits the rate of growth.
>
> (Penrose, 1959)

In short, the resource-based view holds that organizations should find value and competitive advantage as the sum of its resources. In this theory, resources are valued based on three factors: tangibility, heterogeneity, and immobility.

Tangibility: The resource-based view holds that resources which are tangible, or physical, are easily able to be bought or sold in the marketplace, and are thus less valuable than intangible resources, such as brand reputation, intellectual property, personnel, etc. The resource-based view would therefore value a corporation with intangible resources as more valuable than a corporation with a majority of their assets being tangible resources.

Heterogeneity: The resource-based view also values corporations based on the transferability (heterogeneity) of skills and resources from one company to another. If the resources that one company uses can easily be used by a competitor in the same industry, these resources are not deemed as valuable as if those resources are unique to one corporation, not easily transferred or available to another.

Mobility: Finally, the resource-based view holds that resources which are valuable to a corporation are valuable in part since they cannot be easily or quickly moved to another corporation. Brand recognition is one example of an immobile resource, valuable because it cannot be easily moved from one corporation to another, even through a merger or acquisition.

The resource-based view holds that sustainable competitive advantage, often measured in the form of stock price or other quantitative performance metrics, is found through measuring internal resources rather than measuring against external factors. This theory was expanded to the natural-resource-based view in the 1990s through the academic research of Stuart L. Hart, in his 1995 article entitled: "A Natural-Resource-Based View of the Firm" in the *Academy of Management Review* (Hart, 1995). In this article, Hart argued that a corporation's success is tied to its relationship to the natural environment, and introduced that a corporation's relationship to the natural environment should be considered as an internal resource.

The resource-based view was further popularized in the research of J. Barney, who in the 1990s created what is now commonly known as the "VRIO (Value, Rareness, Imitability, Organization) framework" for analyzing and valuing firms' internal resources and capabilities. Barney introduced four attributes useful for analyzing firm resources. Those factors are:

Value: Barney describes a resource as "valuable" when it provides the firm or corporation with the ability to employ strategies that improve efficiency or effectiveness. Value typically shows itself in resources that exploit opportunities or neutralize threats to the corporation.

Rarity: Rare resources are employed by a limited number of competitive entities. These resources could take the form of physical capital, human capital, organizational resources, etc.

Imitability: Firm resources are valuable if they cannot be easily imitable. Firm resources can achieve inimitability for one or a combination of three reasons: 1) the ability of a firm to obtain a resource is dependent upon *unique historical conditions* (the history of the firm or corporation can be directly correlated to its history), 2) the link between the resources possessed by a firm and a firm's sustained competitive advantage is *causally ambiguous* (when the link between firm resources and its sustained competitive advantage are poorly understood), or 3) the resource generating a firm's advantage is *socially complex* (the firm exists in a complex social phenomena that is uncontrollable by the firm itself) (Dierickx and Cool, 1989).

Organization: The resources are organized in such a way as to capture and exploit value.

In more common terms, first introduced by J. Barney in 1991, a corporation's relationship to the natural environment provides a valuable, rare, costly to imitate, and non-substitutable relationship which if handled carefully can present potential for competitive advantage. In the resource-based view, a firm's value can be measured and quantified by the examination of the resources inherent to that firm, without the need to examine outside factors (except where those factors are involved in the value of various resources).

ESG factors and the resource-based view

The factors considered in the resource-based view, value, rarity, imitability, and organization, complement ESG factors well. If one considers environmental, social, and governance factors as resources, then the VRIO framework presented above is an important framework to consider the ability of corporations to utilize these resources. Considering ESG factors as resources in this framework is the first step for investors and corporations alike to begin to utilize environmental, social, and governance factors to full potential.

Porter's five forces model

Michael Porter developed a model for business strategy that involves five competitive forces. At the heart of these competitive forces is the idea that outside threats and circumstances are the most important factors to analyze in examining the health of a corporation or firm. These forces are 1) bargaining power of customers, 2) bargaining power of suppliers, 3) threat of new entrants, 4) threat of substitute products, and 5) rivalry amongst existing competitors. Porter defended the idea that corporations who were able to control these outside forces were well able to build and maintain sustainable competitive advantage. The reader will note that, while the resource-based view concerns itself primarily with evaluating internal contributors to sustainable advantage, Porter's five forces are primarily focused on the external forces related to a corporation's environment (Institute for Strategy & Competitiveness).

ESG factors and Porter's five forces model

1) **Bargaining power of buyers:** Buyers have the power to demand certain actions or behaviors from a corporation, through actions such as positive and negative ESG engagement. ESG engagement can encourage behavior from lower prices, to increased attention to environmental, social, and governance structures. These external factors have been shown to effect corporate policies for positive change.

2) **Bargaining power of suppliers:** Similar to powerful buyers, powerful suppliers can demand certain behaviors from their corporate buyers. This might happen in a service industry, where the supplier of the service might refuse the business until the purchaser conforms to certain environmental, social, or governance structures. The reader might consider unions in demonstrating the bargaining power of suppliers. In this case, union workers might refuse to work under unfair or unwise environmental, social, or governance circumstances.

3) **Threat of new entrants:** Just like it sounds, the threat of new entrants forces prices down as companies compete for consumers. New entrants also provide the potential threat that consumer demands beyond simply pricing will be met by competitors instead of by one's own

firm. Changes in regulation make these even more likely, as new entrants are more quickly able to adapt themselves to environmental and social regulations than established corporations with standard practices might achieve.

4) **Threat of substitute products:** Similar to the above discussion on the importance of rarity and imitability, the threat of substitute products represents the potential of credible competition in products. This can present itself when a product meets the same need as another product (whether this is accomplished with similar methodology).

5) **Rivalry amongst existing competitors:** Related to the bargaining power of buyers, extensive competition helps to drive down prices by increasing the costs of competing. This can erode company profits.

In short, Porter's five forces emphasize the impact of environmental factors on the corporate profitability. Simply put, ESG factors are increasingly being viewed as environmental factors which have the potential to drive both supplier and buyer behavior (Institute for Strategy & Competitiveness).

6.4 Universal owner theory

The universal owners theory, as it is commonly understood today, is linked to the heart of ESG investing growth over the past two decades. In this theory, large institutional investors such as pension funds, insurance companies, and large endowments are invested in virtually every asset class, investment sector, market capitalization, and geography. This asset diversification ties these institutional investors to the economic viability of a vast array of social and environmental factors, as these factors invariably affect investment profitability. By way of example, a pension fund may be invested both an automobile factory and a food-production factory. Poorly regulated emissions from the automobile factory could have a negative impact on the quality of the raw ingredients being used in the food-production factory, which in turn could materially impact the profitability of the food-production company. In this way, negative externalities resulting from poor regulation or sub-par environmental, social, or governance practices could materially impact the profitability of an institutional investor. This reality has the consequence of making institutional investors invested in regulation and focus on positive environmental, social, and governance-related factors. Their sheer size and influence are highly impactful to practices by corporations, which has shown itself in the growth of institutional investing (see Chapter 5 for an in-depth consideration of the prevalence of ESG investing across asset classes, geographies, and investment sectors).

LEARNING PERSPECTIVE 4: Sustainable Development Goals

Aniket Shah is the Head of Sustainable Investing for OppenheimerFunds, Inc. In this role, he is responsible for building and integrating sustainable investing principles throughout the firm's investment strategies and operations. Prior to this role, Aniket was the Program Leader for Sustainable Finance at the UN Sustainable Development Solutions Network, where he was responsible for working with governments, investors, corporations, and non-governmental organizations on sustainable development financing issues. He is a graduate of Yale University and is pursuing his doctorate in Economic Geography at the University of Oxford. This piece is written in his personal capacity.

The Sustainable Development Goals (SDGs) – a guidepost for financial transformation

The simultaneous achievement of economic growth, social inclusion, and environmental sustainability is the imperative of the 21st century. This imperative can be captured in two important words: sustainable development. The 17 Sustainable Development Goals (SDGs) agreed to by 193 member states of the United Nations in September 2015 embody these principles, with quantitative and qualitative targets and timelines through to 2030.

The Sustainable Development Goals (SDGs) provide an opportunity for the financial industry to recalibrate its efforts to support sustainable development. This is an important responsibility of the SDGs given the size and importance of the global financial sector. Recent estimates indicate that the SDGs will require an additional $2.4 trillion of annual public and private investment into low-carbon infrastructure, energy, agriculture, health, education, and other sustainability sectors globally. The financial sector – the task of which is to link the supply and demand of capital for productive investments – will be central to the world's efforts to position itself on a more sustainable path.

The asset management industry will play a particularly important role within the financial sector, given the growing size of investable assets globally and increasing interest on sustainable investing and ESG issues. The total pool of capital within non-bank institutional investors has more than tripled from 2001 to present, with well over $100 trillion today.[1] As of 2016, over $23 trillion of managed assets had some level of ESG integration.[2]

The SDGs can play a powerful role in furthering the investment industry's engagement on sustainable investing. For that to happen, however, it is important for the spirit of the SDGs to not be lost as the goals get translated into action for the financial sector. The spirit that underlies the SDGs is about the transformation of the global economy into a system that simultaneously pursues economic growth, inclusion, and environmental safety. The SDGs are therefore not about simply mapping current practices and revenue streams of issuers to the 17 goals and subsequently being named an SDG-aligned product. That is a superficial treatment of a much deeper transition that is needed and sought after by the SDGs. Keeping with that concept, I believe that the SDGs can be a helpful guidepost to the financial sector in four ways.

First, the SDGs should initiate a structured conversation and governance process within both asset owners and asset managers to understand how they are contributing or detracting from global efforts around sustainability as outlined by the goals. This is simply a first step of the custodians and stewards of capital to more clearly understand how both their international functioning as an organization as well as the external impact of their investments is contributing to the momentum around sustainability. There are no set standards – nor should there be – around how this internal assessment should happen within the boards of asset owners and asset managers, but nonetheless these discussions are an important start.

Second, the SDGs should support the creation of investment products that are *additional* and *intentional* to solving the challenges of sustainable development. Additionality and intentionality are, I believe, the two central aspects of SDG products and investment programs. For an investment product to be aligned to the SDGs, it must be clearly demonstrated how the product lends itself to a non-business-as-usual outcome for whichever sector the fund is investing in. This additionality can be understood in many ways, whether it is shareholder activism and engagement that would likely otherwise not have occurred. It can also mean the deploying of capital to regions and businesses that otherwise may not have had access to private capital. Similarly, in keeping with the spirit of the SDGs, the investment product must have a stated intention to be addressing a sustainable development challenge.

Third, the SDGs should support the creation of multi-stakeholder partnerships between investment firms, issuers, academia, the nonprofit sector, and other sets of actors that must more collaboratively work together for the SDGs to be achieved. One of the biggest challenges for sustainable development to be achieved is the lack of cooperation and coordination between different actors in the global economy. One of the SDGs, SDG 17, explicitly targets this as an issue that must be addressed. The SDGs should drive the creation of platforms that bring together these various actors in an intentional way. Investment firms should be central nodes in these platforms given the significant influence of capital in the global economy.

Fourth, the SDGs should be the central framework used by corporations and governments to create a standard, uniformed, and globally accepted Sustainability Accounting Framework that mandates disclosure of material non-financial information from issuers to investors. The lack of uniformed sustainability accounting standards remains one of the most important challenges and bottlenecks for global efforts around sustainability. The reason that the SDGs can be helpful in this regard is that they have been agreed to by all 193 countries of the United Nations, which gives them an initial legitimacy from which a broader set of efforts can be developed.

The SDGs can be a powerful tool for transformation of the global financial sector, which can then play an even productive and efficient role in connecting capital with investment opportunities for a more sustainable future. For that goal to be realized, the spirit of the SDGs cannot and should not be lost, but rather built upon.

Discussion questions

1) Discuss and identify the differences between shareholder theory and stakeholder theory (LO1)
2) Discuss and identify the differences between material and immaterial information (LO2)
3) Discuss and identify the differences between the resource-based view and the intrinsic value view (LO3)
4) Choose one theoretical perspective and discuss whether that perspective aligns with ESG investing principles and produce reasons to support your view (LO5)
5) Discuss:

   a   Reasons why institutional investors might incorporate ESG investing within their investment portfolio (LO5)
   b   Reasons why institutional investors choose to not incorporate ESG investing in their investment portfolios (LO5)

6) Select a case study within the chapter and describe the contribution the case study had to the efficacy of ESG investing

Notes

1   World Bank (2016). *Global Financial Development Report: Long term finance*. http://documents.worldbank.org/curated/en/955811467986333727/pdf/99100-PUB-REVISED-Box393195B-0U0-9-until-9-14-15.pdf (Accessed: May 11, 2018)
2   USSIF (2017). Report on US Sustainable, Responsible and Impact Investing Trends 2016:

References

Ballantine, H. W., Adolf A. Berle, and Gardiner C. Means. "The Modern Corporation and Private Property." *California Law Review* 21, no. 1 (1932): 78. doi:10.2307/3475545.

Barney, Jay. "Firm Resources and Sustained Competitive Advantage." *Journal of Management* 17, no. 1 (1991): 99–120. doi:10.1177/014920639101700108.

Dierickx, Ingemar, and Karel Cool. "Asset Stock Accumulation and the Sustainability of Competitive Advantage: Reply." *Management Science* 35, no. 12 (1989): 1514. doi:10.1287/mnsc.35.12.1514.

Dodd, E. Merrick. "For Whom Are Corporate Managers Trustees?" *Harvard Law Review* 45, no. 7 (1932): 1145. doi:10.2307/1331697.

"Dodges Sue Henry Ford." *New York Times*, November 3, 1916.

Elson, Charles M., and Goossen Nicholas J., E. Merrick Dodd and The Rise and Fall of Corporate Stakeholder Theory. *Business Lawyer*, May 1, 2017. Available at SSRN https://ssrn.com/abstract=2966331.

Friedman, Milton. "The Social Responsibility of Business Is to Increase Its Profits." *The New York Times Magazine*, September 13, 1970.

Hart, S. L. "A Natural-Resource-Based View of the Firm." *Academy of Management Review* 20, no. 4 (1995): 986–1014.

"Henry Ford Beaten in $60,000,000 Suit." *New York Times*, November 1, 1917.

"Institute for Strategy & Competitiveness." The Five Forces – Institute for Strategy and Competitiveness – Harvard Business School. www.isc.hbs.edu/strategy/business-strategy/Pages/the-five-forces.aspx. Accessed April 8, 2018.

"Newspaper Specials." *Wall Street Journal* (New York), November 4, 1916.

Penrose, Edith Tilton. *The Theory of the Growth of the Firm*. Oxford: Basil Blackwell, 1959.

Keynes, J. M. "The End of Laissez-Faire." *Journal of Political Economy* 36, no. 1 (February 1928): 179–80.

Prahalad, C. K., and G. Hamel. "The Core Competence of the Corporation." *Strategische Unternehmungsplanung/Strategische Unternehmungsführung* (1997): 969–87. doi:10.1007/978-3-662-41482-8_46.

USSIF. 2016 Report on US Sustainable, Responsible and Impact Investing Trends. Report no. 11. The Forum for Sustainable and Responsible Investment. 2016. https://ussif.org/store_product.asp?prodid=34

Wernerfelt, Birger. "A Resource-Based View of the Firm." *Strategic Management Journal* (1984): 171–80.World Bank. "Global Financial Development Report: Long-Term Finance." 2016. http://documents.worldbank.org/curated/en/955811467986333727/pdf/99100-PUB-REVISED-Box393195B-OUO-9-until-9-14-15.pdf. Accessed May 11, 2018.

Chapter 7

Common investor concerns regarding ESG investment strategies

After this chapter, readers should have a well-rounded exposure to the common objections to ESG investing, and have a clearer understanding of the reasons behind the current level of incorporation of ESG investing in portfolio construction and management.

Learning objectives

- Describe forward-looking trends within investing relevant to ESG investing
- Thoughtfully assess and critique investor concerns about the performance of ESG investments
- Thoughtfully assess and critique investor concerns about the policies and obligations of investment managers regarding ESG investments
- Thoughtfully assess and critique investor concerns about the availability of material information within different markets, asset classes, and sectors that would affect the accuracy of ESG rating systems
- Thoughtfully assess and critique investor concerns about regions in which ESG investments may be unavailable or severely restricted

Introduction

Doubts about the effectiveness of ESG research-based investing strategies may be framed by five separate areas of concern:

Return concerns involve the fear that ESG investment strategies limit the investment pool, resulting in the perceived likelihood for lower returns (MacLean, 2012; D'Alessandro, 2011; Duuren et al. 2016)

Investment strategy concerns involve concerns regarding the effectiveness of ESG in passive vs. active investing strategies (Auer and Schuhmacher, 2016; van Duuren, Plantinga, and Scholtens, 2016)

Information concerns involve concerns regarding data accessibility and transparency on environmental, social, and governance issues (Czerwinska and Kazmierkiewicz, 2015; Kiernan, 2007)

Policy concerns are related to current policies that might forbid the use of non-financial screens in investing strategies (Sanders, 2015; Sørensen and Pfeifer, 2011)

Regional concerns involve doubts about the methodology and practice of ESG investing

7.1 Return concerns

This first concern addresses the impact of ESG factors on the accessibility of the investment universe. ESG investing is sometimes perceived to have a likelihood for higher investment risk and/ or lower potential performance because the investor is intentionally limiting investment choices to a smaller universe of investments that are consistent with environmental, social, and governance standards (Cortez, Silva, and Areal, 2012; MacLean, 2012; D'Alessandro, 2011; van Duuren, Plantinga, and Scholtens, 2016). Traditional investors may believe that ESG investing will damper investment performance because of the narrowing or limiting universe element of the methodologies. Investment managers and asset managers may find certain methodologies, such as exclusion, concerning because of the limitation of the investment universe. Even outside of exclusionary screening of securities, integration, impact, and engagement methodologies can directly or indirectly limit an investor's options.

William Sanders, in his article "Resolving the Conflict between Fiduciary Duties and Socially Responsible Investing" (2015), voices a common investor concern that restricting the investment pool to investments that pass the minimum standards of the ESG rating process will reduce the number of possible investments, which may lead to limited returns. However, this assertion that ESG investing strategies limits return potential contradicts much of current portfolio construction theories. In fundamental investing strategies, an investor considers financial ratios and measurements of cash flow such as price-to-earnings, price-to-cash, price-to-book, and price-to-sales as relevant dimensions of financial performance (Gombola and Ketx, 1983; Guerard, 2014; Arinovic-Barac, 2011). The investor would then screen out securities, e.g. equities, that are perceived as unfavorable using these fundamental valuation measurements (Gombola and Ketx, 1983; Guerard, 2014; Arinovic-Barac, 2011). ESG integration provides an additional layer for company valuation, beyond cash flow ratios and general company research (van Duuren, Plantinga, and Scholtens, 2016). Employing fundamental analyses like financial ratios is neither considered imprudent nor is it considered unduly restricting the amount of possible investments (Arinović-Barac, 2011). Therefore, it is reasonable to assume that employing ESG research-based integration should not be considered imprudently restricting the number of potential investments. The investor who employs ESG strategies is able to synthesize a larger amount of research, and more granularly analyze investment options, in order to have a higher opportunity set for return enhancement with a lower risk profile (Czerwinska and Kazmierkiewicz, 2015). ESG investing builds on investment strategies employed by fundamental investors.

A sensible theoretical and commonly reasoned rebuttal to the returns concerns argument is the fact that all investment research and strategy processes narrow the investment universe through their exercise, such is the case with fundamental and quantitative analysis, and all methodologies stretching along the spectrum of discretionary and systematic approaches. A more concentrated universe is not a limitation of opportunity as long as the portfolio is large enough to limit **idiosyncratic risk**, the microeconomic risk associated with a single investment (such as a stock), and which is diversifiable. Idiosyncratic risk protection can be achieved at 28 securities, which is easily feasible, even when considering the limitations ESG methodology implementation might cause. Elton and Gruber (1977), in a study entitled "Risk Reduction and Portfolio Size: An Analytical Solution," conducted a study to measure the relationship between portfolio size and the diversification of idiosyncratic risk. In this study, they discovered that portfolios incorporating approximately 28 securities reduced the total risk of the portfolio to only 20% higher than the minimum total risk (calculated as the variance of the equally weighted population portfolio (Elton and Gruber, 1977). This study's results are widely accepted as an industry standard mathematical assumption for idiosyncratic risk analysis.

Research has also shown that ESG investing has the potential to enhance investment returns. Investors who are hesitant to integrate non-financial factors, such as ESG, might hinder their investment returns. Some investors see ESG investing as distracting, inappropriate, risky, and legally challenging. In response, studies have emerged to show that ESG investing is a growing interest with investors, helps to mitigate financial risks, and does not always represent a financial cost (Rezec, 2016).

The number of public companies reporting ESG information grew from fewer than 20 in the early 1990s to 8,500 by 2014. Moreover, by the end of 2014, over 1,400 institutional investors that manage some $60 trillion in assets had signed the UN Principles for Responsible Investment (UNPRI). Nevertheless, companies with high ESG ratings have continued to be viewed by mainstream investors as unlikely to produce competitive shareholder returns, in part because of the findings of older studies showing low returns from the social responsibility investing of the 1990s. However, more recent studies suggest that companies with significant ESG programs have outperformed their competitors (Kotsantonis, Pinney, and Serafeim, 2016). ESG may also enhance returns by reducing risks when investing in the securities of companies. Empirical evidence shows that institutional investors improve their risk-adjusted returns when incorporating ESG considerations into their investment processes (Nagy, Kassam, and Lee, 2016).

ESG investing in passive and active strategies

There is a perception amongst investors that ESG integration requires an active management strategy, and is incompatible with a passive management strategy (Auer and Schuhmacher, 2016; van Duuren, Plantinga, and Scholtens, 2016). This perception stems from the assumption that making investment decisions based on ESG ratings is the same strategy as actively picking stocks (Auer and Schuhmacher, 2016). However, the research reveals that both active and passive ESG-based investing prove to be more profitable than traditional investments over the long-term (Kocmanova, Karpisek, and Klimkova, 2012; van Duuren, Plantinga, and Scholtens, 2016). In regions with increased environmental, social, or governance risks, limiting the pool of possible investments is an advantage to investors, who, through the method of exclusion or other ESG implementation methodology, are able to diversify risk by investing passively in a volatile market without sacrificing returns. The below case study from Aperio illustrates how ESG-relative passive products are customized for clients in order to not sacrifice index performance or encounter extreme tracking error.

CASE STUDY 7A: passively customized ESG indices by Aperio

Mark E. Bateman, the Director of ESG/SRI Research of the Aperio Group

Mark E. Bateman is Aperio's Director of ESG/SRI Research and is an internationally recognized ESG/SRI/Impact expert and works with Aperio's clients to create customized ESG/SRI/Impact solutions that reflect their values. In addition to his work with Aperio, Mark is the founder of ENSOGO Analytics, a firm offering environmental, social, and governance (ESG) ratings of mutual funds and ETFs. Before founding ENSOGO, he served as the Director of Research at IW Financial (now part of ISS), a leading provider of value-added ESG research. Prior to that, Mark spent 11 years at the Investor Responsibility Research Center (IRRC, now part of MSCI) in Washington, DC, in a range of positions, including Director of the Environmental Information Service, and ultimately, Vice President of Research and Operations. He also served on the original steering committee of the Global Reporting Initiative, helping to develop a sustainability reporting framework for companies. He serves on the board of directors for the Sustainable Investments Institute (Si2), a social proxy research firm. Mark holds a BA from Johns Hopkins University and an MA from George Washington University. Mark lives in

Salem, Oregon, where he serves on the school district budget committee as well as a number of church boards and committees at the local, state, and regional level.

Mark provides an understanding of how Aperio Group uses ESG as part of their passive investing practice. Aperio Group's overall approach to working with clients in the creation of separately managed accounts is to customize in all areas of need for the client. This includes environmental, social, and governance (ESG) issues when requested by the client. Aperio seeks to customize the ESG criteria for a client's account to best reflect the client's expressed values.

Aperio's primary investment style is designed to match index performance as closely as possible. Therefore, Aperio does not manage ESG issues with an eye to seeking alpha from long-term ESG trends. In addition, Aperio is agnostic when it comes to social and environmental values. While as individuals we certainly have our own views of the world, as an asset manager for our clients, it is their environmental and social values, not ours, that are our concern.

Primary tools for aligning values
Aperio uses two primary approaches to integrate ESG criteria into the portfolio construction process to best reflect a client's values: exclusions and tilting.

Exclusions, also sometimes called "negative screening," identify a bright line definition against which companies are evaluated. Companies that match the criteria are then unavailable to the portfolio. We often tell clients when thinking about exclusionary criteria that they eliminate companies from consideration based on one issue, no matter how good the company may be on other issues about which they care.

Tilting, on the other hand, has no absolutes. It does not guarantee the exclusion of a company based on specific criteria, neither does it guarantee the inclusion of a company. Tilting is how the Aperio Group implements ESG integration passively. The process of tilting the portfolio toward "better" companies (as defined by the client's criteria) relies on a way to measure the relative ESG scores of companies. With such a score, Aperio's approach to portfolio construction allows for us to build a "better" portfolio.

In addition to these tools used during portfolio construction, Aperio offers its clients the opportunity to use their ownership in companies to advocate for corporate responsibility. Specifically, Aperio votes client proxies based on a set of socially responsible investing criteria at corporate annual meetings, and interested clients may use some of their investment positions to file shareholder resolutions on topics of concern.

Building a custom values policy
In order to evaluate companies to identify those better aligned with a client's interests, we must first determine the issues that matter to the client and a method of scoring companies. (Note that in evaluating companies, Aperio doesn't refer to "good" or "bad" companies, but to "better" or "worse" companies. We use comparative language, not standards-based language.)

At Aperio, we use several different types of ESG scores as building blocks to reflect a client's values.

Broad-based ESG issues. The first approach is to build an ESG score based on client preferences across a wide range of ESG issues from categories like environment, climate change, human rights, diversity, corporate governance, workforce/labor, and sexual orientation. Within each of these categories, we use individual data elements to build a category score. In Aperio's process, clients can select these data elements. For example, in the Diversity category, a client may be more interested in minority diversity than gender diversity. On this basis, the criteria set might include two data elements: the *percentage of minorities in senior management* and *percentage of minorities in the total workforce*, but might not include the parallel data elements related to women.

Once data elements have been selected in each of the categories of interest to the investor, the client determines the relative importance (or weight) of each category. This step is critical to the customization process. Consider two clients, both interested in environment and human rights, though their prioritizations may be different. One might say that human rights is twice as important as environment, and the other might say the reverse.

Within this broad spectrum ESG scoring system, a client's preferences are customized at three levels: 1) which categories/topics are included in the profile, 2) the relative weight/importance of the categories to one another, 3) the data elements used within each category to represent that topic. Each minor change to one of these will change the scores generated for each company and therefore the optimization process for the portfolio.

Low carbon. A second tilting opportunity available in Aperio portfolio's is to tilt toward a lower carbon portfolio than available in the benchmark index. By using a combination of total carbon emissions and carbon intensity (emissions normalized by revenue) as an ESG score, we use the optimization process to target a specific reduction in the carbon footprint of the portfolio compared to the benchmark, usually an 80% reduction.

Positive exposures. A third tilting opportunity is to identify a set of positive scores, and increase the exposure of the portfolio to these scores. One example Aperio has used in client portfolios is the level of exposure to an MSCI dataset called Clean Technology Solutions. The data measure the percentage of revenues companies have in five areas: green building materials, pollution prevention, sustainable water, alternative energy, and energy efficiency. By using the percentage of revenue from this data as an ESG score, we're able to calculate a weighted average percentage in the benchmark index and then target a higher weighted average in the client portfolio, usually two or three times higher.

Other "positive" attributes we've used to tilt a portfolio include place-based strategies seeking to overweight companies with specific geographic attributes. For instance, a community foundation interested in employment in a specific state has tilted toward higher exposure to employers in that state, or Jewish investors can tilt toward companies with direct ties to Israel.

ESG data
There are four basic kinds of ESG data that Aperio uses: involvement, disclosure, policy, and performance.

Involvement data is most frequently used for exclusionary criteria, but as mentioned above, can be the basis for tilting toward "positive" involvement. This type of data may be collected from a variety of sources that provide an indication of company involvement. In most cases, this involvement is then confirmed based on company sources.

Disclosure data evaluates that level of transparency of a company within a specific issue area by looking at categories or attributes of disclosure. In evaluations of transparency, the information disclosed is not itself evaluated, but the fact of disclosure is noted. Since this is a measure of transparency, the information must be publicly available and therefore anything not publicly available receives a zero in the evaluation.

Policy data evaluates the level of company policy on specific topics. Like with disclosure data, it most frequently looks for attributes of the policy. Policy data is also based on publicly available information. Policies that are not publicly available do not qualify for inclusion in this type of evaluation.

Performance data is usually quantitative and reflects something that took place. It may be pounds of toxic emission, number of women on the board of directors, or dollars spent on lobbying. Performance data may be based on mandatory disclosure or on voluntary disclosure. When Aperio's evaluation of a performance data element is based on voluntarily disclosed data, our methodology penalizes companies that do not make the necessary information available. In these cases, lack of disclosure scores worse than any company that does disclose the necessary information. This creates the possibility of distortion in the dataset, but from Aperio's perspective, it's better to penalize the lack of disclosure rather than create a potential incentive for a company to not disclose bad performance.

Portfolio construction

Aperio is a quantitative manager seeking to match benchmark index performance. We use a multi-factor optimizer to statistically sample the benchmark index, and then optimize (or reweight) the selected names for the portfolio in order to match as closely as possible the factor attributes of the benchmark index. This process allows us to reduce transaction costs associated with owning all securities in the index (think: owning 500 names from the Russell 3,000 rather than all 3,000 names). Note that the goal is to match the risk characteristics "as closely as possible." The optimization process cannot match exactly all factors and each deviation from the benchmark index introduces variability in the expected risk factors and financial performance of the portfolio compared to the benchmark index. The expected difference in financial performance is called tracking error (TE). Tracking error is measured in percent of deviation.

While the process of excluding specific companies alters the universe available to the optimizer, the optimizer functions in the same manner as described above, with the same goal – minimizing the tracking error based on traditional financial and risk factors of comparing the constructed portfolio to the benchmark index.

When tilting the portfolio toward the client's ESG preferences, we are adding to the multi-factor optimization process. Specifically, we add one or more ESG "factors" into the process, usually in the form of an ESG score. The optimization process then uses the same quantitative and statistical tools to construct a portfolio based on all the original factors and the new ESG factor or factors. Left to its own devices, the optimizer would seek to match the inserted ESG component's exposure from the benchmark index in the new portfolio. This is where "tilting" comes in. Aperio assigns a target ESG exposure to the optimizer higher than that of the index.

For example, Aperio scores companies on clients' ESG criteria from 1 to 100, where the higher the score the better the company compared to the client's values. The first job for the optimizer is to establish the total exposure of the benchmark index to this new ESG factor. In this case, it calculates a weighted average ESG score for the benchmark index (sum of each company ESG score X company weight). If the benchmark index starts with a weighted average score of 50, to tilt toward a better reflection of the client's values, we might assign the optimizer a goal of building a portfolio with a weighted average score of 65. The optimizer must achieve this "higher than the benchmark" ESG score while matching as closely as possible the new portfolio's exposure to the original financial/risk factors. The additional deviation from the benchmark caused by tilting toward a higher ESG score for the portfolio results in some increase in tracking error.

The optimization process described here can be used to insert and manage multiple ESG issues into the construction of a portfolio. The only requirement is that there be an ESG score for each additional issue area.

Values intensity
In the example above, we tilted the portfolio above the benchmark average ESG score of 50 to a score of 65, but there is nothing magical about 65. We could as easily have assigned a target of 75 or 85. It's fairly intuitive that the higher the target ESG score, the more necessary the deviation on the financial/risk factors, and therefore the higher the tracking error. Based on the same set of ESG criteria, we can construct an optimal curve that shows ever increasing ESG scores and the resulting increase in tracking error. We call this the Social Efficient Frontier. Every social profile (every client) has a unique Social Efficient Frontier.

SRI Summary Results

Portfolio Name	S&P 500	S&P 500 All Cash	Sample Portfolio - 75	Sample Portfolio - 80	More Idealistic Sample Portfolio - 85
Tracking Error (%)	0.00	0.18	0.34	0.80	1.58
Beta	1.00	1.00	1.00	1.00	1.00
Standard Deviation (%)	13.46	13.54	13.54	13.56	13.63
# of Holdings	505	349	347	258	144
Dividend Yield (%)	2.32	2.34	2.35	2.23	2.23
Social Score	70	70	75	80	85
Benchmark	S&P 500	S&P 500	S&P 500	S&P 500	S&P 500

Figure 7.1 Tracking error in social scores

As the Social Efficient Frontier demonstrates, the application of a client's values in this process is not a binary issue. It's not that the values have or haven't been applied, it's in part a question of the intensity at which the values are applied. The higher the ESG score, the more intensely the values have been applied.

Conclusion

By combining customized values criteria with a portfolio optimization approach to portfolio construction, Aperio allows clients to tackle two persistent perceptions regarding ESG investing:

- That investors can't achieve market rate returns if they use ESG criteria
- That investors must use the values/criteria identified by the money manager

While it is true that many ESG financial products must start with a specified value set because they are co-mingled funds from a variety of investors, Aperio's market offerings are separately managed accounts and for ESG clients, premised on the belief that client values are unique and criteria set can be developed in collaboration with the client to determine criteria that reflect their values.

In addition, we believe that the construction of the portfolio matters as much as the selection of portfolio constituents. The optimization process provides the opportunity to minimize the impact of excluding companies from the portfolio as well as minimize the impact of overweighting "good" ESG companies.

Traditional active management strategies are also augmented by ESG strategies, which provide more information on which to base investment decisions. Whether an investor employs an active management strategy and selects ESG investments based on individual ESG ratings, or invests in ESG indices such as one of the 650+ MSCI ESG indices or a custom product from Aperio, in aggregate, returns are proven to be higher and risks lower (Odell and Ali, 2016; Banerjee and Orzano, 2010; Chelawat and Trivedi, 2013; Pollard, Sherwood, and Klobus, 2018).

Organizations are making efforts to analyze the return implications of ESG investing. The Pension and Lifetime Savings Association (PLSA) commissioned a study from Sustainalytics in order to better understand the ESG risks facing the default funds offered by defined contribution (DC) pension plan sponsors in the United Kingdom (UK). The number of Defined Contribution plan members in the UK is set to increase dramatically over the next ten years. The Pension Policy Institute (PPI) forecasts that by 2030 there could be 17 million members enrolled in DC workplace schemes in the UK, up from 11 million today. The value of the aggregate pension pot held by these DC plan members is forecasted to reach £554 billion by 2030, and could potentially be as high as £914 billion, up from £324 billion in 2015. Close to 90% of these assets are likely to be held in default funds. The decisions made by plan trustees and asset managers about the management and construction of default fund options, including whether to integrate ESG factors, will have significant implications for the future financial security of UK workers (Morrow, 2017).

7.2 Policy concerns

Investors traditionally have hesitated to integrate ESG factors, for the fear that this will violate regulatory policy. **Institutional theory** reveals that there are three forms of law that govern the behavior of institutional investors: regulative, normative, and cognitive (Scott and Meyer, 1994; Galbreath, 2012). **Regulative law** regulates through official rules set in place by government; **normative laws** are underlying values and moral commitments of a society; **cognitive laws** are "common sense laws" which incorporate unspoken common understandings of rational people (Scott and Meyer, 1994, Galbreath, 2012). The institution of **fiduciary obligation** within investing is the result of regulative law. Fiduciary obligation, very simply, is the legal obligation for one party to act in the best interest of another party. Chapter 6 discussed the "principal – agent theory." In fiduciary relationships, the agent has the fiduciary duty to act in the best interest of the principal. This traditionally has been measured by the extent to which the agent acts in the financial interest of the principal, instead of the agent's own financial profit. The result of the institution of fiduciary obligations, is that institutional investors until very recently have ignored normative and cogitative law. There has been a prevailing notion within institutional investing that fiduciary law forbids the use of non-financial screens because the investments that select or reject securities are not based purely on financial performance (Sanders, 2015). However, for an institutional investor, acting in the beneficiaries' best interest, which is the duty of a fiduciary, might include elements of ESG investing, such as socially responsibility (Sanders, 2015).

The United States' Department of Labor issued new guidance in 2015 regarding economically targeted investments (ETIs) and ESG factors. In the new guidance report, the US Department of Labor defines ESG strategies as any investment that is selected in part for its collateral benefits, apart from investment returns (Department of Labor, 2015). In this interpretive bulletin, the US Department of Labor concluded that fiduciaries should not be discouraged from integrating ESG investments into portfolios, as long as the investments were otherwise an appropriate investment in terms of risk levels and expected rate of return (Department of Labor, 2015). Therefore, policy concerns seem to logically contradict legislative rulings and empirical proof as to the qualitative and quantitative value of ESG investing strategies.

CASE STUDY: 7B ESG investing – key trends and a roadmap for institutional implementation

Michael C. Lauer, Alecia DeCuollo, and Trevor Jackson

Summit Strategies Group has a dedicated team of three professionals that focus on developing, enhancing, and sustaining the firm's perspectives and approaches to responsible investing. Leading this group and the responsible investing efforts at Summit is Michael Lauer, the lead author of this case study. Alecia DeCuollo (research analyst) and Trevor Jackson (consultant) also made significant contributions to the original white paper produced by Summit.

Michael C. Lauer *is a consultant at Summit Strategies. He works closely with several of Summit's clients, including corporate and public pension plans, endowments and foundations, and healthcare systems. Prior to his current role, Michael was an intern in the firm's Capital Markets & Risk Management group, where he focused on the development of a healthcare model that views investment risks in a holistic system-wide context. Michael holds a bachelor's degree (with honors) in economics from Loyola University Chicago, a master's degree in business administration from Saint Louis University and a master's degree in health administration from Saint Louis University. He is also active in various nonprofit boards and committees in St. Louis.*

About the case study

The following case study was adapted from a white paper produced by Summit Strategies Group, a leading institutional investment consulting firm, in December 2017. The demand for socially responsible investment strategies has grown tremendously over the past decade. Investors who have implemented successful responsible investing programs typically have dedicated time up front to determine what they wanted out of a responsible investing program (goals and objectives) and built their policy around those goals. In an industry where investment options abound, identifying the preferences of the investor's committee and/or board is critical to success. This case study outlines key investor considerations in the development and implementation of responsible investing policies and strategies.

About Summit

Summit Strategies Group is one of the industry's leading investment consultants focused on developing long-term partnerships with institutional investors. Founded in 1995, we have been serving our clients, including endowments and foundations, hospitals and healthcare systems, public funds and corporations (defined benefit and defined contribution plans), for more than 20 years.

We provide traditional full-service consulting, defined contribution, and outsourced CIO services. Our extensive in-house resources and research capabilities enable us to help clients meet their investment objectives. We have highly experienced professionals in the areas of consulting, capital markets and risk management, manager research, operational due diligence, and performance measurement and analytics.

Introduction

Over the past decade, growth in responsible investing has been driven by amplified concerns about how corporations conduct business. During this time, investors have increasingly allocated capital to investment strategies that support initiatives or endeavors that ultimately benefit society. ESG investing, in particular, is one approach that has garnered investor interest. This case study provides a broad overview of ESG investing, key trends in the ESG community, along with a framework for institutional investors to successfully implement ESG strategies.

Industry statistics

- $22 trillion is invested in responsible investing strategies globally, 53% of which comes from asset owners in Europe (Global Sustainable Investment Alliance)[1]
- $8 trillion is invested in responsible investing strategies in the US, up from $3 trillion in 2010 (US Sustainable Investment Forum)[2]
- +25% of North American institutional investors employ ESG (environmental, social, governance) principles in their portfolios and 60% of investors who do not incorporate ESG criteria state they are open to incorporating ESG in the future (Greenwich)[3]
- Over 1,700 organizations managing $60 trillion have become signatories to the United Nations Principles for Responsible Investing (UNPRI)[4]

Incorporation of ESG factors is growing

The growth of ESG investing has been driven by asset owners becoming more interested in aligning their investment portfolios with their organization's mission/vision/values.

In the marketplace, three major market trends have pushed investors to consider the potential benefits of ESG investing – 1) corporate scandals, 2) the continued generational shift in investment preferences, 3) regulation that allows investors flexibility to incorporate these factors, and 4) performance results that suggest investors can generate attractive long-term returns while adhering to their responsible investing beliefs.

Corporate scandals – avoidance of negative corporate behaviors

Over the past several decades, corporate scandals centered on environmental, social, and governance issues have been a prominent driver for investors to consider responsible investing strategies. In the 1980s, environmental concerns garnished increased attention in the wake of disasters, such as the Exxon Valdez oil spill. In the 1990s, Nike was one the first large retail manufacturers pressured to improve company standards for overseas production after disturbing rep0orts of child labor and sweatshops emerged. More recently, the financial crisis and governance issues at Enron and Volkswagen, among others, have continued to create demand for additional initiatives and awareness in tightening corporate governance and sustainable business practices.

Generational shift in investment preferences – societal evolution

Growing pressures from the millennial generation have reinforced the need for companies to incorporate sustainable business practices and consider their potential influence on society and the environment. A 2015 study by TIAA[5] found that 90% of affluent millennials (vs. 76% of affluent non-millennials) stated interest in promoting positive social and environmental outcomes, in addition to realizing competitive returns from their investments. As the so-called great wealth transfer accelerates – an estimated $30 trillion[6] in wealth will transfer from baby boomers to Generation X and millennials over the next several decades – trends in ESG and responsible investing will continue to be supported.

Regulation – relief of legal roadblocks

Over 50% of assets in Europe are in some way connected to responsible investing according to the 2016 Global Sustainable Investment Review (compared to 22% in the US).[7] This has largely been driven by regulation, where many countries require the disclosure and consideration of ESG factors in the portfolio construction process. The US has since implemented measures that clarify fiduciary duties among pension investment advisors, which has helped support the rise in responsible investing. In 2015, the Department of Labor (DoL), responsible for enforcing the Employment Retirement Income Security Act (ERISA), rescinded its 2008 bulletin on Economically Targeted Investments, which was largely thought to have discouraged fiduciaries for private sector retirement plans from considering environmental and social factors in their investments. The DoL articulated that

> environmental, social, and governance issues may have a direct relationship to the economic value of the plan's investment . . . such issues are not merely collateral considerations or tiebreakers, but rather are proper components of the fiduciary's primary analysis of the economic merits of competing investment choices.[8]

Historical performance of ESG investment strategies – investors desire to have it all

One challenge for institutional investors when considering ESG investment strategies is marrying the goals of responsible investing with long-term return objectives. Due to the newness of ESG investment products, and subsequently a lack of long-term perfor-mance data, historical analysis typically focuses on measuring the performance of indi-vidual companies with strong ESG practices relative to their counterparts, as opposed to investment products themselves. The empirical data is mixed: many studies point to the financial benefit (corporate profits and stock performance) awarded to companies that incorporate sustainability themes into their businesses. Other studies suggest these benefits are already reflected in stock prices, and therefore investors have nothing to gain by incorporating responsible investing factors into their investment strategies.

Summit believes the investment industry is still in the early innings of truly assessing the performance efficacy of ESG strategies. Long-term performance data remains limited, and it will be critical to assess how ESG strategies perform over multiple market cycles and longer time horizons than is currently available.

Helping clients achieve ESG goals and objectives
Summit has dedicated resources to support clients in their responsible investing initia-tives. In particular, we recommend a four-step process that guides investors through the creation and implementation of responsible investing strategies. Board and committee expectations are determined up front, which then inform the manager evaluation and selection process. The first two steps are particularly crucial, as explicit expectations and objectives are essential in selecting managers that best align with the organization's goals.

Four-step process
1   Education
2   Policy development
3   Implementation and manager selection
4   Ongoing due diligence

Education
For clients considering ESG investing, Summit recommends education as the first step. Most often, we start by outlining the potential pros and cons of SRI/ESG/Impact investing, the explicit and implicit goals of each, and how these strategies can aid/detract from performance (both in theory and historical experience). Through this education process, clients come away knowing if they want to be involved and, if so, have a rough idea of where the policy is heading (which is to be developed further).

Policy development
We have extensive experience in developing responsible investing solutions that align our clients' investment objectives with the mission of the organization, whether it be an endowment, foundation, healthcare system, religious organization, or corporation. We have helped create and manage exclusionary lists (e.g., SRI) as well as developed ESG-specific strategies. For example, we recently helped a pension plan (ERISA) inte-grate a holistic responsible investing approach that will advocate ESG investing over time. We also worked with a healthcare organization to set specific ESG guidelines for managers, and assisted a corporate defined contribution plan evaluate the appropriate ESG decisions for interested participants. In all three cases, the discussions with our clients were the most crucial element in developing successful policies.

Regardless of the approach utilized, we believe the first step to a successful program is to identify how responsible investing aligns with the mission and vision of the organization. To assist clients in thinking about this, we developed a series of key questions that we believe investors should answer as part of the consideration process:

1   Alignment. Which responsible investing approach fits best with the mission/vision of your organization (SRI/ESG/Impact)?
2   Value selection. Are there particular values that the committee would like to see integrated into this mandate?
3   Portfolio placement. Should there be a dedicated mandate within the portfolio, or is it an overarching goal for the entire portfolio?
4   Customization. Do off-the-shelf products meet your objectives or does it make sense to create a customized mandate?
5   Performance goals. What are the goals of the mandate (risk/return/tracking error/ societal impact)?
6   Measuring success. How will you measure the success (e.g., benchmarking) of the strategy?

An often-underappreciated point is the third question: from a portfolio construction perspective, investors should consider where ESG mandates fit within their portfolio – they can be bolt-on to traditional mandates, or investors can build a portfolio only utilizing managers that consider ESG factors. If a client is looking for a holistic portfolio solution, a major consideration is that not all asset classes are created equal, as some are further developed in their incorporation of ESG factors (Table 7.1).

Implementation and manager selection

For the past five years, Summit's manager research team has been gathering ESG information from managers and recently began scoring managers (equity and fixed income) along our proprietary ESG spectrum. Given this background, we have a broad understanding of the ESG universe and the various approaches that managers utilize. We use

Table 7.1 ESG strategy availability

	Equity	Fixed income	Alternatives (Hedge funds | real assets)
Prevalence of strategies (# of available options)	High (Global | US) Medium (EAFE | EM)	Medium	Low (hedge funds) Medium (real assets)
Maturity of strategies (track record)	High	Medium (Credit) Low (Government | Other)	Low
Customization capabilities	High	Medium	Low

Note: Private equity is not highlighted above as those strategies focused on ESG themes typically fall under the impact investing trend (not ESG)

this expertise to provide unique perspectives on managers to our clients and help identify those that we believe have the most potential of achieving our clients' goals.

While "off-the-shelf" products exist within all asset classes, equity products offer the most options for investors – both in the absolute number of available products and in length of track record – enabling them to select those that best align with their goals. If an investor has a sizable asset base, a customized mandate may be more appropriate. Investors can utilize an ESG research firm, such as MSCI, to create a customized list of companies that meet specific ESG criteria in which the manager can invest. As an example, we recently helped a client and an investment manager in developing a customized product that incorporated the client's specific religious values and ESG factors.

Our view on manager selection within the ESG space

Investment managers that integrate ESG into their investment processes typically develop proprietary ESG evaluation methods/tools to assess underlying companies and to build portfolios. While each method is unique, we believe managers fall into four broad categories: passive, quantitative, qualitative, and thematic.

1 Passive approach. Managers that take a passive approach to incorporating ESG factors into their process typically overlay ESG scores from a third-party provider onto their portfolio. The scores are then used to tilt the portfolio holdings accordingly. Portfolios built using this type of passive approach are usually built to have a better overall ESG "score" and low tracking error relative to traditional benchmarks.

   IDEAL INVESTOR: For fee-sensitive investors who want to make a statement, but do not want to incur much tracking error relative to a traditional benchmark or peers.

2 Quantitative approach. Quantitative strategies that utilize factor models typically integrate ESG metrics into an existing portfolio construction process to incrementally "enhance" the model from a risk and/or return perspective. There are two variations:

   a Universal integration – Managers integrate ESG scores (developed externally or internally) into their quantitative process for every company within the universe. They will often optimize their models to have a better ESG score than the benchmark or non-ESG strategies.

   b Selective integration – Managers evaluate which ESG metrics should be integrated (by industry, sector, or company), with the ultimate goal of maximizing risk-adjusted return. Differing from universal integration, the selective approach applies those ESG scores to companies or sectors found to be the most relevant for the model. For example, an ESG metric may not be a driver of alpha across all industries (according to a manager) and thus would only be used selectively.

   IDEAL INVESTOR: For investors who want to incorporate ESG into a quantitative process that aims to achieve incremental value-add over a traditional benchmark.

3 Qualitative approach. Managers who utilize qualitative judgments and views in the security selection and portfolio construction process fall into this approach, which is utilized by many managers that offer ESG products. Managers first narrow the universe based on ESG and/or financial metrics, then further consolidate the universe to a target list of portfolio companies based upon qualitative views and analysis.

The entire process is unique to each manager, with their own views on each company and/or portfolio construction serving as the main differentiator. There are three variations:

a Top-down perspective – Managers integrate and weight the portfolio based on top-down views on industries to formulate weights for companies within the portfolio.
b Bottom-up perspective – Managers utilize internal teams that evaluate companies along ESG metrics and rank companies against each other for the security selection and portfolio construction process.
c ESG factor perspective – Managers develop their own definitions of which issues constitute effective ESG investing. From there, they make a qualitative assessment based on their own definitions.

The spectrum of strategies that fall into this approach is broad. It is especially important for investors considering a qualitative approach to clearly define their views to ensure alignment with a strategy. By aligning views and goals, the manager will then target results that fit the investor's preferences.

IDEAL INVESTOR: For investors looking to take a large step into ESG investing and put their capital with a firm that possesses and implements strong views on ESG.

4 Thematic approach. Thematic investing is utilized by managers that want to focus on one or several ESG themes from either a macro or mission perspective. The implementation of a thematic model ranges from managing highly concentrated portfolios utilizing one theme (niche), e.g., a green energy fund, to a diversified group of assets that align with a variety of themes (multi-thematic).

IDEAL INVESTOR: For investors who are passionate about a particular theme (or themes) and want to have a focused mandate bolted onto a core-oriented ESG strategy. These often come with higher fees and are uniquely differentiated.

Manager differentiators

Summit has identified a variety of high-quality managers that offer products utilizing each type of approach discussed above. When evaluating ESG strategies, we conduct both quantitative and qualitative analysis. The quantitative factors that are assessed are similar to any traditional manager, but when it comes to the qualitative differentiators, we focus on five categories:

1 Firm involvement. Is the firm dedicated to ESG investing or is this product used for asset gathering?
2 Team composition. Has the firm established a dedicated team to conduct and/or analyze ESG research?
3 Engagement. How engaged is the firm with portfolio companies on ESG issues?
4 Data sources. What data does the strategy utilize during the portfolio construction process?
5 Strategy goals. What does this strategy aim to accomplish by integrating ESG factors?

Ongoing due diligence

Responsible investing mandates aim to accomplish more than simply outperforming a benchmark. Therefore, monitoring success over time is vital. We aid clients in managing exclusionary screens, ensuring compliance with predetermined ESG guidelines, and monitoring manager success as it relates to the collateral benefits of investing in ESG mandates. For numerous clients, we have established quarterly compliance reviews to ensure adherence to specific guidelines, and in some cases this includes responsible investing metrics and scores.

Conclusion

While still a young trend, ESG investing is here to stay as evidenced by the incredible growth of these strategies in recent years. For managers, the trend demands continual innovation and the development of solutions to meet client goals and objectives. For investors, it is becoming increasingly important to define what ESG means to them in order to determine the best way to incorporate ideas and preferences into investment portfolios. Having a structured process, which begins with education on considerations and options available, is integral to program success.

Summit Strategies has advised clients on responsible investing for over 20 years, including the development and maintenance of responsible investing policies. We have dedicated resources to assist clients in responsible investing initiatives and believe our investment consulting experience enables us to contribute valuable insights to our client partnerships.

7.3 Information concerns

ESG factor integration, by its very nature, requires access to non-financial information that has not historically been included in financial statements or company disclosures (van Duuren, Plantinga, and Scholtens, 2016; Odell and Ali, 2016; Farooq, 2015). According to the traditional approach to investment strategy, investors consider expected rate of return and the level of investment risk in choosing investments (Czerwinska and Kazmierkiewicz, 2015). Such considerations depend on available information about the company's business model and practices (Czerwinska and Kazmierkiewicz, 2015; van Duuren, Plantinga, and Scholtens, 2016). ESG integration even more so requires the disclosure of certain information to pass the minimum requirements for consideration as ESG investments (Dorfleitner, Halbritter, and Nguyen, 2015; Semenova and Hassel, 2015). Investors therefore are concerned that the lack of available information in certain asset classes and markets, e.g. the emerging markets, will limit the availability of ESG investments (Siddiqi, 2011; Kutan, 2004).

Most legislation relevant to socially responsible investments and ESG strategies have only been passed in Europe, while the United States and developing markets lag in legislation and accounting disclosure standards (Renneboog et al. 2008; Gilbert, 2010; Siddiqi, 2011). Outside of Europe, Australia is the only country to implement specific SRI regulations (Renneboog et al. 2008; Galbreath, 2012). Because of the lack of legislation, many companies have no incentive to disclose relevant information for the consideration of ESG factors. However, regulations like Regulation S-K passed by the United States' Securities & Exchange Commission (SEC) continue to develop legislation, requiring companies to disclose financial measures and other information that could be useful for measuring ESG factors (Rashty and O'Shaughnessy, 2014). For example, though emerging markets traditionally lag developed markets in accounting disclosure standards and information (Siddiqi, 2011), global ESG trends suggests progress towards the increased availability of non-financial information in these markets (Stewart, 2015). Organizations like the Sustainability Accounting Standards Board (SASB), the Carbon Disclosure Project (CDP), the Global Reporting Initiative

(GRI), the International Integrated Reporting Council (IIRC), CERES, and the UN Principles for Responsible Investment (UNPRI) are all committed to increasing the availability of information relevant to ESG investing (Stewart, 2015; United Nations, 2006). Each of these organizations, and hundreds more smaller organizations, continue to gather material information and investigation tactics that are improving the flow of non-financial information from companies (Stewart, 2015).

Investors may hold information concerns relative to ESG research and ratings firms. Investors may have difficulty determining which ESG research and ratings firms to use for data, and struggle to distinguish between the value of using an emerging ESG research service, or using a larger well-established firm, such as MSCI or Sustainalytics. Information concerns can also come in the form of the lack of standardization of the research methodologies and ratings data produced by such ESG research and ratings firms. Investors may have concerns on the validity and transparency of ESG information. However, the ever-growing field of ESG research and ratings by independent data service and research providers allow such concerns to be addressed in an unbiased manner. These data and research firms, as discussed in Chapter 3, may also be triangulated in order to reduce informational bias from individual research firms. The quality of information continues to advance at a rapid pace, and as such is advancing the development of cross-sectional data (Sherwood and Pollard, 2017).

7.4 Regional concerns

In the late 1990s, when socially responsible investing was gaining traction amongst institutional investors, institutional investors began reallocating research endeavors towards global sector allocation (Lin, 2013; Fernandes, 2005). The trend towards global sector allocation resulted in a renewed interest in emerging markets as a potential source of alpha that was unrelated to the risk in developed markets (Lin, 2013). A common practice for institutional investors during and after the 1990s was diversifying assets through various regional allocations throughout the developed, emerging, and frontier markets (Lin, 2013; Odell and Ali, 2016; Fifield, Power, and Sinclair, 2002; Pfau, 2011; Lingaraja, Selvam, Vasanth, and Ramkumar, 2015; Fernandes, 2005). However, many investors may raise concerns on the efficacy of ESG investing in various regions. This was briefly noted above in the informational concerns section of this chapter.

ESG approaches may benefit investors in various regions where investing is more volatile and less liquid, such as in the emerging markets (Fernandes, 2005; Chuhan, 1992; Bekaert, Harvey, and Lundblad, 2007; Siddiqi, 2011). Jamieson Odell and Usman Ali (2016) identify ten separate elements specific to emerging markets that contribute to emerging market beta. Odell and Ali divided these elements into environmental risks, social risks, and governance risks in order to frame their relevance to ESG integration. The environmental risks are often due to lack of regulation and lack of available resources, and include climate change, pollution and policy shift, and resource scarcity. The social risks, resulting from weak or inefficient institutions, involve consumers, employees, and communities. The governance risks, propagating from shifting standards and lack of accountability, involve corruption, accounting and disclosure, ownership and alignment of interests, board composition and independence, and shareholder rights and enforcement mechanisms. (Odell and Ali, 2016). Such risks present a difficult obstacle for profitable investment (Fernandes, 2005; Odell and Ali, 2016; Bai and Qin, 2015; Klomp, 2015). The additional lack of information results in the emerging markets analyses often assuming that the investor is prescient, which is an unrealistic implication, and does not present a replicable model (Fifield, Power, and Sinclair, 2002; Fernandes, 2005). Additionally, evidence of bubbles in emerging markets suggests that the market is not perfectly efficient, which, alongside the difficulties in analyzing emerging markets, widened the door for active management to re-enter the emerging markets investing field with the benefits of analyzing ESG factors and non-financial performance information (Hatipoglu and Uyar, 2012; Bekaert,

Hodrick, and Zhang, 2009; D'Ecclesia and Costantini, 2006; Scheicher, 2001). Nuno Fernandes (2005) concludes that, due to high non-diversifiable risk, passive investments in emerging markets no longer add value to global portfolios. Odell and Ali's classification of environmental, social, and governmental risks highlights an advantage of excluding emerging market companies that do not pass minimum ESG research-based standards.

Others have conducted studies which demonstrate the positive influence of ESG integration on emerging markets investments (Halbitter and Dorfleitner, 2015; Banerjee and Orzano, 2010; Chelawat and Trivedi, 2013; van Duuren, Plantinga, and Scholtens, 2016; Himick, 2011; Meziani, 2014; Odell and Ali, 2016). Banerjee and Orzano (2010) conducted a study on the SandP ESG India Index and the SandP CNX Nifty Index in 2009, which revealed that the SandP ESG India Index returned 140.00%, while the non-ESG SandP CNX Nifty Index only returned 76.00%, resulting in 64.00% excess returns attributable to ESG research-based investment strategies. Banerjee and Orzano also showed that ten other ESG indices returned higher than 140.00% in 2009, with only two non-ESG indices yielding returns higher than 140.00% in the same period (Banerjee and Orzano, 2010; Chelawat and Trivedi, 2013). Chelawat and Trivedi (2013) came to a similar conclusion when analyzing the CNX Nifty 50, compared to the S&P ESG India Index in the period from 2008 to 2012.

CASE STUDY 7C: ESG integration in markets and asset classes

Usman Ali is a sustainable investment consultant. Usman's clients include: Treis Partners, a single-family office in London, Degroof Petercam Asset Management in Brussels, and East Capital in Stockholm. Usman was previously an investment analyst at Caravel Management, a New York-based investment manager focused on emerging and frontier markets. He started his career at Royal London Asset Management. Usman has served on the Investor Working Group for the UN Sustainable Stock Exchanges Initiative where he was responsible for engaging with the Board of the Pakistan Stock Exchange.

In your experience, which asset classes are the most saturated with ESG investing practices? Which asset classes are the least saturated?

Equities appear to be the most saturated asset class with respect to ESG investment strategies. This is particularly true with global equity portfolios, though we are yet to see this trend truly take off with emerging market equities. However, it is important to make the distinction between funds which are marketed as ESG funds, and those that implement ESG strategies through ESG integration and portfolio construction, meaning that the risks and opportunities provided by ESG investing strategies are imbedded within the financial models of the underlying securities and positions are sized accordingly. I am specifically referencing those ESG-imbedded funds, as opposed to the funds marketed as ESG funds. The true ESG-integrated funds are rare. The fixed income market is becoming increasingly saturated with ESG investment opportunities, through sovereign bonds looking at country-level issues such as human rights, water risks, and other relevant factors. Corporate bond investors are also increasingly developing proprietary ESG screens and integration techniques, which logically follows, given their focus on downside risks. Private equity and real estate are also highly ESG-saturated, as they already have metrics in place to integrate and measure social and environmental impact.

Integrating ESG strategies within the hedge fund space is trickier, as ESG factors are not always relevant to the investment strategies being adhered to within the specific fund. It is imperative to note that for some asset classes, ESG factors are not always "material."

For example, ESG strategies built on independent rating systems are not necessarily relevant to a short-term investor trading on quantitative financial metrics. However, there is a tremendous opportunity in these asset classes for investors to incorporate ESG factors.

What steps would be necessary to grow ESG integration within the untapped asset classes?

A good deal of the development will be driven by two factors: investor demand, and basic business sense.

Investors are becoming increasingly exposed to ESG investing strategies. The outcome of this is most tangibly displayed by the clamor by pension funds and other asset owners for their investments and investment managers to adhere to ESG investing criteria. The Government Pension Investment Fund (GPIF), a Japanese pension fund with over $1.3 trillion in assets under management, has begun to demand that the passive index funds in which their assets are invested integrate ESG by engaging with the companies in which the indices invest. This type of pressure by large pension funds and endowments develops an opportunity for index funds to increase their focus on engagement teams. In this way, supply will increasingly be driven by the demand from asset owners.

ESG integration will also be driven by basic business sense. As investment managers increasingly offer competitive ESG integrated investments, the pressure mounts for those who are not offering ESG strategies to devote attention to ESG factors, in order to remain competitive within the marketplace. This may also have an impact on performance, as transparency and disclosure laws will reveal companies with poor ESG practices. Overtime, this could logically be reflected in share prices, particularly as investors are constantly exposed to ESG concepts and strategies through the media.

ESG and SRI strategies have become increasingly popular within both developing and emerging markets, and in a variety of asset classes. This is due in part to the recognition of potential higher risk adjusted returns as the result of ESG factors, as well as the tangible impact of investing to have an impact. Though ESG strategies are growing, they are still dominant within developed markets such as Europe, the United States, and increasingly Canada.

LEARNING PERSPECTIVE 5: sustainability and financial performance

Robert G. Eccles is a leading authority on the integration of environmental, social, and governance factors (ESG) in resource allocation decisions by companies and investors. He is also the world's foremost academic expert on integrated reporting. Currently Eccles is a Visiting Professor of Management Practice at the Said Business School, University of Oxford, where he is helping them start the Oxford Said Corporate Accounting and Reporting (OSCAR) Programme and conducting a joint research project with the Ford Foundation on creating more sustainable capital markets. Eccles has been a Visiting Lecturer at the Massachusetts Institute of Technology, Sloan School of Management and is a Berkeley Social Impact Fellow at the Haas School of Business, University of California Berkeley. He was a Professor at Harvard Business School and received tenure in 1989.

Eccles is a member of the board of the Mistra Center for Sustainable Markets at the Stockholm School of Economics, was the founding Chairman of the Sustainability Accounting Standards Board, and was one of the founders of the International Integrated Reporting Council. In 2011, Dr. Eccles was selected as one of the Top 100 Thought Leaders in Trustworthy Business Behavior – 2012 for his extensive, positive contribution to building trust in business. In 2013, he was named the first non-accountant Honorary Fellow of the Association of Chartered Certified Accountants (ACCA), one of only nine since 1999.

Dr. Eccles received an S.B. in Mathematics and an S.B. in Humanities and Science from the Massachusetts Institute of Technology and an M.A. and Ph.D. in Sociology from Harvard University. He currently resides in Lexington, MA with his wife Anne Laurin Eccles and their three dogs Basil, Ivy, and Rowan. His main outside activity is weight lifting where he is quite good at the dead lift, credible at the squat, and pathetic at the bench press.

Sustainability and financial performance: the mounting evidence and the need for case studies

Evidence continues to mount that good performance on material environmental, social, and governance (ESG) issues is associated with superior financial performance. These empirical studies, of course, show correlation, not causation. In this section I will review three particularly important studies, showing how they provide increasingly deeper views on this relationship, followed by a discussion of SAP's 2016 integrated report which is a good example of articulating the relationship between financial and ESG performance. I will then review the results of a global survey of 582 institutional investors that are relevant to this issue and briefly discuss ESG and performance from an investor perspective. I conclude with a brief call for longitudinal case studies to better understand exactly what the mechanisms are for how good ESG performance can contribute to good financial performance.

"The Impact of Corporate Sustainability on Organizational Processes and Performance"

The first study "The Impact of Corporate Sustainability on Organizational Processes and Performance" by Ioannis Ioannou, George Serafeim, and me was published in 2014.[9] This study of US non-financial services companies compared 90 high sustainability firms with a matched pair set of low sustainability firms in terms of sector, total assets, return on assets, return on equity, leverage, turnover, and market-to-book ratio. The high sustainability companies had adopted an average of 40% of 26 environmental and social policies in the Thomson Reuters ASSET4 database in the mid-1990s and 50% by the late 2000s. The low sustainability companies had adopted almost none of these policies in the mid-1990s and only an average of 10% by the late 2000s. This study is based simply on the extent to which environmental and social policies had been put in place; there was no data on how effective these policies were in influencing outcomes, such as reduction in carbon emissions and work days lost due to accidents. The logic behind this approach was that companies which had adopted many policies were more "sustainable" than those which had not.

There are two important findings from this study which make it a frequently cited one in the literature on the relationship between ESG performance and financial performance. The first is that the high sustainability firms had very different characteristics than their low sustainability counterparts in terms of corporate governance, stakeholder engagement, time horizons, and measurement and disclosure.

The high sustainability firms were two to three times as likely to have formal board responsibility for corporate citizenship (52.7%) and to have a sustainability committee

(40.9%). This indicates that "sustainability" wasn't being relegated to an ancillary function but was seen as being core to how the company was being managed. Supporting this is the fact that they were also twice as likely to include environmental (17.6%) and social metrics (35.1%) in the variable compensation of top executives and three times as likely to include external perception metrics (32.4%), such as customer satisfaction. Standard practice has been, and continues to be, to award compensation only on financial performance, and often short-term financial performance. It should also be noted that only one-half or less of the high sustainability firms were using these practices which suggests that there is substantial room for improvement even amongst this group.

The high sustainability firms showed dramatically higher levels of stakeholder engagement (a p-value of <.0001 in all cases), something I think is at the foundation for a company to have a sustainable corporate strategy vs. a sustainability strategy.[10] A sustainable strategy requires stakeholder engagement to identify the material ESG issues which will affect the company's ability to deliver long-term returns for shareholders. There was actually none or very little (13.5% at most) stakeholder engagement by the low sustainability firms in terms of the three phases of stakeholder engagement: 1) prior (opportunities/risks examination, stakeholder identification, and training), 2) during (concerns, grievance mechanism, common understanding, scope agreement, and targets), and 3) after (board feedback, result reporting, and public reports). In contrast, for the high sustainability firms the percentage practicing these aspects of stakeholder engagement ranged from 15% to 45%. The same observation about room for improvement applies here as well.

Sustainability, or better said, "ESG integration," are two sides of the same coin. Consistent with expectations, the high sustainability firms had a greater discussion of long-term (defined modestly as more than one year) vs. short-term (less than one year) issues, although the difference was admittedly modest. However, there was a greater difference in the percentage of long-term vs. short-term shareholders among the two sets of firms, although both sets had more short-term than long-term shareholders which is not surprising given the nature of today's capital markets. A company's investor base is not a purely exogenous variable. It can be shaped by presenting a long-term view to investors. When it's credible, long-term investors will be attracted to this although it will be of little interest to short-term ones.

A long-term view must eventually be supported by performance results, leading to the differences in measurement and disclosure between the two sets of firms. ESG, often called non-financial performance, can be a leading indicator of future financial performance. Measuring non-financial performance also provides a balance or check on simply focusing on short-term financial performance. The high sustainability firms were much more likely to be measuring performance on employee and supplier issues than the low sustainability ones. This was not the case for customer issues, the one hypothesis in this study that wasn't confirmed. To some extent this could be due to measurement difficulties (such as customer lifestyle and the potential lifetime value of a customer) but in other cases (such as historical sales and products bought) this would seem to be fairly straightforward.

For companies to get a benefit in the market from its non-financial performance, these internal metrics must be communicated externally. As would be expected, the high sustainability firms had higher scores than the low sustainability ones in terms of the quantity of non-financial disclosures (ESG disclosure metrics from Bloomberg and

Thomson Reuters), coverage (whether their sustainability report covered their full global activities), and integration (non-financial vs. financial discussion, social data integrated in financial reports, and environmental data integrated in financial reports).

These results point to the essential characteristics for a company to have a sustainable strategy. Support for this must come from the top, starting with the board of directors, which then puts a set of financial and non-financial metrics in place for awarding compensation to senior management. Both characteristics enable the company to have a long-term time horizon in its strategic and capital allocation decisions which it communicates to the market and, in doing so, shapes its investor base to have a larger proportion of long-term investors. A sustainable strategy doesn't attempt to address every sustainability issue in the world. Rather, it focuses on the material ESG ones which affect financial performance. A key part of identifying which ones are material is stakeholder engagement. Even if this is done well, if internal measurement and control systems only focus on short-term performance, the material non-financial issues won't get the attention they deserve in order to create financial value over the long term. Thus, a broad set of metrics must be used internally and communicated externally, ideally through "integrated reporting" which explains to investors the relationship between financial and non-financial performance.[11]

The second important finding, and the one which tends to get the most attention although I think the first one is equally important, is that over an 18-year period, the high sustainability firms consistently outperformed their low sustainability twins in terms of financial performance.

> Investing $1 in the beginning of 1993 in a value-weighted (equal weighted) portfolio of high sustainability companies would have grown to $22.6 ($14.3) by the end of 2010. In contrast, investing $1 in the beginning of 1993 in a value-weighted (equal-weighted) portfolio of control companies would have only grown to $15.4 ($11.7) by the end of 2010.[12]

The former outperformed the latter in 11 of the 18 years and showed lower volatility. The high sustainability firms outperformed the low sustainability firms in terms of both return on assets and return on equity (in 14 of the 18 years). For both stock market and accounting metrics of performance, noticeable differences didn't begin to appear until after six or seven years, further evidence that outperformance from ESG requires patience.

What is missing from this study is why the adoption of these policies resulted in these different characteristics and how the adoption of these policies and these characteristics led to superior financial performance. As with all such empirical studies, this paper shows correlation not causation, although the correlations are and strong and reasons for these relationships can be hypothesized. For example, a company with human resource policies regarding employee welfare, employment quality, and generous fringe benefits will want to measure how well these policies are being implemented and their consequences. This can create awareness of the long-term benefits of building human capital, extending the company's time horizon. Turnover and recruiting costs will decrease and a more dedicated and skilled workforce will produce higher quality products and serve customers better generating higher profit margins, leading to a higher stock price and higher ROE and ROA.

"Corporate Sustainability: First Evidence on Materiality"

The second study, "Corporate Sustainability: First Evidence on Materiality" is by Mozaffar Khan, George Serafeim, and Aaron Yoon and was published in 2016.[13] It provides a deeper level of granularity in understanding the relationship between ESG performance and financial performance. In contrast to the first study which was based on adoption of policies, this one was based on actual performance on ESG issues. There are no data regarding the policies in place, if any, which produced these outcomes. The thesis of this paper was that superior financial performance isn't a result of good sustainability performance in general, but a result of good performance on the material ESG issues. Here materiality is defined in terms of what matters to investors. When all stakeholders are considered, every ESG issue is important to someone. Only a subset of those that matter to stakeholders collectively matter to investors.

For guidance on materiality, the authors used the work of the Sustainability Accounting Standards Board (SASB), a nonprofit organization based in San Francisco, founded by Jean Rogers.[14] I was the Founding Chairman. The current Chair is Michael P. Bloomberg and the Vice Chair is Mary Schapiro. The intellectual foundation for SASB was the paper "From Transparency to Performance: Industry-Based Sustainability Performance on Key Issues" by Steve Lydenberg, Jean Rogers, and David Wood.[15] The key point of the paper is that what are material issues vary by sector, e.g., they are very different for a bank (e.g., incentives and managing systemic risk) compared to an oil and gas company (e.g., carbon emissions and drilling safety) compared to a pharmaceutical company (e.g., access to medicine and safety in clinical trials).

To identify the material issues, SASB created a ten-sector classification system that subdivides into 79 industries. Through Industry Working Groups (IWGs) comprised of people from companies, investors, professional service firms, industry experts, and NGOs, SASB identifies the material issues through the lens of the 10-K. While this is a US orientation, material issues are more sector dependent than country dependent. Their work has shown that a relatively small number of ESG issues are material for each industry.[16] SASB also recommends the key performance indicator for reporting on each material issues. By February 2014, SASB had produced guidance for six sectors (out of a total of ten) that include 45 industries. These sectors were healthcare, financials, technology and communications, non-renewable resources, transportation, and services.

Given the early stages of SASB's work, few companies are reporting according to their standards. In order to get information on performance, Khan et al. used the MSCI KLD database which it mapped to the SASB material issues for each sector. They created portfolios of companies based on the top quartile and bottom quartile of performance on the material issues for that sector. They found that the firms performing well on material issues had better stock price performance and better future performance measured by return on sales, return on equity, and return on assets. Those performing well on immaterial issues did not have better financial performance than those performing poorly.

Tellingly, the best financial performance was delivered by firms performing well on material issues and performing poorly on the immaterial ones. By whatever internal decision-making processes, these companies were allocating resources to the ESG issues that affect financial performance and not to the ones that don't. This makes sense. Every company, no matter how large, has limited resources and must make decisions about how to allocate them. As with the previous study, the financial outperformance from ESG didn't appear until after about seven or eight years.

This is another breakthrough paper because it distinguishes between the material and immaterial sustainability issues from an investor perspective and shows that it is the former that matter. The term "sustainability" now means so many different things to so many people, conjuring up concepts of both value and values, that shifting the focus and language to "materiality" is immensely clarifying. That said, like the first paper, this one shows correlation, not causation, something true of all such empirical studies. There is no explanation for how good performance on the material issues in a sector lead to higher stock prices and higher future accounting returns.

"Total Societal Impact: A New Lens for Strategy"

The third study, a large research project by the Boston Consulting Group, "Total Societal Impact: A New Lens for Strategy" is by Douglas Beal, Gerry Hansell, Rich Lesser, Shalini Unnikrishnan, Wendy Woods, David Young, and me and was published in 2017.[17] Total Societal Impact (TSI)

> is not a metric; it is a collection of measures and assessments that capture the economic, social, and environmental impact (both positive and negative) of a company's products, services, operations, core capabilities, and activities. Adding the TSI lens to strategy setting naturally leads companies to leverage their core business to contribute to society in a way that enhances TSR [Total Shareholder Return].[18]

This paper combined both quantitative and qualitative analysis. Its quantitative analysis is also about correlation, not causation, but it is yet a further step into deeper granularity. This study also benefited from the work of SASB which was supplemented by BCG industry experts regarding the issues they thought were material for their sector. What is different about this study from the previous one is that it focused on specific ESG issues to see if they were related to financial performance. This analysis was done for the period 2013–2015 for 39 biopharmaceutical companies, 97 consumer packaged goods companies, 66 oil and gas companies, and 141 retail and business banking companies. Data sources were MSCI and Oekom.[19] As with other studies, the lack of longitudinal, high-quality, and comparable data on ESG performance is a significant limitation. (Lack of data was the reason this analysis wasn't performed for the technology sector, although it was part of the qualitative analysis.) With better data through better company reporting and alternative data sources, such as the big data approach used by TruValue Labs,[20] it will be possible to do even more in-depth research on the relationship between ESG performance and financial performance.

This study showed positive relationships between a number of ESG issues and EBITDA and gross margins (net income in banking). For example:

- In banking, promoting financial inclusion accounts for an additional 0.5% in net income margin, all else equal.
- In biopharmaceuticals, expanding access to drugs accounts for an additional 8.2% in EBITDA margin.
- In consumer goods, socially responsible sourcing accounts for an additional 4.8% in gross margin.
- In oil and gas, maintaining process-oriented health and safety programs accounts for an additional 3.4% in EBITDA margin.

These findings are extremely important from both a company and investor point of view. For companies, they provide guidance on the financial return from investments made in improving ESG performance. For investors, they provide insights into how to incorporate ESG factors into their models and what questions to ask their portfolio companies. For both they provide a financial language for talking about "sustainability."

This study also showed a relationship between ESG performance and valuation, both for specific ESG issues and for the aggregate of all ESG factors. In each sector, the top performers (90th percentile) for combined performance for the material issues – most of which were related to downside and risk – had higher valuation multiples (when all other measures were equal) than the median performers (50th percentile). The valuation multiple premium was 3% for banking; 12% for biopharmaceuticals; 11% for consumer packaged goods; 12% for biopharmaceuticals; and 19% for oil and gas. In general, we found that adding ESG factors to BCG's SmartMultiple®Fit valuation model added an additional 9% in predictive power to the 74% for financials of a company's stock price. What is important about this finding is that it shows that the market is beginning to price in ESG performance that is not already being reflected in financial performance. With better ESG data, some of the remaining 17% in the regression model might also be accounted for by ESG factors.

As with the previous two studies, this one shows correlation, not causation. But this study had a qualitative element as well based on interviews with over 200 executives in more than 20 companies, as well as dozens of interviews with investors and people who worked for international development organizations and NGOs. Based on these interviews, the report contains a number of examples of how companies are managing ESG issues which contribute to financial performance and to positive total societal impact. While these case studies are not directly related to the quantitative findings, they point the way to how research can be done that shows both the mechanisms for how ESG issues affect financial performance and the extent to which they do so.

SAP's 2016 integrated report

At least one company is already doing this in the context of integrated reporting. On the home page of its 2016 integrated report, SAP provides data on growth (+31%), profitability (+4%), customer loyalty (net promoter score of 19.2%), and employee engagement index (85%).[21] Just below these figures is a diagram on "Making Connections" which reports that a +/–1% change in the employee engagement index has a €45–55 million impact on non-IFRS operating profit, a +/–1% change in employee retention has a €50–60 million impact on non-IFRS operating profit, a +/–1% change in the Business Health Culture index has an €80–90 million impact on non-IFRS operating profit, and a 1% decrease in carbon emissions has a €5 million impact on non-IFRS operating profit.

These relationships are further elaborated on the "Connectivity" page of their 2016 integrated reporting website.[22] It shows a big circle of 11 circles. Four are the corporate objectives (growth, profitability, employee engagement, and customer loyalty), two are environmental indicators (GHG footprint and total energy consumed), and five are social indicators (business health culture index, employee retention, women in management, social investment, and capability building). Clicking on any one of the small circles brings it to the center and arrows show what affects it and what it affects. For example, employee engagement and capability building improve employee retention and employee retention improves growth, profitability, and customer loyalty. Data from SAP and external studies are referenced which validate these relationships. The latter are based on cause-and-effect analyses based on internal and external interviews and linear regressions. This is the kind of rigorous analysis companies need to do in order to have an integrated approach to both ESG and financial performance and to be able to communicate this to their shareholders. This kind of analysis and effective external communications is sadly lacking in most companies, a point raised in the BCG study,[23] and the focus of my own research for many years.

The investing enlightenment: how principles and pragmatism can create sustainable value through ESG

Although evidence on the positive relationship between ESG performance and financial performance for companies continues to grow,[24] there is less evidence that integrating ESG into investment decisions leads to outperformance. The overall finding of these studies is that SRI funds perform about as well as conventional funds.[25] These studies face a number of data and methodological limitations. However, some insights from the investor's perspective can be gained from the white paper "The Investing Enlightenment: How Principles and Pragmatism Can Create Sustainable Value through ESG," by Mirtha D. Kastrapeli and me.[26] This study was based on a survey of 582 institutional investors who were or were planning to implement some degree of ESG integration in their investment process. They were evenly split regionally (Americas, Asia-Pacific, and Europe, Middle East, and Africa), asset owners and asset managers, and equity and fixed income. When asked if ESG integration meant sacrificing financial returns, nearly one half (48%) said it did not, about one-third (35%) said it did, and the rest (17%) said they didn't know. The one-third group shows that there are still those skeptical about ESG integration, even in a group doing or planning to do it. However, this indicates that the view that ESG integration necessarily means sacrificing financial returns is no longer the dominant one.

The first two studies showed the importance of a company having a long-term perspective for getting the financial benefits of ESG integration. This survey confirmed that investors have a similar view. Nearly two-thirds (63%) felt that outperformance from ESG would take between three and ten years. Only 7% expected it in three years or less. Further evidence of the relationship between ESG integration and time frames is the fact that the most frequently cited benefit of ESG integration was fostering a long-term mindset (62%) followed by cultivating better investment practices (48%).

The most dramatic difference, and where the biggest tension lies, is that 70% of investors awarded compensation on an annual basis and only 17% did so based on two years or more. Reasonable time frames for expecting outperformance from ESG integration need to be supported by equivalent time frames for evaluating performance and paying bonuses.

Just as research on the relationship between ESG performance and financial performance needs better ESG data, investors want this as well. In fact, this was the biggest barrier to ESG integration. Sixty percent cited lack of standards for measuring ESG performance and 53% cited lack of ESG performance data reported by companies. But when it comes to data, the issue is not simply more data but having the right data, defined in terms of what is material. When asked if it would be useful for companies to identify and report on what they considered to be the material ESG issues, a remarkable 92% of investors said "Yes."

Respondents were also asked who should determine what is material and could select more than one group. Nearly two-thirds (64%) cited the board of directors, which supports the idea of an annual board "Statement of Significant Audiences and Materiality."[27] More cited the Chief Sustainability Officer (39%) than the Chief Executive Officer (32%). Equally striking was the fact that only 14% cited both the Chief Financial Officer and the Head of Investor Relations, a strong indication that the market thinks that most people in these roles are ill-equipped to explain the relationship between ESG performance and financial performance. At the same time, respondents thought this could be done since two-thirds thought it was possible to build analytical models showing the relationship between ESG and financial performance. The fact that SAP is making real progress on doing this is further evidence that this is not an impossible feat.

Reference
Verheyden, Tim, Robert G. Eccles, and Andreas Feiner. "ESG for All? The Impact of ESG Screening on Return, Risk, and Diversification." *Journal of Applied Corporate Finance* 28, no. 2 (2016): 47–55.

Discussion questions

1) Return Concerns:

   a   Discuss return concerns of an investor (LO1)
   b   Assess whether you believe ESG investment principles are favorable for investment performance and adoption within portfolios (LO1)

2) Assume the role of a chief investment officer that represents an institutional investor, such as a university endowment or pension fund. Discuss how policy concerns influence the use of ESG investment principles. (LO2)

3) Consider if bias against ESG investing might exist because of an institutional investor's fiduciary duty (LO2)

4) Describe how information concerns cause investors to be hesitant to adopt ESG investment strategies (LO3)

5) Assess investor concerns about ESG investing within emerging markets (LO4)

6) Discuss three macro trends which might affect the growth of ESG investing opportunities (LO5)

Notes

1   Results found through the Trends Report 2016 by the Global Sustainable Investment Alliance.
2   Results found through the 2016 edition of the "Report on US Sustainable, Responsible and Impact Investing Trends" by the Forum for Sustainable and Responsible Investment.
3   Results found through the Greenwich Associates Report, detailing the spread of ESG Investing.
4   Number of signatories and AUM of the United Nations Principles for Responsible Investment at the time of writing.
5   Results found through a 2015 study by TIAA Global Asset Management in their Second Annual Practice Management Study.
6   Estimates are provided by a 2016 study conducted by Accenture titled The "Greater" Wealth Transfer: Capitalizing on the Intergenerational Shift in Wealth.
7   Results found through the 2016 edition of the "Global Sustainable Investment Review" by the Global Sustainable Investment Alliance.
8   Information regarding the changes in fiduciary standards can be found on the Federal Registrar, Interpretive Bulletin Relating to the Fiduciary Standard Under ERISA in Considering

Economically Targeted Investments, A Rule by the Employee Benefits Security Administration on October 26, 2015.

9 Eccles, Robert G. Ioannis Ioannou, and George Serafeim, "The Impact of Corporate Sustainability on Organizational Processes and Performance," *Management Science* Vol. 60, No. 11, November 2014, pp. 2835–2857.

10 Eccles. Robert G. and George Serafeim, "The Performance Frontier: Innovating for a sustainable strategy," *Harvard Business Review*, May 2013, pp. 50–60.

11 The International Integrated Reporting Council, http://integratedreporting.org/.

12 Eccles, Ioannu, and Serafeim, p. 2849.

13 Khan, Mozaffar, George Serafeim, and Aaron Yoon, "Corporate Sustainability: First Evidence of Materiality," *The Accounting Review*: November 2016, Vol. 91, No. 6, pp. 1697–1724.

14 Sustainability Accounting Standards Board, www.sasb.org/.

15 Lydenberg, Steve, Jean Rogers, and David Wood, "From Transparency to Performance: Industry-Based Sustainability Reporting on Key Issues," The Hauser Center for Nonprofit Organizations at Harvard University, Initiative for Responsible Investment, 2010.

16 For more information on how SASB determines the material issues for an industry see the "Rules of Procedure" page on their website www.sasb.org/approach/rules-of-procedure/.

17 Beal, Douglas, Robert Eccles, Gerry Hansell, Rich Lesser, Shalini Unnikrishnan, Wendy Woods, and David Young, "Total Societal Impact: A New Lens for Strategy," The Boston Consulting Group, 2017, www.bcg.com/publications/2017/total-societal-impact-new-lens-strategy.aspx.

18 Ibid., p. 6.

19 For a complete description of the methodology see "Appendix: Background and Outputs of Quantitative Analysis," pp. 39–52.

20 TruValue Labs is a big data sustainability company based in San Francisco. I am on the board of directors. www.insight360.io/, accessed November 2017.

21 Impact through Innovation, SAP Integrated Report www.sap.com/integrated-reports/2016/en.html, accessed November 2017.

22 Connectivity of Financial and Non-Financial Indicators www.sap.com/integrated-reports/2016/en/strategy/connectivity.html, accessed November 2017.

23 "Bridging the Investor Divide," p. 17.

24 "Sustainable Investing: Establishing Long-Term Value and Performance," by DB Climate Change Advisors, Deutsche Bank Group, June 2012, www.db.com/cr/en/docs/Sustainable_Investing_2012.pdf. Clark, Gordon L., Andreas Feiner, and Michael Viehs, 'From the Stockholder to the Stakeholder: How Sustainability Can Drive Financial Outperformance," University of Oxford Smith School of Enterprise and Arabesque Partners, March 2015, https://papers.ssrn.com/sol3/papers.cfm?abstract_id=2508281. Friede, Gunnar, Timo Busch, and Alexander Bassen, "ESG and financial performance: aggregated evidence from more than 2000 empirical studies," *Journal of Sustainable Finance & Investment*, 2015, Vol. 5, No. 4, 210–33, http://dx.doi.org/10.1080/20430795.2015.1118917. Subramanian, Savita, Dan Suzuki, Alex Makedon, Jill Carey Hall, Marc Pouey, and Jimmy Bonilla, ""Equity Strategy Focus Point: ESG: good companies can make good stocks," Bank of America Merrill Lynch, December 18, 2016, www.bofaml.com/content/dam/boamlimages/documents/articles/ID17_0028/equitystrategyfocuspoint_esg.pdf. "The PM's Guide to the ESG Revolution," by GS Sustain, Equity Research April 18, 2017 www.gsam.com/content/dam/gsam/pdfs/international/en/institutions/articles/2017/GS_Sustain_The_PMs_Guide_to_the_ESG_Revolution.pdf?sa=n&rd=n.

25 O'Brien, Amy, Lei Liao, and Jim Campagna, "Responsible Investing: Delivering competitive performance," Nuveen TIAA Investments, July 2017, www.tiaa.org/public/pdf/ri_delivering_competitive_performance.pdf. Desclee, Albert, Lev Dynkin, Jay Hyman, and Simon Polbennikov, "Sustainable investing and bond returns: Research study into the impact of ESG on credit portfolio performance," Barclays Bank PLC, 2016, www.investmentbank.barclays.com/content/dam/barclaysmicrosites/ibpublic/documents/our-insights/esg/barclays-sustainable-investing-and-bond-returns-3.6mb.pdf. "Sustainable reality: Understanding the Performance of Sustainable Investment Strategies," Morgan Stanley Institute for Sustainable Investing, March 2015, www.investmentbank.barclays.com/content/dam/barclaysmicrosites/ibpublic/documents/our-insights/esg/barclays-sustainable-investing-and-bond-returns-3.6mb.pdf.

"How and Why SRI Performance Differs from Conventional Strategies: Executive Summary of White Paper: Exploration of the Cross-Sectional Return Distributions of Socially Responsible Investment Funds," Envestnet PMC, 2014, www.envestnet.com/files/Campaigns/PMC-SRI-TrustedAdvisor/images/PMC-SRI-0914.pdf. "Demystifying Responsible Investment Performance: A review of key academic and broker research on ESG Factors," by The Asset Management Working Group of the United Nations Environment Programme Finance Initiative and Mercer, 2007, www.unepfi.org/fileadmin/documents/Demystifying_Responsible_Investment_Performance_01.pdf.

26 Eccles, Robert G. and Mirtha D. Kastrapeli, "The Investing Enlightenment: How Principles and Pragmatism Can Create Sustainable Value through ESG," State Street Corporation, 2017, www.statestreet.com/content/dam/statestreet/documents/Articles/The_Investing_Enlightenment.pdf.

27 Eccles, Robert G. and Tim Youmans, "Restoring Trust after a Scandal," MIT Sloan Management Review, October 23, 2017, https://sloanreview.mit.edu/article/restoring-trust-after-a-scandal/. Eccles, Robert G. and Tim Youmans, "Materiality in Corporate Governance: The Statement of Significant Audiences and Materiality," *Journal of Applied Corporate Finance*, Volume 28, No. 2, Spring 2016, pp. 39–46, www.roberteccles.com/docs/JACF_Materiality_in_Corporate_Governance_070116_bob_website_doc_2.pdf. Eccles, Robert G. and Tim Youmans, "The Board that Embraced Stakeholders Beyond Shareholders," *MIT Sloan Management Review*, June 9, 2016, https://sloanreview.mit.edu/article/the-board-that-embraced-stakeholders-beyond-shareholders/. Eccles, Robert G. and Tim Youmans, "Why Boards Must Look Beyond Shareholders," *MIT Sloan Management Review*, September 3, 2015, https://sloanreview.mit.edu/article/why-boards-must-look-beyond-shareholders/.

References

Arinović-Barac, Željana, "Predicting Sustainable Financial Performance Using Cash Flow Ratios: A Comparison Between Lda and Ann Method," *Sarajevo Business & Economics Review* no. 31 (January 2011): 33.

Auer, Benjamin, and Frank Schuhmacher. "Do Socially (Ir)responsible Investments Pay? New Evidence from International ESG Data." *The Quarterly Review of Economics and Finance* 59 (2016): 51–62. doi:10.1016/j.qref.2015.07.002.

Bai, Min and Yafeng Qin. "Commonality in Liquidity in Emerging Markets: Another Supply-Side Explanation." *International Review of Economics & Finance* 39 (December 2, 2015): 90–106, 2015. Available at SSRN https://ssrn.com/abstract=2698356

Banerjee, Alka A., and Michael Orzano. "Performance Analysis of Two Indian Equity Indices. S&P Indices." S&P Dow Jones Indices, March 2010. https://us. spindices.com/documents/research/PerformanceAnalysis of Two Indian Equity Indices 2010Mar.pdf. Accessed November 2016.

Beal, Douglas, Robert Eccles, Gerry Hansell, Rich Lesser, Shalini Unnikrishnan, Wendy Woods, and David Young. "Total Societal Impact: A New Lens for Strategy," The Boston Consulting Group, 2017. www.bcg.com/publications/2017/total-societal-impact-new-lens-strategy.aspx.

Bekaert, G., R. J. Hodrick, and X. Zhang. "International Stock Return Comovements." *The Journal of Finance* 64, no. 6 (2009): 2591–626. doi:10.1111/j.1540–6261.2009.01512.x

Chelawat, Hemlata, and I. V. Trivedi. "Impact of Ethical Screening on Investment Performance in India." *IUP Journal of Financial Risk Management* 10, no. 4 (2013): 16–34.

Chuhan, P. "Are Institutional Investors an Important Source of Portfolio Investment in Emerging Markets?" 1992. World Bank Working Paper No. 1243.

Clark, Gordon L., Andreas Feiner, and Michael Viehs. "From the Stockholder to the Stakeholder: How Sustainability Can Drive Financial Outperformance." University of Oxford Smith School of Enterprise and Arabesque Partners, March 2015. https://papers.ssrn.com/sol3/papers.cfm?abstract_id=2508281.

Cortez, Maria Céu, Florinda Silva, and Nelson Areal. "Socially Responsible Investing in the Global Market: The Performance of US and European Funds." *International Journal of Finance & Economics* 17, no. 3 (2012): 254–71.

Czerwińska, Teresa, and Piotr Kaźmierkiewicz. "ESG Rating in Investment Risk Analysis of Companies Listed on the Public Market in Poland." *Economic Notes* 44, no. 2 (2015): 211–48. doi:10.1111/ecno.12031.

D'Alessandro, W. "Dow Sustainability Investors Lick Their Wounds." September 13, 2011. http://crosslandsbulletin.com. Accessed October 23, 2016.

D'Ecclesia, Rita L., and Mauro Costantini. "Comovements and Correlations in International Stock Markets." *The European Journal of Finance* 12, no. 6–7 (2006), 567–82. doi:10.1080/13518470500531135.

"Demystifying Responsible Investment Performance: A review of key academic and broker research on ESG Factors." by The Asset Management Working Group of the United Nations Environment Programme Finance Initiative and Mercer, 2007. www.unepfi.org/fileadmin/documents/Demystifying_Responsible_Investment_Performance_01.pdf.

Department of Labor. "Interpretive Bulletin Relating to the Fiduciary Standard under ERISA in Considering Economically Targeted Investments." Department of Labor, October 2015. www.dol.gov/opa/media/press/ebsa/ebsa20152045.htm. Accessed November 2016.

Desclee, Albert, lev Dynkin, Jay Hyman, and Simon Polbennikov. "Sustainable Investing and Bond Returns: Research Study into the Impact of ESG on Credit Portfolio Performance." Barclays Bank PLC, 2016. www.investmentbank.barclays.com/content/dam/barclaysmicrosites/ibpublic/documents/our-insights/esg/barclays-sustainable-investing-and-bond-returns-3.6mb.pdf.

Dorfleitner, Gregor, Gerhard Halbritter, and Mai Nguyen. "Measuring the Level and Risk of Corporate Responsibility – An Empirical Comparison of Different ESG Rating Approaches." *Journal of Asset Management* 16, no. 7 (2015): 450–66. doi:10.1057/jam.2015.31.

Eccles, Robert G. and Mirtha D. Kastrapeli. "The Investing Enlightenment: How Principles and Pragmatism Can Create Sustainable Value through ESG." State Street Corporation, 2017. www.statestreet.com/content/dam/statestreet/documents/Articles/The_Investing_Enlightenment.pdf.

Eccles, Robert G., and George Serafeim. "The Performance Frontier: Innovating for a Sustainable Strategy." *Harvard Business Review* (May 2013): 50–60.

Eccles, Robert G. and Tim Youmans. "Restoring Trust After a Scandal." *MIT Sloan Management Review* (October 23, 2017). https://sloanreview.mit.edu/article/restoring-trust-after-a-scandal/.

Eccles, Robert G., Ioannis Ioannou, and George Serafeim. "The Impact of Corporate Sustainability on Organizational Processes and Performance." *Management Science* 60, no. 11 (November 2014): 2835–57.

Elton, E. J., and M. J. Gruber. "Risk Reduction and Portfolio Size: An Analytical Solution." *Journal of Business* 50 (1977): 415–37.

Farooq, Omar. "Financial Centers and the Relationship Between ESG Disclosure and Firm Performance: Evidence from an Emerging Market." *Journal of Applied Business Research* 31, no. 4 (2015): 1239–44. doi: 10.19030/jabr.v31i4.9298.

Fernandes, Nuno. "Portfolio Disaggregation in Emerging Market Investments: Passive Indexing Strategies Are No Longer Enough." *The Journal of Portfolio Management* 31, no. 2 (2005): 41–9. doi:10.3905/jpm.2005.470577.

Fifield, S., D. M. Power, and C. D. Sinclair. "Emerging Stock Markets: A More Realistic Assessment of the Gains from Diversification." *Applied Financial Economics* 12, no. 3 (2002): 213–29. doi:10.1080/09603100110090082.

Friede, Gunnar, Timo Busch, and Alexander Bassen. "ESG and Financial Performance: Aggregated Evidence from More Than 2000 Empirical Studies." *Journal of Sustainable Finance & Investment* 5, no. 4 (2015): 210–33. http://dx.doi.org/10.1080/20430795.2015.1118917.

Galbreath, Jeremy. "ESG in Focus: The Australian Evidence." *Journal of Business Ethics* 118, no. 3 (2012): 529–41. doi: 10.1007/s10551-012-1607-9.

Gilbert, K. "Asset Managers Find New Source of Alpha – Responsible Investing." October 2010. IMAE.

Gombola, M. J., and J. E. Ketz. "A Note on Cash Flow and Classification Patterns of Financial Ratios." *Accounting Review* 58, no. 1 (1983): 105.

Guerard, J. B. "A Note Regarding the Further Analysis of Efficient Portfolios with the GLER Data." *Journal of Investing* 23, no. 4 (2014): 75–84.

Halbritter, Gerhard, and Gregor Dorfleitner. "The Wages of Social Responsibility – Where Are They? A Critical Review of ESG Investing." *Review of Financial Economics* 26 (2015): 25–35. doi:10.1016/j.rfe.2015.03.004.

Hatipoglu, O., and O. Uyar. "Do Bubbles Spill Over? Estimating Financial Bubbles in Emerging Markets." *Emerging Markets Finance and Trade* (2012): 4864–75.

Heenetigala, K., C. De Silva Lokuwaduge, A. Armstrong, and A. Ediriweera. "An Investigation of Environmental, Social and Governance Measures of Listed Mining Sector Companies in Australia." *Journal of Business Systems, Governance & Ethics* 10, no. 4 (2015): 1–17.

Himick, Darlene. "Relative Performance Evaluation and Pension Investment Management: A Challenge for ESG Investing." *Critical Perspectives on Accounting* 22, no. 2 (2011): 158–71. doi:10.1016/j. cpa.2010.07.002.

"How and Why SRI Performance Differs from Conventional Strategies: Executive Summary of White Paper: Exploration of the Cross-Sectional Return Distributions of Socially Responsible Investment Funds." *Envestnet PMC*, 2014. www.envestnet.com/files/Campaigns/PMC-SRI-Trusted Advisor/images/PMC-SRI-0914.pdf.

Khan, Mozaffar, George Serafeim, and Aaron Yoon. "Corporate Sustainability: First Evidence of Materiality." *The Accounting Review* 91, no. 6 (November 2016): 1697–1724.

Kiernan, M. J. "Universal Owners and ESG: Leaving Money on the Table?" *Corporate Governance: An International Review* 15, no. 3 (2007): 478–85. doi:10.1111/j.1467-8683.2007.00580.x

Klomp, J. "Sovereign Risk and Natural Disasters in Emerging Markets." *Emerging Markets Finance and Trade* 51, no. 6 (2015): 1326–41. doi:10.1080/1540496X.2015.1011530

Kocmanova, A., Z. Karpíšek, and M. Klímková. "The Construction of Environmental Indicators for Determination of Performance of ESG Indicators to Support Decision-Making of Investors." *Business: Theory & Practice* 13, no. 4 (2012): 333–42. doi:10.3846/btp.2012.35

Kotsantonis, Sakis, Chris Pinney, and George Serafeim. "ESG Integration in Investment Management: Myths and Realities." *Journal of Applied Corporate Finance* 28, no. 2 (2016): 10–16.

Kutan, A. M., and T. Aksoy. "Public Information Arrival and Emerging Markets Returns and Volatility." *Multinational Finance Journal* 8, no. 3/4 (2004): 227–45.

Lin, Wenling. "Is There Alpha in Institutional Emerging-Market Equity Funds?" *The Journal of Portfolio Management* 39, no. 4 (2013): 106–17. doi:10.3905/jpm.2013.39.4.106.

Lingaraja, K., M. Selvam, V. Vasanth, and R. R. Ramkumar. "Long-Run Overseas Portfolio Diversification Benefits and Opportunities of Asian Emerging Stock Markets and Developed Markets." *International Journal of Economics and Financial Issues* 5, no. 2 (2015). http://ezproxy.liberty.edu/login?url=http://search.proquest.com.ezproxy.liberty.edu/docview/1678821903?accountid=12085

Lydenberg, Steve, Jean Rogers, and David Wood. "From Transparency to Performance: Industry-Based Sustainability Reporting on Key Issues." The Hauser Center for Nonprofit Organizations at Harvard University, Initiative for Responsible Investment, 2010.

MacLean, R. "ESG Comes of Age." *Environmental Quality Management* 22, no. 1 (2012): 99–108. doi:10.1002/tqem.21321

Meziani, A. Seddik. Investing with Environmental, Social, and Governance Issues in Mind: From the Back to the Fore of Style Investing." *The Journal of Investing* 23, no. 3 (2014): 115–24. doi:10.3905/joi.2014.23.3.115.

Morrow, Douglas. "ESG Risk in Default Funds: Analysis of the UK'S DC Pension Market." Pensions and Lifetime Savings Association, 2017, 1–40.

Nagy, Zoltán, Altaf Kassam, and Linda-Eling Lee. "Can ESG Add Alpha? An Analysis of ESG Tilt and Momentum Strategies." *The Journal of Investing* 25, no. 2 (2016): 113–24.

O' Brien, Amy, Lei Liao, and Jim Campagna. "Responsible Investing: Delivering competitive performance." Nuveen TIAA Investments, July 2017. www.tiaa.org/public/pdf/ri_delivering_competitive_performance.pdf.

Odell, Jamieson, and Usman Ali. "ESG Investing in Emerging and Frontier Markets." *Journal of Applied Corporate Finance* 28, no. 2 (2016): 96–101. doi: 10.1111/jacf.12181.

Pfau, W. "Emerging Market Pension Funds and International Diversification." *SSRN Electronic Journal* (2011). doi:10.2139/ssrn.1267528

"The PM's Guide to the ESG Revolution." by GS Sustain, Equity Research April 18, 2017. www.gsam.com/content/dam/gsam/pdfs/international/en/institutions/articles/2017/GS_Sustain_The_PMs_Guide_to_the_ESG_Revolution.pdf?sa=n&rd=n.

Pollard, Julia, Matthew Sherwood, and Ryan Klobus. "Establishing ESG as Risk Premia." *Journal of Investment Management* 16, no. 1 (2018). Principles for responsible investment. www.unpri. org/. Accessed October 17, 2016.

Rashty, J., and J. O'Shaughnessy. "Reporting and Disclosures Using Non-GAAP Financial Measures." *CPA Journal* 84, no. 3 (2014): 36–9.

Renneboog, Luc, Jenke Ter Horst, and Chendi Zhang. "Is Ethical Money Financially Smart? Non-financial Attributes and Money Flows of Socially Responsible Investment Funds." *Journal of Financial Intermediation* 20, no. 4 (2008): 562–88. doi:10.1016/j.jfi.2010.12.003.

Rezec, Michael. "Alternative Approaches in ESG Investing: Four Essays on Investment Performance & Risk." PhD diss., University of St Andrews, United Kingdom, 2016.

Sanders, William. "Resolving the Conflict Between Fiduciary Duties and Socially Responsible Investing." *Pace Law Review* 35, no. 2 (2015): 535–79. http://digitalcommons.pace.edu/cgi/viewcontent.cgi?article=1889&context=plr.

Scheicher, M. "The Co-Movements of Stock Markets in Hungary, Poland and the Czech Republic." *International Journal of Finance and Economics* 6, no. 1 (2001): 27–39.

Scott, R. W., and Meyer, J. W. *Institutional Environments and Organizations.* Thousand Oaks, CA: Sage, 1994.

Semenova, Natalia, and Lars Hassel. On the Validity of Environmental Performance Metrics." *Journal of Business Ethics* 132, no. 2 (2015): 249–58. doi: 10.1007/s10551-014-2323-4.

Sherwood, Matthew and Julia Pollard. "Risk-Adjusted Return Potential of Integrating ESG Strategies into Emerging Market Equities." *Journal of Sustainable Finance and Investment* 8, no. 1 (June 2017): 26–44.

Siddiqi, H. "A Creative Institutional Response to Twin Problems of Liquidity and Information Gaps in Certain Emerging Markets." *International Review of Finance* 11, no. 4 (2011): 537–52. doi:10.1111/j.1468-2443.2011.01142.x

Sørensen, O. B., and S. Pfeifer. "Climate Change Issues in Fund Investment Practices." *International Social Security Review* 64, no. 4 (2011): 57–71. doi:10.1111/j.1468-246X.2011.01411.x

Stewart, Levi S. "Growing Demand for ESG Information and Standards: Understanding Corporate Opportunities as Well as Risks." *Journal of Applied Corporate Finance* 27, no. 2 (2015): 58–63. doi:10.1111/jacf.12118.

Subramanian, Savita, Dan Suzuki, Alex Makedon, Jill Carey Hall, Marc Pouey, and Jimmy Bonilla. "Equity Strategy Focus Point: ESG: Good Companies Can Make Good Stocks." Bank of America Merrill Lynch, December 18, 2016. www.bofaml.com/content/dam/boamlimages/documents/articles/ID17_0028/equitystrategyfocuspoint_esg.pdf.

"Sustainable Investing: Establishing Long-Term Value and Performance." by DB Climate Change Advisors, Deutsche Bank Group, June 2012. www.db.com/cr/en/docs/Sustainable_Investing_2012.pdf.

"Sustainable Reality: Understanding the Performance of Sustainable Investment Strategies." Morgan Stanley Institute for Sustainable Investing, March 2015. www.investmentbank.barclays.com/content/dam/barclaysmicrosites/ibpublic/documents/our-insights/esg/barclays-sustainable-investing-and-bond-returns-3.6mb.pdf.

United Nations. "Principles for Responsible Investment." *United Nations*, 2006. https://unpri.org. Accessed October, 2016.

van Duuren, Emiel, Auke Plantinga, and Bert Scholtens. "ESG Integration and the Investment Management Process: Fundamental Investing Reinvented." *Journal of Business Ethics* 138, no. 3 (2016): 525–33. doi:10.1007/s10551-015-2610-8.

Chapter 8

Commonly held ESG views and practical considerations

This chapter investigates the drivers behind RI-factor implementation within investors' portfolios. The chapter first analyzes how investors who approach ESG through quantitative reasoning practically differ from investors who approach ESG through qualitative reasoning. This chapter further synthesizes the practical considerations of investors, both on the buy side and on the sell side, who approach ESG investing through specific aspects of environmental, social, and governance as opposed to a holistic view, and analyzes the practical considerations for such viewpoints. This chapter will be structured as an introduction to the investors' views of ESG investing, and some practical considerations which impact investor decisions.

Learning objectives

- Identify and analyze qualitative and quantitative reasoning for RI-factor implementation within investors' portfolios
- Compare and evaluate qualitative and quantitative approaches to implementing ESG investment strategies
- Define and distinguish tenants of a holistic investor approach to ESG investing from tenants of a segmented investor approach to ESG investing
- Synthesize practical considerations of investors who approach ESG through a holistic view as opposed to a segmented view to RI-factor implementation
- Distinguish and assess the value of the holistic investor approach and the segmented investor approach to ESG investing
- Examine the benefits of the holistic investor approach and the segmented investor approach to ESG investing within different markets, asset classes, and investment sectors

After this chapter, the reader should have a basic understanding of the different priorities and lenses through which investors make decisions regarding ESG Investing.

Introduction

The field of ESG investing is broad in scope and serves as an umbrella for a plethora of issues and subject matter specialties. This chapter investigates the drivers and implementation methods behind quantitative and qualitative environmental, social, and governance factor implementation within investors' portfolios.

8.1 Qualitative vs. quantitative models

As has been discussed in previous chapters, ESG factors can be measured quantitatively (as is done with ESG ratings data), or qualitatively, as is done in ESG screening and some forms of engagement. Some investors employ a combination of the two.

Qualitative reasoning is analysis and research that is based on qualitative (non-statistically measured) information. Qualitative reasoning, as it applies to ESG investing, is the approach that gathers information on ESG issues through qualitative metrics. Qualitative research might include gathering information through interviews, discussion groups, controlled experiments, and surveys. In ESG data collection specifically, this may include interviews with the management team and board of directors of a company, analysis of a company's standard policies and code of ethics, or observations of a company's news and key changes that may have a material impact on ESG factors. For example, an ESG investor may examine the issue of the labor standards in a company's supply chain qualitatively as it might be difficult to gather this information through quantitative means. Another example of an ESG investor using qualitative reasoning could be an ESG investor's preference to analyze a company's business ethics. It may be extremely difficult for an investor to gather detailed quantified information on the ethical culture of a company, and they may prefer a qualitative assessment of the company's culture to make a more informed decision. Although an independent research firm may produce a quantitative scoring of business ethics for the company, an ESG investor may feel that their own ethics, or the ethical policies of the institution they represent, differ from the independent research firm, thus fueling the investor's desire to conduct qualitative research and reasoning. In this example, the investor may find that conducting face-to-face interviews and anonymous surveys at the company will provide better insight on the business ethics of the company. This form of data may be an attractive research approach for the ESG investor when variables relative to a specific issue exist beyond what can be gathered quantitatively. Qualitative research may allow an ESG investor the ability to test for hypotheses and make inferences during research and analysis that would not be possible through a pure quantitative approach, and does not require representation through numbers or figures.

Qualitative research can often be a tool for an investor to form opinions when quantitative ESG data is lackluster. As information on ESG issues can be complex and multifaceted in nature, some ESG investors prefer using qualitative research to broaden the data being considered. The reader should note, however, that qualitative research is a broad methodological approach that encompasses many underlying methods and designs. Qualitative research conclusions are often considered propositions (informed assertions) and are often synthesized as such for practical consideration.

An ESG investor may first gather data qualitatively before they organize, sort, and filter data that can be measured and analyzed in a quantitative manner.

An ESG investor may also opt for a **quantitative reasoning** approach to ESG research and analysis. Quantitative research involves a systematic investigation of observable data by way of statistical, mathematical, or computational processes. An investor that elects to use quantitative techniques and models to examine ESG issues does so because of the ability to mathematically standardize data for synthesis and investment decision-making reasoning. Quantitative data can be understood as any data that is in numerical form such as statistics or percentages. While qualitative research is subjective, quantitative reasoning is likely to be substantially more objective (though subjectivity may exist on behalf of data providers who produces quantitative ESG ratings data).

For example, an investor might use a quantitative reasoning approach in measuring board diversity. An investor who seeks to identify corporate boards of publicly traded companies that are inclusive of various ethnicities and female representation may find that this quantitative data is publicly available and easily measurable.

Many investors choose to employ a balance of qualitative and quantitative research methods in their ESG strategies. In a similar way, investors weigh environmental, social, and governance data differently in investment portfolios. Some investors choose to focus on quantitative environmental factors, while other investors choose to focus on qualitative social factors. As environmental, social, and governance investing becomes more popular, many investors choose to focus on specific factors or sub-factors. For example, funds and investors are emerging which use a combination of qualitative and quantitative information to focus on water pollution, climate change, labor practices, board diversity, etc. This next section will provide insight into how and why investors implement these tilts in portfolio construction.

8.2 Environmentally focused investing

Environmentally focused investing is the investment practice that integrates environment factors to create a lens for portfolio analysis, risk management, and ultimately investment. Environmentally focused investing may utilize investment strategies such as exclusion, integration, impact, or engagement methodologies, and is a broad term that covers an array of ideologies and practical considerations. Environmentally focused investing is commonly referred to as green investing.

Broadly speaking, environmentally focused investors concentrate on companies or projects that are committed to the conservation of natural resources, the production and discovery of alternative energy sources, the implementation of clean air and water projects, and/or other environmentally conscious business practices. Importantly, environmentally focused investing also encapsulates investment philosophy that uses the analysis of environmental risks of activities by companies, governments, and natural forces to access and assess information for investment risk and return potential measurement. A broad scope of investors may choose to adopt aspects of environmentally focused investing, based on investor objectives, principles, and guidelines. For example, an institutional investor may be driven to environmentally focused investing because of a mandate set by the board of directors or charitable donors. An asset manager may be drawn to environmentally focused investing because of their view of portfolio risk and sustainable investment process, whereas a retail investor may choose environmentally focused investing because of their love of nature and desire to protect the planet.

Environmentally focused investing is often implemented using an emerging trend referred to as **thematic investing**. Here specific themes are identified by a portfolio management team as the focus of the portfolio. Historically, themes such as disruptive technology and emerging markets have been chosen. Today, environmentally focused investing has made themes such as clean energy, climate change, and stranded assets common. Environmentally focused investing advocates have also highlighted the positive benefits of making investments in companies and projects that are beneficial to both risk and return and the environment.

Environmentally focused investors seek to achieve a higher risk-adjusted return from using environmental research. For example, an investor may buy green bonds with yields that benefit their portfolio as part of their environmentally focused investment strategy. A **green bond** is a term given to certain bonds underwritten by banks or asset managers on the behalf of a municipality, park, or natural resource. Green bonds are often focused on the sustainable development of nature conserving or bio-development in a bio-friendly and environmentally healthy manner. Green bonds may be guaranteed by foundations, governments, or philanthropists. Environmentally focused investors may integrate green bonds within their portfolio for the diversification from traditional corporate and government bonds, as well as the attractive relative returns that the fixed income assets can provide. Investors also seek the benefits of environmentally focused investing through private equity and venture capital impact investments that intend to disrupt traditional industries and businesses through their positive environmentally minded business activities, products, and services. Investors aim to achieve high return targets through sustainable business models that have the objective to capture environmentally conscious consumers. The way an environmentally focused investor practices exclusion may also be to divest from all companies that generate revenue from environmentally harmful business activities.

Environmentally focused investors may implement their practical considerations differently as an investor's policies and views on environmental issues or factors differ, and are often subject to the investor's specific goals. For example, environmentally focused investment managers and asset managers implement investment approaches differently in their considerations relative to the environmental impact of fossil fuels. Consider two environmentally focused investors who both believe that carbon released by global energy consumption is harmful: one of the investors may implement exclusion through the total divestment away from securities that business activities are related to fossil fuels and carbon emissions, whereas the other investor may leverage a non-exclusionary approach through structuring a low-carbon portfolio so that they may continue to have exposure to the sector. It is important to note the fossil fuel divestment movement that was briefly mentioned in Chapter 2 as the movement has been a phenomenon impacting the investment industry and is a major issue for environmentally focused investors.

Fossil fuels divestment is the act of excluding all securities that meet a specific criteria of business activities and practices that generate revenue from fossil fuels. This may be excluding investments in commodities, such as crude oil futures or natural gas futures, or excluding investment in equities that are oil exploration and production or petroleum refining. Investors practicing fossil fuel divestment will screen out such securities from their portfolios by using GICS and other analytics, which have been discussed in Chapter 3. In certain geographies, the fossil fuels divestment movement arose from the advocacy by young adults attending universities, who believe that university endowments should be better aligned with their students and alumni's ideal view of the climate of the future (Cleveland and Reibstein, 2015). Non-governmental forces, predominately led by environmental organizations and institutional investors' beneficiaries, such as the students of universities that have endowments, have put pressure on institutional investors to divest from fossil fuel and carbon emissions-associated investments. The divestment movement has been led by environmental advocate groups that use a range of strategies to shame, pressure, facilitate, and encourage investors in general, and large institutional investors in particular, to relinquish their holdings of fossil fuel securities (Ayling and Gunningham, 2017). Even governmental policies and regulations have played a role in the fossil fuels divestment issue by forcing structural adjustments in the business operations of the energy industry (Ritchie and Dowlatabadi, 2015). For example, the fossil fuel divestment movement has gained political decisions and strong civil support, which increases the significance of climate change concerns in the strategic management of the German electricity giants, namely the top four German energy giants – E.On, RWE, Vattenfall, and EnBW (Kiyar and Wittneben, 2015).

CASE STUDY 8A: GreenFaith

GreenFaith is an interfaith environmental organization whose mission is to educate, inspire, and mobilize diverse religious institutions globally for environmental action. GreenFaith is a classic example of how ESG research from a single organization is tailored to a specific cause, and therefore, isolated research focus.

Fossil fuel divestment
GreenFaith has played a leading role in supporting faith participation in the fossil fuel divestment movement which has resulted in over 125 religious divestment commitments, the most of any sector globally. Beginning in 2013, GreenFaith provided education and

training materials to help faith-based activists promote divestment at both the local congregational and national denominational levels, including a series of webinars that helped introduce the divestment movement to the faith community. GreenFaith provided essays by theologians in support of divestment, sermon materials, religious education lesson plans, and even a divestment comic book! GreenFaith also developed a multi-faith statement, entitled Divest and Reinvest Now, which was signed by over 80 prominent theologians and ethicists globally in support of divestment. GreenFaith's Executive Director, Rev. Fletcher Harper, spoke regularly about the moral imperative for divestment, and GreenFaith convened calls of faith-based divestment campaigners from the US, UK, Canada, Australia, New Zealand, and Europe, helping build momentum behind divestment within the faith community.

As noted in the above example, not all environmentally focused investors who believe that fossil fuels can be harmful to the environment believe in the divestment as part of their environmentally focused investment strategy. Unlike fossil fuel divestment, which practices exclusion, low-carbon investing is a practice adopted by many institutional investors (Cowburn, 2015). **Low carbon investing** (LCI) is a type of environmentally focused investing that investors deploy as to not eliminate exposure to carbon producing securities, such as the debt of an oil company producing fossil fuel reserves or the equities of an automobile company that has poor carbon emissions standards, using analytics-based carbon emissions measurement (Haigh and Shapiro, 2011). Analytics providers, such as MSCI and Sustainalytics, discussed in Chapter 3 offer carbon analytics services of a portfolio. Measuring the amount of carbon investment, or the carbon footprint of a portfolio, allows investors to strategize low-carbon targets or impose investment policy guidelines. Investors, particularly institutional investors and asset management firms may also use their own proprietary method for assessing the carbon investment, or carbon footprint, of the portfolio.

Environmentally focused investors become aligned to certain themes for reasons such as a policy mandate, a personal belief, or a view of risk. Some of the common themes are:

Raw materials use and natural resources use: Some environmentally focused investors maintain a granular lens on corporate use of raw materials and natural resources. Such investors will evaluate investments based on the amount of raw materials and natural resources used for manufacturing, consumed, and/or wasted by companies. This evaluation is integrated into the quantitative models used to choose investments. Proprietary or service provider analytics assist these investors in their materials and resources measurement. These investors may use the factors of raw materials use and/or natural resources use to gain insight into a company's profitability, business practices, and market-relative usage, in addition to monitoring the environmental footprint of the investment portfolio.

Waste management and water stress: Management of the water supply chain is another common theme in environmentally focused investing. Environmentally focused investors capitalize on water management as it is essential for sanitation, drinking, agriculture, manufacturing, and leisure. These investors may aim to optimize the use of water and reduce the impact water use has on the natural environment.

Environmentally focused investors may analyze how much water a company uses as part of their business activities relative to competitors in the same industry or sector. This may involve calculating **water stress**, which measures the amount of demand for water that exceeds the available amount during a certain period. Water stress, calculated through either proprietary measurements or a third-party service provider, is used as a tool for assessing company's water-consumption and sustainability, and provides insight on the investment's impact of the deterioration of fresh water resources in terms of quantity (e.g. water reservoir levels, aquifer over-exploitation, dry rivers, etc.).

Water as an asset class: Though some investors have targeted water portfolios, for most investors it is impractical to hold physical water as part of an investment portfolio. Investors seeking water investments may invest in water-business-based equities, credit, or structured product vehicles, such as mutual funds and exchange-traded funds (ETFs), to achieve exposure to water. Such investors may consider the global long-term demand for water as a sustainable growth investment.

Water as a risk factor: Other investors integrated water use and impact as a risk factor. These investors may consider the sustainability of a company's business model, products, or services based on how they manage water and water stress. Such investors view water usage and management as a risk, as a company may be threatened by further growth and development if consumers and/or shareholders have a negative perception on the company's water management practices. Investors may also use water as a lens for the company's financial efficiency, such as a measure of cost efficiency and ongoing cost requirement of producing goods.

CASE STUDY 8B: KBI Global Investors

KBI Global Investors was established in 1980, in Dublin, Ireland. Its original Irish client base required a faith-based approach to investing, and so the firm implemented negative screens into the process as far back as the early 1980s, in order to incorporate various "ethical" criteria such as humanitarian and animal welfare issues for its clients. Today, its investment process has evolved from the simple negative screens utilized for its original faith-based clients to a fully integrated, decisive commitment to Responsible Investing, serving endowments, foundations, and institutional investors across the globe.

Eoin Fahy, Head of Responsible Investing, has been with the firm since 1988 and has seen much change over the period.

"In the 1980s and 1990s, almost all of our clients were Irish and the term 'ESG' just wasn't used. Some clients certainly wanted to avoid investing in what they regarded as 'unethical' companies, such as those involved with tobacco, adult entertainment, or weapons manufacturing, and it was not difficult to incorporate those constraints into the management of their portfolios – though often in a fairly basic way."

By the turn of the century, however, the firm identified the global shortage of clean, safe water and energy as emerging "Global Megatrends." It launched two investment strategies, a Water strategy investing in companies providing solutions to the global shortage of safe and clean water, and an Energy Solutions strategy taking the same approach to clean Energy. (A similar strategy targeting safe Food was launched in 2008.)

"In the early years of these strategies," Fahy said, "ESG was arguably not really incorporated into the investment process at all. The fact that a company was involved in providing clean energy or safe water or food was the only ESG factor which was considered. This was of course vitally important, but as time passed we became significantly more sophisticated in the way we used ESG performance indicators in our investment process."

Why ESG?

Before getting into the detail of *how* ESG factors are incorporated into the investment process for the firm's Natural Resource strategies, it's important to understand *why* the firm uses them. It does so because it believes that companies with strong governance and whose products and services enhance social or environmental goals should meaningfully outperform over time. Such companies are more likely to have long, durable, sustainable business models.

"We don't believe that there's a trade-off between better financial performance and achieving social, environmental or governance goals for society. To us, companies that take care to manage environmental, social or governance issues are also likely to be well-managed companies in a more general sense," says Fahy.

So, for the firm's Natural Resources strategies, incorporating ESG factors into the investment process is aimed at achieving better financial performance, as well as contributing to society's environmental or social goals.

ESG in the investment process

The investment team uses a proprietary model to calculate the likelihood of a stock price reaching their upside, or optimistic, price target, and in parallel the likelihood of the stock price reaching their downside, or pessimistic, price target.

Four factors are built into that model and two of those four are ESG factors, as below:

> **Environmental and social:** do the company's products enhance society's environmental and/or social/sustainable goals?
> **Governance:** does the board of the company sufficiently represent the interests of shareholders, particularly minority shareholders? If not, can it be changed?

A specific score is given to each security under each of those two factors – a score which is awarded based on the portfolio manager's own judgment though taking into account external ESG research – and that feeds directly into the proprietary model which calculates the probability of the stock price reaching the upside or optimistic price target.

"The advantage of this approach," Fahy explains, "is that the ESG performance of each company is assessed directly by the Portfolio Manager who knows the company best, and not by a separate team in the company who may be on a different floor of the building – or in a different building! – with little real-world communication between the two."

This approach strengthens the ESG credentials of the strategies. The first ESG element is that each strategy is based entirely on investing in companies that are providing solutions to global problems (shortages of food, clean energy, safe water, etc.). Then the second ESG element – and just as important to some investors – is that each company is also assessed on its ESG performance – in other words, a company that is in the "right" industry, but has poor ESG performance on other fronts, is less likely to be in the portfolio than a company in the same line of business but with superior ESG performance.

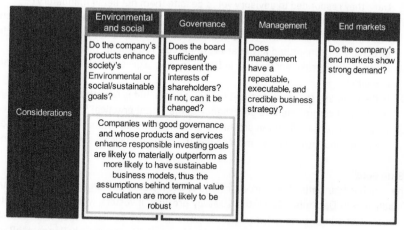

Figure 8.1 ESG: an integral part of investment process

The Portfolio Managers know their companies well – there are only 30–45 stocks in each portfolio. But can they genuinely assess the ESG performance of each stock?

"Very much so," says Fahy. "Of course the PMs have the benefit of detailed ESG research reports from external suppliers such as MSCI ESG Research and Institutional Share-holder Services, as well as from some mainstream brokers. But more importantly they also meet company management teams, conduct onsite visits to company facilities (not just to head offices), and monitor relevant specialized industry publications. This allows them to focus on the ESG issues that really matter to us."

He also points out that the specific criteria on which they assess companies is published on the firm's website, in the interests of transparency (below is the list of Governance criteria – there is also a published list of Environmental and Social factors).

Governance
Do we honestly believe that the board is representing stakeholders' interests and espe-cially minority shareholders?

1   Is there a majority shareholder with potentially conflicting interests?
2   Has the board responded to continued management disappointments?
3   Have there been poor capital allocation decisions?
4   Has the board exercised reasonable oversight of compensation policies for senior management?
5   Is the board seeking controversial changes or fighting logical changes in the annual meetings?

6   How difficult would it be for us to change the board's makeup if needed (relevant factors include company domicile, differentiated voting rights, board classification, etc.)?

7   Has the company and/or responsible board member(s) tried to reach out to investors on any matters that we're aware of?

8   Have they responded to advisory votes despite them not being mandatory?

9   Is the board composition and governance in line with or close to best practice (including for example gender balance, number of independent directors, designated lead director, well constituted key board committees, reasonable board turnover)?

10   Is the company resident in a market/country where governance/regulatory oversight is poor?

11   Is the company too small to meet best standards, but is nonetheless showing a generally good commitment to governance to the extent practical?

12   Have our external ESG input providers, or shareholder activists, expressed a material concern about governance, and if so has the company given a satisfactory response?

"Blue Gold"

The firm has four natural resource strategies, but Water is the largest by some distance. Established in December 2000, the strategy provides investors with the opportunity to achieve strong long-term returns and potential portfolio diversification from investing in companies providing solutions to arguably the greatest resource challenge of all – the scarcity of safe, clean water.

Water – sometimes called **Blue Gold** given its importance – is a key resource that will need significant investment to ensure its adequate provision to a growing global population, and investing in water stocks offers exposure to a number of long-term growth themes:

• Inadequate supply and access: Less than 1% of the world's water is available for use (the remainder is saltwater, polluted, in polar ice caps, or otherwise unavailable) and this is increasingly threatened by pollution and depleting aquifers.[1]

• Increasing demand: The demand for clean water is growing rapidly, due to population growth and industrialization. Water demand is already growing at twice the rate of population growth.

• Increasing infrastructure investment: An estimated $7.5 trillion of infrastructure will be required by 2030 to address urgent global requirements for water and water services worldwide.[2]

• Increasing regulation and government support: Across the world, governments are insisting on higher standards for water and water waste services, as evidenced by the Safe Drinking Water Act in the US, the Water Framework Directive in Europe, and China's water standards. Regulation – both economic and environmental – has been a backbone of support for investment in water.

KBI believes that investors can help to finance solutions to the growing need to address water scarcity, while also gaining exposure to the long-term growth themes referred to above. This can be done by investing in companies that are providing those solutions across a range of business areas: companies that increase water supply and access, improve water quality, or reduce water waste across the industry, agriculture, and household sectors.

The long-term drivers above have driven the strong returns of the strategy since inception in 2000. "Since inception in December 2000, the strategy has outperformed its benchmark (MSCI All Country World index) by more than 2.5% per annum, net of management fees," explains Fahy.[3] This puts investors in the happy position of being invested in a strategy which is addressing a major problem for society, and which outperformed the broad equity market at the same time.

Active engagement

The firm also has an extensive Engagement programmer with the companies in which it invests.

"We don't have a principled objection to investors who simply divest from companies whose ESG performance is unacceptably low – we will do that if necessary. But we do believe that in most circumstances it is worthwhile to seek to change that undesirable behavior rather than sell out of the stock because of it," explains Fahy.

This Engagement will usually commence with an approach to the company by the relevant Portfolio Manager(s), outlining their concerns. This will preferably be an in-person meeting or a direct phone call with the appropriate personnel at the company in question, though the Engagement could commence with a letter or email.

The firm outlines its concern and asks the company to respond, either at the time or (more usually) at a later date having had time to consider the issue.

The team then considers the company's response and either closes the Engagement if a satisfactory response has been obtained or pursues it further, usually via escalation to the Company Chairperson or designated independent/lead director, as appropriate.

The process continues until closed. Engagement can finish either because the firm has obtained a satisfactory result or because it feels that a satisfactory outcome is unlikely, in which case it will consider divestment, if it judges it to be in the best interests of its clients.

Reporting impact

Investors in these Natural Resource strategies know, as a matter of common sense, that their investments are addressing important global problems. But how does KBI **measure** the impact of the investments?

"With difficulty!", says Fahy. In an ideal world, he explains, companies would report on their contribution to society and the environment in a standardized, quantifiable way, but that is not the case – at least to date.

"We can measure the carbon footprint of the portfolio with reasonable accuracy as most companies now realize that their carbon emissions are important to investors, and must be reported to investors in a usable format. But that is the exception rather than the rule," says Fahy. He points out that while an increasing number of companies now publish Sustainability Reports, each company picks a different set of indicators to report on (perhaps, he notes, choosing only those that show their company in the most favorable light). So, as an investment manager it's very difficult, and in fact all but impossible, to collect comparable data from all, or even most, companies in the portfolio.

The company works with investor organizations like the Institutional Investors Group on Climate Change, the Principles for Responsible Investing, the CERES Investor Network on Climate Risk, and others to push for standardized reporting of impact data. It is also embarking on a project to "map" the investments in its Natural Resources strategies to the United Nations Sustainable Development Goals, as many investors, especially in Europe, are very interested in seeing how their investments can contribute to the achievement of those goals.

Energy efficiency: Many environmentally focused investors use energy efficiency as a theme for investment analysis and portfolio consideration. Such investors may practice investing through the lens of energy efficiency because of the financial sustainability and long-term optimization of energy-efficient companies and renewable technologies (Ritchie and Dowlatabadi, 2015), while others do so because of the positive environmental impacts.

These investors analyze their portfolios and investment universe for securities, e.g. equities and corporate credit, for companies and investment opportunities (e.g. development projects) that display energy efficient characteristics, often relative to the industry or sector in which the business operates. Many of these investors incorporate renewable energy investments. Outside of pure environmental consciousness, these investors believe that energy efficient businesses can provide attractive financial returns because of the adoption by consumers and the vast market potential (Liu et al. 2017). Renewable energy provides an alternative to fossil fuels. Wind, solar, and hydropower are popular renewable energy focuses being capitalized by investors.

Wind power is the generation of energy using windmills or turbines to transform natural wind into usable energy. This commonly takes place in wind farms, which are a grouping of many individual wind turbines that are connected to an electric transmission network, also known as the grid, to supply power. Wind energy investors may invest in companies that own, construct, or maintain wind farms.

Solar power is the method of converting sunlight into energy using photovoltaics (e.g. solar panels or solar tape), concentrated solar power, or a combination of both. Photovoltaic (PV) cells convert light into an electric current for electricity use, while concentrated solar power systems use mirrors or lenses and tracking systems that focus a large amount of sunlight into a small beam. Investors may consider investing in solar energy through companies that produce solar photovoltaic panels for residential use or through large-scale solar farms for concentrated solar power production that feed electric grids. Investments in solar systems have been profitable for many projects and can supplement energy production for large populations (Liu et al. 2017).

Hydropower is the harnessing of water currents to generate power. Niagara Falls, a massive natural waterfall in New York, United States supplies a significant amount of electricity to the Canadian and United States power. Investors may seek hydropower investments, such as the hydraulic facilities at Niagara Falls, or tidal generation-based systems to access hydropower investments.

Investors that prioritize energy efficiency are often attracted to renewable energy investments because of the positive impact to the environment, the plentiful abundance of the power supply source, and the financial incentive, particularly when the cost of such renewable energy sources is comparable to traditional fossil-fuels-burning energy sources. Governmental subsidies and tax breaks for investors and corporates further encourage the financial incentive (Richardson, 2009).

Environmentally focused investors who prioritize energy efficiency often integrate research on **clean technologies** as part of their investment process.

Clean technologies are commonly understood as technologies that improve the impact of business activities, e.g. the production of products or processes. It is important to note that clean technologies may consist of various applications and are not limited to the production of energy or the harvesting in natural resources. One such clean technology that energy efficient-minded investors access is **green building**. Green building is "a building that, in its design, construction or operation, reduces or eliminates negative impacts, and can create positive impacts, on our climate and natural environment. Green buildings preserve precious natural resources and improve our quality of life" (World Green Building Council, 2016). Clean technology and green building are particularly relevant to environmentally conscious investors who focus on the theme of **pollution**.

Pollution is the introduction of contaminants into the natural environment that may potentially lead to adverse consequences. Naturally, pollution is closely related to other issues on which environmentally focused investors focus, such as greenhouse gases, carbon emissions, and water pollution. These environmentally focused investors may be critical of companies that emit industrial pollutions as the act is both harmful to the sustainability of society and is not a long-term sustainable business practice due to regulatory pressures and consumer scrutiny risk (Sueyoshi and Goto, 2014). Therefore, investors may include pollution to air, water, or land in their corporate analyses. Empirical research shows that pollution is negatively related to stock returns, even when controlling for other variables (Levy and Yagil, 2011). This being the case, investors analyzing pollution gain greater insight on the long-term path of a company's securities. These investors may choose to analyze granular aspects of pollution, such as the biodiverse land use, toxic waste, toxic emissions of a company, in order to measure the appropriateness for their portfolio, whether on a basis of environmental mindfulness or performance potential.

Environmentally focused investors are typically driven by one of two motivators: either the positive impacts that prioritizing such factors may have on the environment, or return enhancement and risk management. Regardless whether an environmentally focused investor chooses such themes because of environmental concern, policy, mandate guidelines, downside risk management, return enhancement, or another motivation, environmentally themed investing is a mainstream practice employed by asset managers, institutions, and retail investors. This practice is specifically focused on the environment and, although under the ESG umbrella, is differentiated from the broader holistic practice of ESG investing because of the isolated and granular focus on environmental issues.

CASE STUDY 8C: Varma Pension Plan

Kaskela Hanna – Director of Responsible Investing

About Varma: Varma provides pension insurance for work carried out in Finland. Varma handles the earnings-related pension coverage of some 860,000 people. With EUR 45 billion in investment assets, Varma is the largest private investor in Finland. Varma's mission is to accumulate assets received as pension contributions in order to pay present and future pensions.

Climate policy of Varma

One of Varma's responsibility targets is mitigating climate change, which has substantial financial, social, and environmental implications for current and future generations.

Varma was the first Finnish earnings-related pension company in 2016 to publish a climate policy that steers its investments. The policy covers all of the company's asset classes and outlines how Varma mitigates climate change in its investment operations by, among other things, reducing the carbon footprint of its investments. Mitigating climate change is one of Varma's CSR targets.

Climate change is one of the most significant factors that investors must prepare for in the long term. Greenhouse gases from human activities have already changed the climate. Emissions arising from fossil fuel combustion, from changes in land use and from agricultural and industrial processes have led to an increase in greenhouse gas concentrations in the atmosphere and global warming.

Climate change will have substantial financial, social, and environmental impacts on current and future generations. The operating conditions of several sectors and companies will change in the long run. In certain sectors, such as energy production, the change can already be seen.

Mitigating climate change calls for substantial and long-term restrictions on emissions, as the future development will largely be determined by the total volume of greenhouse gas emissions. The goal of the Paris climate agreement is to limit the increase in the global average temperature to well below 2°C above pre-industrial levels. The goal requires shifting to a low-carbon economy as well as an appreciable reduction in the use of fossil fuels.

Varma recognizes the importance of climate change to its investment activities and the long-term development of the economy. Varma also supports actions to mitigate climate change and adapt to the upcoming changes and is committed to develop its investment operations such that investments and investment processes comply with the two-degree target. This means focusing investments in the longer-term on investees that are low-carbon or whose climate strategy aims for a low-carbon society.

In the short term, Varma's goal is to reduce the carbon footprint of our investments. The goal is to reduce the carbon footprint of our listed equity investments by 25% and that of listed corporate bond investments by 15% in relation to the companies' revenue, and the carbon footprint of real estate investments by 15% in relation to gross square meters by the year 2020.

Carbon footprint of Varma's investments in dramatic decline 2015–2017
The carbon footprint of Varma's investments fell substantially over the past two years. Varma achieved in two years the CO_2 reduction target it had set for 2020 in all asset classes.

The greatest change took place in listed equities, where carbon footprint was 27% smaller at the end of 2017 than in 2015. This result was due to focusing on low-emissions industries and reducing investments in energy-intensive companies. Varma had already 2015 excluded electricity companies that generate more than 30% of their electricity with coal from its direct equity investments. In addition, Varma does not invest in coal mining operations and has a negligible number of direct oil stock holdings in its direct equity portfolio.

An increasing number of industries are being shaken up by both regulation and changes in consumer behavior. This means that investors can't focus merely on the energy sector or coal.

The carbon footprint of listed corporate bonds declined 22% in two years. Compared to the benchmark, the CO_2 footprint of corporate bonds is as much as 57% smaller. In 2017, Varma also began investing in green bonds. The debt capital raised through the issuance of a green bond is earmarked for environmentally friendly investments. By the end of 2017, the green bond portfolio was valued at approximately EUR 300 million.

The carbon footprint of real estate investments declined by 18% 2015–2017. This positive development is partly due to the change in Varma's real estate base, but credit also goes to the measures taken to boost energy efficiency in the properties. Reducing the carbon footprint of buildings demands an improvement in energy efficiency, which is something Varma has done for a long time now, meeting its energy-savings targets ahead of time in the energy efficiency program for business premises. In addition, Varma has built solar power plants in its properties, and rental flats have partly transferred to green real estate electricity.

Now that Varma has achieved the shorter-term goals, Varma will focus on developing the portfolio towards meeting the longer-term two-degree target agreed in the Paris climate conference.

Investor's opportunity to influence

As a major investor, Varma has the opportunity to influence companies and encourage them to reduce their carbon footprint. Varma has signed the CDP (formerly Carbon Disclosure Project), and joined the Montréal Carbon Pledge initiative supported by the Principles for Responsible Investment (PRI) and the United Nations Environment Programme Finance Initiative (UNEP FI). Under the Montréal Carbon Pledge, investors commit to measure and publicly disclose the carbon footprint of their listed equity investments on an annual basis. Starting from 2018 Varma also supports TCFD initiative. The FSB Task Force on Climate-related Financial Disclosures (TCFD) will develop voluntary, consistent climate-related financial risk disclosures for use by companies in providing information to investors, lenders, insurers, and other stakeholders. The Task Force will consider the physical, liability, and transition risks associated with climate change and what constitutes effective financial disclosures across industries.

In its ownership policy Varma also states that it expects clear assessments and reporting transparency from companies on the current and future impacts climate change will have on the company's operations and growth potential. The reporting should cover how climate change is included in the company's governance, strategy and risk management, especially in emissions-intensive industries. By reporting on the targets and indicators set by the company, it is possible to monitor the company's progress.

Sustainable equity portfolio part of responsible investments

Varma also has a thematic equity portfolio built on sustainable development. The investment universe of the portfolio is developed markets, excluding oil and coal companies. The investment strategy of the portfolio is to use sustainability to: 1) minimize risks regarding portfolio companies; 2) analyze costs benefits sustainable business model gives and; 3) find possible business opportunities from which companies could benefit. The portfolio invests in listed companies in developed markets and there are three different type of companies in the portfolio: companies 1) which benefit from climate change mitigation; 2) which are not too exposed to climate change risks; and 3) whose aim is to decarbonize. Those companies should be also sustainable on S and G, not just on part of E. That for example means that companies comply with international agreements and standards like the UN Global Compact initiative on corporate responsibility, the OECD guidelines for multinational enterprises and the ILO labor conventions.

8.3 Socially focused investing

Socially focused investing, otherwise referred to as **socially responsible investing** is the investment practice that uses elements of social responsibility, social action, and social impact as a lens for investment decision-making, risk management, and portfolio analysis. This practice may utilize exclusion, integration, impact, or engagement methodologies, and is a broad term that covers an array of ideologies and practical considerations, often referred to as socially focused issues, factors, or topics (Matloff and Chaillou, 2013).

Chapter 2 of this book discussed the history of ESG, which was largely driven by socially focused investing characteristics embodied in **faith-based investing**. Faith-based investing is understood as an investment practice that is driven by adherence to the beliefs and values of a religion. Faith-based investors may come in the form of institutional investors (a Catholic Church endowment), an asset manager (a money manager that manages ministers' retirements), or an individual investor that is guided by their personal beliefs. Faith-based investors often utilize exclusionary methodologies to screen out investments from the portfolio that are in opposition by their religion. The phrase "sin stocks" has been commonly to refer to investments which are restricted based on an asset owner's faith principles (Czerwonka, 2015). These issues may include, but are not limited to abortion, alcohol, gambling, and adult entertainment/pornography. These faith-based investors prioritize their investment policy and potential investment universe limitation based purely on policy, and thus, are not guided by financial performance of any excluded securities from their portfolio (Trinks and Scholtens, 2017).

Socially responsible investing (SRI) is a broader method for investors that are guided by a view or standpoint on an issue not solely based on religious principles (Junkus and Berry, 2015). Socially responsible investors often encompass a wider range of issues than faith-based investors. These potentially controversial issues may include abortion, sex trafficking, animal testing, contraceptives, controversial weapons, fur, gambling, genetic engineering, meat, nuclear power, pork (embryonic) stem cells, and tobacco. For example, in the mid-1900s many socially focused investors excluded South African investments due to Apartheid policies.

Corporate social responsibility (CSR) is a derivative of SRI, and measures the extent to which a corporation's activities and policies benefit their communities (including shareholders and stakeholders). SRI practitioners may use CSR measurements to negatively screen poorly perceived companies out of the investment universe, or for integration, engagement, or impact in order to include favorably perceived companies in the investment universe. Socially responsible investors may view CSR data as a resource to identify opportunities to manage risk or enhance financial returns, as correlations have been found between corporate social performance and financial performance (Hill et al. 2007).

The implementation of SRI practices may differ in scope based on belief system, social cause, and adherence to policy. Culture and regional acceptance also directly impacts socially focused investing. One analysis of the Nordic countries of Denmark, Finland, Norway, and Sweden analyzed the differences in socially responsible investment practices between the four countries. This study found that economic openness, the size of the pension industry, the cultural values of masculinity and femininity, and avoidance of uncertainty can be directly linked to differences in SRI in the four countries (Scholtens and Sievänen, 2013). SRI has become a common practice amongst institutional investors as many institutional investors represent beneficiaries that are drawn together by a common value system or culture. Such institutional investors have motivated asset managers, advisors, and consultants to adopt and implement SRI (LaMore, Link, and Blackmond, 2006). Many of these institutional investors have a fiduciary duty to abide by socially responsible investment guidelines (Sanders, 2015).

Some socially focused investors may purely be focused on using social issues or factors as indicators to enhance returns and mitigate risk. These investors might use social trends to predict the return distributions of various industries or sectors. These social indicators serve as data points to help guide the investor regardless of the investor's personal belief system. This practice of socially focused investing is motivated by the view that the practice provides exceptional insight into long-term value creation and risk protection.

Some socially focused investors will examine potential investments based on their positive impact on society (LaMore, Link, and Blackmond, 2006). These investors desire two outcomes: achieve favorable risk-adjusted returns, and play a positive role in improving the community and social groups through their investing (Trinks and Scholtens, 2017). That said, there are other socially focused investors, often philanthropic foundations and individuals, that prioritize positive social impact with their investment capital more than the return value of their investment.

Academics and investors often debate whether SRI portfolios detract or enhance financial performance (Filbeck, Krause, and Reis, 2016). Empirical research is largely mixed on the performance differential between socially focused investing and traditional investing. However, a plethora of long-term studies have found that there is no statistically significant performance disparity between the SRI investment and traditional investments, though outperformance trends have been discovered in some SRI-integrated investments (Rahul, 2016). The data contradicts the myth that social-based investing provides lower long-term returns (Schueth, 2003). For example, empirical evidence shows that SRI hedge funds on average significantly outperform similar non-SRI hedge funds on average by between 1.50% and 2.67% annually (Filbeck, Krause, and Reis, 2016). Socially focused equity portfolios have been observed to match, and often outperform, traditional equity portfolios over time (Kempf and Osthoff, 2007). This can be attributed to the positive and negative impact that social impact can have on the financial performance of certain industries and companies. Particularly in the 20th-century implementation of SRI, the market appears to reward good corporate charitable giving and an absence of nuclear and defense work, and it appears to penalize firms that provide family related benefits such as parental leave, job sharing, and dependent care assistance (Diltz, 1995).

Socially focused investors, and the social investing movement as observed through history, place emphasis on corporate responsibility, accountability, transparency, and sustainability (Waddock, 2008). Socially focused investing can be a stand-alone practice, or can be implemented in conjunction with environmentally focused investing and governance-focused investing.

8.4 Governance-focused investing

Governance is a broad category encompassing the structure of corporate ethical surveillance throughout the organization's hierarchy and structure. **Governance-focused investing** focuses on themes such as corporate leadership, compensation and labor rights, audits and internal controls, and shareholder rights. Assessing corporate governance allows an investor to gain insight into the company's operations that is otherwise unattainable through traditional research and analysis of a company's fundamentals. Governance-focused investors also examine governance factors to gain insight into corporate public accountability (Aysan, Nabli, and Véganzonés-varoudakis, 2007).

A governance-focused investor evaluates the securities of a company or government based on the quality of the governance structure. These investors favor organizations that display good governance, and view such securities associated with poor governance as less favorable and subject to higher risk. After corporate governance scandals, such as Enron and WorldCom, many investors became more conscious of the impact of corporate governance on stock prices (Duffy, 2004).

Investors often use corporate governance metrics to identify potential growth enhancers and detractors within a corporation. Understanding a company's governance structure is useful for assessing the risk of ownership of a company's debt and equity. Maximizing shareholder value can be a theme of governance-focused investing, if it is not at the expense of the long-term sustainability of the company (Lazonick and O'sullivan, 2001). A corporate governance structure that is transparent to investors, clear in process and policy, and maintains the highest standards relative to a company's industry and the broader market reduces investment risk. Risks related to corporate governance can negatively impact a company's operability, consumer perception, profitability, and sustainability. Like company news and events related to environmental and social issues, headlines related to governance issues can be extremely damaging to the asset prices of the company. However, better corporate governance benefit companies through greater access to financing, lower cost of capital, better performance, and more favorable treatment of all stakeholders (Claessens, Stijn, and Yurtoglu, 2015).

There are many governance-associated themes that an investor may prioritize as part of their research and analysis. These governance themes may be analyzed as a whole, in various parts or groupings, or in a granular focus of a specific issue (Lazonick and O'sullivan, 2001). A number of these governance issues are briefly discussed below.

Business ethics

This may be the most commonly known governance theme analyzed by investors and studied by academia. A governance-based investor may evaluate a company's business policies and practices regarding potentially controversial issues, such as insider trading, bribery, and discrimination. Business ethics are subjective in nature, and investors may differ on what constitutes ethical conduct. Business ethics may also differ greatly by company culture and industry. Governance-focused investors examine a company's business ethics to help determine the extent to which the company displays positive governance structures. Business ethics is a subject matter that is also commonly associated with socially focused investing because of the moral and fiduciary nature of the corporation.

Ownership and stakeholder opposition

Governance-focused investors may also analyze the ownership of an organization to identify characteristics of control, demography, and overall composition. This allows an investor to determine how much of the company the current employees own, thus providing insight on employee-based motivation for shareholder growth and sustainability. An organization's ownership may give the governance-focused investor insight into proxy voting and shareholder resolutions. Evaluating the ownership of a company also allows the ownership of a company to identify the company's stakeholders. The largest group of stakeholders are the shareholders who hold the most voting power. As such, governance-focused investors are interested in those shareholders' relationship with the company's board and management team. Some stakeholder opposition can be beneficial for a company's equity growth (refer back to engagement activism in Chapter 4), but for the most part stakeholder opposition causes internal conflict and turmoil in the organization and might be negatively perceived by the company's consumers.

Board diversity and management team diversity

Institutional investors may examine the composition of a management teams and boards to identify the composition of the hierarchy and leaders of the organization. An investor may want to determine if the company is aligned with the population of businesses and individuals who are buying their products and services. Institutional investors may draft policies, often a form of ESG integration, that require a percentage of their assets to own companies that have minority and female representation on their management teams and boards. Furthermore, some institutional investors have policies that require them to invest a percentage of their assets with minority-owned enterprises (MBE), in which the majority ownership is of a minority population or comprise a diverse population, and women-owned enterprises (WBE), which are companies where the majority ownership is female.

Labor management and labor practices

Governance-focused investors may analyze how a company manages and treats their employee base. Investors may consider labor standards as established by the United Nations in addition to data providers of labor standards within an industry or region. Investors may also use governmental regulation and national labor laws to measure corporate governance. Governance-focused investors may examine a company's policies on specific labor practices such as working hours, workplace safety, healthcare insurance coverage, retirement benefits, maternity and paternity leave, workers' conditions, and other issues related to a company's labor pool.

Supply chain labor standards

Many investors look further than just a company's labor practices and consider the labor practice standards of the organizations with which the company engages in business. These standards may be in the form of compensation, safety, and worker treatment. For example, an investor may examine a Canadian-based technology company that outsources phone center operations to a Malaysian-based company. This investor may investigate how the workers of the Malaysian-based company are compensated, traded, and offered corporate benefits and welfare. Another example might be a German clothing company that produces shirts in Peru. An investor may evaluate the labor management throughout the German company's supply chain and investigate the Peruvian company for set criteria such as child labor, working hours, and healthcare.

Human capital development and compensation

As governance-focused investors examine a company's labor management, practices, and standards, they may also evaluate how a company develops their human capital. This could involve analyzing a company's educational advancement and training programs. It may also entail the analysis of compensation, such as measuring if the lowest-level employees' wages increase with inflation or the management teams' wage growth. An investor may find companies with corporate enrichment programs as more favorable to growth than companies that don't have such programs and policies (Lazonick and O'sullivan, 2001). The governance-focused investor may use human capital development and compensation factors as insight on the sustainability and growth of a company.

Health and chemical safety

Safety is an aspect of governance that is important to many investors. The overall health of employees is vital to productivity. Investors may examine the company's policies and procedures regarding working with dangerous equipment, hazardous materials, and chemicals. The governance-focused investor may investigate how the safety standards affect a company's workers, environment, and communities where the company operates.

Product safety and product quality

The safety of the products that a company produces is also important to measure for many governance-focused investors. Governance-focused investors may take a granular lens to understand a company's product quality as compared to similar competitor products. Understanding product quality allows the investor to both gain insight on the management team's ability to price and market a product in the consumer marketplace, as well as any risks that might be incurred because of poor and ineffective product quality.

Cyber security and data management

As information becomes an increasingly powerful tool for business and the security of such data is constantly under threat from malicious actors, cyber security and data management is ever important for the governance-focused investor. Cyber security is the way a company protects secure data from harmful risks such as viruses. Cyber security protects non-public information such as the personal data and financial information of their consumers and employees. A governance-focused investor may analyze the factors of a company's cyber security and data management in order to best understand the cyber risks that the company may face.

Accounting standards

Accounting standards is a key issue that a governance-focused investor analyzes. Accounting standards and practices may differ greatly between countries and regulatory bodies. Corporate accounting standards and practices can be a critical due diligence factor of a governance-focused investor research as it can have a major impact on a company's assets. Measuring accounting standards and practices can be quite a difficult task for an investor. Even with set standards such as the Generally Accepted Accounting Principles (GAAP), which are a collection of commonly followed accounting rules and standards for financial reporting, flexibility still allows companies to use accounting to manipulate the reporting of income, debt, and cash flow through balance sheet measures (Wahab et al. 2008). A governance-focused investor may investigate accounting standards to better understand a company's practices around using debts and cash as a resource, taxation, and the management of accounts payable and receivable.

The emergence of new institutions, combined with reinforcement by international institutions in the form of the UN-backed Principles for Responsible Investment, global indexes and international CSR guidelines (Jun, 2016) have led to investors acting as notable change agents of corporate governance. This may be a factor of the inability of corporate boards and management teams to recognize problems within their governance structure because of corporate bureaucracy and long term. Active investors, through their ownership and actual participation on boards, improve corporate governance by reducing the gap between ownership and control (Haarmeyer, 2007).

Governance-based investing is largely driven by the demands and pressure of large shareholders. Institutional ownership is related to corporate governance because institutions own a large number of shares on behalf of a population that the institutional investor serves (Wahab et al. 2008). Institutional investors play a principal role in improving corporate governance (Lin, Song, and Tan, 2017). Changes in corporate governance are often a product of the engagement of large shareholders, such as institutional investors or large mutual funds (Sarkar and Sarkar, 2000). Large asset owners, such as sovereign wealth funds, have been able to have an influence on corporate governance issues because of their ability to take large stakes in corporations and, then, influence corporate boards (Rose, 2012).

Government, through regulations or initiatives, can also play a role in encouraging or enforcing corporate governance. For example, in 2001, Malaysia undertook important corporate governance reforms, which saw the integration of the Malaysian Code on Corporate Governance (MCCG) into Kuala Lumpur Stock Exchange (KLSE) Listing Rules and the establishment of the Minority Shareholder Watchdog Group (Wahab et al. 2008). Government-implemented structural reforms like financial development, trade openness, and human development affect investment decisions (Aysan, Nabli, and Véganzonés-varoudakis, 2007). Governance factors can play a significant role in private investment decisions, as well as publicly traded securities (Aysan, Nabli, and Véganzonés-varoudakis, 2007). Empirically, in a study of private investments in the Middle East and North Africa (MENA), governance in private investments is important, especially in the case of "administrative quality" in the form of control of corruption, bureaucratic quality, investment-friendly profile of administration, law and order, as well as for "political stability" (Aysan, Nabli, and Véganzonés-varoudakis, 2007).

LEARNING PERSPECTIVE 6: the future of capitalism is feminine

Lawler Kang, *Co-Founder of the League of Allies, began his career working for a Japanese chemical firm helping to establish US operations, while simultaneously starting a socially responsible importing firm out of Yogyakarta, Indonesia. He then attended The Wharton School at the University of Pennsylvania where he studied Entrepreneurial Management and Finance. Post-Wharton, he did M&A strategy consulting, while starting an internet firm on the side, and then transitioned to technology and turnaround consulting, with an eye on clients that could help the common good (ethical software, bio-tech, etc.).*

He then published his first book, Passion at Work *(Pearson Prentice Hall), which led to a speaking/workshop business helping individuals and teams find purpose, passion, values, and dreams in their work. Clients include: Cisco, Pfizer, EY, Oracle, and HP. He was then drawn back to the client side, serving in roles such as Chief People Officer at a leading eCommerce concern and a software consultancy focused solely on healthcare applications. During these tenures, he wrote his second book,* The E Ticket, *a fictional thriller which, with the support of ~200 footnotes, makes the case women are bio-evolutionarily better suited to lead. It was research for this book that led him to start the League of Allies.*

Business overview: League of Allies is a services firm focused primarily on gender parity, balance, and inclusion in the workplace. The League is co-founded by Patrick Moran, who brings two years of running JPMorgan's global Diversity & Inclusion (D&I) efforts sandwiched between six years on the trading floor. He also draws on eight years of strategy consulting experience with a focus on PE due diligence, a COO position at a sustainable energy company that raised $85 million, and Wharton, SAIS, and Boston College degrees.

The League's value proposition is based on our ability to make a data-driven case to other male executives as to the accretive power of balanced inclusion. We offer a variety of products, from D&I set up, structuring and governance services, to functional and leadership reviews and improvement roadmaps for both operating (mature/PE portfolio, and growth stage) businesses and investment (due diligence, GPs, and Asset Management) firms. These are supported by a library of presentations, workshops, and online content that elicits the mental changes at the individual level needed for scaled organizational impact.

Responding to the 1929 meltdown-induced tumult of the Great Depression, on May 27, 1933, President Franklin D. Roosevelt signed the Securities Act of 1933 into law. It was quickly followed by the Securities Exchange Act of 1934. These efforts replaced the prevailing and dodgy state-owned and operated "blue sky" rules with a federal charge to disclose information deemed to be material to the decision-making process of buying or selling a stock or bond. The economy frantically needed investment to grow, however investors were justifiably skittish as the lack of available and credible data had recently cost them a fortune. Desperate times called for pragmatic measures.

At first, business was resistant to the changes. New York Stock Exchange president Richard Whitney regarded any alterations to his "perfect institution" as a personal threat and facilitated what has been called "the biggest and boldest, the richest and most ruthless lobby Congress had ever known" to emasculate the legislation. Companies viewed the requirement to disclose information to investors and the government – the Securities and Exchange Commission (SEC) came out of these actions – as irksome, if not downright anti-American. Accusations from business quarters that Communist sympathizers were infiltrating the government made the media rounds. At this time, 100% of the companies listed on the US exchanges were directed, managerially and at the Board level, by men.

Examples of the kind of disclosures that caused all the ruckus include: information about the issuer's management, third-party certified financial statements, and documents such as the 10-K, an annual snapshot of the company's well-being. This information is regarded as standard, accepted, and expected today. In fact, no CFO in their right mind would think of reporting results without using these protocols for one very simple, and profitable, reason: investors like data, in consistent and understandable formats. The more they have, the more they can understand and evaluate the degrees of risk and reward the company faces. This impacts their revenue and cost projections, and the relative amount of uncertainty they will have in meeting them (known as a discount rate; the lower the better). Concomitantly, having more data can also impact a company's cost of capital, the interest rate they will pay lenders for their money. Again, the lower the better.

Which is precisely what happened. Some prescient firms, such as Pacific Gas & Electric and packing titan, Swift & Company, used these new materiality standards to raise debt, and investors repaid adherence with capital at reasonable rates. Everyone quickly followed; it was in their financial best interest.

This system survived, with occasional amendments, for 40 years. In 1973 however, to try and avoid increasing political influences, the Financial Accounting Standards Board (FASB) was created. FASB's charter is to establish and continually improve Generally Accepted Accounting Principles (GAAP), the global bedrock of financial reporting. Arguably once-esoteric financial products such as junk bonds, mortgage-backed securities, and credit-default obligations – all very helpful financial instruments if not used primarily for personal gain – would not have been able to come to market without this guidance.

The key terms above are "if not used primarily for personal gain," a caveat it seems many men have a difficult time upholding. Why is this so? In his book *Women After All: Sex, Evolution, and the End of Male Supremacy*, Dr. Melvin Konner presents a compelling hypothesis: our evolutionary biology, particularly the relative degrees of testosterone and estrogen between genders, has been the primary driver of our political, economic, and social mores since the time property was needed to be farmed, and defended. To be sure, there are many other bio-chemicals and environmental factors that affect our actions, however the overarching influences these two possess seem to be intractable.

As a daily baseline, men carry up to nine times the amount of testosterone as women, and can produce 20 times more per day. In addition to physical size, musculature, and a lower voice (all of which historically correlate with power/authority), testosterone has been linked with confidence extending to hubris, aggression, sex drive, criminality, irrational financial decision-making, self-centeredness/lack of generosity, and triggering the classic fight or flight response when faced with crises (like having to follow new rules). Estrogen, while no means a perfect hormone, manifests itself in nurturing/empathy, clear thinking, multi-tasking, better memory, and, when faced with difficult decisions, defaults to tending and befriending.

In 2012, a groundbreaking management survey was published in the *Harvard Business Review*. 64,000 global employees were asked to rank desired leadership competencies of modern leaders. Eight out of the top ten were deemed to be viewed as "feminine" by the participants, i.e., "expressive," "reasonable," "loyal," "patient," "intuitive," and "collaborative." The two traits considered to be "masculine" were "decisiveness" and "resiliency." While the respondent's correlation of traits with gender is certainly being influenced by prevailing social mores and degrees of confirmation bias, the links to our basic biochemistry are difficult to shake. Subsequent studies by top tier consulting firms such as Bain and McKinsey reflect these competencies, underscore their importance in leading, and correlate impacts on organizational performance, particularly in the leadership function.

This preference for "feminine" management styles would seem to manifest itself quantitatively in "engagement," the degree of passion and energy employees have for their work. Employees who feel cared for, are recognized and grown, etc. are more engaged, which both significantly impacts productivity and innovation, and reduces numerous costs: hiring, retention, absenteeism, and healthcare. Gallup, a leading engagement survey provider, reports that of the 12 questions they use, employees who report to women score better on 11 than those who report to men. The likelihood a female manager will be engaged is six points higher than a male, and there is a five point greater difference gracing the scores of blended teams run by women. Male-run and occupied teams average five points less than this and female-run and occupied teams score five points more.

These percentage differences may not seem like they would have much impact. However, per a 2016 study by Lean In and McKinsey, women currently occupy only 19% of C-suite positions, 27% of upper management, and 37% of lower management. If numerical managerial parity were achieved, the potential top and bottom line impacts would be massive. Indeed, McKinsey also projects an additional $25 *trillion* in global GDP growth by 2025 from advancing gender parity, which would dwarf any government-initiated policy shift or stimulus program.

And as capitalism thrives, instability – the risk of conflict, which is generally bad for most businesses – falls. This observation could be a significant reason why Goldman Sachs launched their *10,000 Women* initiative in 2008 to help educate, network, and provide capital to women entrepreneurs in emerging markets. While research in those markets reveals men's biology tends to spend its disposable income on alcohol, tobacco, weapons, and premium branded products for self-glorification, women's fuels economic growth by allocating its money to clothing, food, education, consumer durables, financial services, and insurance. Goldman Sachs has committed to raising up to $600 million to fund these efforts. In addition to the fact investing in women produces greater risk-adjusted returns, reductions in country or regional risk means a better overarching environment for business.

Balancing out testosterone-based groupthink with different perspectives also seems to be extremely accretive. Per a 2016 report from Morgan Stanley, companies with merely more women in them have lower execution risk, as measured by volatility of earnings and stock-trading ranges. Conceptually, this should lower companies' discount rates and their cost of capital, which is in fact happening; recently, Trillium, an asset manager, publicly lowered their discount rate on eBay due to its board-level gender diversity efforts. Further, a study done by Sodexo, a 400,000-employee global food services company, revealed gender-balanced teams, defined as 40–60% female, on average generated 12% greater client retention, 13% more organic growth, and 23% more gross profit. It should be noted the optimal proportion was 60% female.

Combining these two dynamics – the benefits of engagement and the ability to present new viewpoints without being dismissed – could provide rationale behind the results of a recent Credit Suisse and Bloomberg study (N>3,000). It concluded that companies whose senior front-office (revenue generating) positions were 50% female generated roughly 60% better share price growth over the last eight years. "Where women account for the majority in the top management, the businesses show superior sales growth, high cash flow returns on investments, and lower leverage (less debt)."

There are also numerous studies that correlate female participation on boards with markedly higher metrics: share price growth, return on sales, return on invested capital, etc. The data also indicate the greater the number of women, the better the company performs. While the type of industry probably plays a role in these numbers, the prevailing hypothesis of different and less risky perspectives, and engagement to varying degrees (women tend to show up more often for board meetings, as a starter), seems to be driving these results. Last year (2016) marked the highest percentage of women ever, 18.8%, serving as Fortune 1000 board members and there are significant efforts underway to rapidly increase these numbers. Per the numbers, it would seem to be in shareholder's best interests.

There is also a growing body of evidence that a newer demographic of women, at least on paper, are more qualified than older men to fill these pivotal positions, whose mandates have been rapidly expanding over the last decade to address capitalism's sketchier impacts on the world – i.e., climate disruption, resource scarcities, human rights, etc. It appears that it is finally in capitalism's best interests to become actively involved as a force for good.

The notion of socially responsible investing (SRI) has been around a long time. One of the first recorded references came from John Wesley, a founder of the Methodist church, who in a sermon called "The Use of Money" outlined its basic principles: make sure your business doesn't hurt your neighbor and avoid businesses that treat people poorly. Fascinatingly, the "sin" stocks – guns, alcohol, and tobacco – have been shunned by the more religious investors for centuries.

SRI has progressed over time, with a few notable lapses that include enslavement, aspects of industrialization, weapons and war machines, and the seeds of climate change. It has been a man's world. Then, in the mid-1980s, after 20 years of simmering, SRI was thrust into the global spotlight with the Apartheid divestment movement. It was a full-blown mainstream retail, foundation, endowment, and institutional investor revolt, which underscored the fact that individuals with money, organized and at scale, can make different rules.

In 1989, the year of the Exxon Valdez catastrophe, a nonprofit named the Coalition for Environmentally Responsible EconomieS (CERES) was founded by Joan Bavaria, an asset manager, with the mission to "mobilize investor and business leadership to build a thriving, sustainable global economy." CERES, coincidentally, is the name of the Roman goddess of agriculture and fertility. Roughly ten years later, The Global Reporting Initiative (GRI), with UN support, was spun out of CERES. It brought to market the first international set of standards that businesses, governments, and other organizations could use to identify, track, and report their impacts on the environment, climate change, corruption, and human rights. As of 2015, GRI has accumulated 7,500 signatories that include many Fortune 500 firms. Mutual funds marketing various flavors of SRI started popping up in the early 2000s.

At the time, it was a generally accepted principle that investors in SRI products were sacrificing a portion of their returns in exchange for their sustainable and ethical attributes. This started to change however, with the introduction of terms such as "triple bottom line," which implied environmental and social profit, in addition to the standard financial implication. Eventually, drawing on GRI themes, factors categorized as environmental, society, and governance (ESG) started wheedling their way as additional inputs into investment analyses. Not surprisingly, a study by the Haas School of Business (N>1,500) reveals that companies with women on their boards are more likely to focus on addressing a multitude of ESG factors, which coincidentally mitigate a multitude of malevolent effects emanating from "controversy" or "headline" risks. BP has estimated the total costs of its Deepwater disaster to be $61.5 billion.

These efforts would eventually culminate in a study published in the *Harvard Business Review*, which showed that ESG factors, depending on the industry, could have varying degrees of material financial impact on a company's revenues and costs, assets and liabilities, and/or cost of capital. The factors used in the report came from a nonprofit enigmatically named Sustainability Accounting Standards Board (SASB).

SASB is the brainchild of Dr. Jean Rogers whose first job, after earning her Ph.D. in Environmental Engineering, was with a superfund clean-up company. The work was disheartening: how could anyone let things get so bad? (Perhaps not by coincidence, the percentage of women with senior business decision-making authority in the chemical, petro-chemical, and mining industries is at the very low end of the range.) After a stint with Deloitte Consulting to understand the business side of things, she found herself embarking on her life's work, bringing complex issues to light by developing ways to measure them. This led her to a Loeb Fellowship at the Harvard Graduate School of Design, where she studied the link between finance and sustainable business practices. It was this research, and a cast of progressive characters, led by Bob Eccles, a legendary Harvard Business School professor, and Robert Massie, who at the time was the executive director at CERES, that solidified her beliefs that ESG-related changes could be made by aligning respective interests. It was a near-death experience, a neck fracture while sailing in the San Francisco bay, which apparently melded these beliefs with her life's work.

Up to this point in time, SRI investments were relatively narrowly focused on specific issues, i.e., sin stocks, environmental issues, etc., and to this day, there are distinct degrees of dissonance between how funds are marketed and the precise practices of the companies in them. The real gating factor that was constraining potentially trillions of dollars of investment capital being allocated along sustainable and ethical lines was the lack of industry-agreed upon standards for the bevy of ESG factors *on a sector-by-sector basis*. Water scarcity has little impact on banking; however it is a big deal when it comes to semiconductor manufacturing. This was viewed as a Herculean task, one that would require immense fortitude, patience, and probably a bit of existential lunacy. Dr. Rogers fit the bill perfectly, noting the referenced male scale of the effort.

The first few years were harrowing. Dr. Rogers was eternally raising money, courting partners and board members from a broad swathe of backgrounds, and building and guiding the organization, while raising a family. Then, in 2014, Michael Bloomberg agreed to chair the board. Goldman Sachs and BlackRock, the world's largest asset manager with $5.4 trillion under management, would join as corporate sponsors. The Ford Foundation would make a significant grant with a video from Darren Walker, its President, endorsing the organization's purpose and its impacts on the world. SASB would have the resources to meet its mission.

SASB intends to button up its standards, presently broken down to 30 factors across 49 industry types, in the first quarter of next year and, given its momentum, it will set the bar for US, and perhaps one day, global reporting. What is particularly compelling is that, going back to the language of the original securities' laws of the 1930s, the material impacts its standards have on investors' buy-sell decisions would seem to necessitate their inclusion in annual SEC-mandated corporate reporting. Irked or not, companies may need to disclose more data. However, similar to what happened 80 years prior, using SASB should help them attract and retain investment from the $62 *trillion* in assets whose signatories have committed to upholding the Principles of Responsible Investing (PRI) issued by the UN. And depending on the means of investment, they will conceivably secure these funds at a lower cost. The leverage these standards could have on where money is invested, essentially screening for more estrogen-influenced returns, could be profound. And regardless of what happens with the SEC, data reveals the train is leaving the station.

A good example is what is evolving in the alternative investment, or private equity (PE) space, a notoriously male-dominated sector. A recent study by Pitchbook, a data and technology provider, reveals that upwards of 60% of the people with the money (pension funds, foundations, endowments, family offices, etc.) consider the ESG practices of a fund vis-à-vis their investments to be "Important" to "Essential" in determining whether they will commit money to that fund. Per David Rubenstein of The Carlyle Group, a leading PE shop, "I don't really think many limited partners (people with the money) for much of history gave much more than lip service to ESG concerns. Now I think they are very serious about it. And I think GPs (PE funds) that aren't serious about it will suffer."

It turns out that the people with the money, due in considerable part to their shareholder's desires, want sustainable and ethical returns. It should also be noted that 70% of women, who are projected to control two-thirds of America's wealth (~$14 trillion) by 2030, and 92% of millennials have similar investment preferences. While 2016 was a blowout year for PE fundraising – almost $600B was collected – there is a trend amongst some of the larger LPs to downsize the number of GPs (sometimes by a ratio of 10 to 1) and the GPs that are remaining tend to be larger, more established outfits, often with buyout intent, that have invested in integrating ESG into their investment theses and post-transaction operations. It is becoming increasingly difficult to raise the next round of capital, the lifeblood of the industry, without focused attention on the holistic impacts this money will have. In the closing days of 2017, both the New York State and NYC Pension Funds (top 20 largest such funds on the planet with combined assets under management of nearly $400B), followed the Norwegian Sovereign Wealth Fund (largest in the world with $1T) in publicly declaring their portfolios will become free of fossil fuels.

Another recent outgrowth off the SRI/ESG root system is the budding rise of benefit corporations. US corporate structures have traditionally been centered on maximizing shareholder value. Board members have a fiduciary responsibility to these ends. This philosophy came into serious question however, with the rise of ESG factors, and pension fund managers who noticed the competitive dynamics of companies in their portfolios weren't having the nicest accents on the environment, climate, people, etc. While for-profit benefit corporations allow prioritization of other functions, such as purpose and corporate citizenship, both arguably more feminine-focused, before maximizing share-holder value.

Benefit Corporations can be certified as "B Corporations" via a grueling, ESG-in-fused process. And while household names such Patagonia, Ben & Jerry's, Warby-Parker, and Etsy may be perceived as playing on the fringes, a company called Laureate, backed by Kolhberg Kravitz Roberts (KKR), one of the world's largest PE players, went public last year as a B Corp. Currently, B Labs, the nonprofit that issues the credentialing, is responding to market demands by working on ways to allow both private and publicly traded multinationals to become certified, as the current process cannot accommodate the complexities of their legal structures. Soon, both Ben & Jerry's, and its parent, Unilever, could be putting their missions first.

Perhaps the best reflection of the acceptance of ESG materiality is its inclusion in short-term incentive plans. A Goldman Sachs report of this year found that 20% of the non-financial services firms on the S&P 500 had incorporated ESG factors into their management's bonus calculations. Employee health and safety topped the lists, particularly in the heavy industries; however there were growing showings in risk factors ranging from environmental impacts to product safety and workforce diversity to employee engagement. It has only taken 100+ years for predominantly male bosses, especially in industries that employ a lot of metal, to be compensated based on worker safety.

By 2021, for every 100 men in the US who graduate with a degree – bachelor to Ph.D. – 148 women will receive similar designations. This is a global phenomenon and the US is actually at the lower end of the developed world spectrum. The impacts this inexorable trend will have on our social, economic, political, and business landscapes will be profound, irreversible and long, long overdue. From personal experience, having attended Vassar College, which has been predominantly female since its conception in 1868, perhaps the most influential unintended consequence of this imbalance is that men, for the first time in their lives, will be significantly outnumbered by more mature women, presuming gender acceptance rates flex with the number of applications. And if they don't move, the increased competition amongst women for those slots means those who do matriculate will be more mature and more intelligent and accomplished, which will high-light the disparity. I hope these women will be as vocal with their views as my college colleagues, of both genders, continue to be today. The environment is certainly ripe.

While this enlightenment may not be realized without addressing some anxiety-pro-voking unknowns – good enlightenments rarely do – the end product will be men much more conditioned for equality on a scale previously unseen and probably unimagined. Indeed, this trend is already happening as a recent survey of younger male workers reveals only 23% want to be viewed as having "masculine" traits – tough, strong, and respected – vs. the clear majority who desire to be perceived as intelligent, caring, humorous, and friendly. Job descriptions and promotion criteria may need to evolve a bit.

Modern capitalism, like most other governing systems – political, legal, social, religious, and the media – has been created and codified by men, for men, and would seem to be intractably influenced by their biology. The fact a convicted rapist can be released after serving four months in jail, by the letter of the law, is an infuriating reminder of this legacy. It would seem though, if left unfettered and to their own devices, without balance, these codes won't perform optimally, and could inevitably destroy themselves. Numerous reports identify testosterone as the leading cause of financial crises, the 2008 version being the most recent and potentially systemically devastating. Conflict, spanning a myriad of intolerances peaking with war with radiation, is another exemplary manifestation of this syndrome. Our partitioned Congress is currently 19.6% female, roughly one point more than female representation on Fortune 1000 boards, and there are currently pronounced efforts, at least within one party, to increase these numbers. This would also seem to be in shareholders' best interests.

The significance of the diminutive yet sassy Fearless Girl statue confidently staring down the Wall Street bull is profound, even to those who have little understanding of the mechanics of financial markets and don't know the backstory. It was funded by State Street, a $2.5 trillion financial force, as a call for more women on boards. Her hands-on-hips stance, positioned squarely in the path of the Goliath-sized bull's imminent charge, is precisely how and where she currently needs to be. In time, however, as her immense and innate value is recognized, accepted and expands, a more apt rendering might be a similarly strong, yet trotting icon of growth being guided by a woman, at her side. Together, they could be called The Fearless Femme and Ferdinand.

The future of capitalism is feminine. The future of the world is not far behind.

Discussion questions

1) Generate examples of how an investor might approach analyzing RI and ESG factors through quantitative measurement (LO2)
2) Generate examples of how an investor would use qualitative measurement to analyze RI and ESG factors (LO2)
3) Segmented investor approach:

    a   Discuss why an investor might be interested in a specific viewpoint of Responsible investing, such as focusing on one aspect of environmental, social, and governance (LO3)
    b   Further discuss themes within environmental, social, and governance investing that might be applicable to certain investors, and not others (LO3)

4) Discuss practical considerations an investor might make for implementing ESG factor analysis within their portfolio (LO4)
5) List the pros and cons of the holistic investor approach to ESG investing and the segmented investor approach to ESG investing (LO6)

Notes

1   McKinsey Global Institute, "Resource Revolution: meeting the world's energy, materials, food, and water needs" Nov. 2011. Exhibit 19.
2   McKinsey & Co "Bridging Global Infrastructure Gaps" June 2016.
3   Source: KBI Global Investors. Performance based on a representative account in the strategy as of end October 2017 in USD, net of management fees of 85 bps per annum.

References

Alvarez, Marta, and Javier Rodríguez. "Water-Related Mutual Funds: Investment Performance and Social Role." *Social Responsibility Journal* 11, no. 3 (2015): 502–12.

Ashley, Colette. "Can a Low-Carbon Economy Grow GDP?" *Chicago Policy Review* (Online) (2017): 1.

Ayling, Julie, and Neil Gunningham. "Non-State Governance and Climate Policy: The Fossil Fuel Divestment Movement." *Climate Policy* 17, no. 2 (2017): 131–49.

Aysan, Ahmet Faruk, Mustapha Kamel Nabli, and Marie-Ange Véganzonés-varoudakis. "Governance Institutions and Private Investment: An Application to the Middle East and North Africa." *The Developing Economies* 45, no. 3 (2007): 339–77.

Behm, Katri, Roope Husgafvel, Catharina Hohenthal, Hanna Pihkola, and Saija Vatanen. "Carbon Handprint – Communicating the Good We Do." VTT research report. VTT, 2016.

Bello, Zakri Y. "Socially Responsible Investing and Portfolio Diversification." *Journal of Financial Research* 28, no. 1 (2005): 41–57.

Berry, Thomas C., and Joan C. Junkus. "Socially Responsible Investing: An Investor Perspective." *Journal of Business Ethics* 112, no. 4 (2013): 707–20.

Bullard, Nathaniel. "Fossil Fuel Divestment: A $5 Trillion Challenge." White Paper, Bloomberg New Energy Finance, August 25, 2014.

Campiglio, Emanuele. "Beyond Carbon Pricing: The Role of Banking and Monetary Policy in Financing the Transition to a Low-Carbon Economy." *Ecological Economics* 121 (2016): 220–30.

Child, Curtis. "Mainstreaming and Its Discontents: Fair Trade, Socially Responsible Investing, and Industry Trajectories." *Journal of Business Ethics* 130, no. 3 (2015): 601–18.

Claessens, Stijn, and B. Burcin Yurtoglu. "Corporate Governance in Emerging Markets: A Survey." *Emerging Markets Review* 15 (2013): 1–33.

Cleveland, Cutler J., and Richard Reibstein. "The Path to Fossil Fuel Divestment for Universities: Climate Responsible Investment." 2015. https://papers.ssrn.com/sol3/papers.cfm?abstract_id=2565941

Cowburn, Sarah. "Feature: Low-Carbon Investing – What the Low-Carbon Drive Means for UK Pension Funds." *PensionsWeek*, September 21, 2015.

Czerwonka, Monika. "The Influence of Religion on Socially Responsible Investing." *Journal of Religion and Business Ethics* 3, no. 1 (2015).

David Diltz, J. "The Private Cost of Socially Responsible Investing." *Applied Financial Economics* 5, no. 2 (1995): 69–77.

Dorfleitner, Gregor, Gerhard Halbritter, and Mai Nguyen. "Measuring the Level and Risk of Corporate Responsibility – An Empirical Comparison of Different ESG Rating Approaches." *Journal of Asset Management* 16, no. 7 (2015): 450–66.

Duffy, Maureen Nevin. "Corporate Governance and Client Investing." *Journal of Accountancy* 197, no. 1 (2004): 43.

Dyck, A., Lins, K., Roth, L., and Wagner, H. "Do Institutional Investors Transplant Social Norms? International Evidence on Corporate Social Responsibility." Working Paper, Rotman School of Management, 2016.

England, Richard W. "Three Reasons for Investing Now in Fossil Fuel Conservation: Technological Lock-in, Institutional Inertia, and Oil Wars." *Journal of Economic Issues* 28, no. 3 (1994): 755–76.

Fama, E., and French, K. "Common Risk Factors in the Returns on Stocks and Bonds." *Journal of Financial Economics* 33 (1993): 3–56.

Filbeck, Greg, Timothy A. Krause, and Lauren Reis. "Socially Responsible Investing in Hedge Funds." *Journal of Asset Management* 17, no. 6 (2016): 408–21.

Fishburn, P-C. "Mean Risk Analysis with Below Target Returns." *American Economic Review* 67 (1977): 116–26.

Godfrey, P. C., C. B. Merrill, and J. M. Hansen. "The Relationship Between Corporate Social Responsibility and Shareholder Value: An Empirical Test of the Risk Management Hypothesis." *Strategic Management Journal* 30 (2009): 425–45.

Haarmeyer, David. "The Revolution in Active Investing: Creating Wealth and Better and Better Governance." *Journal of Applied Corporate Finance* 19, no. 1 (2007): 25–41.

Habberton, Colin V. "The Role of Democracy in the Governance of Institutional Investing in South Africa." *Development* 58, no. 1 (2015): 103–11.

Haigh, Matthew, and Matthew A. Shapiro. "Carbon Reporting: Does It Matter?" *Accounting, Auditing & Accountability Journal* 25, no. 1 (2011): 105–25.

Halbritter, Gerhard, and Gregor Dorfleitner. "The Wages of Social Responsibility – Where Are They? A Critical Review of ESG Investing." *Review of Financial Economics* 26 (2015): 25–35.

Harlow, W. V. "Asset Allocation in a Downside-Risk Framework." *Financial Analysts Journal* 47 (1991): 28–40.

Hebb, T. *The Next Generation of Responsible Investing*. London: Springer, 2011.

Hill, Ronald Paul, Thomas Ainscough, Todd Shank, and Daryl Manullang. "Corporate Social Responsibility and Socially Responsible Investing: A Global Perspective." *Journal of Business Ethics* 70, no. 2 (2007): 165–74.

Hutton, R. Bruce, Louis D'Antonio, and Tommi Johnsen. "Socially Responsible Investing: Growing Issues and New Opportunities." *Business & Society* 37, no. 3 (1998): 281–305.

"Importance of Analytics-Based Carbon Emissions Reporting for Integration in Investment Management."

Jo, H., and H. Na. "Does CSR Reduce Firm Risk? Evidence from Controversial Industry Sectors." *Journal of Business Ethics* 110 (2012): 441–56.

Jun, Hannah. "Corporate Governance and the Institutionalization of Socially Responsible Investing (SRI) in Korea." *Asia Pacific Business Review* 22, no. 3 (2016): 487–501.

Junkus, Joan, and Thomas D. Berry. "Socially Responsible Investing: A Review of the Critical Issues." *Managerial Finance* 41, no. 11 (2015): 1176–1201.

Kabler, Laura. "Money in the Game: Executing a Governance-Based Hedge Fund Strategy." *Standard Journal of Law, Business & Finance* 12 (2006): 121.

Kempf, Alexander, and Peer Osthoff. "The Effect of Socially Responsible Investing on Portfolio Performance." *European Financial Management* 13, no. 5 (2007): 908–22.

Kiyar, Dagmar, and Bettina B. F. Wittneben. "Carbon as Investment Risk – The Influence of Fossil Fuel Divestment on Decision Making at Germany's Main Power Providers." *Energies* 8, no. 9 (2015): 9620–39.

LaMore, Rex L., Terry Link, and Twyla Blackmond. "Renewing People and Places: Institutional Investment Policies That Enhance Social Capital and Improve the Built Environment of Distressed Communities." *Journal of Urban Affairs* 28, no. 5 (2006): 429–42.

Lazonick, William, and Mary O'sullivan. "Maximizing Shareholder Value: A New Ideology for Corporate Governance." *Economy and Society* 29, no. 1 (2000): 13–35.

Levy, Tamir, and Joseph Yagil. "Air Pollution and Stock Returns in the US." *Journal of Economic Psychology* 32, no. 3 (2011): 374–83.

Lin, Yuchen, Yuchen Lin, Yangbo Song, Yangbo Song, Jinsong Tan, and Jinsong Tan. "The Governance Role of Institutional Investors in Information Disclosure: Evidence from Institutional Investors' Corporate Visits." *Nankai Business Review International* 8, no. 3 (2017): 304–23.

Liu, Yanfeng, Tao Li, Yaowen Chen, and Dengjia Wang. "Optimization of Solar Water Heating System under Time and Spatial Partition Heating in Rural Dwellings." *Energies* 10, no. 10 (2017): 1561.

Lohmann, Larry. "Climate as Investment." *Development and Change* 40, no. 6 (2009): 1063–83.

Matloff, Roger, and Joy Hunter Chaillou. "Socially Responsible Investing." *Nonprofit Investment and Development Solutions: A Guide to Strategies and Solutions for Thriving in Today's Economy* (2013): 111–20.

Meziani, A. Seddik. "Investing with Environmental, Social, and Governance Issues in Mind: From the Back to the Fore of Style Investing." *The Journal of Investing* 23, no. 3 (2014): 115–24.

Rahul, Rangotra. "Analysis of Risk and Return of Traditional and Socially Responsible Investing (SRI): An Empirical Study of Asia and India." *Advances in Management* 9, no. 3 (2016): 1.

Richardson, Benjamin J. "Climate Finance and Its Governance: Moving to a Low Carbon Economy Through Socially Responsible Financing?" *International & Comparative Law Quarterly* 58, no. 3 (2009): 597–626.

Ritchie, Justin, and Hadi Dowlatabadi. "Divest from the Carbon Bubble? Reviewing the Implications and Limitations of Fossil Fuel Divestment for Institutional Investors." *Review of Economics and Finance* 5 (2015): 59–80.

Rose, Paul. "Sovereign investing and corporate governance: Evidence and policy." *Fordham Journal of Corporate & Finance Law* 18 (2012): 913.

Sanders, William. "Resolving the Conflict Between Fiduciary Duties and Socially Responsible Investing." *Pace International Law Review* 35 (2014): 535.

Sandoval, Ricardo. "How Green Are the Green Funds? Fiscal and Philosophical Ups and Downs of Environmental Investing." *Amicus Journal* 17 (1996): 29–33.

Sarkar, Jayati, and Subrata Sarkar. "Large Shareholder Activism in Corporate Governance in Developing Countries: Evidence from India." *International Review of Finance* 1, no. 3 (2000): 161–94.

Scholtens, Bert, and Riikka Sievänen. "Drivers of Socially Responsible Investing: A Case Study of Four Nordic Countries." *Journal of Business Ethics* 115, no. 3 (2013): 605–16.

Schueth, Steve. "Socially Responsible Investing in the United States." *Journal of Business Ethics* 43, no. 3 (2003): 189–94.

Sireklove, Jennifer. "Fossil-Free Investing." *The Journal of Index Investing* 6, no. 4 (2016): 129–33.

Sueyoshi, Toshiyuki, and Mika Goto. "Investment Strategy for Sustainable Society by Development of Regional Economies and Prevention of Industrial Pollutions in Japanese Manufacturing Sectors." *Energy Economics* 42 (2014): 299–312.

Trinks, Pieter Jan, and Bert Scholtens. "The Opportunity Cost of Negative Screening in Socially Responsible Investing." *Journal of Business Ethics* 140, no. 2 (2017): 193–208.

Waddock, Sandra. "Building a New Institutional Infrastructure for Corporate Responsibility." *The Academy of Management Perspectives* 22, no. 3 (2008): 87–108.

Wahab, Effiezal, Aswadi Abdul, Janice How, and Peter Verhoeven. "Corporate Governance and Institutional Investors: Evidence from Malaysia." *Asian Academy of Management Journal of Accounting and Finance* 4, no. 2 (2008): 67–90.

World Green Building Council. "Annual Report 2015/2016." *World Green Building Council* (2016).

Chapter 9

Methods for modeling risk and return for traditional investments

This chapter will analyze traditional performance measurement models used by investors. These traditional performance models will include the Sharpe ratio, the Omega ratio, the Sortino ratio, and the CAPM model, amongst others. This chapter will first discuss the history and development of such models, and then assess the relevance of such models as they apply to the performance measurement of ESG investing. The chapter will evaluate the strengths and weaknesses of such models for the investor in terms of both quantitative and qualitative considerations. This chapter will also provide vocabulary and a high-level overview of momentum and "smart beta" strategies, as cutting-edge developments to ESG investment strategies. It will also build upon concepts discussed in Chapter 7 regarding risk-based investor concerns, and concepts discussed in Chapter 3 regarding ESG risk and the positive performance potential that that risk may provide.

Learning objectives

- Describe traditional performance measurement models used by investors
- Explain the history and development of traditional performance measurement models used by investors
- Utilize traditional performance measurement models used by investors in the context of investment portfolios
- Utilize traditional performance measurement models used by investors specifically in the context of momentum and "smart beta" strategies
- Evaluate the strengths and weaknesses of traditional performance models
- Assess the strengths and weaknesses of utilizing traditional performance models in the context of ESG investments

After this chapter, readers should have a thorough understanding of how models measuring risk and return are developed. Readers should also understand the industry trend towards a model developed specifically for measuring ESG investment risk and return, and be prepared with the foundation to understand the process of developing such a model.

Introduction

As discussed in Chapter 8, ESG investing can be quantitative in nature, though some ESG factors have been traditionally limited to the depth of qualitative data. There are several common quantitative models that investors use in portfolio construction. Investors are currently in the process of testing the extent to which these traditional models can support the integration of quantitative ESG data. ESG data may have a meaningful role as an input to several models, but may also not be applicable in others. On the flip side, ESG data can also be an output of some adapted traditional analytical models. This chapter will discuss the various ways ESG investing has changed the way investors use traditional models, and the perspective investors now take on factors of risk and return within portfolio construction due to the rise in ESG data availability.

9.1 Fundamental analysis

Fundamental analysis is a method of research used to measure the intrinsic value of a security through the examination of economic, financial, and qualitative factors. Fundamental analysis includes the study of all factors that may affect a security's value. The goal of fundamental analysis is to produce a calculated assumption of value that an investor can compare to an asset or security's current price. This method indicates if the price of an asset or security is undervalued or overvalued. For corporate securities, a core fundamental analysis factor is **cash flow**.

Cash flow

Cash flow is the net amount of cash and cash equivalents that move in and out of a business. A positive cash flow indicates that there is a positive increase in the company's assets. A negative cash flow suggests that a company's assets are decreasing. Operating cash flow represents the cash of a company's net income. The Generally Accepted Accounting Principles (GAAP), discussed in Chapter 8, requires accrual accounting which includes non-cash items and stock-based compensation, amortization, and expense that have been incurred but not paid. Jensen and Posner (1986) proposed the idea of free cash flow, but did not provide a specific calculation for Free Cash Flow (FCF). Since Jensen's thesis, free cash flow has become an essential parameter, but there is still much variation in the way that it is calculated. One of the main issues with cash flow is that firms with stable cash flows and low information asymmetry could be construed as investments with lower risk profiles, specifically in volatile markets when investor sentiment is weak.

ESG investors may also place an emphasis on cash flow, and free cash flow, in their valuation of companies. The ESG investor may also take a granular lens to the governance structure around the cash flow. For example, an ESG investor may qualitatively analyze the historical use of cash flow to see whether cash was historically used to benefit or harm the shareholder. The ESG investor may research the potential for cash to be distributed to the investor through dividends, or be used for investment into research & development projects for further growth, or be used for a sustainable environmental or socially responsible project. The same investor may evaluate the likelihood that cash will be used to benefit the management team through frothy executive bonuses or on expansion away from the company's business, competitive market, or industry. An ESG investor may also engage with a company that they own on how to use the cash in a sustainable and responsible way.

One method of analyzing cash flow is using a **discounted cash flow** (DCF) model. Discounted cash flow considers the time value of money. DCF models are often used to determine how attractive an investment will be in the future. This method is done by using a free cash flow (FCF) model which makes projections and discounts them to estimate present value which in turn is then used to evaluate the potential of the investment. DCF valuation forecasts the value of a company by the present value of its future cash flows. One issue with DCF models is that the exact values and the duration of the cash flow may not be known. Fundamental analysis valuation models such as a DCF are a crucial component of forecasting.

Global investors accept the practice of DCF valuation, although the use of DCF models have empirically produced better results for companies in the developed markets than the emerging markets. This is perhaps because emerging markets can be both poorly regulated and less transparent than developed markets. ESG investors may use DCF valuation as part of their own equity valuation work. An ESG investor may integrate an assumption on the sustainability of a company's products or services as an adjustment to the terminal value of a company. In this way, an ESG investor can assume that the sustainable or responsible nature of the corporation, or lack thereof, can increase or decrease the terminal value of the company. Further, an investor may use informational assumptions on ESG factors to add or discount the growth rate of a company as an input to the DCF valuation. In this way, an ESG-minded investor may make a more informed decision on the valuation of a company through the inclusion of such ESG criteria. For a detailed explanation and example of how this may be observed, see below Case study 9A.

CASE STUDY 9A: integrating ESG in DCF valuation: AllianceBernstein's Global Core Equity

AllianceBernstein's Global Core Equity strategy is an active, fundamentally driven service managed by a small team of stock-pickers. Their integrated approach embeds ESG factors into their discounted cash flow analysis. As a global asset manager, AllianceBernstein has embraced responsible investing in spirit and in practice. With a global perspective, deep industry knowledge, and collaborative research culture, responsible investing at the firm is all about exploration, collaboration, and relentless improvement. Integrating ESG factors into investment processes has been a key focus for many years.

The Global Core Equity team invests in companies defined as "value creators" – those that can expand their businesses without tying up too much capital. Companies must simultaneously maintain a sharp focus on growth, profitability, and asset efficiency. A company that's making good use of its assets is capable of growing earnings while rewarding shareholders via buybacks and dividends. Alternatively, companies may also create value by shrinking unprofitable businesses, which allows them to unlock capital.

The team incorporates ESG into their process using the principle of three pillars.

1   First, the team takes a top-down view to eliminate a small number of companies from the investment universe. These include those that operate in controversial industries, the cluster munitions or tobacco, for example.
2   Second, the team takes a bottom-up approach to ensure that ESG risk is effectively quantified and appropriately compensated for in the portfolio.
3   Third, through company engagement, ESG-related issues can be addressed.

In the second step, when pricing companies, ESG is an important part of the return component of a company valuation. Owning companies with severe ESG issues comes with a potential cost should these issues emerge, but they also call into question the sustainability of a business model.

In the team's investment model, a target price is generated by a discounted cash flow model. To predict the upside potential of a new investment, analysts implement forecasts into their models to compute the expected price of a company. To invest, potential investments must pass a specific upside threshold from the current share price (typically +20%), as well as being a company that the team believes can create value over time. Each company is assigned a discount rate to represent the time value of money, adjusted for the following risk premia:

1   Cyclicality – a measure of a company's operational risk against the economic background
2   Financial leverage – to address the additional risk of owning higher-geared companies
3   Country – to account for instances of more than normal political or market-governance risk
4   ESG

By adjusting the discount rate, companies with or without ESG issues can be compared more fairly. Penalizing a poor ESG company by applying a higher discount rate raises the bar for investing in the company, ensuring adequate compensation for taking on additional risk. In some cases, the impact to the model can preclude investing at all.

Evaluation

Importantly, it is not just whether a company is exposed to an ESG risk, but also how well company management is equipped to address it. Evaluating company management's ability to address ESG issues is an important part of evaluating ESG factors. In specific industries ESG risk is an inherent part of company operations – there is an environmental impact from oil explorers and a social impact from alcoholic drink manufacturers – which are in addition to other ESG risks such as worker safety or supply chain management that companies can face.

Downside risks are evaluated on the exposure to the issue and whether it is an issue that a good management team can handle and control. In some cases, there will always be a risk, even though there is competent management – in these cases it is about the tail risk for the company and how that is weighed against the potential return.

Governance issues are assessed on multiple factors: business ethics; how management is incentivized and compensated; board corporate governance principles, structure and oversight. These issues are evaluated and compared to market norms. On governance only, the team assigns a small benefit in cases that a company has excellent stewardship of capital, aligning with the concept of value creators.

Model

A proprietary quantitative scoring model is used to compute the discount rate adjustment for environmental, social, and governance factors that is an input to the valuation framework. In this model, the lower the score, the more attractive the investment.

Company discount rates are adjusted within certain bands. As part of an ongoing review and development cycle these bands may be adjusted over time. Currently the maximum and minimum are set as follows:

•   The maximum penalty of +0.5% for environmental- and governance-related issues is based on the conclusion that these issues have the greatest probability of having a negative impact on a company's stock price.

Table 9.1 ESG-related discount rate adjustments

Discount rate adjustments	Environmental	Social	Governance
Minimum	0	0	−0.25%
Maximum	0.50%	0.25%	0.50%

- Social has a maximum penalty of +25 BP, on the basis that company management is better able to reduce or correct such issues.
- The minimum benefit for environmental and social is zero, meaning the best environmental and social companies are not given an undue advantage which may be captured elsewhere in the analysis, for example in terms of a competitive moat.
- For governance, a discount rate benefit of up to −0.25% may be assigned for excellent capital stewardship companies, as an indication of strong value creation.

Analysts also engage in a thorough fundamental assessment of the company and fundamental views can overrule the quantitative model. As the model uses external data vendors as an input, the team controls for stale or missing data, or data that could be weighted too far to a past occurrence.

Engagement
The quantitative framework gives an indication about management quality on certain issues. If the model identifies a company as an outlier, or suggests a discount rate at the extreme of its allowable bands, the team will look to discuss it with management. As part of a large, global asset management company, analysts have access to management and an ownership level that makes these conversations relevant. Ultimately, if there is an opportunity for management to improve any ESG issues, they believe it will be better for the fair value assessment of the company.

Example
Introduction. Company XYZ is a large multinational, US-domiciled internet services provider. The company faces increasing risks of being targeted by regulators on antitrust and tax avoidance fronts globally. The company has strong privacy and data security commitment and policies, which are enforced with best-in-class structures such as adopting a "privacy-by-design" approach, advance encryption, and privacy enhancing technologies. However, it has not been immune to privacy and data security controversies.

Evaluation. To account for any potential left-tail and non-normally distributed risks associated with ESG exposures and management that was not captured in their direct modeling of economic profit forecasts.

Analysis. Although the company has historically added value to shareholders, continued spending on non-core projects and a reluctance to pay dividends is value destructive. This was already captured by the financial forecast for the company, but the potential future inability to respect shareholder value was not. A potential lack of stewardship leads to further value destruction that needs capturing in the DCF model (1).

The company is struggling with a global approach to local and/or regional clients and regulators. Business ethics that are accepted in the US might be at odds with European regulators, exposing them to fines and restrictions related to anti-competitive behavior. Such risks are not fully captured in the financial forecasts and are therefore included in the discount rate adjustment framework (1 and 2).

Privacy and data security are increasingly of greater concern for individuals and regulators. With a high number of users, the company is largely exposed to any potential data breach and an obvious target for hacking. Despite their best in class management of such risks, it is likely that the company could one day be the victim of a successful cyber-attack (2).

Column 1: Incremental – this represents the quantitative data analyzed through the Discounted Cash Flow (DCF) Model.

Column 2: Adjustments – this represents the adjustments made to the DCF Model, based on risk premia factors (including ESG factors).

Column 3: Upside – this represents the estimated upside return potential for the investment.

ESG model adjustments (see column 2: Adjustments)

1) Company XYZ's ownership and board structure, combined with a less-than-perfect approach to shareholder value earns the company a 0.50% addition to its discount rate.
2) Despite very strong data security management, the company is highly exposed to a potential breach, which earns the company a 0.1% addition to its discount rate.

Conclusion

The potential upside of the company, represented by the difference between the current share price and the team's conclusion for its intrinsic value, is materially affected by governance issues. The upside falls from 15% to 9%, which significantly changes the viability of the investment being considered for the strategy.

Table 9.2 Discounted cash flow model adjusted for ESG factors

Discount rate	Incremental	Adjustment	Upside
Real market implied discount rate (global developed)	4.00%	15.00%	15.00%
Operational leverage and cyclical impact	0.10%	−2.00%	13.00%
Financial leverage	−0.25%	3.50%	16.50%
Environmental	0.00%	0.00%	16.50%
Social (2)	0.10%	−1.50%	15.00%
Governance (1)	0.50%	−6.00%	9.00%
Country risk premium	0.00%	0.00%	9.00%

Price-to-earnings (P/E) ratio

Another factor of fundamental analysis is the price-to-earnings (P/E) ratio. P/E is one of the most common measures of stock valuation, and the P/E and DCF models are the two most common valuation models used by fundamental analysts. Many studies that incorporate the P/E ratio focus on whether the variations of P/E ratio can be explained by macroeconomic factors and firm fundamentals such as risk-free interest rate, inflation, equity risk premium, firm size, leverage ratio, dividend payout ratio, earnings growth, and price volatility. Generally, empirical studies commonly find that the P/E ratio has a positive relationship with dividend payout ratio, firm size, and growth of earnings, but a negative correlation with risk-free rate, equity risk premium, and leverage ratio. Investor sentiment may also contribute to movements in P/E. For example, after investor sentiment is factored into equity pricing, if the stock price suddenly jumps, the company earnings may not reflect the movement in price.

An investor may use the P/E ratios of publicly traded companies to measure the relative market sentiment on a company's valuation within their industry, which can then be used as a benchmark against their own ESG research. An ESG-minded investor may consider the equity valuation of companies that have favorable ESG factors and low P/E ratios as attractive and companies with undesirable ESG factors and high P/E ratios as unattractive. As such, an ESG investor may incorporate P/E ratios in their equity valuation research to gain an understanding of a company's valuation in combination ESG analysis, and the market inferences on a company relative to their competitors and industry.

Price-to-Book (P/B) Ratio

Another widely recognized tool of fundamental analysis is the **price-to-book (P/B) ratio**. The P/B ratio is defined as the market value of a firm's equity divided by the book value of its equity. The P/B ratio can be used to determine if the price of a stock reflects the overall valuation of the market. Deviations from the permanent earnings benchmark are usually explained by the fact that most firms use historical cost accounting to value their operating assets with the consequence of lower book values.

An ESG-minded investor may use P/B ratios as a tool for their equity valuation of a company. This becomes a particularly useful method for an EG investor because it may help them identify where the market price of an equity is dislocated from the investor's view of the book value of a company. For example, a company may be employing dishonest accounting practices, wherein the financial office carries excess losses forward through accounting measures that can conceal such losses from the public. As such, these losses would not be factored into the P/B ratio of publicly used data providers and research firms. In this case, an investor integrating ESG practices would factor in the poor governance structures of the company, and thus may use their knowledge, gained through an investigation of the company's accounting practices to avoid or short sell the equity.

9.2 Quantitative analysis

Quantitative analysis seeks to understand or evaluate assets or securities using mathematical measurements, statistical modeling, and company research. Quantitative analysis includes the study of economic behavior in the financial markets. The practice of quantitative analysis as it relates to the financial markets is dependent on the movement of prices determined by supply and demand.

ESG investing uses quantitative analysis in various fashions. For example, ESG investors may incorporate the supply and demand variables of commodities or carbon emissions. ESG investing cultivates the use of ESG factors in factor analysis and risk premia modeling, uses ESG data as components for principal component analysis (PCA), and integrates ESG news as input of quantitatively derived automated algorithms. As in the case of fundamental analysis, quantitative analysis and quantitative money management can be enriched with the practice of ESG investing.

Correlation

Traditional quantitative analysis often uses measures of **correlation**, which is a metric commonly used to test the interdependency of two random variables. For example, in fixed income, high positive correlation, measured between 0 and +1, indicates that yields are highly dependent and move in the same direction. High negative correlation, measured between −1 and 0, suggest a long dependency; however, the trend will move in opposite directions. Using correlation models enables an investor to assess the drivers behind changes in prices.

Correlation measurement helps investors better understand the relationship between two variables. ESG investors use traditional correlations to measure hypotheses on trades, manage portfolio risks, and research new opportunities through the use of correlation analysis. For example, ESG ratings produced by independent service providers can be used to measure ESG rating correlations between different securities and individual securities against a sector or asset class. ESG ratings can be used to measure trends in the movements that can be used as insight for the quantitative research, analysis, and trading (MSCI). One academic example of correlation analysis with ESG methodology comes from research conducted by Dr. Nenavath Sreenu, in which he studied the relationships between corporate finance decisions, governance, and financial performance in emerging market equities. The objective of his research was to find the correlation between these three factors in the context of the Indian market. Sreenu concluded that corporate governance and corporate financial performance are correlated, and that governance assessments of companies have a significant positive impact on financial performance. It is important to note that practitioners of ESG investing, based on their integration approach or policy view, may discount or credit the book value of a company for assets or liabilities that may not be perceived as sustainable or for ESG-related issues and factors.

Capital asset pricing model (CAPM)

The **capital asset pricing model (CAPM)** is another common model used in quantitative analysis. Investors use the CAPM model to assess the value of a security and price it accordingly based on two factors: the **time value of money** and the risk of the asset. The time value of money refers to the concept that money in the present is worth more than the identical sum of money in the future, due to the potential for earnings on that sum. CAPM uses the market equilibrium, where the expected excess return on a risky asset is comparative to the expected excess return on a market portfolio (a portfolio with a beta of 1, or a portfolio that tracks perfectly with the market). To establish an equilibrium value for the expected return of an asset, an investor must calculate the asset's **beta** (correlation to the overall market), the expected return on the market portfolio, and the risk-free rate of return (often represented by the yield on short-term government bonds). ESG investors may incorporate their own methodologies into the CAPM model. For instance, an ESG investor could choose a risk-free rate that is aligned with a certain ESG policy or use one of the thousands of ESG-based indices offered by index providers. An ESG investor could consider the time value of money through the lenses of potential earnings growth offered by using ESG strategies, meaning that the investor acts on research demonstrating higher long-term performance through ESG integration.

Variance

Another tool of quantitative analysis is **variance**, sometimes referred to as **mean–variance**. Variance measures how far one data point in a given set of data is from the **mean** (the average). Variance calculation requires measuring the statistical difference between the data points in the dataset and the mean, squaring the difference and dividing the sum of the square by the number of data points in the set. Mean-variance modeling is an essential part of modern portfolio theory, and seeks to allocate the investments in a portfolio in such a way that lower volatility and higher volatility assets are mixed to create the optimal risk-return ratio.

Harry Markowitz popularized the use of mean-variance analysis in portfolio theory through his research in 1952. Since then, many institutional investors use modern portfolio theory or an alternative mean-variance modeling technique as a practice for determining target asset allocations. Many ESG-minded investors will use ESG-adjusted volatility assumptions on assets, ESG-relative passive indices, and other ESG information as adjusted inputs for mean-variance modeling. ESG investing and ESG issues can have a material impact on traditional mean-variance modeling. By integrating ESG in mean-variance modeling, asset owners can strengthen systemic frameworks, communicate the importance of ESG performance to their investees and investors, and align their efforts with those of governmental and non-governmental organizations to limit **systemic risk** (risk associated with an overall economic system, as opposed to one specific asset or asset class). Investment managers that use modern portfolio theory, such as private wealth managers and institutional investors, are likely to have a greater understanding of their portfolio risks and be better prepared for systemic risk when they integrate ESG policy and insights into their modeling.

Technical analysis

Technical analysis, another form of quantitative analysis, uses distinctive formations created by movements in the prices of securities on a chart. Lines connecting common price points over time are an indication of these patterns. The information from these charts is then used to identify trends to predict future price movements.

ESG investors will use technical analysis as a tool for entering, building, and exiting investment positions as well. Technical analysis is useful for measuring where the historical market participants have provided levels of support or resistance for securities. ESG investors can also use technical analysis to identify differences in their ESG-aligned valuation of a security with that of the open markets' perception of at what price the security should be trading. Technical analysis may also be applied to measuring of ESG ratings' time series in order to generate assumptions of future ESG rating quality and speculative ESG ratings' forecasts.

Mean reversion

Another factor of quantitative analysis is **mean reversion**. Mean reversion is the theory that prices and returns will eventually move back toward their mean. Mean reversion trading capitalizes on the profit from changes in the pricing of a security as it moves closer to its mean. Mean reversion models have gained popularity in various asset classes and derivatives as technology, such as high-freely algorithmic trading, allows investors to understand mean reverting spreads continuously in real time. Most mean reversion models use the Ornstein-Uhlenbeck process which randomly oscillates around the long-term mean with a constant mean reversion rate to permit dependence. ESG investors may use mean reversion for insight on entering or exiting positions, as well as the measurement of sustainability factors and probable outcomes within a portfolio. ESG investors may also use mean reversion analysis when controlling a variable weighting to a sensitive area within their portfolio. For example, an environmentally focused investor may use mean reversion analysis to help with the weighting of energy, such as oil and gas, exposure within their portfolio as to not be too underweighted to an upward price action cycle, while still controlling for the amount of carbon in their portfolio. Mean reversion and regime switching are a crucial feature of commodity prices.

Skew

Quantitative analysis includes an assessment of **skew**. Skewness describes the asymmetry of normal distribution in a statistical dataset. Skewness is essential to finance because most prices and asset returns do not follow a **normal distribution**. The value of skew can be either positive or negative, with positive indicating a longer tail on the right side and a negative indicating a longer tail on the left side. A zero skew, or a symmetrical skew, would indicate a relatively constant distribution on both sides of the mean. A symmetrical skew pattern is the embodiment of an equilibrium of risk (see Figure 9.1). Mathematically, the equation is as follows:

$$\text{Skew} = \frac{\sum (X - x - bar)^{3}}{(N-1)S^{3}}$$

Symmetry in skewness that results in a change in kurtosis can achieve a materialized desired impact on return distributions. Investors often use options pricing, the implied volatility of such derivatives, to identify the skew of their portfolio, which allows them to identify their risk management probabilities (Ross, 2015). The options' call market provides insight on the future probability distribution of risk to the upside, and is called the right tail. Whereas the options' put market provides insight to the future probability distribution of risk to the downside, or left tail. Skew is a forward-looking metric, as it is used to predict future return distributions.

ESG investors may use insight gained from skewness in the traditional sense, but may also integrate their insights on the probability distribution of a security as projected from ESG analysis. ESG investors may also use skewness-like derivation to develop ESG ratings probability distributions using cross-sectional ESG ratings data. Such data may be weighted relative to sector industry and asset class as forward-looking indistinctive probabilities of future security price performance (Pollard, Sherwood, and Klobus, 2018). In simple terms, ESG ratings data may be integrated to provide insight into future returns using the skew of ESG ratings data in correlation with the skew of financial returns.

Kurtosis

The related concept of **kurtosis** measures the weight of the tails in a distribution relative to the center of the distribution. Kurtosis is sometimes described as the "skew of the skew."

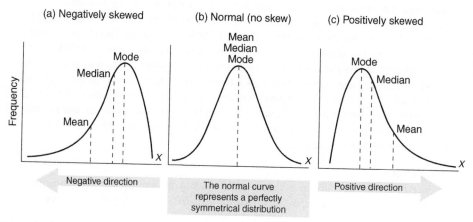

Figure 9.1 Skewness relative to normal distribution

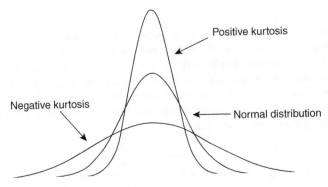

Figure 9.2 A view of kurtosis

Kurtosis can be measured quantitatively and is often done through an examination of skewness. Higher peaks indicate that a distribution also has fatter tails and that there are more chances of extreme outcomes compared to a normal distribution. The analysis and measure of kurtosis enables an investor to better understand the way in which their returns are distributed relative to their objective distribution.

ESG investors may measure the probability distribution of ESG-based investments to model their portfolio relative to a desired kurtosis. Skewness and kurtosis can be useful tools when using exclusionary methodologies to understand how the negative screening of such ESG issues-relative securities may affect the return distribution. Similarly, ESG integration methodologies may leverage the statistical power of skewness and kurtosis as a quantitative guide to address the degree of integration and how to integrate ESG factors in a way that does not dramatically alter a desirable skewness and kurtosis as a result of the integration.

CASE STUDY 9B: eight oil, gas, and coal companies

Hannah G. Commoss, Partner – Spruceview Capital Partners

Hannah has nearly 20 years of institutional investment management and financial analysis experience in both the public and private sectors. In her role at Spruceview, Hannah is responsible for building and managing marketable securities portfolios and multi-asset class ESG solutions. Hannah also served as the Deputy CIO, Public Markets and Director of Strategic Initiatives for the Massachusetts Pension Reserve Investment Management (PRIM) Board. There she oversaw the public markets investment program, which at the time was approximately $35 billion, and implemented a $4.2 billion direct hedge fund program. Additionally, Hannah directed the PRIM Board's investment policy initiatives including all facets of investment restrictions/divestment, proxy voting customization and execution, and targeted investment programs across asset classes. Prior to PRIM, she was at HarbourVest Partners, a private markets investment firm.

Background
As investors, we have grown accustomed to wading through a sea of acronyms to measure success and failure, with the likes of ROE, EPS, and P/E part of our everyday

vernacular. And we have had to familiarize ourselves with the alphabet soup that all too often summarizes investment strategies and vehicles, ETF, UCITS, CAT, SPV, etc., all of which keep allocators on their toes, and financial dictionaries at their fingertips. What we have observed over time, as product offering has come and gone and asset classes have moved in and out of favor, is an increase in questioning from allocators and asset owners as to where and how their assets are being put to work, and what they might be actively or passively supporting along the way. There is a sea change in investor behavior, one that places an ever-increasing importance on the double bottom line – strong financial return and meaningful and measurable impact. The fall out of this investor awareness is the rise of ESG, environmental-, social-, and governance-related discussion and investing. This is an acronym you need to know. Hold outs in the investor community are quick to shrug off ESG as "emotional alpha"; however environmental-, social-, and governance-related focus goes hand in hand with pro-active risk management, increased corporate accountability, and strong long-term returns. In fact, according to combined Harvard Business School and London School of Economics research, companies that incorporate environmental and social practices generate higher long-term stock returns than those that don't.[1]

While the appetite for ESG-related investment options is increasing, how to best approach ESG within a portfolio or asset allocation remains unclear to many of even the most sophisticated and experienced institutional investors. The acknowledgement that ESG is an important factor for consideration is generally followed by a series of questions – Where should I start? What should I focus on? How do I define it? How do you measure it? These are queries which many still struggle to answer.

As a long-term institutional investor, I have seen the industry tackle many social, humanitarian, and health issues on a one-off basis – tobacco, firearms, Sudan, and Iran – to name a few. Unlike the campaigns that came before, which sought to target single issues or regimes, ESG is more of a multifaceted philosophy for which there is no concrete definition. Lack of uniformity around definition presents headwinds with regards to holistic ESG adoption, as asset owners regularly grapple with where to begin from an implementation perspective. That said, a segmented approach with focus on a single broad-reaching component of ESG can be a very effective place to start. Enter climate change. The rise of climate change awareness, and the far-reaching negative impacts that it poses, is hard to deny. Global financial stability stands to be wholly upset by the far-reaching effects of climate change with health and well-being, food and water availability, and increased human migration pressures amongst them. As a result, the "E" in ESG is garnering an increasing amount of attention from both investors and policy makers alike, and is a meaningful and impactful place to begin any ESG conversation.

Practical analysis
With that background, in the fall of 2017 I co-authored the paper "A Methodology for Assessment of Corporate Responsibility on Climate Change: A Case Study on the Fossil Energy Industry," which was published in the *Journal of Environmental Investing*.[2] This paper discusses a quantitative metric developed by the Union of Concerned Scientists, as published in October 2016, which provides a framework for the assessment of corporate accountability related to climate change, with specific focus on the fossil fuel industry.[3]

The metric is made up of 30 different indicators, derived from publicly available sources, spanning four broad categories:

- Renouncing disinformation on climate science and policy
- Planning for a carbon-constrained economy
- Supporting fair and effective policies
- Fully disclosing climate risks

The *Journal of Environmental Investing* paper highlights the initial application of the metric, which focused on eight publicly traded oil and gas and coal companies – Chevron, ExxonMobil, BP, Royal Dutch Shell, ConocoPhillips, Peabody Energy, CONSOL Energy, and Arch Coal – between January 2015 and May 2016.[4] Nearly 15% of industrial carbon emissions, between 1751 and 2010, can be attributed to these eight names alone.[5] The metric translates five qualitative ratings, ranging from "Advanced" to "Egregious," into corresponding quantitative rankings. The quantitative rankings provide rigor and consistency to the methodology, and provide a measure by which one can track progress over time.

Case study findings

The initial results highlight that there was considerable disparity between the practices of the eight companies across the four categories during the sample period.[6] While their areas of deficiency differ, each of the companies analyzed has considerable room to improve as it relates to their role in climate change advocacy, disclosure, policy, and planning.

One of the unique aspects of the metric is that in utilizing publicly available data, with emphasis on non-financial disclosures, it looks beyond emissions and seeks to get to the heart of what fossil fuel producers are doing from a policy and action perspective to inform their role in emissions and climate change going forward. Why is this significant? While it is important to recognize the role that companies played in historical emissions, it is critical to monitor and understand their level of corporate accountability prospectively. Do they support climate change initiatives and policies? Do they align with groups that cast doubt on climate change rather than acknowledge it? Are they seeking to change their business operations to be more climate aware? Intuition and initial results both confirm that there is considerably more work to be done.

The application of the metric can be multifaceted. The early days of implementation of ESG and socially responsible investments tended to focus on negative screening and divestment, leading to wholesale elimination or avoidance of entire industries from an asset allocation. This metric provides asset owners and allocators with the ability to evaluate individual companies along a spectrum of behavior, whereby allowing for distinctions in actions and allegiances. In addition to divestment and exclusionary orientated assessment, the metric may inform shareholder engagement and legal proceedings related to corporate accountability as described in the *Journal of Environmental Investing* paper. Further work on the metric is being contemplated to expand its breadth and depth with regards to companies, industries, and geographies.

There is no denying that ESG is here to stay, as hardly an investment discussion passes without some mention of it. And while holistic ESG integration should be the norm for all asset owners and investors seeking strong, long-term returns, it can be met with resistance given challenges around definition, measurement, and resources. To overcome some of those headwinds, concentration on a single facet of ESG, for example climate change as described herein, can be an effective and meaningful place to begin.

9.3 Development of common method of risk and return

It is important to identify an investor's perspective toward investment research and analysis to better understand risk and return methodology. Understanding how investors approach investing is also helpful in illustrating commonalities, differences, and adaptations ESG investing approaches. It is imperative to first consider the difference of "top-down" and "bottom-up" investment approaches.

Top-down

A top-down investing research approach is an investment strategy that looks at the macro, or big picture, and focuses on assessing the overall macro-economy. Once the overall market picture is assessed, the top-down investor then determines various individual components that equate to the big picture perspective. The top-down approach includes a selection of economic variables that can be chosen by analysts that contribute to macroeconomic movements. These macroeconomic variables include Gross Domestic Product (GDP), trade-data, currency movements, inflation, and interest rates.

An ESG investor may use top-down analysis as their research approach. An ESG investor may apply top-down analysis in conjunction with their methodology for implementing ESG. For example, an ESG investor that utilizes an integration-based methodology to create a low-carbon portfolio, without eliminating exposure to the energy industry, may use the top-down analysis of the supply and demand schematic of oil and gas production to help them in knowing when to be higher and lower on their carbon exposure, as well as guiding them in their renewable energy investment allocation.

ESG investors may use top-down analysis as a research lens for prioritizing ESG issues within their ESG investment approach. The big picture that the macro-economy provides allows ESG investors to gain insight on ESG issues or themes that may be in line with their ESG investment policy, signal risks, or indicate potential for an investment opportunity. The top-down approach is viable to the application of ESG in many various ways and is a chosen approach for many ESG investors. For example, a top-down approach to ESG investing can analyze the sustainability and ethical conduct of a large technology company whose supply chain for electronics components is broad in its global reach and may have parts produced in geography that have association with poor labor rights and child labor. An ESG investor might also identify a theme of social opposition against a specific industry, region, or asset as an indicator of investment risk. This was the case for many investors who divested in South African bonds, equities, and credit in the 1980s because of the Apartheid. This resulted in the massive flow of funds away from South Africa by institutional investors and sovereign wealth funds due to the public injustice.

A top-down approach to investing is a mainstream strategy because it takes into account overall macroeconomics in a way that a bottom-up approach does not account for. Understanding macroeconomic trends is helpful to investors in studying market trends. Countries with volatile macroeconomic patterns pose a risk to investors while countries with stable macroeconomic trends can provide investors with a more stable investment. An example of this, as it applies to ESG investing, could be the act of measuring the quality of governmental bonds in the emerging markets by analyzing macro ESG factors of government corruption, natural resources' export dependency, citizen oppression and human rights, and United Nations adherence by the sovereign issuers.

Bottom-up

Bottom-up investing is a factor of fundamental analysis. Bottom-up investors focus on micro issues and specific companies, such as a single stocks rather than focusing on economic and market cycles. The thesis for this approach is that an investor assumes that an individual company can outperform the industry it operates in. Bottom-up analysis can provide investors with an analysis of systematics risks and provide a risk-adjusted benchmark.

One example of how researchers used bottom-up analysis comes from research conducted by L'Her, Stoyanova, Shaw, Scott, and Lai, in which the researchers used a bottom-up approach to assess the risk-adjusted performance of the buyout fund market. During the research, a bottom-up approach was used to identify risks of underlying companies in buyout funds in order to establish a risk-adjusted benchmark. After the risk-adjusted factors were taking into consideration the researchers concluded that there was no significant outperformance of buyout fund investments when compared to their public market equivalents. This research was beneficial to the investment community because it proved that buyout funds can provide value for institutional investors.

A bottom-up approach to investing is widely recommended by money managers. This approach has an advantage to the top-down approach because of its focus on individual companies. This analysis is helpful for money managers because it does not focus on market patterns and instead focuses on the actual companies. While a top-down approach can be beneficial in understanding the overall markets, the top-down approach does not look at individual companies to the extent in which the bottom-up approach does. A bottom-up approach is necessary for active managers while a top-down approach would be considered for passive investing.

ESG investors often incorporate ESG research into their bottom-up analysis. Much of ESG data is associated with bottom-up analysis as it brings a lens on specific actions of companies and investment projects. Without having a view of a sector or industry's performance, ESG investing can allow an investor to generate bottom-up views on a specific security vs. its peer group beyond what traditional fundamentals can provide. ESG factors used in bottom-up research can consist of various issues such as executive compensation, corporate social responsibility, accounting practices, product quality and safety, and more.

Investors may often use a combination of top-down and bottom-up research as their approach to investing. ESG investors may first examine ESG issues and themes as they impact the macroeconomy and then identify the specific securities that are best positioned against their industry or sector, or vice versa. Investors may blend the two approaches simultaneously or conduct the analysis in a consecutive fashion.

Alpha

Alpha is the intercept in the time series regression of an asset's excess returns on those of a market index. In simple terms, alpha measures an asset's performance relative to the market. Alpha is often considered the active return on investment because it gauges the performance of an investment against a benchmark. Alpha is depicted as a single number percentage which represents how a portfolio performed when compared to a benchmark index. For example, an investment's alpha might be depicted as 3, which represents a 3% outperformance of the benchmark. The analysis of cross-sectional returns, such as used in the Fama-French four factor model uses alpha to measure outperformance. Many investors integrate ESG factors because of the belief that it will help them achieve greater alpha. This is because such investors assume that the insight gained from ESG data, research, and analysis will help them in reducing downside risk and expanding their opportunity for excess return over the broader markets. Alpha, as the outperformance of a benchmark or the market, is essentially an outperformance of beta.

Beta

Beta is an asset's equitably distributed share of the market risk. Beta measures the connotation of systematic risk. The benchmark has a beta of 1. Assets are measured against the benchmark. An asset with a beta of 1 tracks perfectly with the movements of the benchmark. Assets with a beta of -1 move exactly opposite of the benchmark. Beta is calculated using regression analysis and represents the trend of a security's returns to react to swings in the market. In order to calculate the beta of a security the covariance and the benchmark's returns are divided by the variance of the benchmark's returns over a specified period.

ESG investors may use beta, or beta input, similar to traditional investing, but adapting for their investable universe and market perspective. For example, an investor that is excluding certain equities from their investment universe may choose a benchmark index that does not include the GICS code, industry, or sector classification of such securities. As noted in Chapter 3, index providers produce many ESG-relative indices. MSCI produced more than 650 ESG indices alone. Using a benchmark index that is aligned to an ESG investor's strategy or methodology is a better representation of beta for the investor's analysis, as well as understanding of risk and return potential. Further, the use of a proper benchmark for beta allows the investor the ability to better analyze and identify where their investment portfolio is capturing alpha. For example, an investor wishing to measure the correlation between a non-ESG benchmark and its ESG counterpart might measure the beta of the ESG investment using the non-ESG benchmark.

R-squared

Another tool investors use in measuring their risk and return potential is **R-squared**. R-squared is a statistical measure, often associated with quantitative analysis, that represents the percentage of a fund or security's movement. R-squared values range from 0 to 1 and are represented as percentages. An R-squared of 100% indicates all movements from a security are defined by movements in the index. A high R-squared, between 85% and 100%, indicates the fund's performance patterns are in line with the index. A fund with a low R-squared, of 70% or less, indicates the security does not act much like the index. ESG investors may use R-squared measurements to assess how specific ESG investments correlate with the movements of the broader market or peer group, or to identify how different their portfolios may be from portfolios that are similar in asset allocation but use traditional, non-ESG, indices.

Fundamental, quantitative, and technical analysis methods continue to develop, and are being influenced by the integration of ESG factors. Though ESG factors are increasingly being incorporated in traditional performance models, a gap still exists where a quantitative model built around ESG integration might demonstrate the performance impact of ESG integration.

CASE STUDY 9C: integrating ESG at Candriam Investors Group

Wim Van Hyfte, Global Head of Responsible Investments at Luxembourg-based Candriam Investors Group provided the following information on how Candriam integrates ESG research and analysis through an internal, independent, team.

Candriam launched our first ESG equity and fixed income funds in 1996, followed by a range of ESG asset allocation funds in 2000, and established an independent in-house ESG research and analysis team in 2005. Twenty-seven percent, or $36.5bn, of Candriam's total assets is dedicated to ESG strategies. In 2006 Candriam were one of the founding signatories of the UN Principles of Responsible Investment (PRI).

Candriam's ESG research structure is not only the result of two years of organic growth at Candriam, but also designed to best align with the current ESG "zeitgeist" among intuitional investors.

Candriam has an independent, dedicated team of 14 in-house specialists focusing specifically on ESG. This team is made up of both of research analysts as well as analysts focused on engagement and proxy voting. Each of our ESG research analysts is an industry specialist much like traditional research analysts, but their aim is to analyze and rank companies based on ESG performance relative to peers.

The research analysts use a proprietary database, created back in 2006, to identify and monitor quantitative and qualitative data from a wide range of data sources (sustainability agencies, the media, NGO reports, industry experts, and associations). This data is then supplemented with information gathered from company publications, reports, and direct engagement with management and investor relations teams.

This proprietary research database together with the application of one of two custom analysis frameworks – one for corporate analysis and another for sovereign analysis – empowers the ESG research team to grade, rank, and compile ESG investment universes for a wide variety asset classes, investment strategies, and vehicle structures (e.g. separately managed accounts or co-mingled funds).

An independent ESG research team has two benefits. Firstly, it ensures that the team can operate without undue conflict and friction from other investment teams. Secondly, it shows commitment on the part of the investment manager and provides reassurance to investors that it takes ESG seriously as dedicated ESG teams and proprietary research require a non-negligible financial commitment.

LEARNING PERSPECTIVE 7: ESG and investment risk

Lloyd Kurtz is Head of the Social Impact Investing team at Wells Fargo Private Bank, and a lecturer at the Haas School of Business at UC Berkeley and the University of Münster. He also serves on the Sustainability Accounting Standards Board. His academic work has focused primarily on the impact of ESG factors on investment risk and portfolio performance. He did much of the initial quantitative work on the Domini Social Index in the 1990s, and has co-authored two papers for Journal of Investing *on its risk characteristics and performance. His 2013 book,* Looking Forward, Looking Back, *reviewed the academic literature of responsible investment in the years up to and immediately following the financial crisis. His recent work focuses on the relationship between ESG and portfolio quality, and the significance of systemic risks such as corporate governance and climate change.*

Introduction

The relationship between environmental, social, and governance (ESG) factors and investment risk is complex, but great progress has been made in understanding the effects that are at work. Strong risk management tools have been developed that make incorporation of ESG factors into portfolio construction a much more tractable process than it once was, but significant challenges remain. William Sharpe once said that risk is "a complicated feature, and one that human beings have trouble processing."[7] This is particularly true with ESG factors, which may be difficult to measure, and which may operate on different levels of risk. So how you think about ESG risks depends, to a very great extent, on who you are and what problem you are trying to solve.

We will discuss ESG effects on investment risk at three levels: systematic risk, unsystematic risk, and systemic risk.

In Sharpe's classical formulation, there are two types of risk: unsystematic risk, which can be (mostly) diversified away, and systematic risk, which even a well-diversified investor is stuck with. A well-diversified institution will therefore have a very different view of ESG risk as compared to a concentrated hedge fund. In the modern era, a third dimension of risk has emerged: *systemic* risk, which gained prominence with the global financial crisis of 2008–2009 and the continuing progression of the problem of climate change.

Systematic risk

One of the key insights of modern finance is that much of the uncertainty in portfolio returns can be eliminated through diversification. Two stocks may have the same expected return and volatility, but combined together as a portfolio they will have less volatility together than either one alone. Volatility will continue to decline as stocks are added to the portfolio, and there is a diversification benefit even when there are already hundreds of stocks in the portfolio, as illustrated by Statman (1987). Once idiosyncratic risk has been diversified away, the investor need only be concerned with systematic risk.

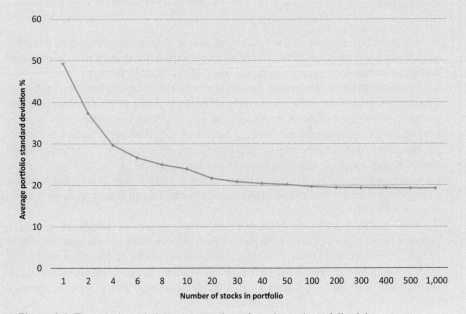

Figure 9.3 The relationship between number of stocks and portfolio risk

For responsible investors, the critical question then becomes whether their portfolios can be adequately diversified. If the effects of ESG investment policies were largely random, investors could simply purchase a large number of securities, weight them in such a way that the portfolio's exposure to common investment factors was similar to the benchmark, and thereby earn benchmark-like returns. Markowitz (2012) examined this question analytically:

> [I]t seems safe to say that an ethics screen which reduced available securities from about 8,000 to about 4,000 would have to be quite strange to make it impossible to select a reasonably liquid, well diversified portfolio with returns comparable to those [one] usually finds in portfolios of well-established companies with similar levels of volatility.

Many studies have provided empirical support for this idea. Studies of North American responsible investment indexes have consistently shown that their relative performance is driven primarily by common investment factors such as beta, size, and investment style (e.g., growth vs. value). Here are summary results of performance attributions of two such indexes over long time periods:

Table 9.3 Performance attributions of Domini/KLD 400 and Calvert Social Index

Index	Domini/KLD 400	Calvert Social Index
Time period	1992–2010	2000–2014
Active return % (annualized) of which . . .	0.72	−0.99
% attributable to common factors	0.6	−1.06
% attributable to stock selection	0.12	0.07
Benchmark	S&P 500	Russell 1000

In each case, differences from the benchmark appear to be driven primarily by common factors. The stock selection factor, where we would expect to see any ESG-related alpha, is positive for both indexes, but not statistically distinguishable from zero in either case.

The discovery that optimization can greatly reduce the tracking error introduced by ESG policies means that investors can often achieve a high degree of alignment between portfolio holdings and personal or institutional values without a significant loss of portfolio efficiency. Optimization has therefore become a core element in modern responsible investment practice, with numerous firms offering strategies that use optimization to meet ESG goals while maintaining low levels of tracking error vs. the benchmark. A US exchange-traded fund, the iShares MSCI US ESG Select ETF (ticker: SUSA), has provided a portfolio of stocks with high ESG ratings, optimized to a North American equity benchmark, since 2005.

Optimization may be used increase exposure to positives, as in SUSA, or to reduce exposure to negatives without creating undue tracking error. A recent example, described by Rao and Brinkmann (2014), is a project to reduce portfolio carbon exposure by the pension funds AP4 (Sweden) and FRR (France). Working in collaboration with the risk management firm MSCI, this project demonstrated that institutions could significantly reduce carbon exposure while maintaining tracking error at surprisingly low levels. For example, an investor seeking to reduce carbon exposure solely through the elimination of coal stocks would achieve a reduction in carbon exposure of about 25%, at the cost of incurring approximately 30 basis points of annual tracking error vs. the MSCI ACWI (global) index. The project demonstrated that investors could do much better than that: by using optimization to reweight the portfolio, MSCI shows that it was possible to reduce carbon exposure by over 60% with the same level of tracking error. Given a tracking error budget of 100 basis points, MSCI was able to show a reduction in carbon exposure of more than 90%. This is a remarkable finding and demonstrates the power and efficacy of modern tools in managing portfolio tracking error.[8]

Unsystematic risk

The world we've described so far represents a very good outcome for responsible investors. Markets are big and liquid and differential performance appears to be driven largely by common factors. And, it seems that portfolio managers can treat ESG impacts as a random draw, easily redressed through optimization. But over the past decade there has been new work that shows that some ESG factors do matter for both fundamentals and returns – and that we shouldn't be overly confident modeling these impacts as the result of a random draw.

Moreover, not all investors are well diversified. A hedge fund charged with focusing on its best ideas might hold a highly concentrated portfolio. For these investors, ESG analysis functions as an important additional risk assessment tool. In a recent *Financial Times* report, Brian Schorr, chief legal counsel for Trian Partners, stated that his firm employs ESG analysis precisely because its portfolio is *not* broadly diversified:

> It was important to understand potential environmental risks and opportunities before we made the investment. We have a very concentrated portfolio and we wanted to be sure that if we invested, we had assessed what their existing and environmental exposure was.[9]

Even indexes may have significant firm-specific risk. For example, at the end of Q1 2018 the MSCI USA ESG Select Index held a 5.1% position in Ecolab, vs. a 0.15% weighting in a comparable MSCI broad market index.[10] Investors who hold the ESG Select in preference to a broad market benchmark must be comfortable that this significant overweighting in a particular name is justified. For these types of investors, ESG risk takes on a different character. It is no longer just a source of tracking error, it becomes integral to the asset selection process.

For many years there was skepticism that ESG factors could directly impact company fundamentals, or that markets did not fully understand the implications of strong firm-level ESG policies. Theorists viewed investor interest in (for example) firms with good human capital policies as a "taste" or "preference," but were highly skeptical of the idea that such policies could be drivers of portfolio performance. Strong papers by Edmans (2011) and Edmans, Li, and Zhang (2015) have shown that the firms with strong employee relations globally have a higher propensity for positive earnings surprise, and that markets have not historically fully incorporated this into valuations – a situation that adept active managers might be able to exploit. Flammer (2015), using a different methodology, shows that stocks tend to react positively when shareholders approve human capital-related shareholder resolutions are passed.[11]

While the work of Edmans and numerous other researchers has focused on a partic-ular issue, the usefulness of overall ESG ratings has also received close scrutiny in recent years. The concept of ESG Momentum seems particularly promising: Giese et al. (2017) show that stocks in firms with improving MSCI ESG ratings have materially outperformed those with declining ratings since the financial crisis:

Efforts are underway to identify which ESG factors matter most for fundamentals in each industry. In the United States the Sustainability Accounting Standards Board (SASB) has published ESG preliminary disclosure standards for US corporations, and is expected to finalize these standards in 2018. These standards are focused on financial materiality, and are the product of years of research and consultation with issuing firms, analysts, industry associations, and experts in ESG issues. In assuming chairmanship of SASB in 2014, Michael Bloomberg stated that "30 years ago I started a company on the idea that greater market transparency leads to better investment decisions, and that idea is at the heart of SASB's mission."[12]

While the incorporation of ESG factors into company-specific investment analysis is still in its early stages, there is some evidence that ESG performance already functions as a supplemental indicator of firm quality, even after accounting for well-known com-mon performance factors. Nofsinger and Varma (2014) show that responsible investment funds in the United States outperformed the broad market – net of conventional risk fac-tors – during the 2008–2009 crisis, but underperformed in non-crisis periods. Kurtz (2016) and Hale (2017) find that better ESG performers are judged by Morningstar to have more economically sustainable business franchises (wider business "moats"), and that this might be the source of responsible portfolios' perceived higher quality. This appears to be a promising area for further research.

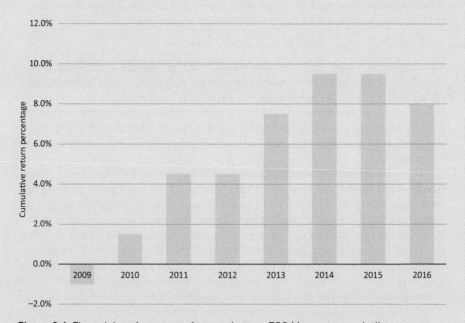

Figure 9.4 Financial performance of top vs. bottom ESG Momentum quintile

Systemic risk

In June 2017, Robert Litterman, former head of risk for Goldman Sachs and a leader in the field of quantitative finance, spoke to a group of investors at a conference in Germany. His topic was climate risk. Climate has traditionally been treated as a policy matter, and sometimes as an economic matter, as in Nordhaus (2013). But Litterman argued that as concentrations of atmospheric carbon rise, uncertainty about climate outcomes also increases, and this uncertainty and the resulting economic imbalances are ultimately the concern of financial markets.

Institutional interest in systemic risk has increased significantly in recent years, and this area will likely be the source of the greatest analytical challenges going forward. It may be useful to think of the difference between systemic and the similarly named systematic risks as follows: *systematic* risk is uncertainty in portfolio returns that cannot be diversified away – it is what you get when you hold a broadly diversified portfolio. *Systemic* risk describes situations where the underlying system itself is potentially endangered, as we saw in the financial crisis. Put more bluntly, systematic risk is when your screen says your portfolio has gone down, systemic risk is when the power goes out and your screen goes blank.

Systemic risk matters especially for institutions because of their size. In 2015 Anne Simpson, director of global governance at CalPERS, stated that "because of our size and the fact we are globally invested we believe [ESG] is part of the multi-faceted nature of the risks we face. At $307 billion we can't hide if there is systemic risk."[13]

Note that systematic risks do *not* need to be highly probable to deserve attention. What matters is the possibility of very large negative impacts, even if they are considered unlikely. A high level of uncertainty about a severe outcome, Litterman argues, strengthens the case for bringing a risk perspective to the problem. "If a scientist gets up and talks about worst-case scenarios, they're often criticized for being alarmist," he said. "If you're a risk manager, that's your job."

Systemic risk may take many forms. Climate is one example, but in the wake of the financial crisis institutions also became concerned about the health of global financial markets and regulatory systems. Some analysts argue that the appropriate spectrum of interest is even wider: DiBartolomeo and Hoffman (2015) find that market returns have historically been negatively correlated with geopolitical conflicts. This is particularly true for debt markets because "wars are expensive, driving up yields, losers in war can't pay and there is no 'upside' for lenders even if their borrower wins a war."

One of the most pernicious aspects of systemic risk is that severe outcomes – market meltdowns, climate-related disasters, etc. – may occur very quickly, leading to "time compression." Most problems humanity faces are tractable if they are well-characterized and there is time to adjust and respond. The most dangerous situations are the ones where there is not time to prepare, or where the time available to prepare has been wasted. As Litterman puts it: "a risk becomes a catastrophe when you run out of time."

As global suppliers of capital, institutions' concern for systemic health is understandable. There is little consensus on the right way to approach the problem, however, so organizations' responses to systemic risk vary widely. They may include partial or complete avoidance of a particular factor, such as AP4's efforts to reduce carbon exposure; or direct dialogue with companies to promote better performance, as seen with CalPERS's corporate governance program. Many other organizations' efforts remain in the formative stages.

Concluding thoughts

It is now well established that ESG factors bear on the assessment of portfolio risk. But, since it is impossible and prohibitively expensive to manage every conceivable risk, it is crucial to think clearly about what types of risk matter most in a given situation, and what ESG factors we believe bear on them. A large, well-diversified institution will have a very different approach to risk management than a hedge fund.

In some areas the news is surprisingly good: at the systematic risk level, thanks to modern risk management tools, the handling of ESG impacts on portfolio tracking error is usually a manageable problem. At the unsystematic/stock specific level the impacts are not as well understood, but strong research progress is being made, and the publication of final disclosure standards by SASB should move best practices forward in the years to come.

Systemic risk, however, is both potentially extremely important and poorly understood. Portfolio managers and risk management professionals should do everything possible to understand their portfolios' exposures to systemic risk before problems arise, and – when appropriate adjustment strategies are unclear – to promote research into how to best manage them.

Discussion questions

1) List the major risk and financial performance measurement models used by investors (LO1)
2) Discuss the history and development of financial performance models (LO2)
3) Discuss why it might be difficult to measure the impact of ESG investment implementation on performance through traditional performance measurement models (LO4)
4) Do you feel traditional performance-based models accurately measure risk-adjusted return within ESG-based investing strategies? Why or why not? (LO5)

Notes

1 Eccles, R., Ioannou, I., Serafeim, G. 2012. The Impact of Corporate Sustainability on Organizational Process and Performance. Online at www.hbs.edu/faculty/Publication%20Files/SSRN-id1964011_6791edac-7daa-4603-a220-4a0c6c7a3f7a.pdf

2 Goldman, G., Mulvey, K., Frumhoff, P., Pfirman, S., Sethi, R., Commoss, H. 2017. A Methodology for Assessment of Corporate Responsibility on Climate Change: A Case Study on the Fossil Energy Industry Journal of Environmental Investing 8, no 1. 2017.

3 Mulvey, K., Piepenburg, J., Goldman, G., Frunhoff, P. 2016. The Climate Accountability Scorecard. Online at www.ucsusa.org/global-warming/fight-misinformation/climate-accountability-scorecard-ranking-major-fossil-fuel-companies#.Whwrbqqosy8

4 Goldman, G., Mulvey, K., Frumhoff, P., Pfirman, S., Sethi, R., Commoss, H. 2017. A Methodology for Assessment of Corporate Responsibility on Climate Change: A Case Study on the Fossil Energy Industry Journal of Environmental Investing 8, no 1. 2017.

5 Heede, R. 2014. Carbon Majors: Accounting for carbon and methane emissions 1854–2010, Methods & Results Report, Table 14. Online at: http://carbonmajors.org/wp/wp-content/uploads/2014/04/MRR-9.1-Apr14R.pdf

6 Goldman, G., Mulvey, K., Frumhoff, P., Pfirman, S., Sethi, R., Commoss, H. 2017. A Methodology for Assessment of Corporate Responsibility on Climate Change: A Case Study on the Fossil Energy Industry Journal of Environmental Investing 8, no 1. 2017.

7   "Revisiting the Capital Asset Pricing Model." Dow Jones Asset Manager, May/June 1998. Link: web.stanford.edu/~wfsharpe/art/djam/djam.htm
8   In 2014 MSCI launched a line of low-carbon indexes. Link: www.msci.com/msci-low-carbon-indexes
9   "Why activists are cheerleaders for corporate social responsibility." *Financial Times*, December 26, 2017. Link: www.ft.com/content/6f9dc2cc-e512-11e7-97e2-916d4bac0da
10 MSCI USA ESG Select Index fact sheet, March 30, 2018. Link: www.msci.com/documents/10199/5b30f74d-8bdd-4efd-9824-c77c05eb64d8
11 Note that Flammer's methodology focused only on closely contested resolutions, as it would be difficult for the market to discount the outcome of these close votes beforehand.
12 "Finance powerhouses Michael Bloomberg and Mary Schapiro to lead SASB." Greenbiz, May 1, 2014.
13 "CalPERS gives its managers ESG ultimatum." top1000funds.com, May 22, 2015. Link: www.top1000funds.com/news/2015/05/22/calpers-gives-its-managers-esg-ultimatum/

References

DiBartolomeo, Dan, and Howard Hoffman. "Seeing the Big Picture: Financial Markets, Conflict and Corruption." Working paper, Northfield London Seminar, April 2015. www.northinfo.com/documents/642.pdf

Edmans, Alex. "Does the Stock Market Fully Value Intangibles?" *Journal of Financial Economics* (2011).

Edmans, Alex, Lucius Li, and Chendi Zhang. "Employee Satisfaction, Labor Market Flexibility, and Stock Returns Around The World." European Corporate Governance Institute (ECGI) – Finance Working paper No. 433/2014, June 24, 2015.

Flammer, Caroline. "Does Corporate Social Responsibility Lead to Superior Financial Performance? A Regression Discontinuity Approach." *SSRN Electronic Journal* (2012). doi:10.2139/ssrn.2146282.

Giese, Guido, Linda-Eling Lee, Dimitris Melas, Zoltan Nagy, Laura Nishikawa. "How ESG Affects Equity Valuation, Risk, and Performance." *Foundations of ESG Investing – Part 1*, MSCI, November 2017.

Hale, Jon. "Sustainability and Quality Go Hand in Hand." *Morningstar*, March 16, 2017. http://news.morningstar.com/articlenet/article.aspx?id=798237.

Jensen, Michael C., and Richard A. Posner. "Agency Costs of Free Cash Flow, Corporate Finance, and Takeovers." *Corporate Bankruptcy* 76 no. 2 (1986): 11–16. doi:10.1017/cbo9780511609435.005.

Kurtz, Lloyd. "Moats and Sustainability." CQAsia Conference, Hong Kong, November 2016.

Kurtz, Lloyd, and Dan DiBartolomeo. "The Long-Term Performance of a Social Investment Universe." *Journal of Investing* (Fall 2011).

Litterman, Robert. "Pricing of Climate Risk and the Effect on Portfolio Construction." Speech to Uhlenbruch GmbH Annual Portfolio Management Conference, June 2017. www.youtube.com/watch?v=iFZ7r4b8lYw

Markowitz, Harry. "Can You Do Well While Doing Good?" *Index Fund Advisors*, July 20, 2012. www.ifa.com/pdfs/can-you-do-well-while-doing-good.pdf.

Nofsinger, John, and Abhishek Varma. "Socially Responsible Funds and Market Crises." *Journal of Banking and Finance* (November 2014).

Nordhaus, William. *The Climate Casino*. William Nordhaus: Yale University Press, 2013.

Oikonomou, I., C. Brooks, and S. Pavelin. "The Impact of Corporate Social Performance on Financial Risk and Utility: A Longitudinal Analysis." *Financial Management* 41 (2012): 483–515.

Rao, Anil, and Sebastian Brinkmann. "Transition to a Low Carbon Economy: Optimized Low Carbon and Ex Fossil Fuel Indexes." MSCI presentation, UC Berkeley Haas School of Business, October 2014.

Ross, Steve. "The Recovery Theorem." *The Journal of Finance* 70, no. 2 (2015): 615–48. doi:10.1111/jofi.12092.

Statman, Meir. "How Many Stocks Make a Diversified Portfolio?" *The Journal of Financial and Quantitative Analysis* (September 1987).

Trunow, Natalie, and Josh Lindner. "Perspectives on ESG Integration in Equity Investing: An Opportunity to Enhance Long-Term, Risk-Adjusted Investment Performance." Calvert Investments, 2015.

Conclusion

The field of ESG investing is a vast universe that spans research, analysis, and investment strategy. This book has established standardized nomenclature and definitions, as well as a clear construct on the various approaches and methodologies that have been adopted by the investment industry and in academia. Understanding the growth of ESG investing through history provides insight into how the field has evolved, and how ESG investing may continue to emerge as a significant investing trend. The cultivation of ESG investing through history, and the traction of the practice in recent years, lays the foundation for the further development in theory and practice.

Investors adopt ESG strategies in a manner that is relevant to their needs, which can encompass one, or a combination of, the exclusion, integration, impact, or engagement approaches. This customization lends itself to various asset classes and geographies, providing ESG strategies with a geographic and longitudinal influence.

This book provides a high-level overview of the academic theoretical frameworks surrounding ESG investing, such as the shareholder theory, materiality, and the universal owner theory. A summary of concerns, namely return, policy, information, and regional, were identified. These concerns provide a lens to the opinions often used in the arguments of the critics of ESG research and analysis. The book reviewed the differences between qualitative and quantitative ESG research. Individual factors, the underlying sub-components, of "E," "S," and "G," are identified to illustrate the various issues that environmental, social, and governance-based investors consider. These factors may be prioritized individually, in groupings, or holistically depending on the investor and the investor's objectives. Practical implementations of ESG, such as ESG discounting within a discounted cash flow valuation and ESG as a factor within a multi-factor model, are outlined. Understanding how ESG is implemented and applied within traditional financial models allows for the learner to use ESG research and discover how non-financial performance factors can optimize the risk and return schematic of investing.

The research and practice of ESG investing is still at its infancy, as the investment and academic communities continue to evaluate and adopt ESG research practices and implementation techniques. The evolution of incorporating and implementing non-financial performance factors as part of the investment process is likely to continue as asset owners demand such informational insight. Remember that history illustrates the fact that ESG investment practices and the adoption of ESG approaches origins came from the asset owners and institutional investors. This evolution has not only experienced significant traction, but may very well experience further momentum as new innovations in ESG research and theory emerge. Looking forward in the evolution of ESG investing, it is reasonable to assume that the asset management and investment management industry will produce more active and passive strategies to meet the needs of investors. A split in views between traditional money managers, namely those who adopt ESG and those who do not, may continue to widen. And, new money managers, both asset and investment managers, that center their businesses on a foundation of ESG approaches and methodologies will continue to emerge. As institutional investors continue to publicize their ESG investing efforts, retail investors will represent a greater share of the ESG investment landscape. Being that the flow of funds will likely continue its pace to ESG approaches and investment strategies, ESG research, ratings, and reporting firms will grow and new competitors are likely to emerge.

Like many mainstream techniques adopted by investors, ESG methodologies and approaches will likely continue to be more efficiently researched and measured as standardization of qualitative and quantitative practices grows in acceptance by the consensus. An assumption may be made that the quantification of ESG research, such as what is observable in the context of ESG ratings, will likely continue as the quantitative data analysis of ESG becomes more and more mainstream. New theory on how to quantify such non-financial performance factors may also continue to surface in the future. It is believed that ESG investing will continue to flourish and prosper as a research and analytical field in academia. Whereas, currently for example, 80% of the students at Massachusetts Institute of Technology ("MIT") take at least one course on sustainability, colleges and universities may not only offer courses on ESG-relative subject matter, but also offer majors and core concentrations on ESG-relative subject matter. ESG investing will be considered a core competency, like other financial research and analysis specializations, under the broader finance and economics umbrella. Furthermore, as the investment industry continues to evolve the practice and adoption of ESG, students will be required to have adequate academic training for their future employment.

Nevertheless, it is important to remember that ESG investment strategies are new only in the sense that they present a market and an opportunity to monetize the consideration of such factors. In this comes both an opportunity and a warning. Investors practice ESG investing for various reasons and not all ESG strategies provide a quantifiable positive impact on the underlying environmental, social, and governance structures on which it is dependent. Similarly, not all ESG strategies provide characteristics of return enhancement and risk reduction. Some might argue that ESG ratings data and the increased documentation of such information, as well as its classification as risk, generates attention on the issues in a way that forces positive change. Others might argue that ESG investing itself is dependent on the existence of ESG issues. These contrarians would argue that if ESG investing remains popular amongst institutional investors and their underlying beneficiaries, companies will continue to focus on momentum in ESG factors, rather than achieving acceptable levels of environmental, social, and governance standards. The opportunity and the warning are here: that ESG investing may be an opportunity for real change to be initiated by investors or may be manipulated by the ever-shifting standards of environmental, social, and governance factors within corporations, geographies, industries, and governments.

When you first began this textbook, you may have already been familiar with some of the common terms and current methods of incorporating ESG into traditional investing strategies. For some, the information presented in this text might have been completely new. In either case, this text provides a holistic picture of the historical, geographical, and cultural atmosphere in which ESG investing exists. Here is a quick review of the main points from each chapter:

Chapter 1: This text began with an introduction to the difference in terminology and the need to standardize wording and phrases in order to have consistency for investors and academia. This chapter introduced the subject matter and provided the contextual framework for the book.

Chapter 2: An introduction to the history of ESG investing was provided. We discussed the development of ESG investment strategies, from the preliminary screening of the Methodists and Muslims, to the advanced integration methodology that is in practice today. This introduction to ESG history provided context which built the foundation for ESG factor implementation in a variety of geographies, investors, asset classes, and sectors.

Chapter 3: We next discussed the recognition and development of ESG risks, through the ESG rating systems. We delved into the development of various ESG ratings methodology, and discussed how the cross-sectional development of third-party ESG analysts would lead to the increased effectiveness of integrating the data into portfolio construction to mitigate risk and enhance returns. In this section, we also discussed the concept of risk premia, and theorized about ways that ESG could be considered an independent form of risk premia. This section expounded upon the theory of ESG risk and the potential for risk premium, by outlining various portfolio risks specifically related to ESG factors. These specific portfolio risks were referred to as policy risk, headline risk, and performance risks.

Chapter 4: The text next detailed the four ESG investment approaches. These approaches are commonly referred to as exclusion-based, integration-based, impact-based, and engagement-based ESG investing. These structures provide the investor with a way to identify a methodology that is consistent with their investment goals.

Chapter 5: This chapter identified the current integration levels of ESG investments (categorized in the four structures discussed in Chapter 4) across geographies and asset classes. This chapter first discussed legislation related to ESG in Europe, Canada, the United States, and Asia, and then covered how and to what extent ESG strategies were integrated across geographies.

Chapter 6: This chapter provided an overview of several key investment theories which have bearing on the ways ESG factors are integrated. These theories include the shareholder vs. stakeholder theory, the material information theory, the resource-based view vs. Porter's five forces model, and the universal owners theory. These theories provide a helpful foundation for how and why ESG information is incorporated as it is currently. These theories also help to track the trend for how academics will continue to approach ESG investing strategically.

Chapter 7: The text next identified some common concerns with integrating ESG factors, and suggestions for responses to these concerns. This chapter is geared towards equipping students with how to think about how ESG factors develop and opportunities the industry has to utilize the information.

Chapter 8: Chapter 8 provided the reader a broad overview of how individual investors might implement ESG factors thematically and idiosyncratically. The manner in which ESG research can be conducted was reviewed. A lens on investors that focus specifically on environmental, social, or governance-based factors was reviewed. Further specific ESG factors are presented and explained.

Chapter 9: The final chapter of the book reviewed fundamental and quantitative research and analytical instruments and examined how ESG might apply to such instruments. The instruments are industry standard models and tools, which may be useful within the practical considerations of ESG, are summarized and examined for use in the construct of ESG investment strategy, research, and analysis.

Whether an investor implements an ESG investing approach because of policy or the belief that non-financial performance factors catalyze into financial performance and risks, ESG investing continues to grow in adoption and evolve in nature. What began as an investment practice by the asset owners of the world is now intertwined throughout the consultant, service provider, asset management, and academic community. Now that an introduction to the ESG investment field has been established, you are equipped with the knowledge to explore the depth of the many facets of the field. Be encouraged to research and study any of the factors, approaches, methodologies, and analytical capacities that you developed an understanding in from this book.

Index